THE REGULAR EDUCATION INITIATIVE:
ALTERNATIVE PERSPECTIVES ON CONCEPTS, ISSUES, AND MODELS

John Wills Lloyd
Nirbhay N. Singh
Alan C. Repp
Editors

SYCAMORE
PUBLISHING COMPANY

Library of Congress Cataloging-in-Publication Data

The Regular education initiative : alternative perspectives on
  concepts, issues, and models / [edited by] John W. Lloyd, Nirbhay
N. Singh, Alan C. Repp.
    p.   cm.
  Includes bibliographical references and indexes.
  ISBN 0-9625233-3-X
  1. Handicapped children--Education--United States.
2. Mainstreaming in education--United States. 3. Educational
change--United States.   I. Lloyd, John, Ph.D.   II. Singh, Nirbhay
N. III. Repp, Alan C.
LC4031.R396 1991
371.9'046--dc20   90-25261
                                                          CIP

Copyright © 1991 Sycamore Publishing Company

Sycamore Publishing Company
P.O. Box 133
Sycamore, IL 60178
815-756-5388

Sycamore Publishing Company is dedicated to publishing effective approaches to educating persons with diverse abilities

EDUCATING PERSONS WITH DIVERSE ABILITIES

For our exceptional children

Corey Johannah
— JWL

Ashvind and Subhashni
— NNS

Erin
— ACR

Contents

Part II: CATEGORICAL PERSPECTIVES

CONTRIBUTORS

Joni Alberg, Ph.D.
Center for Research in Education
Research Triangle Institute
P.O. Box 12194
Research Triangle Park, NC 27709-2194

Mark Alter
Department of Teaching and Learning
New York University
New York, NY 10003

Diane Shaner Bassett, M.A.
Special Education Department
University of New Mexico
Albuquerque, NM 87123

Mary Bay, Ph.D.
College of Education/Special Education
Box 4348 (m/c 147)
University of Illinois at Chicago
Chicago, IL 60680

Tanis Bryan, Ph.D.
College of Education/Special Education
Box 4348 (m/c 147)
University of Illinois at Chicago
Chicago, IL 60680

Michael Bullis, Ph.D.
Teaching Research Division
Western Oregon State College
345 N. Monmouth Avenue
Monmouth, OR 97361

Douglas W. Carnine, Ph.D.
Teacher Education
University of Oregon
805 Lincoln Street
Eugene, OR 97401

Mavis Donahue, Ed.D.
College of Education/Special Education
University of Illinois at Chicago
Box 4348 (m/c 147)
Chicago, IL 60680

Douglas Fuchs, Ph.D.
Department of Special Education
George Peabody College
Vanderbilt University
Nashville, TN 37203

Lynn Fuchs, Ph.D.
Department of Special Education
George Peabody College
Vanderbilt University
Nashville, TN 37203

Christine Gambatese, B.A.
Curry School of Education
University of Virginia
Charlottesville, VA 22903

Alan Gartner
The Graduate School and University Center
The City University of New York
New York, NY 10036-8099

Barbara W. Gottlieb
Department of Specialized
  Services and Education
Herbert Lehman College of the
  City University of New York
Bronx, NY

Jay Gottlieb
Department of Teaching and Learning
New York University
New York, NY 10003

Anne M. Hocutt, Ph.D.
Research and Development Services
N.C. State Department of Public Instruction
217 W. Jones Street
Raleigh, NC 27603-1332

James M. Kauffman, Ed.D.
Department of Curriculum, Instruction
  and Special Education
405 Emmet Street
University of Virginia
Charlottesville, VA 22903

Thomas R. Kratochwill, Ph.D.
Department of Educational Psychology
School Psychology Program
University of Wisconsin-Madison
1025 West Johnson Street
Madison, WI 53706

Dorothy Kerzner Lipsky
Senior Research Scientist
The Graduate School and University Center
The City University of New York
New York, NY 10036-8099

John Wills Lloyd, Ph.D.
Curry School of Education
University of Virginia
Charlottesville, VA 22903

Norma Lopez-Reyna, Ph.D.
College of Education/Special Education
University of Illinois at Chicago
Box 4348 (m/c 147)
Chicago, IL 60680

Edwin W. Martin, Ph.D.
Human Resources Center
201 N. Willets Road West
Albertson, NY 11507

James D. McKinney, Ph.D.
Special Education and Reading
University of Miami
P.O. Box 248065
Coral Gables, FL 33124

Maynard C. Reynolds, Ph.D.
Special Education Programs
Department of Educational Psychology
University of Minnesota
242 Burton Hall, 178 Pillsbury Dr., SE
Minneapolis, MN 55455

Susan M. Sheridan, Ph.D.
Department of Educational Psychology
School Psychology Program
University of Utah
327 Milton Bennion Hall
Salt Lake City, UT 84112

Robert E. Slavin, Ph.D.
Center for Research on Effective
 Schooling for Disadvantaged Students
Johns Hopkins University
3505 N. Charles Street
Baltimore, MD 21218

Deborah Deutsch Smith, Ed.D.
Special Education Department
University of New Mexico
Albuquerque, NM 87131

Martha E. Snell, Ph.D.
Department of Curriculum, Instruction
 and Special Education
Curry School of Education
University of Virginia
Charlottesville, VA 22903

Susan Stainback, Ed.D.
College of Education
University of Northern Iowa
Cedar Falls, IA 50614

William Stainback, Ed.D.
College of Education
University of Northern Iowa
Cedar Falls, IA 50614

Robert J. Stevens, Ph.D.
Center for Research on Effective Schooling
 for Disadvantaged Students
Johns Hopkins University
3505 N. Charles Street
Baltimore, MD 21218

Hill M. Walker, Ph.D.
Center on Human Development
College of Education
University of Oregon
Clinical Services Bldg.
901 East 18th Avenue
Eugene, OR 97403

Frederick J. Weintraub
The Council for Exceptional Children
1920 Association Drive
Reston, VA 22091

Preface

The purpose of this book is to provide a collection of thoughtful treatments of issues that are a part of the Regular Education Initiative (REI). The REI was perhaps the most widely-discussed topic in special education during the 1980s and promises to continue to be of concern in the 1990s. In our view, however, this discussion has had several shortcomings:

- Proponents and opponents presented diverse views in the pages of journals and books and from podia and lecterns. Often the nature of these presentations was not so much discussion as it was argument. People advocated positions and marshalled evidence and reason to support those positions. None of the participants seemed to believe that other participants understood what they were saying.
- Although many of the articles on the REI appeared in special sections or issues of journals devoted to the topic, many more articles were not published as parts of collections. They appeared instead as separate entries. Often, responses to both articles that appeared as a part of a series and articles that appeared separately were not published until much later. Furthermore, the articles were published in quite diverse journals. As a result, the literature on the REI has been somewhat disjointed.
- Some of the presentations about the REI addressed more general issues but others focused on narrow matters. There were papers on both philosophy and practice, but these occurred primarily by happenstance rather than plan.

We chose to prepare a book that we hoped would correct these shortcomings of the discussion about the REI. We wanted to have a book in which a reader could find:

- Lively rhetoric focused on issues and free of <u>ad hominem</u>;
- Diverse views presented side-by-side;
- Presentations addressing not just the REI as a whole, but also its implications for different students and different methods of integrating students;
- A systematic approach to the issues and commentaries on the discussions of these issues.

We wanted to remove the discussion from the realm of advocacy and cast it in the light of legitimate concern about the future of education for children and youth with handicaps. Thus, we hope that readers of this book do not seek to identify a winner (unless the winner is the children and youth of our schools), but rather to gain from the book a broader and deeper understanding of the issues, possibilities, and hopes that are inherent in the debate over the Regular Education Initiative.

We want to acknowledge the chapter authors who acquiesced to a somewhat brutal schedule and to editorial suggestions of a similar nature. Their contributions are the substance of this book and we greatly appreciate their efforts and patience. We want to obviate the argument that chapter authors have ulterior motives for their positions; we are thoroughly convinced that all these authors presented their cases because of honest concerns for the appropriate education of children and youth.

We also wish to express our thanks to people who provided substantial help to us in completing this book, particularly Don Roe, Cynthia Nicholson, and Kathy Kendall. We extend special appreciation to Joan Mueller Cochrane, who served as the production editor for the book.

John Wills Lloyd
Nirbhay N. Singh
Alan C. Repp

INTRODUCTION

1

REFORMING THE RELATIONSHIP BETWEEN REGULAR AND SPECIAL EDUCATION: BACKGROUND AND ISSUES

John Wills Lloyd and Christine Gambatese
University of Virginia

Contentious issues do not spring forth fully formed and are rarely simple. They develop over time, growing and changing with the addition of new supporters and the discovery of new relationships with other issues. And they are composed of many smaller issues, often those contributed by the new supporters or added in reaction to detractors. The development and complexity of such topics also sometimes make them difficult to grasp.

As a contemporary issue in education, the "regular education initiative" has developed similarly. It is the product of many events, much discussion, and extensive modification. And it is sometimes difficult to understand the breadth and depth of the topic. This book includes chapters by many individuals who have been at the forefront of discussions about the regular education initiative, many of whom have contributed to its development and complexity; these chapters provide a deep and broad consideration of the topic.

In this chapter, we introduce the topic. In our introduction we hope to frame the issue in such a way that the following discussions become readily comprehensible and informative. To do so requires that we describe the background from which

the regular education initiative developed and the issues that comprise it.

BACKGROUND

Although the regular education initiative is primarily an educational matter with roots in criticisms of special education practices and policies, it has some roots in another parallel movement called deinstitutionalization. These two influences--deinstitutionalization and critiques of special education--form the content of this section.

Deinstitutionalization

Prior to the late 1960s and early 1970s, very many individuals with handicaps such as mental retardation or severe behavior disorders were placed in large residential facilities often called state hospitals. Such facilities became the focus of strong criticism by many individuals, criticism particularly well expressed by Nirje (1969a, 1969b). Pictorial essays (e.g., Blatt & Kaplan, 1966; Rivera, 1972) drew public attention to the deplorable conditions in state hospitals and, in concert with empirical and logical analyses of the effects of institutionalization (e.g., Wolfensberger, 1972), helped to launch the *normalization* movement in the area of mental retardation. Essentially, the normalization principle refers to providing individuals with mental retardation "patterns and conditions of everyday life which are as close as possible to the norms and patterns of the mainstream of society" (Nirje, 1969a, p. 181).

Deinstitutionalization resulted in the development of many community residential facilities for individuals--particularly those with mental retardation--who would otherwise have been placed in a state hospital. Advocates hoped that providing such facilities in the community--group homes--would lead to more nearly normal behavior on the part of people with mental retardation, more humane treatment, greater social and vocational opportunities, greater community acceptance of people with mental retardation, and other similar benefits.

Advocates of the integration of children and youth into regular education classrooms have hoped that such integration will produce similar benefits. Indeed, many of the ideas and much of the rhetoric of the integration movement has parallels in the normalization movement.

Critiques of Education

The United States witnessed tremendous political, social, and economic changes during the 1980s. A decade of

economic growth, fundamental changes in the political structure of foreign countries, and other marks of progress contrasted with homelessness, AIDS, drug abuse, governmental debt, and other problems.

Education was one of the areas of public policy that received the greatest emphasis during this remarkable decade (Balz, 1989). In *A Nation At Risk*, we were warned about a rising tide of mediocrity in our educational system, apprehension that a decreased level of competence in our schools jeopardized our future (National Commission on Excellence in Education, 1983). Education was painted as generating products of inferior quality, functioning inefficiently, sheltering ill-prepared or even incompetent teachers, and losing touch with the concerns of the general citizenry; education was simply not doing well enough--it was ill. And, although overall spending on education increased, commissions repeatedly criticized educational practice and the structure of schools. Politicians contended that increases in funding were not an appropriate means of improving the quality of education provided to pupils. Just as was true in other areas of social service, education must learn to do more with less.

Not only was education in general an issue of the 80s, but special education was a specific area of concern. Early in the decade, schools were contending with the substantial changes necessitated by implementation of Public Law 94-142, the Education of All Handicapped Children Act (EHA) (1978). Many considered the passage of EHA to be a landmark in civil rights legislation, in part because it mandated federal support of special education programs for individuals who had long been neglected.

But even before the passage of EHA, some people questioned the usefulness of special education programs. The titles of several papers illustrate this point:

[1]Others, however, became one of the ubiquitous sights of big cities: homeless people. By the early 1980s the population of institutions had decreased to one-fourth of the level it was in 1955 and as many as 90% of the people in shelters for the homeless may have "diagnosable mental illness" (Bassuk, 1984, p. 42). Although there are many homeless children (see, Kozol, 1988), Bassuk's sample consisted mostly of adults. One should not construe that a like percent of all homeless individuals, particularly all homeless children, suffer from mental illness.

- "Special Education for the Mildly Retarded--Is Much of It Justifiable?" (Dunn, 1968);

- "Providing Special Education without Special Classes" (Budoff, 1972);

- "Down With (Most) Special Education Classes" (Kraft, 1972).

One of the bases for these position papers was what is often called *efficacy research*--studies of the effectiveness of different systems for delivering educational services to pupils with handicaps. Studies of the effectiveness of special education services and service arrangements had at least a 40-year history at the time of the passage of EHA. Table 1 presents a list of some of these studies. Many of them are discussed in greater detail in subsequent chapters.

Not long after the passage of EHA, some professionals continued to raise questions about education of pupils with handicaps, particularly in light of the tremendous political changes taking place as part of the Reagan presidency. Perhaps one of the most important events in the raising of such questions was a meeting held at Wingspread, a conference center near Racine, Wisconsin, in September of 1981.

Participants in the 1981 Wingspread conference addressed an array of broad questions about the relationship between public policy and education of pupils with handicaps. Among the issues raised were many that presaged the issues discussed in this text. For example, the conference participants were asked to address the questions listed in Table 2.

At the 1981 Wingspread meeting, Reynolds and Wang (1983) identified many of the aspects of special education that would become issues of concern as a part of the regular education initiative: indefensible labeling of students, inappropriate funding systems, development of miniature bureaucracies serving each of the various categories of students, adaptation of regular education learning environments, extension of services to children with learning problems who were not officially identified as handicapped, and others. These concerns were echoed by others, particularly Stainback and Stainback (1984). One of the biggest boosts for the fledgling movement came when Madeline Will (1986), the Assistant Secretary of Education for the U. S. Department of Education, spoke at a subsequent meeting (1985) at Wingspread. Drawing many ideas from earlier critiques of special education, Will called for regular and special educators to share the responsibility of teaching students with learning problems. Her comments were later published as a paper in *Exceptional Children* (Will, 1986).

Around this time, the term "regular education initiative" came into common use, though the origins of the term are unclear. In October, 1986, the Teacher Education Division (TED) of the Council for Exceptional Children issued a statement describing recommendations about reform being forwarded by members of the federal government and special educators. In this document, TED used the term regular education initiative (REI) to describe attempts to "revise instructional program options for low-performing students" (p. 1).

Although it is difficult to identify the earliest use of the term REI, there have been many historical events that reflect on the question of whether, or to what extent, learners with handicaps should be educated beside their peers who do not have handicaps. There have been many efforts to provide separate or integrated education for individuals with handicaps, as Table 3 shows. For discussion of the implications of these and other historical events, see the chapter by Hocutt and her colleagues in this book.

The events and ideas in the preceding paragraphs show concern about educa-

Table 1: Selected Efficacy Studies

Year	Authors	Study Title
1932	Bennett	A Comparative Study of Sub-Normal Children in the Elementary Grades.
1936	Partsch	A Comparative Study of the Progress of Sub-Normal Pupils in the Grades and in Special Classes.
1957	Carriker	A Comparison of Post-School Adjustment of Regular and Special Class Retarded Individuals Served in Lincoln and Omaha, Nebraska, Public Schools.
1957	Lapp	A Study of Social Adjustment of Slow Learning Children Who Were Assigned Part Time to Regular Classes.
1958	Baldwin	The Social Position of the Educable Mentally Retarded in the Regular Grades in the Public Schools.
1958	Blatt	The Physical, Personality, and Academic Status of Children Who are Mentally Retarded Attending Special Classes as Compared with Children Who Are Mentally Retarded Attending Regular Classes.
1962	Johnson	Special Education for Mentally Handicapped--A Paradox.
1962	Kern & Pfaeffle	A Comparison of Social Adjustment of Mentally Retarded Children in Various Educational Settings.
1965	Goldstein, Moss, & Jordan	The Efficacy of Special Class Training in the Development of Mentally Retarded Children.
1971	Sabatino	An Evaluation of Resource Rooms for Children with Learning Disabilities.
1972	Bersoff, Kabler, Fiscus & Ankley	Effectiveness of Special Class Placement for Children Labeled Neurologically Impaired.
1973	Gottlieb & Budoff	Social Acceptability of Retarded Children in Non-Graded Schools Differing in Architecture.
1973	Gottlieb & Davis	Social Acceptance of EMR's During Overt Behavioral Interaction.
1974	Gampel, Gottlieb, & Harrison	Comparison of Classroom Behavior of Special-Class EMR, Integrated EMR, Low IQ, and Nonretarded Children.
1975	Gottlieb, Gampel & Budoff	Classroom Behavior of Retarded Children Before and After Integration into Regular Classes.
1976	Budoff & Gottlieb	Special Class EMR Children Mainstreamed: A Study of an Aptitude (Learning Potential) x Treatment Interaction.
1976	Myers	The Efficacy of the Special Day School for EMR Pupils.
1980	Carlberg & Kavale	The Efficacy of Special vs. Regular Class Placement for Exceptional Children: A Meta-Analysis.

Table 2: Questions Directed to Participants of the Wingspread Conference

1. What does the current system for allocating and serving handicapped children look like and how does it work?

2. What do we know about the effectiveness of *current practice*, and to what extent is best practice a part of current practice. [*sic*]

3. *How can public policy contribute to the quality of teaching* in programs for handicapped children and youth?

4. *How is the special education system actually or potentially integrated with other systems?*

5. Is there a need for general restructuring of the special education area and of its relations with "regular" education? What lessons can be learned from the experience of implementing legislation for other special *populations which are applicable to the special education area?*

NOTE. From "Symposium on public policy and educating handicapped persons" by M. C. Reynolds, J. Brandl, & W. C. Copeland, 1983, *Policy Studies Review*, Volume 2, Special No. 1, p. 12. Copyright 1983 by Policy Studies Organization. Reprinted by permission.

tion, people with handicaps, and the education of children and youth with handicaps. By the 1980s, there was general agreement that education needed to change. And there was continuing concern about making the lives of people with handicaps more closely approximate normalcy. And there was agreement that special education needed reform. But people disagreed about what changes were needed and how reforms should be achieved. This disagreement ranges over many issues.

ISSUES

As we noted previously, the regular education initiative is not a simple topic. The REI is not solely about the question of whether special educational services should be delivered in separate or integrated settings. Though setting is the central issue, the REI includes many related issues: labeling, testing, roles of specialists, and so forth. In this section we identify issues that are related in important ways to the topic.

Because our purpose in identifying these issues is not to resolve each of them, we shall not engage in debate about them. Instead, we pose a series of questions that are addressed in the subsequent chapters.

- Are regular educators prepared to work with pupils who have disabilities? Do they have the expertise? Are they willing to have more students with handicaps in their classes? Do they have the requisite administrative and institutional support?

- Are many of the problems confronting atypical learners and their schools symptomatic of problems in how the larger society addresses handicaps? Does society as a whole consider people with handicaps to be less worthy, less human, less capable? Is it the responsibility of schools to blunt such an attitude? What changes are needed to make regular education more amenable to serving atypical learners?

- Do non-handicapped pupils receive a better education when they have more frequent and more direct contact with their peers who have handicaps? Does placing pupils with handicaps in regular classrooms hinder the educational progress

Table 3: Historical Events Reflecting Ambivalence about Separate or Joint Schooling of   Handicapped and Non-Handicapped Students

1760's Thomas Braidwood established a separate facility, Academy for the Deaf and Dumb, in Britain.

1760 Abbe de l'Eppe opened a public school for the handicapped (Institution Nationale des Sourds-Maits in Paris), a first attempt to teach a large class rather than provide tutoring.

1778 Samuel Heinicke established state school for handicapped children in Germany.

1784 Valentin Huay, an associate of Abbe de l'Eppe established the National Institution for Young Blind People in Paris.

1792 London Asylum for the Deaf opened

1793 Henry Dannett established an asylum for the indigent blind in Liverpool; it was intended to be a vocational school instructing the blind in musical or mechanical arts. In 1800 it became the School of Industry for the Blind.

1810 Johann Wilhelm Klein began to promote the principle of education of blind children in local schools for non-handicapped children.

1812 The General Institution for the Instruction of Deaf and Dumb Children was established in Birmingham, England.

1817 Thomas Hopkins Gallaudet established the first American public residential school for deaf students in Hartford, CN. It is now known as the American School for the Deaf.

1819 Arrowsmith published *The Art of Instructing the Infant Deaf and Dumb* which recounted how his deaf brother had learned to speak (by imitating the other children and using lip reading) when he attended an ordinary school. Arrowsmith advocated that deaf children should attend ordinary schools.

1819 Johann Wilhelm Klein prepared a guide to assist regular classroom teachers who had blind children enrolled in their classrooms.

1824 Samuel Gridley Howe founded the Perkins School for the Blind in Watertown Mass.

1837 Edward Seguin established a residential school for people with retardation in Paris.

1840's James Donaldson of Scotland left his fortune to establish a residential school for the education of destitute children. The school accepted one deaf child for every two destitute children with normal hearing.

1842 The government of Lower Austria issued an official statement indicating that wherever possible the education of the blind should be incorporated into regular public schools

1844 The Kurtz Foundation in Munich was subsidized by the state and became the first instance of the education of crippled children by public funds.

1848 Eduard Seguin became superintendent of the newly opened Massachusetts School for Idiots and Feeble-Minded Youths.

1852 Massachusetts became the first state to enact compulsory education laws; however, these laws expressly permitted exclusion of children with handicaps from required attendance.

1854 Congress authorized establishment of a school for the deaf, dumb and blind, which became Gallaudet College for the education of the deaf.

1855 A residential community school for child with retardation was established in Boston.

1865 The National Industrial Home for Crippled Boys opened in Kensington, England; it enrolled only pupils with disabilities.

1868 A blind boy was admitted to the Mid-Parish School at Greenock, England, and was taught beside and with the help of sighted pupils. By 1874, 50 blind students were being taught this way.

1869 Boston established a special class for deaf students.

1871 Authorities in New Haven, CT, opened an ungraded class for truant, disobedient, and insubordinate children.

Table 3 (continued)

1873 The First International Conference of Teachers of the Blind at Vienna resolved that blind students should only be educated with sighted students in the absence of something better.

1874 William Stainer was appointed Superintendent of the Instruction of the Deaf in London and he requested a room in a public school and opened a class for deaf children there. By 1888, 373 deaf children were being instructed in such centers, all of which were within ordinary public schools.

1874 New York established a special class for unruly or truant boys.

1875 Wynter argued for the benefits of mixing "imbeciles" with "sane" members of society. His idea was that through the power of imitation, the imbeciles would learn from those of greater intelligence. The segregated setting was viewed as intensifying idiocy.

1876 Charity Organization Society's Special Committee published a report expressing the view that blind children should be educated with sighted children in the public elementary schools until the age of 15 when industrial training should begin. Institutionalization should be the exception. (In the end, it was this approach--the approach recommended by the First International Conference of Teachers of the Blind made in 1873--that the London School Board followed.)

1878 London School Board Inspector Marchant Williams published a report stating that blind children should spend only part of their day in special classes and the remainder of the day in ordinary schools near their homes.

1886 Nelson's Royal Readers (braille books) became available. These were used in many board schools so that blind children could read the same books and be taught beside sighted children

1888 By this date, 133 blind children in London were being educated as recommended in the London School Board's report. There were 23 centers attached to ordinary schools, and the children divided their time between the center and regular classrooms and playgrounds with sighted children.

1896 A separate day class for retarded pupils ("problem children") was established in Providence, RI.

1898 Alexander Graham Bell, in an address to the National Education Association, suggested that an annex to the public school be formed to provide special classes for deaf, blind, and mentally deficient.

1899 The Education Commission of Chicago urged establishment of special, ungraded classes and parental schools for pupils who could not be managed in the regular classes.

1900 Compulsory attendance laws had been enacted widely. Providing for all minors, including those with handicaps, introduced new problems. Initially, schools attempted to educate them, particularly those with mild mental retardation, within regular classes, but they either failed or were left back. Many behavior problems occurred, and thus the special class emerged.

1902 Alexander Graham Bell argued that special education programs in local schools, should function as he had recommended in 1989; children should not have to leave their homes to attend institutions and the National Education Association should actively pursue such educational provisions.

1902 Supervisor of Primary Schools in New Haven, CT, noted that ungraded classes were receiving three distinct groups of students in the special classes--incorrigible boys, defective children, and non-English speaking pupils.

1905 New York City established its first non-residential school (PS 120 in Manhattan) for truants, delinquents, and incorrigible children. Part of the rationale for this school was that the removal of those students whose behavior is disruptive would benefit the other students in the schools.

1913 Roxbury, MA, established a special class for partially-sighted pupils.

1920 Lynn, MA, established a special class for pupils with hearing losses.

1930 Studies comparing the efficacy of special class placement began to be conducted (see Table 1).

1945 The Council for Exceptional Children annual meeting included a panel discussion of segregated educational practices and concluded that children with educable mental retardation should be included in regular education settings.

1946 New York City established the so-called "600 Schools" specifically to educate pupils with emotional disturbance. Some of these were day schools, others residential diagnostic treatment centers. A bureau in the Division of Child Welfare was created to provide a therapeutic school environment

Table 3 (continued)

for students who could not be taught effectively in the regular schools and whose behavior could not be tolerated in the classroom.

1948   By this date, 41 of 48 states had enacted laws authorizing or requiring school districts to make special educational provisions for at least one category of students with handicaps (most often those with mental retardation).

1954   The U. S. Supreme Court ruled that separate schools for black and white students were unconstitutional (*Brown versus Board of Education*).

1950s   Studies compared the self-esteem, social acceptance, and achievement of children with
-70s   handicaps in the mainstream to those in special education classrooms.

1962   G. O. Johnson's review of literature concluded that special classes were of little academic value to pupils with mild retardation.

1966   Bureau of Education for the Handicapped was established within the U. S. Office of Education to promote the development of better programs for pupils with handicaps.

1968   Lloyd Dunn's article ("Special Education for the mildly retarded--Is much of it Justifiable?") accompanied widespread reevaluation of the establishment of special classes.

1972   *Pennsylvania Association for Retarded Citizens v. Commonwealth of Pennsylvania*, a class action suit brought on behalf of children in state-operated institutions, was settled by a consent agreement. The agreement required that the state must provide access to free appropriate public education for retarded children of Pennsylvania.

1972   *Mills v. Board of Education of District of Columbia* led to a court order that required the public schools to provide for pupils with handicaps even if they did not fit the currently available array of services.

1975   U. S. Congress passed Public Law 94-142, the Education of All Handicapped Children Act which legally specified a preference for the least restrictive environment.

1977   National Education Association Teachers Rights Committee formed a panel to investigate the experiences of selected school systems in carrying out PL 94-142 and state special education laws.

NOTE. We consulted the following sources in developing this table: Berkowitz and Rothman (1967), Cullinan, Epstein, and Lloyd (1983), Dunlop (1977), Dunn (1962), Gearheart and Weishahn (1984), Hobbs, 1975; Hoffman (1975), Kauffman (1989), Kaufman (1985), Massie (1978), Pritchard (1963), Schwartz (1984), Stephens, Blackhurst, and Magliocca (1982), and Wallin (1955).

of pupils who do not have handicaps?

• Does identifying and labeling students as handicapped cause them harm? Do labels cause stigma? Is labeling itself essentially discriminatory? Is it necessary?

• Are our systems for classifying students defensible? Are our instruments measuring what they are supposed to measure? Does anyone really know where to draw the line between normal and retarded achievement? How precise and trustworthy are test scores? Should a difference of one or two points on one test-- between otherwise identical people--make the difference between labels? Do our criteria for classification take into account other factors in children's lives (abuse, poverty, hunger, sleeplessness) which may be effecting their achievement and behavior?

- Does the matter of integration depend on the type of handicap a pupil has? Should students be integrated into the mainstream regardless of the kinds of problems they may manifest? Is integration more appropriate for certain pupils during certain times of the day?

- What is the least restrictive environment? Should regular education classrooms be considered the least restrictive environment and, therefore, the recommended placement for all pupils? Under what conditions is it appropriate to use specialized settings away from regular classrooms?

- Is special education effective? Is regular education effective for learners with handicaps? On what metrics do we base our answers to these questions? How trustworthy is the evidence bearing on them?

- What is the place of evidence in making educational policy? Should policies be based solely on evidence?

- Is provision of educational services outside of the regular classroom a violation of a fundamental right? Does requiring student with handicaps to participate in regular classrooms violate a right to needed services? Is separate education on the basis of learning characteristics inherently unequal?

- Is it fair to spend more money on one child than on another? What is the source of the enormous amount of money required for special education?

Are our special education dollars being used wisely? Would schools be more effective if they were no longer required to devote certain funds to special education and were free to allot that money to serve a wider variety of students with learning problems?

These are complex questions that cannot be answered with a simple "yes" or "no." A person's answers to some of the questions may conflict with her or his answers to other questions. But, answering such questions helps to elucidate one's views on the regular education initiative.

In the following chapters, authors with substantial experience in special education address the issues raised here (and other issues), often arriving at different conclusions. They bring to their discussions arguments from diverse sources. The ideas they present must be considered in the context of decisions about where and with whom to educate children and youth with handicaps that have been made over the past 200 years, discussions of mainstreaming during the 1970s, exchanges about the effectiveness of special education from the 1950s through the present, arguments about normalization in the 1960s and 70s, disputes about the reform of education during the 1980s, and disagreement about the appropriate role of social institutions in American society during the 1980s. This context makes clear that the controversy over the regular education initiative is the current version of a continuing debate about how to provide the most beneficial educational services to our children and youth.

REFERENCES

Baldwin, W. K. (1958). The social position of the educable mentally retarded in the regular grades in the public schools. *Exceptional Children, 25,* 106-108,112.

Balz, D. (1989, December 12). A decade of doubts about social policy. *The Washington Post*, pp. A1, A18-A19.

Bassuk, E. L. (1984). The homlessness problem. *Scientific American, 251*(1), 40-45.

Bennett, A. (1932). *A comparative study of sub-normal children in the elementary grades.* New York: Teachers College, Columbia University.

Berkowitz, P. H., & Rothman, E. P. (1967). *Public education for disturbed children in New York City.* Springfield, IL: Charles C Thomas.

Bersoff, D. N., Kabler, M., Fiscus, E., & Ankley, R. (1972). Effectiveness of special class placement for children labeled neurologically impaired. *Journal of School Psychology, 10*,157-163.

Blatt, B. (1958). The physical, personality, and academic status of children who are mentally retarded attending special classes as compared with children who are mentally retarded attending regular classes. *American Journal of Mental Deficiency, 62*, 810-818.

Blatt, B., & Kaplan, F. (1966). *Christmas in purgatory: A photographic essay on mental retardation.* Boston: Allyn and Bacon.

Budoff, M. (1972). Providing special education without special classes. *Journal of School Psychology, 10*, 199-205.

Budoff, M., & Gottlieb, J. (1976). Special class EMR children mainstreamed: A study of an aptitude (learning potential) x treatment interaction. *American Journal of Mental Deficiency, 81*, 1-11.

Carlberg, C., & Kavale K. (1980). The efficacy of special vs. regular class placement for exceptional children: A meta-analysis. *Journal of Special Education, 14*, 295-309.

Carriker, W. R. (1957). *A comparison of post-school adjustments of regular and special class retarded individuals served in Lincoln and Omaha, Nebraska, public schools* (Study prepared pursuant to Contract SAE-6445, U. S. Department of Health, Education, and Welfare). Lincoln: University of Nebraska.

Cullinan, D., Epstein, M. H., & Lloyd, J. W. (1983). *Behavior disorders of children and adolescents.* Englewood Cliffs, NJ: Prentice-Hall.

Dunlop, K. (1977). Mainstreaming: Valuing diversity in children. *Young Children, 32*(4) 26-32.

Dunn, L. M. (1962). *Mental retardation: Readings and resources.* New York: Holt, Reinhart, & Winston.

Dunn, L. M. (1968). Special education for the mildly handicapped--Is much of it justifiable? *Exceptional Children, 35*, 5-22.

Education of All Handicapped Children Act of 1975, 20 U.S.C. 1401 (1978).

Gampel, D. H., Gottlieb, J., & Harrison, R. H. (1974). Comparison of classroom behavior of special-class EMR, integrated EMR, low IQ, and nonretarded children. *American Journal of Mental Deficiency, 79*, 16-21.

Gearheart, B. R., & Weishahn, M. W. (1984). *The exceptional student in the regular classroom.* St Louis: Mosby.

Goldstein, H., Moss, J. W., & Jordan, L. J. (1965). *The efficacy of special class training in the development of mentally retarded children.* Cooperative Research Project No. 619, Washington D.C.: US Office of Education.

Gottlieb, J., & Budoff, M. (1973). Social acceptability of retarded children in non-graded schools differing in architecture. *American Journal of Mental Deficiency, 78*, 15-19.

Gottlieb, J., & Davis, J. E. (1973). Social acceptance of EMR's during overt behavioral interaction, *American Journal of Mental Deficiency, 78*, 141-143.

Gottlieb, J., Gampel, D. H., & Budoff, M. (1975). Classroom behavior of retarded children before and after integration into regular classes. *Journal of Special Education, 9*, 307-315.

Hobbs, N. (1975). *The futures of children.* San Francisco: Jossey-Bass.

Hoffman, E. (1975). A study of child variance: Vol 3 Service Delivery Systems. *Journal of Special Education, 9*,415-423.

Johnson, G. O. (1962). Special education for mentally handicapped--A paradox. *Exceptional Children, 19*, 62-69.

Kauffman, J. M. (1989). *Characteristics of behavior disorders of children and youth* (4th ed.). Columbus, OH: Merrill.

Kaufman, M. (1985). *Mainstreaming learners and their environments.* Cambridge, MA: Brookline Books.

Kern, W. H., & Pfaeffle, H. (1962). A comparison of social adjustment of mentally retarded children in various educational settings. *American Journal of Mental Deficiency, 67*, 407-413.

Kozol, J. (1988). *Rachel and her children: Homeless families in America.* New York: Fawcett Columbine

Kraft, A. (1972). Down with (most) special education classes. *Academic Therapy, 8,* 207-216.

Lapp, E. R. (1957). A study of social adjustment of slow learning children who were assigned part time to regular classes. *American Journal of Mental Deficiency, 62,* 254-262.

Massie, D. (1978). Update. *Today's Education, 67*(3), 60-62.

Myers, J. K. (1976). The efficacy of the special day school for EMR pupils. *Mental Retardation, 14*(4), 3-11.

National Commission on Excellence in Education. (1983). *A nation at risk: The imperative for educational reform.* Washington, DC: Author.

Nirje, B. (1969a). The normalization principle and its human management implications. In R. B. Kugel & W. Wolfensberger (Eds.), *Changing patterns in residential services for the mentally retarded* (pp. 179-195). Washington, DC: President's Commission on Mental Retardation.

Nirje, B. (1969b). A Scandinavian visitor looks at U. S. institutions. In R. B. Kugel & W. Wolfensberger (Eds.), *Changing patterns in residential services for the mentally retarded* (pp. 51-57). Washington, DC: President's Commission on Mental Retardation.

Partsch, C. F. (1936). *A comparative study of the progress of sub-normal pupils in the grades and in special classes.* New York: Teachers College, Columbia University.

Pritchard, D. G. (1963). *Education and the handicapped 1760-1960.* New York: Humanities Press.

Reynolds, M. C., & Wang, M. C. (1983). Restructuring "special" school programs: A position paper. *Policy Studies Review, 2*(1), 189-212.

Rivera, G. (1972). *Willowbrook.* New York: Random House.

Sabatino, D. A. (1971). An evaluation of resource rooms for children with learning disabilities. *Journal of Learning Disabilities, 4*(2), 27-35.

Schwartz, L. L. (1984). *Exceptional students in the mainstream.* Belmont, CA: Wadsworth.

Stainback, W., & Stainback, S. (1984). A rationale for the merger of special and regular education. *Exceptional Children, 51,* 102-111.

Stephens, T. M., Blackhurst, A. E., & Magliocca, L. A. (1982). *Teaching mainstreamed students.* New York: John Wiley & Sons.

Teacher Education Division. (1986). *A statement by the Teacher Education Division, Council for Exceptional Children, on the regular education initiative.* Reston, VA: Author.

Wallin, J. E. (1955). *Education of the mentally handicapped children.* New York: Harper & Row.

Will, M. C. (1986). Educating children with learning problems: A shared responsibility. *Exceptional Children, 1986, 52,* 411-416.

Wolfensberger, W. (1972). *Normalization: The principle of normalization in human services.* Toronto: National Institute on Mental Retardation.

PART I

2

HISTORICAL AND LEGAL CONTEXT OF MAINSTREAMING

Anne M. Hocutt
North Carolina State Department of Public Instruction

Edwin W. Martin
Human Resources Center

James D. McKinney
University of Miami

The purpose of this chapter is to present the historical and legal context of mainstreaming. Mainstreaming may be defined as:

> the temporal, instructional, and social integration of eligible exceptional children with normal peers based on an ongoing, individually determined, educational planning and programming process and requires clarification of responsibility among regular and special education administrative, instructional, and supportive personnel (Kaufman, Gottlieb, Agard, & Kukic, 1975, p. 4).

The key concepts of integration of children, continuous individualized services, and clear roles and responsibilities for professionals are fundamental; mainstreaming is not merely a matter of placement. Clearly, mainstreaming is a complex idea that is likely to be difficult to implement adequately in real life settings. Yet, it is an ideal for those who are dedicated to providing the most appropriate education for handicapped students.

We are now in the middle of a debate on the extent to which atypical learners should be, and can be, accommodated within regular education. The increased practice of mainstreaming in the public schools is a goal of a movement called the Regular Education Initiative (REI) (Will, 1986). Proponents of the REI have argued that the current system for serving handicapped students in some combination of regular and special classes has created a dual educational system which is dysfunctional, ineffective, and excessively costly (Lilly, 1986; Stainback & Stainback, 1984; Reynolds & Wang, 1983). They believe that this system burdens schools with costly classification and placement procedures, and also that there is considerable evidence that special education is not effective for many handicapped students; consequently, they argue strongly for "restructuring" (Reynolds, Wang, & Walberg, 1987). They call for comprehensive, but experimental, mainstream education programs that would feature regular educational practices found to be effective (Reynolds et al., 1987). In short, they argue that regular education can accommodate "the full range and types of exceptional children" (Wang, 1987, p. 7).

Others have cautioned against the wholesale mainstreaming of handicapped students in regular classrooms. Some point out that it is illogical to advocate placing atypical learners in a regular education system that has come under major criticism in this decade (Keogh, 1988a). The research on the efficacy of special education is seriously flawed (Hallahan, Keller, McKinney, Lloyd, & Bryan, 1988; Wang & Baker, 1986)--as is the research on the effectiveness of educating atypical learners in regular education (Hallahan et al., 1988; Bryan & Bryan, 1988; Fuchs & Fuchs, 1988). Additionally, there are few methodologically sound comparisons of special versus regular class placement (Madden & Slavin, 1983), and the results of any comparisons are equivocal (Hocutt & Schulte, 1987; Madden & Slavin, 1983; Carlberg & Kavale, 1980; Goldstein, Moss, & Jordan, 1965). The assumptions of the regular education initiative, e.g., that student failure is due to deficits in schools rather than deficits in children, have been questioned (Kauffman, Gerber, & Semmel, 1988). Finally, there are serious questions about the extent to which regular educators are, or will be, willing to accept still more mainstreamed handicapped children (Gersten, Walker, & Darch, 1988; Gerber & Semmel, 1984; Walker & Rankin, 1983).

Given these issues, we believe that it is helpful to view the Regular Education Initiative, particularly its emphasis on mainstreaming, in the context of the historical and legal context of mainstreaming. The legal and historical context both illuminates the values (e.g., equality of opportunity) that make mainstreaming an educational ideal and the problems (e.g., the concern of regular educators, and the problems encountered in regular education) that make its implementation so difficult. Additionally, in our opinion, the legal and historical context instructs us about where the debate has "gone wrong," i.e., become unproductive, for the education of handicapped children.

SIGNIFICANT HISTORICAL EVENTS

In this section, we underscore some of the most significant historical events. Whereas the discussion in Chapter 1 reported the events, we describe their impact on and contribution to contemporary thinking.

Social Reform: Late 19th Century to the Early 20th Century

Special education began in this country in 1823 with the establishment of the first state school for the deaf in Kentucky. During the 19th century, other state schools and institutions for handicapped persons who had specific conditions were begun. By the end of the century, the typical service delivery pattern was state schools or institutions for the deaf, the blind, and the "feebleminded." Federal involvement in special education began in 1857 with the establishment of the Columbia Institution for the Instruction of the Deaf and Dumb, and the Blind (now known as Gallaudet College). The remarkable thing about these institutions is that they went counter to the idea prevalent throughout most of human history, that is, only a small number of presumably intelligent elite was worthy and capable of education.

Public school education for handicapped students began in 1869 with a public day school for the deaf in Boston; five years later, New York City began special education classes. In 1896, the city of Providence, Rhode Island, began special education classes for mentally retarded students. Nearly 20 years later, Minnesota instituted State aid for each child attending public school and even required special certificates for teachers of exceptional children. In 1913, Cleveland began a "sight saving class" in which children spent part of the day in a regular class with normal peers and the remainder of the day in a special class, which was perhaps the first attempt at what we currently call mainstreaming.

During the early 20th century, the combination of immigration, compulsory school attendance, and other reforms resulted in large numbers of children being served by public schools. Education of the masses was seen as a means to improve the quality of living and increase our economic productivity. Consequently, it was desirable to separate children who might be problematic in some way in the interest of school efficiency (Skrtic, 1987). Concurrently, the development and increasingly common use of the IQ test could be used to justify placement in special classes (Wang, 1987). Thus, special class placement became the preferred setting for those students whose academic or behavioral problems might be disruptive to the other students.

On the other hand, the growth of special classes rather than institutions was a movement to integrate handicapped children in the home and community (Kirk & Gallagher, 1979). It was not the case that the well-being of exceptional students was thought to be violated: In 1923, at the first meeting of the Council for Exceptional Children, a major speaker stated that "the special class is one of the new school tools" to improving the self-concept of mildly handicapped students (Woods, quoted in Hallahan & Kauffman, 1982, p. 425).

Through the first half of the 20th century and on into the 1960s, special education continued to be provided in self-contained classes for children having specific conditions (Weintraub, 1971). Special class placement was clearly preferred over residential placement wherever special education programs had been established. However, it was in-

evitable that eventually another question would be asked: Is regular class placement preferable to special class placement (Polloway, 1984)?

Civil Rights and the Concept of Equity: The Mid-Twentieth Century

The first major challenge to special class placement appeared in 1968 when Dunn published his now famous indictment of special class settings. Dunn stated that (a) no available evidence suggested that the academic progress of mentally retarded children in special, separate classes was better than the academic progress of mentally retarded children in regular classrooms; (b) labels accompanying special class placement were stigmatizing; (c) regular education was capable of providing effective individual instruction to slow or mentally retarded pupils; and (d) self-contained classes for mentally retarded children also tended to segregate black children from white children, as black children were disproportionately enrolled as a result of virtually complete reliance on IQ testing for placement decisions.

During the same period, a series of court cases in California questioned the standards and tests applied to assign students to special education in general and to label them handicapped--primarily as having educable mental retardation (EMR). The context in which these cases (e.g., *Diana v. State Board of Education* in 1970 and *Larry P. v. Riles* in 1972) were brought was the overrepresentation of minorities in classes for mildly retarded children in relation to their prevalence in the total school population. These cases resulted in injunctions against group testing, in requirements that tests be developed and standardized for different cultural and language subgroups in society, and requirements that parents give their consent for a child to be placed in special education. The entire thrust of these cases was to prevent special education classes from being dumping grounds for slow or difficult to teach children (Kirk & Gallagher, 1979).

It was, of course, no coincidence that concerns about the disproportionate percentages of minority children in separate classes and the separation of handicapped children from normally achieving children rose to the surface during the 1960s. The civil rights movement was the most powerful domestic force of the time, and it was entirely antithetical to ideas of unequal treatment of minority students and separation of black and white children. Potential discrimination of any kind--on the basis of race, sex, handicapping conditions--was a major concern. There was so strong a negative reaction to the fact that such a disproportionate number of minority children had been classified as mentally retarded that in 1973 the American Association of Mental Deficiency redefined mental retardation so that only those with an IQ below 70 qualified for services.

Legal decisions began to specify the criteria to be followed with regard to placement decisions. The consent agreement in *Pennsylvania Association for Retarded Children v. Commonwealth of Pennsylvania* (PARC) specifically stated that "placement in a regular public school class is preferable to placement in a special public school class and placement in a special public school class is preferable to placement in any other type of program of education and training" (PARC, 1971, Section 117). Similarly, in *Lebanks v. Spears*, 1973, the consent order reinforced the desirability of placement in regular education classrooms--with appropriate support service--over placement in special classes removed from the mainstream of public education.

At the federal level, leadership in the Bureau of Education for the Handicapped (BEH)--the forerunner of the Office of Special Education--began to push for a change in federal policy toward handicapped children. The change involved a move from federal support of education

for handicapped children through grants for research and teacher education to a fundamental commitment to special education for all children. Sidney Marland, then Commissioner of Education, followed the lead of the Bureau leadership and publicly called for a goal of education for all children by 1980. However, the President's Office of Management and Budget was concerned about the financial implications of such a goal and rejected a major increase in federal funding. BEH funded a major grant to the Education Commission of the States (ECS), which adopted the goal and added impetus to state efforts (Martin, 1971b).

The Council for Exceptional Children (CEC) had received a BEH grant to develop model state statutes that could be used or adopted by individual state governments (see Weintraub, Abeson, Ballard, & LaVor, 1976, pp. 195-211, for these statutes). Section 102 of Part 1 (Policy), entitled Preference for Regular Programs, is almost word for word the same language about the least restrictive environment that later became public law. This section reads:

> To the maximum extent practicable, handicapped children shall be educated along with children who do not have handicaps and shall attend regular classes. Impediments to learning and to the normal functioning of handicapped children in the regular school environment shall be overcome by the provision of special aids and services rather than by separate schooling for the handicapped. Special classes, separate schooling or other removal of handicapped children from the regular educational environment, shall occur only when, and to the extent that the nature or severity of the handicap is such that education in regular classes, even with the use of supplementary aids and ser-

vices, cannot be accomplished satisfactorily. (p. 196)

BEH and CEC then assisted ECS in holding a series of conferences attended by state legislators, school board members, and state administrators at which the model statutes were presented. These conferences made a tremendous difference in state-based special education programs; many states responded to the goal of education for all handicapped children, some adopting the model statutes word for word.

This activity at the local level was accompanied by Congressional activity. In the Senate, Harrison A. Williams of New Jersey, chairman of the Senate Committee on Labor and Public Welfare (now the Committee on Labor and Human Resources), established a standing Subcommittee on the Handicapped in 1971. The existence of this new Subcommittee meant stronger Congressional concern for the education of handicapped children. Under the chairmanship of Jennings Randolph of West Virginia, it immediately began work on Senate Bill 6, which was introduced in January, 1972.

Although some of the language in Senate Bill 6 changed considerably between its original introduction and its enactment as PL 94-142 in November of 1975, its provisions were taken largely from the CEC model statutes and the court orders and consent decrees. Section 612(5) of PL 94-142 requires the states to establish:

> procedures to assure that, to the maximum extent appropriate, handicapped children, including children in public or private institutions or other care facilities, are educated with children who are not handicapped and that special classes, separate schooling, or other removal of handicapped children from the regular educational environment occurs only when the nature or severity of the

handicap is such that education in regular classes with the use of supplementary aids cannot be achieved satisfactorily.

Section 614(C)(iv) requires local education agencies to provide full educational opportunities to all handicapped children, including:

> to the maximum extent practicable and consistent with the provisions of section 612(5)(B), the provision of special services to enable such children to participate in regular educational programs.

During consideration of this legislation, there was a great deal of discussion in the Congress about just what "to the maximum extent appropriate" and a phrase from Section 612(2)(b)--"appropriate public education"--actually meant in terms of implementation. No one knew exactly how to define "appropriate," and the debate in executive sessions was lively, with considerable differences of opinion about just how much mainstreaming the members could anticipate as a result of enactment of the legislation. In testimony before the House Select Education Subcommittee, BEH Director Martin explained the Executive Branch's view that "appropriate" would be that program defined by the school with parental participation through the IEP process--a local decision (Martin, 1971a).

Additionally, several senators had heard from the regular educators in their state education agencies and were expressing some reservation about wholesale mainstreaming of most or all handicapped children. Another issue that was brought up was the extent to which teachers would be held responsible for children's achieving the goals and objectives of their IEPs; teachers were assured that the IEP was a plan for services that must be delivered in good faith, but not a document meant to guarantee that those services had to succeed, or that the teacher, therapist, or other caregiver was accountable for their success.

In the end, the philosophy that was accepted was based on a "cascade of services" (Reynolds, 1973). Available options in every Local Education Agency (LEA) would range from full-time placement in the regular classroom (with or without support services) to full-time placement in special classes, the home, or hospitals and residential institutions. The "cascade of services" concept was built into both law and the regulations promulgated pursuant to the enactment of P.L. 94-142. The ultimate decision about which of these placement options was the least restrictive environment appropriate for a child would be made by the parents at the meeting of the local IEP committee.

While the bills that became PL 94-142 were being considered and during the period immediately after enactment of P.L. 94-142, staff in the BEH were called upon time and again to explain the concept of least restrictive environment to worried regular educators. Across the country, regular educators at the local level expressed concern that the intent of the law was to place moderately and severely handicapped students in regular classroom settings. National organizations, e.g., the National Education Association and the National School Boards Association, expressed concern about the impact of the law on regular education teachers and students. However, regular educators were not the only concerned professionals. Special educators themselves, who endorsed the concept, were worried about the "mad dash" to mainstream children without full recognition of the barriers (e.g., the preparation of regular teachers) that would have to be overcome (Martin, 1974).

The concept of mainstreaming, however, was widely accepted in principle, and, in 1976, CEC officially endorsed it

within the context of a continuum of services:

> Mainstreaming is a belief which involves an educational placement procedure and process for exceptional children, based on the conviction that each such child should be educated in the least restrictive environment in which his educational and related needs can be satisfactorily provided. This concept recognizes that exceptional children have a wide range of special educational needs, varying greatly in intensity and duration; that there is a recognized continuum of educational settings which may, at a given time, be appropriate for an individual child's needs; that to the maximum extent appropriate, exceptional children should be educated with non-exceptional children; and that special classes, separate schooling, or other removal of an exceptional child from education with non-exceptional children should occur only when the intensity of the child's special education and related needs is such that they cannot be satisfied in an environment including non-exceptional children, even with the provision of supplementary aids and services (quoted in Hallahan & Kauffman, 1982, p. 426).

The Late Twentieth Century: The Regular Education Initiative and A Nation at Risk

Over the years since enactment of PL 94-142 (Education of All Handicapped Children Act of 1975), the principle of mainstreaming has been widely accepted by special educators. PL 94-142 requires that the Department of Education annually report to Congress about the implementation of the law; one feature of these reports is an accounting of the percentage of pupils participating in the mainstream. The Second Annual Report to the Congress on the Implementation of Public Law 94-142 (U.S. Department of Education, 1980) shows that the percentage of handicapped children in regular classes had increased from 58 percent in school year 1976-77 to 61.1 percent in school year 1977-78. "Regular classes" was one of four broad categories; the others were separate classrooms, separate school facilities, and other environments (e.g., home or hospital). This increase in regular class placement was accompanied by a decrease in the three other placements. particularly separate school facilities. The Tenth Annual Report to the Congress on the Implementation of Public Law 94-142 (U.S. Department of Education, 1988) shows that 67 percent of handicapped students received special education in regular classes, or a combination of resource room and regular class, and that an additional 24 percent received services in separate classes within a regular education building.

To the extent that exceptional children are being served in regular classrooms across the country, the principle of mainstreaming also has been accepted, at least to some degree, by regular educators. However, the continuing debate over mainstreaming has been fueled by a number of factors: continuing concerns about the overidentification of minority children and separate placement in special education classes; lack of definitive research results about the efficacy of either special or regular class placement; the issue of stigma associated with students separated from their peers; and a belief that instructional strategies found effective with normally achieving students will be equally effective with all mildly handicapped students and perhaps with all students.

The debate is now occurring within the context of a major reform movement in regular education based on deep concerns about its quality. In 1983, the National Commission on Excellence in Education published *A Nation At Risk*, a short document that accused the nation's educational system of being "a rising tide of mediocrity." This was followed by reports and studies, among them *A Report on Secondary Education in America* (Boyer, 1983), *A Place Called School: Prospects for the Future* (Goodlad, 1984), *Horace's Compromise: The Dilemma of the American High School* (Sizer, 1984), and *A Nation Prepared: Teachers for the 21st Century* (Carnegie Forum on Education and the Economy, 1986).

The impetus for these reports was a deep concern about America's ability to compete in world markets. A high general level of education was, and is, viewed as the key to continued economic productivity. The critics argue that in the communication age, with a knowledge-based economy, we have made a fundamental mistake in emphasizing basic levels of competence and, consequently, not ensuring that all children reach those levels of competence required in a competitive world economy. They advocate strongly for an education that promotes critical thinking skills such that the entire work force can "think for themselves . . . act independently and with others . . . can render critical judgment and contribute constructively to many enterprises, whose knowledge is wide-ranging and whose understanding runs deep" (Carnegie Forum on Education and the Economy, 1986, p. 20).

The criticisms of the regular education system made by these and other critics can be briefly summarized as follows:

- Typically, teachers stand in front of classes imparting knowledge; students listen to lectures, fill in the blanks in workbooks, and generally regurgitate rote lessons;

- Class sizes are too large in general, and the average of 150 students per day handled by secondary teachers is too many for the teacher to realistically know and remember;

- A core curriculum is needed, especially at the secondary level (among the various proposals, the emphasis should be on literature, history, Western civilization, science, mathematics, foreign language, the arts, and civics or U.S. government, the idea being that students should understand that they are part of a community beyond themselves); and

- Teachers need to be paid more, and a way of providing greater compensation to the best teachers needs to be worked out.

As a result of these and other criticisms, regular educators are attending to the research on effective schools and on effective teaching. There is much discussion about holding schools and school systems accountable, and much emphasis is being placed on outcomes; e.g., higher student performance on achievement and mastery tests, lower dropout rates, higher attendance rates, higher graduation rates, and better performance by graduates attending colleges and universities. Additionally, there is much more emphasis on teaching higher order skills in addition to the basic skills. Thus, some states are even using academic course enrollments (especially for advanced courses at the high school level), the amount of homework given or completed, and SAT scores as outcome variables (Kaagan & Coley, 1989).

The *State Education Indicators*, a document published by the Council of Chief State School Officers, (1988), shows that most states now have programs designed to promote greater achievement for all students. These programs fall in the categories of instructional leadership, ef-

fective teaching, school climate, professionalism/collegiality, regular assessment and use of results, and comprehensive effective school programs. The names of specific state programs give a clue to priorities: Effective Teaching Through Higher Achievement, Student Assessment Program, Teacher Performance Appraisal System, Teacher Quality Improvement Program, and Educational Effectiveness Administrative Training Program. The names of various state laws, such as The Excellence in Education Act of 1985, the State Education Reform Act of 1982, and the Quality Basic Education Law, are equally reflective of regular educational priorities.

On the surface, this major educational reform effort looks positive in light of the mainstreaming initiative. Many specific reforms that are mentioned (e.g., smaller classes, interactive teaching, use of teaching strategies such as peer coaching and mastery learning) are familiar to special educators. However, we believe that the overall picture is not as positive with regard to mainstreaming as it might appear.

Equity, or equal opportunity for all children, is one of two major values underlying the reform effort, but discussions of equity in the reform literature are limited to children largely served in regular education classes. The effective schools research model and other efforts pay considerable attention to the needs of poor, minority, and inner-city students (Edmonds, 1982; Stedman, 1987; Lezotte, 1989). In some states, analyses of data focus on outcomes of these students by using indices composed of parent education or occupation, or of percentage of students receiving Aid to Families with Dependent Children or receiving Federal assistance in a school lunch program (Kaagan & Coley, 1989). However, the silence about the needs of, or outcomes for, handicapped children in the current reform movement is deafening.

Obviously, excellence is the other value driving the reform effort. The focus on excellence recognizes the fact that, as pointed out by Keogh (1988a, 1988b), schools are not working even for regular students, and especially are not working for regular students who come from disadvantaged homes or from different culture/ethnic groups. We point to criticisms listed above with regard to overburdened and underpaid teachers, large classes and large teacher loads, and of rigid and out-of-date organizational structure as likely factors in this failure. These problems, which have not yet been changed to any significant degree, may also account in part for the failure of the regular system to accommodate handicapped students successfully, as witnessed by their referral for special education.

The drive toward excellence is hardly surprising, given the impetus to supply workers equipped to handle a changing world economy and a communication age and knowledge-based economy. Unfortunately, the consequent emphasis placed on performance on achievement and mastery tests, enrollment in advanced academic courses, and development of higher order thinking skills likely create a problem for many, if not most, exceptional students. These barriers have been recognized by some special educators (Schumaker & Deshler, 1988; Shepard, 1987). Until and unless this movement toward excellence is accompanied by fundamental changes in the organization of schools, especially at the secondary level, as well as by effective staff development, it will be extremely difficult for even the ablest exceptional students to measure up to expectations fostered by the school reform movement.

Finally, there is another unfortunate problem in regular education that likely affects the success of mainstreaming. Data show that teachers are being drawn, to a greater extent than ever before, from general education programs--secondary programs that are not designed to prepare students for college work. Additionally,

the SAT scores of students contemplating teaching careers consistently have lagged behind the SAT scores of the average college-bound senior (Carnegie Forum on Education and the Economy, 1986). Data in at least one state show that the SAT scores of those who remain in teaching after five years are lower than those who leave teaching within five years of finishing college (Hocutt, 1989).

THE FUTURE FOR MAINSTREAMING WITHIN THE CONTEXT OF CONTINUING EDUCATIONAL REFORM

If there is anything that should be shown by the legal and historical context of mainstreaming, it is that the various components of our educational system are extraordinarily complex. In our opinion, this calls for more analysis, as opposed to advocacy, about the potential benefits of increased mainstreaming and also for more consideration of the barriers in regular education that could prevent the implementation of mainstreaming as defined at the beginning of this chapter (McKinney & Hocutt, 1988a, 1988b; Martin, 1974). We hope that the current reform movement in regular education will prove beneficial in terms of the principle of mainstreaming and that a vastly improved regular education system will be much more responsive to the needs of handicapped students with regard to instruction and social integration. There is no argument with the principle of mainstreaming.

Nevertheless, the consideration of the physical location of placement to the exclusion of all other factors should not be the primary consideration in the education of handicapped students. The legal and historical context that we have laid out and the research we have very briefly alluded to clearly indicate that primary consideration should be given to what is most appropriate for a given child under specific circumstances. Existing state and public laws clearly state that each child's education should be "appropriate." The history of mainstreaming, especially the current context of the reform movement, shows that there are excellent reasons for advocating mainstreaming, as well as excellent reasons for being cautious about its implementation. Consequently, we would argue that the primary concern should be to educate handicapped students in whatever setting promotes the most effective learning and adaptive functioning.

More important than a simple argument over placement is the fundamental need to determine very carefully the answers to questions such as: "Do these students finish school or drop out?," "What percentages of these students go on to community or four-year colleges?," "What percentages become employed on a full-time basis after schooling?," "What is the self-concept of this student compared to others?," and "What roles in social and community life does this student play?"

We believe that these questions are valid indices of effectiveness. If an education program demonstrates success in this kind of "outcome analysis," issues of placement adequacy are less consequential. Appropriateness must precede placement as a criteria of adequacy of programming. We cannot allow our belief in the promises of mainstreaming to blind us to the need to evaluate the outcomes of our programs if we are responsible professionals.

REFERENCES

Boyer, E. (1983). *High school: A report on secondary education in America.* New York: Harper and Row.

Bryan, J., & Bryan, T. (1988). Where's the beef? A review of published research on the adaptive learning environment model. *Learning Disabilities Focus, 4*(1), 15-23.

Carlberg, C., & Kavale, K. (1980). The efficacy of special class versus regular class placement for exceptional children: A meta-analysis. *Journal of Special Education, 14,* 295-309.

Carnegie Forum on Education and the Economy. (1986). *A nation prepared: Teachers for the 21st century.* New York: Author.

Council of Chief State School Officers. (1988). State education indicators. Washington, DC: State Education Assessment Center.

Diana v. State Board of Education. Civil No. C-70, 37 RFP (N.D. Cal., January 7, 1970, and June 18, 1973).

Dunn, L. (1968). Special education for the mildly retarded--Is much of it justifiable? *Exceptional Children, 35,* 5-22.

Edmonds, R. (1982). *Programs of school improvement: An overview.* Paper presented at the National Institute of Education Conference, Washington, DC.

Education of All Handicapped Children Act of 1975, 20 U.S.C. 1401 (1978).

Fuchs, D., & Fuchs, L. (1988). Evaluation of the adaptive learning environments model. *Exceptional Children, 55,* 115-127.

Gerber, M., & Semmel, M. (1984). Teacher as imperfect test: Reconceptualizing the referral process. *Educational Psychologist, 19,* 137-148.

Gersten, R., Walker, H., & Darch, C. (1988). Relationships between teachers' effectiveness and their tolerance for handicapped students: An exploratory study. *Exceptional Children, 54,* 433-438.

Goldstein, H., Moss, J., & Jordan, L. (1965). *The efficacy of special class training on the development of mentally retarded children.* Urbana: University of Illinois Press.

Goodlad, J. (1984). *A place called school: Prospects for the future.* New York: McGraw Hill.

Hallahan, D., & Kauffman, J. (1982). *Exceptional children: Introduction to special education* (2nd ed.). Englewood Cliffs, NJ: Prentice-Hall.

Hallahan, D., & Keller, C., McKinney, J., Lloyd, J., & Bryan, T. (1988). Examining the research base of the regular education initiative: Efficacy studies and the adaptive learning environments model. *Journal of Learning Disabilities, 21,* 12-18.

Hocutt, A., & Schulte, S. (1987). *A study of noncategorical special education: A literature review*. Research Triangle Park, NC: Research Triangle Institute.

Hocutt, A. (1989). *Facts and questions about secondary education in North Carolina*. Raleigh, NC: State Department of Public Instruction.

Kaagan, S., & Coley, R. (1989). *State education indicators: Measured strides, missing steps*. Princeton, NJ: Educational Testing Service.

Kauffman, J., Gerber, M., & Semmel, M. (1988). Arguable assumptions underline the regular education initiative. *Journal of Learning Disabilities, 21*, 6-11.

Kaufman, M., Gottlieb, J., Agard, J., & Kukic, M. (1975). Mainstreaming: Toward an explication of the construct. *Focus on Exceptional Children, 7*, 1-12.

Keogh, B. (1988a). Improving services for problem learners: Rethinking and restructuring. *Journal of Learning Disabilities, 21*, 29-35.

Keogh, B. (1988b). Perspectives on the regular education initiative. *Learning Disabilities Focus, 4*(1), 3-5.

Kirk, S., & Gallagher, J. (1979). *Educating exceptional children* (3rd ed.). Boston: Houghton Mifflin.

Larry P. v. Riles, Civil No. C-71-2270, 343 F. Supp. 1306 (N.D. Cal, 1972).

LeBanks v. Spears. Civil No. 71-2897 (E.D. La., April 24, 1973).

Lezotte, L. (1989). Base school improvement on what we know about effective schools. *American School Board Journal*, 18-20.

Lilly, S. (1986, March). The relationship between general and special education: A new face on an old issue. *Counterpoint, 6*(1), 10.

Madden, N., & Slavin, R. (1983). Mainstreaming students with mild handicaps: Academic and social outcomes. *Review of Educational Research, 53*, 519-569.

Martin, E. (1971a). Congressional testimony in *Hearings, Financial assistance for improved educational services for handicapped children, H.R. 70*. Subcommittee on Select Education, 93rd Congress, 2nd Session, U.S. House of Representatives.

Martin, E. (1971b). New public priorities: Education of handicapped children. *Compact* (The Journal of the Education Commission of the States), *5*(4), 4-7.

Martin, E. (1974). Some thoughts about mainstreaming. *Exceptional Children, 41*, 150-153.

McKinney, J., & Hocutt, A. (1988a). The need for policy analysis in evaluating the regular education initiative. *Journal of Learning Disabilities, 21*, 12-18.

McKinney, J., & Hocutt, A. (1988b). Policy issues in the evaluation of the regular education initiative. *Learning Disabilities Focus, 4*(1), 15-23.

National Commission on Excellence in Education. (1983). *A nation at risk*. Washington, DC: Author.

Pennsylvania Association for Retarded Children v. Commonwealth of Pennsylvania, 334 F. Supp. 1257 (E.D. Pa., 1971).

Polloway, E. (1984). The integration of mildly retarded students in the schools: A historical review. *Remedial and Special Education, 5*(4), 18-28.

Reynolds, M. (1973). Two policy statements approved by CEC delegate assembly. *Exceptional Children, 40*, 71.

Reynolds, M., & Wang, M. (1983). Restructuring "special" school programs: A position paper. *Policy Studies Review, 2*, 189-212.

Reynolds, M., Wang, M., & Walberg, H. (1987). The necessary restructuring of special and regular education. Exceptional Children, 53, 391-398.

Schumaker, J., & Deshler, D. (1988). Implementing the regular education initiative in secondary schools: A different ball game. *Journal of Learning Disabilities, 21*, 36-42.

Shepard, L. (1987). The new push for excellence: Widening the schism between regular and special education. *Exceptional Children, 53*, 327-329.

Sizer, T. (1984). *Horace's compromise: The dilemma of the American high school*. Boston: Houghton Mifflin.

Skrtic, T. (1987). *An organizational analysis of special education reform*. Paper presented at the annual meeting of the American Educational Research Association, Washington, DC.

Stainback, W., & Stainback, S. (1984). A rationale for the merger of special and regular education. *Exceptional Children, 51*, 102-111.

Stedman, L. (1987). It's time we changed the effective schools formula. *Phi Delta Kappan*, 215-244.

U.S. Department of Education. (1980). *'To assure the free appropriate public education of all handicapped children." Second Annual Report to Congress Handicapped Act.* Washington, DC: Author.

U.S. Department of Education. (1988). *"To assure the free appropriate public education of all handicapped children." Tenth Annual Report to Congress on the Implementation of the Education of the Handicapped Act.* Washington, DC: Author.

Walker, H., & Rankin, R. (1983). Assessing the behavior expectations and demands of less restrictive settings. *School Psychology Review*, 274-284.

Wang, M. (1987). *Implementing the integration mandate of the Education of All Handicapped Children Act of 1975.* Paper presented at the Bush colloquium on policy implementation. Chapel Hill, NC.

Wang, M., & Baker, E. (1986). Mainstreaming programs: Design features and effects. *Journal of Special Education, 19,* 504-521.

Wang, M., Reynolds, M., & Walberg, H. (1985). *Rethinking special education.* Paper presented at the Wingspread conference on the education of students with special needs. Sponsored by the Learning Research and Development Center. University of Pittsburgh.

Weintraub, F. J. (1971). Special education and the government. In *The Encyclopedia of Education* (Vol. 8). New York: Macmillan and Free Press.

Weintraub, F. J., Abeson, A., Ballard, J., & LaVor, M. (1976). *Public policy and the education of exceptional children.* Reston, VA: Council for Exceptional Children.

Will, M. (1986). Educating children with learning problems: A shared responsibility. *Exceptional Children, 52,* 422-415.

3

CLASSIFICATION AND LABELING

Maynard C. Reynolds
University of Minnesota

A pervasive system of classification is used in the field of special education. It results in labels for children, programs, and teachers; it controls program structures and funding. This chapter provides a critical appraisal of procedures now used for classification and labeling, and also suggests criteria for improved conceptualizations and practices. It distinguishes between taxons and classes, between categorical and dimensional analysis, and offers other basic considerations relating to classification. It examines critically formal cluster algorithms for detecting classes for uses in special education. Comment is provided on problems that arise when classification procedures correlate with differences in race, sex, and social class. A brief review is provided on how labels for students are sometimes useful, but also may be stigmatic, thus influencing expectations for learning and/or social acceptance in school and elsewhere. It is proposed that a major "gestalt switch" is required to emphasize prediction of disposition to respond to particular features of instruction as an approach to classification. A case is made for pursuing the regular education initiative, based mainly on the lack of justification for removal of mildly handicapped students "by category" from mainstream classes and schools.

Human classification on the basis of shared characteristics is an inevitable aspect of ordinary social life. It provides economy to memory and contributes to the predictability and order of life. Classification of persons on a formal basis and the relating of classes to other situations and processes is also the basic stuff of the human sciences.

Classification can overemphasize shared characteristics to the neglect of the uniqueness of individuals, or it can fail to recognize important commonalities and thus fail in the useful ordering of knowledge. At the extremes, human classification can be a demeaning process, causing stigma and leading to the isolation and neglect of those in unfavored classes; it conversely, can be the basis on which extraordinary services and favors are rallied in support of select groups.

Human classification is, at once, a scientific enterprise and a social act. It is a proper subject not only for inquiry and creative work, but also for the applied work of the teacher, school psychologist, social worker, and others. In the schools, several varieties of specialists often work together and with parents to make classifications and to organize related work; such teamwork is often difficult, but is important and useful.

It would simplify the situation if one could assume that all of the classes or categories used for humans are "carved by nature" in some permanent form, waiting only to be discovered in cumulative fashion by means of human inquiry. But this is not always so. We might wish that all professions would agree on a proper system of classification. But they do not and should not. To illustrate, the physician may classify "the blind," for example, according to the specific causes of the blindness, but the teacher classifies students with visual impairments according to the most promising methods for teaching reading (and such methods will surely change over time). When Louis Braille invented the tactile reading system, the whole outlook for people with visual handicaps changed and new modes of classification were required. So it is that human classification is, at least in part, a changing and creative enterprise--both in its basic scientific aspect and in social implications-- and often looks different to the various professions and at different times.

Researchers have a basic need and responsibility to be clear about the subjects included in their studies. That has been a major problem in fields such as mental deficiency, for example, where even now the major scientific journals have difficulty making it clear what classes of mentally retarded persons are being reported upon in research (Taylor, 1980). Problems are also severe in speech pathology, special education, and many other fields. The problem of being clear about the definition of classes is particularly acute in that largest-of-all special education categories--learning disabilities (LD). When even the researchers are unclear about the boundaries for the classes of subjects whom they study, teachers and other practitioners have great difficulty in assembling knowledge relevant to their work.

We face especially challenging problems in the matter of human classification at this time. The reasons for this are complex; but, at least in part, the difficulties may be attributed to political actions over recent decades that have favored the establishment of programs in rather narrow streams, involving categorization of individuals into various entitle-

ment groups. For example, to qualify their school districts for special financial supports, children with handicaps must now be classified and reported to state and federal governments by categories, such as retarded, emotionally disturbed, or learning disabled. Health care providers face similar problems in the classification of diseases and deviations if they are to qualify for the various forms of third-party payments. As classification processes are turned into entitlement and funding categories, expansions and distortions occur, which may provide profit for some and stigma for others, and great resistance to changes may occur because of threatened changes in the flow patterns of money. Also, many dollars are spent to perform gatekeeping functions across the wide span of programs and, ultimately, to pay for litigation where classification processes have become controversial. What started as a program of noble purpose sometimes turns to a procedural morass, general discouragement, and potential reversal of public sentiments because problems of classification have been allowed to grow without resolution.

Another broad set of social actions has occurred in the domain of civil rights by establishing protected classes and affirmative action requirements to redress neglect and discrimination of the past. In recent years, major protected classes have been created in wave-like fashion to cover race, sex, and disabilities. Difficult questions have come to the civil rights authorities and to the courts about the disproportionalities in making assignments of various sex and racial groups to disability categories. This has been an extraordinarily difficult problem area for special educators (Heller, Holtzman, & Messick, 1982).

A TWO-STEP PROCESS

For the child whose school situation is problematic and who has been referred for study, special education usually begins through a two-step process. First, a decision is made as to whether the child fits into one of the government-approved categories, such as learning disabled (LD), seriously emotionally disturbed (SED), or mentally retarded (MR). Second, a decision is made about whether the child needs special instruction and services. If both decisions are positive, the child is entitled to such forms of special education and related services as may be judged "appropriate" by teams of educators and parents that are written out in an individualized educational plan (IEP). All of this follows from Public Law 94-142 and related regulations.

The programs of special education and of specialized teacher preparation and licensing tend to be organized according to the same government-approved categories as used in the first of the steps described in the previous paragraph. For example, children classified as learning disabled are taught by teachers of the learning disabled in special programs for learning-disabled students. Very often, the special programs are conducted in special places, requiring that the student be removed (full- or part-time) from general education classes. The view offered here is that, at least for the mildly handicapped students who comprise three-fourths or more of the clients of special education (Algozzine & Korinek, 1985), this pervasive system of classification and separation represents a large and expensive error. A "gestalt switch" to different procedures is indicated.

In the first step of diagnosis in special education, the decision as to whether a student is handicapped and assignable to one (or perhaps several) of the categories, it is assumed that a context-free classification can be made. The student is judged to be, or not to be, mentally retarded, or to be, or not to be, emotionally disturbed, and so on.

A question can be raised about whether the first step in classification can be made without reference to the school context. When is a child mentally retarded or emotionally disturbed? According to what criteria? In 1969, the President's Committee on Mental Retardation issued a major report titled, *The Six-Hour Retarded Child*; the title implies that some children are retarded only during school hours. In such cases, the students would not be viewed as retarded if they were not in school (i.e., free of the school context). During World War II, it was noted that the traditional psychiatric classifications were useful in no more than about 10% of the psychiatric casualties (American Psychiatric Association, 1965). Application of a context-free classification system in that situation would have missed 90% of the psychiatric casualties. Perhaps the situation is similar in education; i.e., the basic classification needs to be context-specific to education.

These are some of the frequently-noted problems about special education practices in classification:

- *Nonreliability.* Differences in rates and methods of classification across school districts go well beyond all scientific bounds and reflect basic reliability problems. Researchers at the University of Minnesota have shown that 80% of the general school population could be classified LD by one or more of the methods used in the schools (Ysseldyke, Algozzine, & Epps, 1983).

- *Nonvalidity.* Classifications show no distinct relations with instructional approaches that are useful in serving the pupils involved (Brophy, 1986). This observation puts in doubt most parts of the classification system, including the separateness of teacher preparation and licensing systems, which assumes distinctive knowledge bases for teaching in the several categorical programs.

- *Nonrelevant variables.* Recent studies have shown how economic and political factors (such as power position of parents, program availability, race, and other factors having no valid implications for instruction) have entered into classification decisions (Ysseldyke, 1987). Enormous shifts have occurred in the rates of classification in special education. In a recent period, for example, the number of children classified as MR was reduced nationally by more than 300,000; in the same period, the number of children labeled LD increased by more than a million (Reschly, 1988). These shifts were not made on clearly established professional grounds. As shown by Tucker (1980), school districts find it quite easy to change the classifications of children--for example, from MR to LD-- when one label becomes more stigmatic than another.

- *Stigmatic labeling.* Through use of negative terms such as "retarded," "disturbed," and "disordered," and practices resulting in segregation (part-time or full-time) of selected students within the schools, there tends to be a degree of public labeling and stigma for special education students. Research evidence does not clearly associate stigma directly with the classification or labeling process (the stigma might be associated with child behavior present before labeling), but it is evident that many parents, especially minority parents, perceive the public labeling that inheres in special education placements of mildly handicapped students to be stigmatic (MacMillan & Meyers, 1979). The field of special education continues to be the object of criticism (Heller, Holtzman, & Messick, 1982) and even of costly legal battles because minority children tend to be given stigmatic labels at disproportionately high rates (*Larry P. v. Riles*, 1972). It seems likely that there would be less parental objection to the labels if the programs for which they were entitled had high value; but evidence for such value is lacking. Semmel, Gottlieb, and Robinson (1979) put it this way: "There is an absence of a conclusive body of evidence which confirms that special education services appreciably enhance the academic and/or social accomplishments of handicapped children beyond what can be expected without special education" (p. 267).

Commenting specifically on the *Larry P. v. Riles* case, Anne Cleary (1980), then chair of the American Psychological Association Committee on Psychological Tests and Assessments, said, "The problem is the special education classes. There would be no controversy about testing if kids blossomed when they were put into special education classes" (p. 7).

A recent study estimated that the cost of initial appraisal of children for special education averaged $1,300 per child (Moore, Strong, Schwartz, & Braddock, 1988). If one adds the cost of transportation to deliver children to labeled classrooms, such costs can be very large indeed, even before instruction begins. Simpler and less costly methods of initial identification of exceptional children exist (Tucker, 1985), and it is well demonstrated that most special education can be conducted in neighborhood schools, eliminating most, if not all, special and highly expensive transportation costs.

The late Nicholas Hobbs, in one of the last of his many statements on child labeling, described the special education classification system as a barrier to, rather than a facilitator for, appropriate education for handicapped children and their families (Hobbs, 1980). Scriven (1983) described diagnostic practices in special education as "scandalous." There is, indeed, good reason for reconsidering practices in special education classification.

SOME BASICS

In moving to a consideration of ways to improve the situation, it may help to recount some basic ideas about classification.

Purpose

As stated by Robbins (1966) in his classic statement on the subject, the choice of categories in a classification system "implies that the category chosen is good for something" (p. 5). The most fundamental purpose of child classification in the schools ought to be to facilitate appropriate instruction. Classification is sometimes oriented to discovery of etiology or to general prognostics (how the problem is likely to develop over time), but each of these purposes is more related to diseases than to instruction and thus has a limited place in education. More important is the allocation of the child to a promising program of instruction. Such a framework is meaningful only when one has alternatives about instruction and choices to make. Prognostication is thus multiple and complex; the etiology of learning problems may be, but usually is not, relevant to planning for better instruction.

Typological versus Dimensional Approaches

There are two basic ways of approaching the diagnosis of persons, one according to classes or types, and the other by dimensions on which variations may be continuous. One can think of persons dichotomously as either mentally retarded or not mentally retarded, in which case we are using a typology. Thinking in terms of dimensions, we might speak of a person as having an IQ of a certain level, along with other characteristics, such as social adaptivity, at various levels. In the dimensional mode of thinking, one sees individuals in terms of continuous variables in a complex hyperspace in which various dimensions intersect; that saves uniqueness for individuals, even though each of the dimensions used may be commonplace. An analogy is provided in the case of weather, where one uses such variables as temperature, cloud cover, barometric pressure, and wind velocity to describe a unique moment and place (Reynolds & Balow, 1972). If, of course, through studies of many individuals, regions of density begin to appear in a hyperspace, it may be considered that the dimensional analyses reveal meaningful classes. Researchers who do formal cluster analyses of characteristics of handicapped children appear to believe that, by using algorithmic approaches, one can start with dimensions and end with classes (McKinney, Short, & Feagans, 1985). I doubt that such procedures are useful as a basic approach to human classification, especially in the educational framework where efficient allocation to treatment is the goal. Meehl (1982) makes the point that classical cluster analytic procedures "have not been responsible for discovering a single taxon in psychopathology or...in organic medicine," or even in clarifying "taxonomic controversies" (p. 141).

At present, special education operates in accord with a typological system, as applied to both individuals and programs.

The field would be better served through a dimensional approach, at least as far as mildly handicapped students are concerned.

Taxons versus Classes

In the schools, many categories or classes are set by using a "cut point" on a continuous variable. For example, the class of first graders is established by choosing a cut-off birth date, resulting, in most members being between 68 and 80 months in chronological age at time of entrance. Similarly, a student may be classified as learning disabled when the discrepancy between measured achievement and "expectations" for achievement (based perhaps on IQ score) reaches some specified magnitude. The classes so created are not defined causally; they are not "types" in any fundamental way. They are invented, more or less, as administrative conveniences rather than as true types. Such classes are not totally arbitrary; they are more like standards for admission to college. They are much influenced by the adaptive capacity of the schools, local and state definitions or criteria for categorization, the amounts of money for special funding provided by state legislatures, how bothersome pupils are to their teachers, the persistence and special perceptions of advocacy groups, and similar factors. These are classes, but they are not taxonic. They show relatively low taxonicity.

Taxa, on the other hand, are "nature carved at its joints." They exist regardless of whether special education exists. Down's Syndrome is a taxon, while the broader class of mental retardation, as used in the schools, is not.

All taxa are classes, but not all classes are taxonic. The categories used in special education are classes, not taxons. They are created, as Burton Blatt once noted, by committees of professional organizations meeting in smoke-filled rooms. In a very important sense, the classification of children for special education represents a political process at least as thoroughly as a scientific enterprise.

Classification in special education can become a scientifically validated procedure, not simply by adhering to procedures for classification advanced by the American Association on Mental Retardation (Grossman, 1983), or the American Psychiatric Association (1987), or any other such professional group, but only by demonstrating that the classification and the decisions supported by it result, or are likely to result, in enhancement of learning by the students involved. The special task force appointed by the National Academy of Science to study placement procedures in special education made that point succinctly in these words:

> It is the responsibility of a placement team that labels and places a child in a special program to demonstrate that any differential label used is related to a distinctive prescription for educational practices...*that lead to improved outcomes* (Heller et al., 1982, pp. 101-102, emphasis added).

Orders of Disposition

In diagnosis and classification, one may engage in an orders of disposition analysis. For example, when a child is not learning well from lessons being offered in reading, one can undertake a surface level description of the problem, such as how many words the child can recognize, the rate of reading in well-defined texts, the ability of the child in syllabification and blending, and so on. This would be diagnosis at the "level of the lesson." The stimulus material used in the diagnosis is the same as that used in teaching, and one attempts to describe exactly what the child knows and can do in the domain of instruction.

If one proceeds beyond the level of the lesson and gives an IQ test, for example, and interprets results to show how rapidly we could "expect" the child to learn to read, then one has moved one order of disposition beyond the level of the lesson. Classifications of children of this one-order-removed kind are very common in special education. The distinction between mentally retarded and learning-disabled students depends upon such one-order-removed analysis. The LD child is one whom we think has a disposition such that he or she should be expected to read well, whereas less should be expected from the child who is retarded. Of course, if we knew enough, every child would be reading exactly as well as expected. Nevertheless, there is much preoccupation by special educators with discrepancy analyses.

The process can go to still more complicated dispositional analysis and to levels still more remote from the "level of the lesson." It might be asserted, for example, that the child is brain injured and that this accounts for dispositions at a first-removed level (low IQ, for example), as well as at the "level of the lesson" (poor reading ability, for example). Still further, it might be found that the brain injury could be understood by means of environmental analysis (for example, widespread use of lead paint in the child's environment), in which case we have moved to a fourth order of disposition.

In diagnosing problems of students, it is common to involve a variety of specialists who work at various levels or orders of disposition. The psychologist may tell about intelligence, personality factors, and cognitive processes; the physician about basic health and neurological integrity; and the social worker about family background and environment. Educators tend to turn their diagnostic problems over to professionals who work at one or more orders of disposition removed from the level of the lesson. As a result, teachers often find the diagnostic for-mulations offered to them to be irrelevant or meaningless in the instructional framework. The current trend toward wider use of curriculum-based assessments in diagnosis is beginning to correct excesses of remote dispositional analysis and to bring more educational meaning to diagnostic findings (Tucker, 1985).

Labeling Programs, But Not Children

Special educators and school psychologists tend to put the labels primarily on children rather than on programs. Perhaps this is because funding systems have been tied to labeled children. School districts usually qualify for special funding whenever a child has been given one of the accepted labels and enrolled in a special program. The money comes on the input side and without regard to whether the program does the child any good.

It would be possible, however, to put the labels primarily on programs, instead of on the children, and to tie funding to the programs instead of to children. One can imagine a school situation in which one has programs such as the following:

The Braille Reading Program
The Reading Recovery Program
The Intensive Basic Skills Program
The Social Skills Program
The White Cane and Mobility Program
The Speech Correction Laboratory
The Total Communications Assistance
  Program
The "Time-Out" Program
The Persistent Life Needs Curriculum
  and Program
The Behavior Management System

Some years ago, Nicholas Hobbs (1975) suggested that the schools might de-emphasize the use of categories and labels for children and put the emphasis instead on the "services required...in the interest of the child's fullest development" (p. 234).

Perhaps it is inevitable that a degree of public labeling of children would occur even if the labels were shifted mainly to programs, but it seems likely that some gains for the children would be made. But more is implied, because if we are clear about programs and shift funding to them, it's likely that more evaluations will result on the outcome (as against input) side. For example, one could examine carefully the Reading Recovery Program in terms of progress shown by pupils assigned to it and the influence of the program on the rates of pupil failure in a school or school system. Such evaluations at the program level and on the outcome side, in addition to the evaluations of progress made by individuals through the recurring IEP process, could be a very healthy development for the whole field of special education.

Predicting Dispositions to Respond to Treatment

As we are more explicit about the kinds of programs conducted in the field of special education, it becomes possible to examine closely the characteristics of students who profit most from enrollment in the various programs. In such a framework, the purpose of diagnoses becomes one of predicting the dispositions of individuals to respond to particular forms, levels of intensity, or levels of instruction. Educators are not alone in advancing the idea that diagnosis, to be useful, must be oriented to choice of treatment. Speaking from a clinically-oriented perspective, Skinner (1981) proposed that "if a classification is to be clinically useful, then the information it provides must enhance decision making with respect to what treatment intervention is most appropriate for a particular patient or group of similar patients" (p. 77).

Selection-Rejection versus Placement Decisions

Most institutions in our society are permitted to make selection-rejection decisions. In such cases, the institution selects some persons as its employees, students, or team members; others are rejected. Little, if any, responsibility rests with the institution to serve those whom it rejects. Until 1975, the schools of the nation were permitted to make selection-rejection decisions to some degree. However, with the enactment of PL 94-142, it became the policy of the nation that the schools were no longer permitted to reject any student. Every child, no matter how seriously disabled, was to be enrolled in school and offered an *appropriate* program, one that would be beneficial to him or her.

When literally *all* children were required to be provided a place and appropriate program in the schools, the whole category of selection-rejection decision processes was eliminated, or should have been eliminated. The schools were, in effect, ordered to discontinue making selection-rejection decisions and to make placement decisions instead. The terms *selection-rejection* and *placement* are used here in the ways proposed by Cronbach and Gleser (1965). Placement decisions involve an assumption that *everyone* is included and that the problem is to design a program for each individual or to fit individuals into programs that offer consistently promising or beneficial results.

The schools have been overloaded for decades with test results and procedures that are oriented to prediction and to selection-rejection decisions. Indeed, Alfred Binet's work early in the 1900s in Paris on the intelligence test was oriented to mere prediction of academic success. The Binet test, when it came into broad use, was used to reject or to set aside in special classes those students who were not expected to perform well in regular schools. As Cronbach (1967) put it, "when ability tests became available they were used by the schools--to put it bluntly--to decide which pupils should be allowed to drop by the wayside or to vegetate in an undemanding slow class-room" (p. 24).

Even in the 1990s, there is a tendency to try to put new wine in old bottles; i.e., to use procedures designed for selection-rejection decisions when placement decisions are what is required. The concept of aptitude-treatment-interactions, the idea that one needs to consider simultaneously program differences and individual differences, and subsequently to make allocation decisions clearly oriented to the benefit of individuals, was born in this new context for special education; but new ways of thinking and new practices emerge very slowly.

Institutional versus Individual Payoff

Placement decisions are oriented to pay off or to provide value for individuals rather than to institutions. If the goal is to maximize institutional payoff, such as to make more profit or to have a higher average score on reading tests, then it is to the advantage of the institution to select high performers and to reject low or unpromising performers. Any device that makes it possible to predict with some accuracy how well individuals will perform can be used to make selection and rejection decisions and, thus, to increase institutional payoff. Tests, such as general intelligence tests, which tend to predict academic performance across many domains, are very useful in making selection-rejection decisions and in improving institutional payoff. But precisely because procedures, such as IQ test results, predict in many situations, they are not very useful in choosing between situations. High IQs predict high achievement in many curricula, but don't help very much in choosing between curricula for individuals. Similarly, broad-based tests (such as IQ tests) tend to predict low performance in many domains for low-scoring pupils. However, such tests are very limited in usefulness in choosing among educational programs. Sadly, millions of children have been dropped by the wayside when they are placed in special classes for "the retarded," not because there is evidence that they will profit more from the special class, but only because of the prediction that they will perform relatively less well than others in regular classes. Today, when the accountability checks run to what is good for each child, decisions based on simplistic predictive schemes that are oriented mainly to institutional payoff cannot be justified.

A SUMMARY VIEW

Considering the several "basics" just reviewed, and recognizing that many children have extraordinary problems and needs in the schools, what can be said in a summary way about classification and labeling? I believe that the present categorical system in special education, at least in aspects that deal with mildly deviant pupils, is flawed and needs to be revised. The trouble is with the ways in which we partition our work and children into categories such as LD, ED, and MR. The two-step system that first requires a context-free identification of the students by category is faulty. There is no such thing as a context-free identification process that has meaning in the schools. The categories are classes, not taxa. We would do better to think and to work in terms of dimensional analysis than of a typology. It would be helpful if we could be more explicit about the special forms of instruction that we offer and then orient diagnosis to the prediction of dispositions to respond to particular instructional approaches. In our present state of knowledge, it would be best to limit diagnostic work mainly to the "level of the lesson," rather than to engage in analysis of remote orders of disposition, which deal all too vaguely with expectations, underlying psychological processes, neurological disorders, and like matters.

Special educators, I believe, would serve their clients better by focusing on what works instructionally. Remote dispositional analyses of educational problems should be admitted into school practices only when evidence for relevance is compelling and related to instructional decisions.

While insisting on careful monitoring of the progress of each individual child, we also should evaluate with much care the general outcomes of each program. In such evaluations, it will be extremely important to search for whatever evidence there is that shows interactions of pupil characteristics and program differences. At present, it appears that the program differences which are most important for exceptional students are those relating to intensity or density of instruction and of time on task. Students who show least progress in school need more instruction over longer periods of time and more highly structured instruction, but not a different kind of instruction than do other pupils. As Brophy (1986) put it in a review of research:

> Main effects tend to be much more frequent and powerful than interactions, and the interactions that do occur tend to be ordinal interactions indicating that some students need more (of the same kind of) instruction rather than disordinal interactions indicating that some students need to be taught one way but other students need to be taught in a different way (p. 121).

If we move generally in the directions proposed here, it will be important to be open to renegotiation of relations not only between special and regular education, but among the several varieties of categorical programs as well. There is no evidence of separate and distinct knowledge bases, or of the need for different instructional practices, relevant to LD pupils and Chapter I (economically disadvantaged) students; and it is wasteful in the extreme to force separate identification and instructional systems upon these two groups. Similarly, there is great need for coordinated efforts that will cut across domains now separated for migrant children, children showing problems in social behavior, and children in remedial reading programs. The goal in every school ought to be to operate efficient, well-coordinated programs for all pupils, including those who show extraordinary problems and needs.

THE DEBATE OVER THE REGULAR EDUCATION INITIATIVE

Suppose there were agreement that the categorical approaches now widely used in special education for mildly handicapped students cannot be justified, that the approach is unreliable, lacks validity, is extremely expensive, sometimes results in harmful labeling, and contributes to an inefficient disjointedness in school operations. I believe that the evidence supports all of these conclusions, and I find myself among those who find the situation frustrating in the extreme, both intellectually and morally. Can we go on preparing teachers by categories and ask school psychologists to make differential allocations of children to categorical programs when there is so little evidence that the procedures have true value? Perhaps most observers would agree that all forms of special education "have been effective for some students, all have failed with some" (Kauffman & Pullen, 1989, p. 13), but the challenge is to know with some degree of precision who will profit from what. Otherwise, random allocations would suffice. It's at this more detailed and very expensive level of decision that the present operations fail to meet decent standards. Is it reasonable for special educators to lock themselves and their students into separate and narrow categorical streams of work when broader and newer needs are emerging very rapidly in the schools? Will special educators join in broad efforts to serve all children and be ready to help restructure programs and schools as necessary?

It is much too early to say what new forms of special education may be necessary. But it seems clear that major revisions of present practices and programs are necessary and that this will involve basic renegotiation of relations with regular education. Separation by administrative arrangements is likely not to be very important; how instruction is offered is likely to be more important.

It is in this framework that some of us have advanced the "waiver for performance" idea. This strategy proposes that existing governmental controls be waived for limited periods of time and without financial disincentives for school districts and possibly for states that wish to try new approaches of service for exceptional students (Reynolds, Wang, & Walberg, 1987). In return for the waivers, school officials would accept responsibility for careful evaluation of the outcomes of their innovations; thus, the "for performance" aspect of the strategy. In this way, perhaps special education of the future can be built on a firmer foundation of research and evaluation than has been true of the past.

There is a significant and growing knowledge base about what enhances the learning of children. There are not different knowledge bases for what we know as special education and regular education, and what is known about learning is not fully applied in any part of education. So, in experimental efforts for improvement, we can travel much distance together, all of us, in special and regular education, attempting to improve attention to individual differences and to provide more effective education. As part of the Regular Education Initiative, I see efforts for improvement going forward in a framework of complete collaboration among regular and special educators and across all categorical programs, both within and beyond special education as now conducted.

All of this starts with disaffection for the narrowly-framed, limiting system of categorization, which is now so pervasive but so little justified in the field of special education. To break away from that system will involve a major gestalt switch and this will be difficult to conceptualize; and it will be difficult to achieve in the face of resistance by those who are comfortable and well rewarded in the present structures. What I suggest is not an early rewriting of laws and policies, but only a modest breakthrough by granting waivers to those who have carefully developed plans and exhibit a willingness to be accountable for outcomes. This is a call for deeply penetrating revisions and evaluation of educational practices, but it does not prescribe exactly how those revisions should occur. It seems likely that many new ideas will emerge if the situation can be opened to innovation.

The late Ray Graham, director of special education for the State of Illinois, often said that it is one of the duties of special educators to get well ahead of the law and the related regulations and then to help them catch up! The field of special education in the United States, for somewhat more than a decade, has been very busy implementing an important law and the policies embodied therein--PL 94-142. There have been many good and helpful outcomes of that process. But it is past time now for special educators to recognize problems that exist and the fact that some of them are growing. It is time to try a revised course, one that will acknowledge special education as an integral part of education as a whole and also provides some of the developmental capitol (Deno, 1970) for educational renewal.

REFERENCES

Algozzine, B., & Korinek, L. (1985). Where is special education for students with high prevalence handicaps going? *Exceptional Children, 51*, 388-394.

American Psychiatric Association. (1965; 1980; 1987). *Diagnostic and statistical manual* (2nd ed., 1965; 3rd ed., 1980; 3rd ed. rev., 1987). Washington, DC: Author.

Brophy, J. (1986). Research linking teacher behavior to student achievement. In B. I. Williams, P. A. Richmond, & B. J. Mason (Eds.), *Design for compensatory education: Conference proceedings and papers* (pp. 121-179). Washington, DC: Research and Evaluation Associates.

Cleary, A. (1980). [quoted in] *APA Monitor, 11*(1), p. 7. Washington, DC: American Psychological Association.

Cronbach, L. J. (1967). How can instruction be adapted to individual differences? In R. M. Gagne (Ed.), *Learning and individual differences* (pp. 23-39). Columbus, OH: Merrill.

Cronbach, L. J., & Gleser, G. C. (1965). *Psychological tests and personnel decisions*. Urbana: University of Illinois Press.

Deno, E. (1970). Special education as developmental capitol. *Exceptional Children, 37*, 229-240.

Grossman, H. J. (Ed.). (1983). *Classification in mental retardation* (rev.). Washington, DC: American Association on Mental Deficiency.

Heller, K. A., Holtzman, W. H., & Messick, S. (Eds.). (1982). *Placing children in special education: A strategy for equity*. Washington, DC: National Academy Press.

Hobbs, N. (1975). *The futures of children*. San Francisco: Jossey-Bass.

Hobbs, N. (1980). An ecologically oriented service-based system for the classification of handicapped children. In S. Salzinger, J. Antrobus, & J. Glick (Eds.), *The ecosystem of the "sick" child: Implications for classification and intervention for disturbed and mentally retarded children*. New York: Academic Press.

Kauffman, J. M., & Pullen, P. L. (1989). An historical perspective: A personal perspective on our history of service to mildy handicapped and at-risk students. *Remedial and Special Education, 10*(6), 12-14.

Larry P. v. Riles. (1972). Civil Action N.C.-71-2270, 343 F. Supp. 1306 (N.D. Cal.).

MacMillan, D. L., & Meyers, C. E. (1979). Educational labeling of handicapped learners. In D. Berliner (Ed.), *Review of research in education* (Vol. 7). Washington, DC: American Educational Research Association.

McKinney, J. D., Short, E. J., & Feagans, L. (1985). Academic consequences for perceptual-linguistic subtypes of learning disabled children. *Learning Disabilities Research, 1*(1), 6-17.

Meehl, P. (1972). Specific genetic etiology, psychodynamics and therapeutic nihilism. *International Journal of Mental Health, 1*, 10-27.

Moore, M. J., Strong, E. W., Schwartz, M., & Braddock, M. (1988). *Patterns in special education service delivery and cost*. Washington, DC: Decision Resources Corp.

President's Committee on Mental Retardation. (1969). *The six-hour retarded child*. Washington, DC: Government Printing Office.

Reschly, D. J. (1988). Minority mild mental retardation overrepresentation: Legal issues, research findings, and reform trends. In M. C. Wang, M. C. Reynolds, & H. J. Walberg (Eds.), *Handbook of special education: Research and practice* (Vol. 2, pp. 23-41). Oxford: Pergamon Press.

Reynolds, M. C., & Balow, B. (1972). Categories and variables in special education. *Exceptional Children, 38*, 357-366.

Reynolds, M. C., Wang, M. C., & Walberg, H. J. (1987). The necessary restructuring of special and regular education. *Exceptional Children, 53*, 391-398.

Robbins, L. L. (1966). An historical review of classifications of behavior disorders and one current perspective. In L. D. Eron (Ed.), *The classification of behavior disorders*. Chicago: Aldine.

Scriven, M. (1983). Comments on Gene Glass. *Policy Studies Review, 2*(Special No. 1), 79-84.

Semmel, M., I., Gottlieb, J., & Robinson, N. M. (1979). Mainstreaming: Perspectives on educating handicapped children in the public schools. In D. C. Berliner (Ed.), *Review of research in education* (Vol. 7, pp. 223-279). Washington, DC: American Educational Research Association.

Skinner, H. A. (1981). Toward the integration of classification theory and methods. *Journal of Abnormal Psychology, 90*(1), 68-87.

Taylor, R. L. (1980). Use of the AAMD classification system: A review of recent research. *American Journal of Mental Deficiency, 85*(3), 116-119.

Tucker, J. A. (1980). Ethnic proportions in classes for the learning disabled. *Journal of Special Education, 14*(1), 93-105.

Tucker, J. A. (1985). *Exceptional Children, 53*(3), entire issue.

Ysseldyke, J. E. (1987). Classification of handicapped students. In M. C. Wang, M. C. Reynolds, & H. J. Walberg (Eds.), *Handbook of special education: Research and practice* (Vol. 1, pp. 253-271). Oxford: Pergamon Press.

Ysseldyke, J. E., Algozzine, B., & Epps, S. (1983). A logical and empirical analysis of current practice in classifying students as handicapped. *Exceptional Childen, 50*, 160-166.

4

RESTRUCTURING FOR QUALITY

Dorothy Kerzner Lipsky[1]
Alan Gartner
The City University of New York

The current system of special education needs to be changed for a basic reason: It does not work. That is, it fails to serve well the students. Although particular practices are faulty, the cause is not in practice but in basic conception.

THE NECESSITY FOR CHANGE

For us, the topic of (re)structuring an educational program begins with addressing two interrelated questions: (a) "For what are we preparing the students?", and (b) "Of what are the students capable?"

For What Are We Preparing Students?

One of the ways of answering this question is to examine what have been the outcomes for those who have been served by the present special education system.[2]

[1] The order of authors does not represent seniority.

[2] We are aware that this is a somewhat unusual way to address the topic. More typically, such discussions emphasize statements of philosophy and goals. Although we value such statements, and will include them later, we emphasize outcomes for students here for two reasons: First, little educational discussion is about them and second, because we are advocating for a total change in the education of students labeled as handicapped, it is essential to show the failure of the present model in terms of outcomes for students labeled as handicapped.

Let us examine briefly outcome measures including student learning, graduation rates, return to general education, and post-school education, employment, and community living. (For a fuller discussion of these outcomes, see Gartner & Lipsky, 1989.)

Although more than a third of school districts presently excuse students labelled as handicapped from the standardized tests that all other pupils take, the results available indicate the schools' failure in terms of academic knowledge acquired by these students. According to the recently released report of the National Longitudinal Transition Study (Wagner & Shaver, 1989), almost one in four students with disabilities failed to pass any part of the minimum competency tests they were required to take, a third passed some of the test, and four in ten passed the entire test.

Although there are no systematic data collected regarding drop-out rates for students labelled as handicapped, the information available from the latest report of the Department of Education on the implementation of PL 94-142 shows drop-out rates a fifth or more greater than those for students in general education. Among those students labelled as learning disabled, generally among the least impaired, the drop-out rate was 47 percent of all those over age 16 (*Tenth Annual Report*, 1988).

As for graduation rates, the National Longitudinal Transition Study (Wagner & Shaver, 1989) reports that in a two year period, 56 percent of special education exiters left secondary school by graduation. Of this group, 79 percent received a regular diploma (M. Wagner, personal communication, *May 6, 1989*). Thus, of 3,045 special education exiters in the Study's sample, 1,347 (44%) graduated with a regular diploma.

National data concerning the return to general education for students who have been in special education and then declassified are not available. Although the federal government collects voluminous amounts of data, it does not collect this essential outcome marker. Such information would be difficult to collect, but it should be no harder to collect than other data collected by the government. Our earlier estimate (Gartner & Lipsky, 1987), based on reports from large city school districts, that indicated the figure would be in the low single digits, has been confirmed by the National Longitudinal Transition Study (Wagner & Shaver, 1989) report that approximately 5 percent of secondary youth enrolled in special education programs were annually declassified from special education.[3]

Rather than the difficulty of collecting such data or even the bleak picture it presents as the reason that such data are not collected, we believe the reason is more insidious: Namely, that students labelled as handicapped and served in special education programs are not expected to achieve and, as a result, return to general education. Thus, there is no reason to collect such data.

Even more troubling is the report that 31 percent of the youth with disabilities who had been out of school for more than a year had not been engaged "in any productive activity in that year" (Wagner & Shaver, 1989, p. 11). This is particularly disturbing given the broad definition of a "productive activity" as including: not taking any courses from any postsecondary educational institution; not working for pay full- or part-time, either competitively or in a sheltered environment; not engaging in a volunteer job or unpaid work; not receiving job skills training from other than a family member; or, if a female, not being married or reported to be involved in child raising. In short, not engaged in a "productive activity" means doing nothing. And this was true of nearly a third of the youth with disabilities.

Of What Are the Students Capable?

Let us now turn to the second question. The answer inherent in the current special education system is a bimodal one; that is, it sees two groups of students: those who are "handicapped" and those who are not so designated. This is based upon the following paradigm:

- Disability is a condition that individuals have;

- The distinction between disabled and typical (or handicapped and not handicapped) is an objective and useful distinction; and, therefore,

- Special education is a rationally conceived and coordinated system of services that help children labelled as handicapped. (Bogdan & Kugelmass, 1984, p. 93)

Our view is contrary to each aspect of the current conceptualization. Rather than believing that a bimodal distinction is accurate, no less useful, we believe that:

- Children are more alike than different, and

---

[3] These national data challenge an earlier report from a four-city study of significantly higher declassification rates (Singer, 1988).

- All children differ one from another.

Thus, it is neither appropriate nor efficacious to divide students for instructional purposes[4] between those labelled as handicapped and those not.[5]

Furthermore, contrary to the present system which is based upon a deficit model and expects little of the students, we believe that students labelled as handicapped are "capable of achievement and worthy of respect" (Lipsky & Gartner, 1987, p. 69). The current special education system, however, reflects the opposite of this. Rather, it is a system that (a) assumes the problem is solely located in the individual, emphasizing the impairment rather than understanding that the handicap results from the interplay between impairment and environment--built and attitudinal; (b) is built, as is much of the human services, upon a medical and deficit model; and (c) has lower expectations for those it serves as well as rewards their failure. Describing the findings of his pioneering work in both classroom and laboratory settings, Gardner (1989) speaks of a "motley collection of human skills and abilities, with level of performance in one realm seldom serving as a reliable predictor of a person's competence in some other endeavor" (p. 95). Challenging the current special education formulation, he goes on to note that "individual strength or weak

ness in one [mental capacity] could have no predictive power about a person's strengths or weaknesses in other intellectual domains" (p. 96). Based upon his concept of multiple intelligences, Gardner (1983) says the task of education is to identify each person's intelligences, and to craft an education program based upon them. (For a fuller discussion of his ideas on education, specifically as an alternative to the current special education design, see Goldman & Gardner, 1989).

Our call is for fundamental changes in education, so as to create schools that serve and succeed for all students. The current system of special (and remedial) education is a result of the failure of education in general to appropriately serve the growing population of children. Particularly vulnerable are those children dubbed as at risk, that is, those children of color, or living in poverty, or labelled as handicapped. Too often, these children are all three. Special education is not the problem; it is only the flawed response to the problem.

THE NEEDED CHANGES

As we have indicated earlier, the changes needed begin at the level of conceptualization--about the students and their parents, and about the purpose of their schooling. We turn now to this topic and then to the practices based upon such conceptualizations, some now in effect in schools across the country.

New Conceptualization

Society's attitudes toward disability are deeply ingrained in professional practice (Gartner & Joe, 1987). This is particularly evident in the social-psychological literature, where disability is based on the following assumptions:

- Disability is biologically based.

---

[4] As a tactical matter of the moment, we do not object to the PL 94-142 requirement that students be assigned to particular categories of handicapping conditions and that they be counted as such. What we do object to--and what we believe PL 94-142 does not require--is the division of these students by such categories for instructional purposes. In the longer run, as we indicate in a subsequent section, we do reject the entire labelling activity.

[5] We are aware of the numerous and accurate critiques of the present classification systems (see esp. Ysseldyke, 1987); our point here is that the problem is not in implementation but in conceptualization.

- Disabled persons face endless problems that are caused by the impairment.

- Disabled persons are "victims."

- Disability is central to the disabled persons' self-concept and self-definition.

- Disability is synonymous with a need for help and social support. (Fine & Asch, 1988a)

Similar assumptions hold in special education. The child is considered impaired, instruction is disability-focused, professional personnel are often trained and certified to work only with children with specific disabilities, and attention to societal issues is often considered too political and not the business of educators. Additionally, the child's parents are often treated as both part of the problem and disabled themselves. (For a fuller discussion of parental treatment and the need for their involvement, see Lipsky, 1989; see also, Ferguson & Asch, 1989; Fewell & Vadasy, 1986; Lipsky, 1985; Sarason & Doris, 1979; Turnbull & Turnbull, 1985.)

This view of students labelled as handicapped adversely affects expectations regarding their academic achievement, often causing them to be separated from other students, to be exposed to a watered-down curriculum, to be excused from standards and tests routinely applied to other students, to be given grades that they have not earned, and in some states to be awarded diplomas that have not been earned.

The rationale given for such watered-down expectations is that they are in the best interests of the child. Professionals often suggest that a child be placed in an environment where he or she will be "safe...because he would never be asked to do things there 'we know he cannot do'" (Granger & Granger, 1986, p. 26).

The medical or clinical model that undergirds special education inextricably leads to the belief that persons with impairments, especially those with severe disabilities, are not capable of making choices or decisions. This conceptualization diminishes

> our ability to see them as individuals capable of ever making a choice, let alone the right choice. Seldom, if ever, is the person with the handicapping condition involved in the process of determining how their behavior, or the behavior of those around them, will be modified. The end result is more control for the caregivers and less control for the person being cared for. (Guess, Benson, & Siegel-Causey, 1985, p. 83)

(For our purposes, substitute 'teachers' for 'caregivers' and 'student' for 'the person being cared for.')

Human services practice, including education and particularly special education, operates from a deficit model. That is, the consumer (the student in education) is seen as having some inadequacy, short-coming, failure, or disease. The provider (the teacher in education) is seen as knowing something, doing something, or having something that will overcome the deficit, fix the problem, or cure the disease. Central to this formulation is the assumption that in exchange for accepting and not challenging the expertise of the provider, the consumer is excused from normal obligations. That is, the consumer is allowed to be dependent, and thus, not autonomous. Such a deficit-based model stands at odds with the beliefs that undergird autonomy.

Having denied individuals with disabilities autonomy and decision-making authority--in effect, denying them a function given to people whom society respects--we then excuse their behavior, ascribing it to the disability.

Autonomy, that is, self-determination or control over decision-making, is something granted to persons who are valued. For individuals to be autonomous, or to be granted decision-making authority, reflects acceptance of three interrelated beliefs. They are:

- A statement as to the *right* to control one's own life;

- An expression of belief in the individual's *capacity* to do so; and

- A recognition of the *benefits* to the individual of doing so.

For persons with disabilities, autonomy is limited by at least three factors. These include:

- The limitations consequent upon the *impairment*;

- The broad *societal attitudes* toward persons with disabilities; and

- The nature of current *human services practice*.

Currently, it is the first of these that has the most effect. Specifically, it is assumed that having a disability in itself precludes (or at least substantially limits) being autonomous. Although the impairment itself may warrant some limitations on autonomy, such limits should come about only *after* the limits caused by societal attitudes and human services practices are removed. Even then, great care must be exercised in coming to *a priori* assumptions about the extent of such limitations. Until an accommodating society is established, the full range of an individual's capacity, and the extent to which apparent limitations are inherent or are a function of

externally-imposed barriers, will be unknown.[7]

In a recent Supreme Court decision, *School Board of Nassau County v Arline*, Justice Brennan captured the point, writing: "Congress acknowledged that society's accumulated myths and fears about disability and disease are as handicapping as are the physical limitations that flow from actual impairment" (quoted in "On cases of contagion," 1987, p. A21).

The educational reforms needed encompass the whole of the educational system, not only that part called special. Indeed, the origin, growth, and shape of special education has in many ways been defined by general education and the attitudes and behaviors of mainstream educators toward students declared to be disabled. There has been a narrowing of the definition of what is considered normal, accompanied by the growth of ever expanding programs for those declared to be special. Not only does this have deleterious consequences for these students, there is consequence for those students who remain in general education classrooms:

> every time a child is called mentally defective and sent off to the special education class for some trivial defect, the children who are left in the regular classroom receive a message: no one is

[6] This denial of autonomy and respect is especially the case for women with disabilities. See esp. Fine & Asch, 1981, 1988b.

[7] This being the case, it is particularly disturbing that special education as a field gives so little attention to the larger world of disability. Thus, for example, there can be no doubt that the most important current piece of legislation concerning the lives of students now labeled as handicapped is the Americans with Disabilities Act. Pending for over a year and developed over a longer period of time, no special education journal has addressed it and its meaning for the lives of the students. There is a growing body of literature from a policy and political perspective about disability and disability rights (see especially Berkowitz, 1987; Hahn, 1989; Scotch, 1984; Stone, 1984).

above suspicion, everyone is being watched by the authorities; non-conformity is dangerous. (Granger & Granger, 1986, p. xii)

The problem is not special education or general education alone. "In a sense, regular and special education teachers have colluded to relieve regular teachers of responsibilities for teaching children functioning at the bottom of their class" (Shepard, 1987, p. 328). The pressure to succeed--to produce high test scores and work with the very large class sizes that make individual attention extremely difficult--increases the chances that teachers will seek uniformity of students rather than diversity. To put it more sharply, there is, in effect, a deal between special and general education. The former asserts a particular body of expertise and a unique understanding of special students, thus laying claim to both professional obligation and student benefit. The latter, because of the lack of skills and resources, or because of prejudice, is often happy to hand over these students to a welcoming special education system. The

deal is sanctioned, on the one hand, by the clinicians who provide an intrapsychic justification for the referral, and, on the other hand, by those in the role of advocacy who see increasing numbers of students in special education as providing evidence of their effectiveness. (Lipsky & Gartner, 1987, p. 59)

And as Lilly (1989) points out, a similar situation exists in professional preparation programs, separating special- and regular-education teacher training.

Skrtic (1986) argues that the assumptions about disability that underlie the current special education system are challenged by different understandings of disability, ones less rooted in biology and psychology, "and derive more from sociological, political, and cultural theories of deviance, and which provide many different

perspectives on virtually every aspect of special education and 'disability'" (p. 6). Skrtic (1987) argues that

current school organization creates, and can do nothing but create, students with mild disabilities as artifacts of the system. Furthermore, [current] efforts to reform the system--without replacing it with an entirely different configuration--do little to eliminate mild disabilities or their effects, produce even more students with mild disabilities, and create a new and largely hidden class of student casualties. (p. 3)

Stainback and Stainback (1984, 1989, 1990; see also, Stainback, Stainback, & Forest, 1989) emphasize the shared characteristics of students. They argue that there are not two distinct groups of students, regular or normal students and others who deviate from the norm. They believe that all students vary across a range of physical, intellectual, psychological, and social characteristics. Single characteristic definitions inevitably fail to capture the complexity of people--indeed, they trivialize them. The issue is to craft for each student the individualized education program from which she or he can benefit. This can only be done in an integrated or unitary system.

The conception of a unitary system requires a fundamental change in the way differences among people are perceived, in the ways educational programs in schools are organized, and in how the purpose of that education is viewed. Unlike the current system, with its deviance model, ascription of the problem to the individual, and resolution to one or another treatment modality, the unitary system requires adaptations in society and its institutions, including school systems.

Placing the Student at the Center

The new design, as we have indicated, must go beyond changes for the education of students now labelled as handicapped. As an avalanche of studies have documented, since the publication in 1983 of *A Nation At Risk*, the educational system as a whole is fundamentally flawed. The early rounds of post-1983 school reform have had limited effect. In part this is because of the limited period of time. But, it is also because they focussed on external factors--higher standards (for example, strengthened graduation requirements, competency statements, exclusion of students with failing grades or poor attendance from participation in extracurricular activities), new and mandated curricula, strengthened teacher certification requirements, differentiated salary schedules, and salary and other expenditure increases of more than a thousand dollars per pupil between the 1982-83 and 1987-88 school years. More recently, a second wave of school reforms have focussed on the roles of the adults--teacher empowerment, school-based management, and parental choice. It shifts the locus of attention from state capitals to districts and individual schools, from mandated and "quick fix" activities to collaborative, cooperative, and protracted efforts. The changes necessary will require a new way of thinking--in Kuhn's (1962) term, a paradigm shift. Rather than focussing on the adult providers of educational services or the balance of responsibility among national, state, and local authorities, the needed new formulation places the student at the center of educational reform. It recognizes that it is the student who is the producer of the educational outcome, learning. It is a shift not merely from inputs to outputs--what teachers do (teach) to what we hope students do (learn); it is a shift from means to results.

As generations of frustrated teachers have realized, they cannot learn *for* their students; it is the *student* who must do the learning. Moreover, there is not a one-to-one equivalence of teaching and learning. Indeed, each can go on without the other

occurring--there can be teaching without learning and learning without teaching. Ultimately, it is the student--and *only* the student--who does the learning for herself or himself, acquires knowledge, develops skills, gains insights, (re)shapes understanding, and develops values. The work of learning is the student's.

The next and third wave of school reform needs to increase the productivity of students as workers in their own learning. Giving students respect, building upon their knowledge, providing them control over the learning process and appropriate materials, helping them to see the connection between subjects, and encouraging cooperation among students are the necessary predicates to the increases in student learning, the bases for school improvement that will produce enhanced school outcomes of substantial magnitude for all students, including those now labelled as handicapped.

To make students more effective workers in their own learning, two things are essential: They need to be shown respect and they must become actively engaged in the learning process.

Students do their best when they are respected. As former U. S. Commissioner of Education Harold Howe says, "If [young people] are treated with understanding, care and respect, and if they are helped to find some genuine interest and purpose in what they are asked to do, then they are very likely to respond favorably to it" (Howe, 1989, p. 3). Yet, schools generally focus on student weaknesses and what is not known--a deficit model. This is reflected in the instructional methodology of educators and in the emphasis of most schools to track and sort students. Although this is most particularly the case for those students labelled at risk and handicapped, it is true about education in general. An alternative to the deficit model is to build programs based upon the strengths and capacity of students. Adoption of the school effectiveness literature's correlate of high expectations for all students (Edmonds, 1979) is a starting point toward establishing respect for all students. (See also Lezotte, 1989, for the relationship of the school effectiveness formulation to special education.)

So, too, the perspective of Gardner (1983) about multiple intelligences can be the basis of school reform. He points out that currently schools are organized as if intelligence can be conceptualized as a single construct that encompasses all cognitive processes of significance, one that changes very little over time and can be adequately summarized as a single metric. His reconceptualization emphasizes that individuals exhibit a jagged profile of intelligences; were schools organized in a way that respected and built upon multiple intelligences a wider range of students would be respected and expected to learn.[8]

The traditional concept of schooling, largely unchanged by current reform efforts, puts the student in a passive role, as the recipient, the object of teaching. A new educational paradigm will place the student at the center, as an active, engaged worker. The learning process will become less that of memorizing answers and more one of discovery and higher level thinking. "Students must participate in learning endeavors in which they engage in the process of learning. That is, learning is not seen as students sitting at a desk listening to a teacher lecture. Students are doing things" (Benjamin, 1989, p. 8).

New Practices

A student's development is enhanced when she or he is an active participant in structuring the environment. The student needs to confront the environment as it is and then to have a role in modifying it by

changing either the environment (physical or social) and/or adapting her/his behavior. In so doing, the student develops a sense of competence and mastery.

Engaging students in the work of learning is the basis for new instructional strategies and curriculum efforts. Cooperative learning (Johnson & Johnson, 1984; Slavin, 1987) and peer tutoring (Hedin, 1986; Jenkins & Jenkins, 1981; Lipsky & Gartner, 1990) are to be encouraged. Involving students in the active work of preparing material, sharing information with other students, acting as tutors, monitoring their own performance, and other such activities have been found in extensive research to offer both affective and cognitive benefits. (Much of this research is summarized in Lipsky & Gartner, 1990.) For students who themselves are at risk, tutoring programs are of particular value. The *Harvard Education Letter* reports, "[T]utors learn at least as much as the students they teach--and tutors who are far behind academically gain even more" ("Big kids teach little kids", 1986, p. 2). This learning-through-teaching concept has been incorporated in programs where students with disabilities themselves are tutors both to others with disabilities and to non-disabled students, again with particular benefits to the tutors--who may be students labelled as handicapped (*Handicapped Children as Tutors*, 1984; Lipsky & Gartner, 1990; Osguthorpe & Scruggs, 1986).

In addition to cooperative learning and peer programs, educational practices that fit the new paradigm include curriculum-based assessment, adaptive curricula, alternative measurement procedures, and programs that teach students how to learn, including self-scheduling.

New Roles for School Adults

Although we have focused on a new conceptualization which places students

---

[8] Gardner has launched several educational activities, described in Gardner (1989) and Goldman and Gardner (1989). The Key School in Indianapolis has been built upon these concepts.

at the center in roles for them, of course this view has consequences for the adults in schools, also. Recognition of the centrality of the student is enhanced when decision-making is closer to them, at the school building level rather than the district office or a distant state education department. It is at the building level where the action of student learning takes place and, thus, it is at the building level where the responsibility and accountability must be located. The particulars of the balance of responsibilities between administrators and teachers is less important than the fact of placing the locus of decision-making at the school level. Indeed, the conceptualization of the student as producer of learning requires it.

With decision-making at the building level, teachers become the key resources to enhance student productivity.

> [A] teacher must connect with what students already know and come up with a set of pedagogical representations, metaphors, analogies, examples, stories, demonstrations, that will connect with [the students'] prior understandings, that will make them visible, will correct them when they are way off base, and will help the student generate, create, construct, their own representations to replace them. (Shulman, 1989, p. 10)

Far from narrowing the role of teachers, recognizing the student as the producer of learning will enhance it. The new characteristics of effective teachers will be:

- Teachers will transcend narrow categorical responsibilities of subject matter to become broader enablers of student learning;

- Teachers will have opportunities to work more collegially with other teachers across the disciplines;

- Teachers will have the opportunity to engage in a greater variety of interactions with students, including whole-class instruction, small-group work, individual tutoring, organizing peer-learning networks, monitoring of self-scheduled learning; and

- Teachers will have broader involvement with other adults, including out-of-school learning resources and parents.

FORCES FOR CHANGE

These changes in both concept and practice are fundamental, involving basic shifts in school organization and functioning, in roles for students and adults alike and for those students labelled as handicapped and not. In assaying the forces for change, we will focus in particular on the factors concerning students labelled as handicapped. These of course include the larger changes occurring in education. They provide both context and potential force for the changes affecting the students labelled as handicapped.

The changes in general education produce momentum and a concern for educational restructuring that can have potential benefit for those students now labelled as handicapped. This is especially the case given two aspects of the second wave of school reform: first, increasing attention to at-risk students and second, increasing recognition that the changes necessary must be fundamental, not tinkering at the margin. That being the case, there is we believe, an opportunity to struggle for the fundamental changes necessary to establish schools that serve and succeed for all students.

Speaking of the turmoil created in a high school characterized by "the wrongs of racial discrimination and segregation and the treatment of the handicapped" and its efforts to reform, Albert Shanker (1988), president of the American Federation of Teachers, points out that "a school is...a moral community...[which cannot] be 'good' for only a small, privileged handful at the expense of discriminating against or excluding many others" (p. E7). A community, indeed a "moral community," is the result of human choice. People with disabilities can be full participants in a community, as friends, neighbors, workers, citizens, and family members. Whether this is the case is a result of decisions both at the larger societal level and that of the school system that prepares people, both those labelled as handicapped and not. Indeed, that decision is one of the basic decisions the school system makes for itself and for the larger society. The goal of a life of full participation can be achieved only if we shape school systems that include all students, systems that are both consonant with, and build toward, an inclusive society.

There are of course various reform efforts underway concerning special education. Some of them involve making the separate special education system work better. Others introduce efforts to bridge the gap between the separate regular and special education systems, including pre-referral programs, consulting teacher models, and efforts toward mainstreaming (see Lipsky & Gartner, 1989, chapter 14). Although beneficial, each of these reforms assumes, at bottom, the continuing of two separate systems, perhaps with the boundaries shifted or made more permeable or both. The concepts of Least Restrictive Environment (LRE)--a continuum of placements, and a cascade of services--were progressive when developed but do not today promote the *full* inclusion of *all* persons with disabilities in *all* aspects of societal life, nor do they serve as guiding principles for the

education that is the necessary means toward that goal's achievement. As Taylor (1988) powerfully points out, there are seven conceptual and philosophic flaws in LRE.

- The LRE principle legitimates restrictive environments.

- The LRE principle confuses segregation and integration on the one hand with intensity of services on the other.

- The LRE principle is based on a "readiness" model.

- The LRE principle supports the primacy of professional decision-making.

- The LRE principle sanctions infringements on people's rights.

- The LRE principle implies that people must move as they develop and change.

- The LRE principle directs attention to physical settings rather than to the services and supports people need to be integrated into the community.

Beyond the broad wave of educational reform, other factors particular to the education of students labelled as handicapped encourage change. These include growing professional recognition that changes are necessary and the often heated debate about the Regular Education Initiative, a modest step in the right direction, suggests something of this. Furthermore, the increasing number of children--beneficiaries of PL 94-142's provision of access--who are now completing school ill-prepared for life, has led to increasing parental pressure for better results.

The emerging and growing involvement of adults with disabilities can have a positive impact on the education of students labelled as handicapped. They will be less likely to tolerate an educational system that does not recognize the capabilities of students with impairments and that fails to prepare them to deal with the realities of the outside world.

It is the force of a mobilized community of persons with disabilities that has been missing in the struggle for quality integrated education. Their involvement is essential. Unlike minority-group students and others ill-served by the schools, most students with disabilities are not born into a community of shared experience. They need to partake of the strength that comes from those who are "ready with the armor and anger to fight to preserve their sense of themselves that the [larger] world [tries] to shatter" (Asch, 1984, p. 551).

The involvement of the community of adults with disabilities goes beyond the standard call for role models.

It goes to the power of mutual support, the understanding of shared experiences and shared strength, the anger at oppression which powers advocacy and social action. Individuals with disabilities are less likely to tolerate a system which is disdainful of the capability of students with handicapping conditions; a system which fails to prepare them well for the larger world; a system which in the name of compassion and understanding gives caring and love but fails to provide education; a system which is special in its resources, but not its results; a system which sees the problem located solely in the biology of the individual; and ultimately a system which fails to prepare students to recognize and then to confront and change a disabling environment. (Lipsky & Gartner, 1987, pp. 72-73)

We have already noted the critical role of parents. They are central both to the process of education of their children and to the advocacy necessary to make that education effective.

Increasingly, organizations are championing the cause of fundamental change. Several of the parent-assistance centers established under the auspices of PL 94-142 have taken a prominent role here, through both their publications and their training activities; outstanding examples include the national TAPP Center and the Peak Center in Colorado. A leading role is being played by TASH (The Association for Persons with Severe Handicaps), that blends together a parent and professional membership. And several professional organizations have supported various aspects of restructuring. For example, the National Association of School Psychologists (NASP), the National Association of Social Workers, and the National Coalition of Advocates for Students have developed and are promoting the "rights without labels" concept. And NASP has published collections identifying new alternative strategies (see especially Graden, Zins, & Curtis, 1988).

And in practice, promisingly, there are increasing efforts to craft solutions that do not consign some to permanent second-class status. These include school systems such as Johnson City, NY, as well as several of the Roman Catholic Separate School Boards in the metropolitan Toronto area and the Woodside district in New Brunswick; state education department efforts in Colorado, Delaware, Iowa, Pennsylvania, and Wisconsin; individual schools such as the Ed Smith School in Syracuse, NY, and the Key School in Indianapolis; the efforts in the San Diego City Schools and the plans of the Denver schools to end remedial education in favor of a common core curriculum where all students are expected and helped to learn; multi-district efforts such as Ted Sizer's Coalition of Essential Schools and Tom Joe's New Futures Schools; and new conceptualizations such as Howard Gardner's multiple intelligences and Harry Levin's accelerated schooling.

PL 94-142, right for its time, has assured access. Now, it is time to achieve quality.

REFERENCES

Asch, A. (1984). Personal reflections. *American Psychologist, 39*, 551-552.

Berkowitz, E. D. (1987). *Disabled policy: America's programs for the handicapped.* New York: Cambridge University Press.

Benjamin, S. (1989). An ideascape for education: What futurists recommend. *Educational Leadership, 47*(1), 8-14.

Big kids teach little kids: What we know about cross-aged tutoring. (1987). *Harvard Education Letter, 3*(2), 1-4.

Bogdan, R., & Kugelmass, J. (1984). Case studies of mainstreaming: A symbolic interactionist approach to special schooling. In L. Barton & S. Tomlinson (Eds.), *Special education and social interests* (pp. 83-97). London: Croom-Helm.

Edmonds, R. (1979). Some schools work and more can. *Social Policy, 9*(5), 25-29.

Ferguson, D., & Asch, A. (1989). What we want for our children: Perspectives of parents and adults with disabilities. In D. Biklen, P. M. Ferguson, & A. Ford (Eds.), *Schooling and disability* (pp.108-140). Chicago: National Society for the Study of Education.

Fewell, R. R., & Vadasy, P. F. (1986). *Families of handicapped children: Needs and supports across the life span.* Austin, TX: Pro-Ed.

Fine, M. & Asch, A. (1981). Disabled women: Sexism without the pedestal. *Journal of Sociology and Social Welfare, 8*(2), 233-248.

Fine, M., & Asch, A. (1988a). Disability beyond stigma: Social interaction, discrimination, and activism. *Journal of Social Issues, 44*, 3-22.

Fine, M., & Asch, A. (Eds.). (1988b). *Women with disabilities: Essays in psychology, culture, and politics.* Philadelphia: Temple University Press.

Gardner, H. (1983). *Frames of mind: Theories of multiple intelligences.* New York: Basic Books.

Gardner, H. (1989). *To open minds: Chinese clues to the dilemma of contemporary education.* New York: Basic Books.

Gartner, A., & Joe, T. (Eds.). (1987). *Images of the disabled/disabling images.* New York: Praeger.

Gartner, A., & Lipsky, D. K. (1987). Beyond special education: Toward a quality system for all students. *Harvard Educational Review, 57*, 367-395.

Gartner, A., & Lipsky, D. K. (1989, June). *Equity and excellence for all students.* Presentation before the National Council On Disability, National Study on the Education of Students with Disabilities. Washington, DC.

Goldman, J., & Gardner, H. (1989). Multiple paths to educational effectiveness. In D. K. Lipsky & A. Gartner (Eds.), *Beyond separate education: Quality education for all* (pp. 121-139). Baltimore, MD: Paul H. Brookes Publishing Co.

Graden, J. L., Zins, J. E., & Curtis, M. J. (1988). *Alternative educational delivery systems: Enhancing instructional options for all students.* Washington, DC: National Association of School Psychologists.

Granger, L., & Granger, B. (1986). *The magic feather.* New York: E. P. Dutton.

Guess, D., Benson, H. A., & Siegel-Causey, E. (1985). Concepts and issues related to choice-making and autonomy among persons with severe disabilities. *Journal of the Association for Persons with Severe Handicaps, 10*(2), 79-86.

Hahn, H. (1989). The politics of special education. In D. K. Lipsky & A. Gartner (Eds.), *Beyond separate education: Quality education for all* (pp. 225-242). Baltimore, MD: Paul H. Brookes Publishing Co.

Handicapped Children as Tutors. (1984). Salt Lake, UT: David O. McKay Institute of Education, Brigham Young University.

Hedin, D. (1986). *Students as teachers: A tool for improving school climate and productivity.* A Paper Prepared for the Task Force on Teaching as a Profession, Carnegie Forum on Education and the Economy, Rochester, New York.

Howe, H., II. (1989, August). Letter. *Educational Excellence Network,* 1-5.

Jenkins, J. R., & Jenkins, L. M. (1981). *Cross age and peer tutoring: Help for children with learning problems*. Reston, VA: The Council for Exceptional Children.

Johnson, D. W., & Johnson, R. T. (1984). *Circles of learning: Cooperation in the classroom*. Washington, DC: Association for Supervision and Curriculum Development.

Kuhn, T. K. (Ed.). (1962). *The Structure of scientific revolutions*. New York: Basic Books.

Lezotte, L. (1989). School improvement based on the effective schools research. In D. K. Lipsky & A. Gartner (Eds.), *Beyond separate education: Quality education for all* (pp. 25-37). Baltimore, MD: Paul H. Brookes Publishing Co.

Lilly, M. S. (1989). Teacher preparation. In D. K. Lipsky & A. Gartner (Eds.), *Beyond separate education: Quality education for all* (pp. 143-158). Baltimore, MD: Paul H. Brookes Publishing Co.

Lipsky, D. K. (1985). A parental perspective on stress and coping. *American Journal of Orthopsychiatry,55*,614-617.

Lipsky, D. K. (1989). The roles of parents. In D. K. Lipsky & A. Gartner (Eds.), *Beyond separate education: Quality education for all* (pp. 159-180). Baltimore, MD: Paul H. Brookes Publishing Co.

Lipsky, D. K., & Gartner, A. (Eds.). (1989). *Beyond separate education: Quality education for all*. Baltimore, MD: Paul H. Brookes Publishing Co.

Lipsky, D. K., & Gartner, A. (1987). Capable of achievement and worthy of respect: Education for the handicapped as if they were full-fledged human beings. *Exceptional Children, 54*, 69-74.

Lipsky, D. K., & Gartner, A. (1990). Students as instructional agents. In W. Stainback & S. Stainback (Eds.), *Support systems for educating all students in the mainstream* (pp. 81-94). Baltimore, MD: Paul H. Brookes Publishing Co.

On cases of contagion. (1987, March 4). New York Times, p. A21.

Osguthorpe, R. T., & Scruggs, T. E. (1986). Special education students as tutors: A review and analysis. *Remedial and Special Education, 7*(4), 15-26.

Sarason, S., & Doris, J. (1979). *Educational handicap, public policy, and social history*. New York: Free Press.

Scotch, R. K. (1984). *From good will to civil rights: Transforming federal disability policy*. Philadelphia: Temple University Press.

Shanker, A. (1988, June 11). Doing right wrong: The lesson of Hamilton High. *New York Times*, p. E7.

Shepard, L. A. (1987). The new push for excellence: Widening the schism between regular and general education. *Exceptional Children, 53*, 327-329.

Shulman, L. S. (1989, June). Toward a pedagogy of substance. *AAHE Bulletin*, 8-13.

Singer, J. D. (1988). Should special education merge with regular education? *Educational Policy, 2*,409-424.

Skrtic, T. (1986). The crisis in special education knowledge: A perspective on perspective. *Focus on Exceptional Children, 18*(7), 1-16.

Skrtic, T. (1987). *Prenuptial agreements necessary for wedding special education and general education*. Paper presented to the American Education and Research Association, Washington, DC.

Slavin, R. E. (1987). Cooperative learning and the cooperative school. *Educational Leadership, 45*(3), 7-13.

Stainback, S., & Stainback, W. (1989). Integration of students with mild and moderate handicaps. In D. K. Lipsky & A. Gartner (Eds.), *Beyond separate education: Quality education for all* (pp. 41-52). Baltimore, MD: Paul H. Brookes Publishing Co.

Stainback, S., Stainback, W., & Forest, M. (1989). *Educating all students in the mainstream of regular education*. Baltimore, MD: Paul H. Brookes Publishing Co.

Stainback, W., & Stainback, S. (1984). A rationale for the merger of special and regular education. *Exceptional Children, 51*, 102-111.

Stainback, W., & Stainback, S. (1990). *Support networks for inclusive schooling: Interdependent integrated education*. Baltimore, MD: Paul H. Brookes Publishing Co.

Stone, D. A. (1984). *The disabled state*. Philadelphia: Temple University Press.

Taylor, S. J. (1988). Caught in the continuum: A critical analysis of the principle of least restrictive environment. *Journal of the Association for Persons with Severe Handicaps, 13*(1), 41-53.

Tenth Annual Report to the Congress on the Implementation of the Education of the Handicapped Act. (1988). Washington, DC: U.S. Department of Education.

Turnbull, H. R., III, & Turnbull, A. P. (Eds.). (1985). *Parents speak out: Then and now* (2nd ed.). Springfield, OH: Charles C. Merrill.

Wagner, M., & Shaver, D. M. (1989). *Education programs and achievements of secondary special education students: Findings from the national longitudinal transition study.* Menlo Park, CA: SRI International.

Ysseldyke, J. E. (1987). Classification of handicapped students. In M. C. Wang, M. C. Reynolds, & H. J. Walberg (Eds.), *Handbook of special education: Research and practice: Learner characteristics and adaptive education* (Vol 1, pp. 253-271). London: Pergamon Press.

5

RESTRUCTURING IN SOCIOPOLITICAL CONTEXT: RESERVATIONS ABOUT THE EFFECTS OF CURRENT REFORM PROPOSALS ON STUDENTS WITH DISABILITIES

James M. Kauffman
University of Virginia

Education might be restructured in a variety of ways, but the instant case is the restructuring proposed by advocates of the regular education initiative (REI). The REI is difficult to define precisely, being a loosely connected set of propositions and proposals for reform of the relationship between special and general education (see Hallahan, Kauffman, Lloyd, & McKinney, 1988). More specifically, the REI suggests restructuring what has been called a "dual system" of special and general education such that special and compensatory or "second system" programs are merged into a single structure (cf. Gartner & Lipsky, 1989; Wang, Reynolds, & Walberg, 1988). Evaluation of the REI requires attention to structures and how they are articulated in the education of children in public schools.

Epstein (1988) describes school structures as comprised of several elements: tasks set for students, authority to make choices, rewards for progress, grouping for instruction, evaluations of standards, and time or rate of learning. Cuban (1988) offers the following definition:

> The structure of schools includes the formal and informal goals used to guide funding and organizing activities, including such things as who has authority and responsibility for governing schools and classrooms; how time and space are allotted; how subject matter in the curriculum is determined; how students are assigned to classes; how those classes are organized; how the different roles of teachers, principals, and superintendents are defined; and how such formal processes as budgeting, hiring, and evaluating are determined and organized. To a large extent, these structures shape the roles, responsibilities, and relationships within schools. (p. 344)

These definitions appear to encompass all aspects of restructuring envisioned by proponents of the REI. However, most of the literature on the reform of special education has focused on grouping for instruction, locus of authority, and funding mechanisms as the structural components of primary concern.

The REI is a multifaceted set of proposals, reflecting the multiplicity of issues involved in the structures of schooling. This volume attests to the variety of perspectives and specific questions to be addressed. In the limited space provided, I shall address four questions: (a) What is the case against the current structures of special and general education? (b) What is the case for alternative structures? (c) How can the REI be understood in its sociopolitical context? (d) What are some alternatives to the REI?

THE CASE AGAINST CURRENT STRUCTURES

In addition to more specific charges regarding failures of the current structures of special education, REI advocates draw the general conclusion that pull-out programs per se are failures. Biklen and Zollers (1986), for example, concluded that "even when all measures are taken to coordinate the pullout program with the work of the regular class, *students do not benefit from this special education*" (p. 581). Similarly, Gartner and Lipsky (1989) stated,

> What is known about the education of students labelled as handicapped? First, separate special education does not work. It does not do so by any measure of assessment--learning, development of self-esteem and social skills or preparation as student, worker, or citizen. Its failure is costly in several currencies--in dollars, in public confidence and, most importantly, in students' lives. (p. 26)

Reynolds (1989) commented, "There was no evidence in the past and there is no evidence now showing that removing disabled children from the mainstream and putting them into special classes or schools is an advantage for them" (p. 8). The conclusions of these writers seem to me to go somewhat beyond the data. Considerable empirical evidence may in-

dicate that special education is often poorly practiced. But as a juror I have reasonable doubt that structure accounts for the majority of special education's failures and that special education has been overwhelmingly a structural failure. A reasonable skeptic might ask, for example: Is there really no evidence whatsoever that any special classes of any kind (even resource) for any disabled children have benefited students?

Some research studies have yielded findings at odds with the conclusions of REI advocates (e.g., Marston, 1987-88; O'Connor, Stuck, & Wynne, 1979). Moreover, alternative conclusions have been reached by others who have reviewed findings on special education's effects (e.g., Hallahan, Keller, McKinney, Lloyd, & Bryan, 1988; Robert Wood Johnson Foundation, 1988; Singer, 1988; Wiederholt & Chamberlain, 1989) or obtained a national sample of the opinions of parents, teachers, and children (Harris, 1989). Beyond the findings of academic researchers, it is difficult to reconcile conclusions like those of Biklen and Zollers (1986), Gartner and Lipsky (1989), and Reynolds (1989) with national survey findings that 94% of educators believe that education for children with handicapping conditions is better now than 12 years ago and that 77% of parents of handicapped children are satisfied with the special education system (Harris, 1989). Furthermore, 74% of parents of children in regular classrooms stated that the current extent of integration was best for their children, and 7% said less integration would be better. The International Center for the Disabled's "Report Card" on special education (Harris, 1989) noted problem areas and needed improvements in special education; it did not, however, support the conclusion that special education, separate or integrated, does not work.

Finally, in response to sweeping charges that special education pull-out programs "do not work" (Gartner &

Lipsky, 1989) and that students do not "benefit" (Biklen & Zollers, 1986) or gain "advantage" (Reynolds, 1989), one must ask what is meant by these charges. It is apparent that little consideration has been given to the outcomes we might expect, were special education to "work" (Kauffman, 1990).

THE CASE FOR RESTRUCTURING (REI)

Proponents of the REI assert that alternatives to the current structure have been shown to work. For example, "It is recognized that integrated programs work, and that preparation for full lives can only occur in integrated settings" (Gartner & Lipsky, 1989, p. 26). "All types of students can be accommodated in ALEM [Adaptive Learning Environments Model] classrooms" (Biklen & Zollers, 1986, p. 583). The restructuring envisioned by REI advocates typically is described as comprised of such elements as these: not separating children for special instruction (i.e., no pull-out instruction), holding high expectations or high demands for performance, teacher consultation or collaboration, amalgamating all special programs, peer tutoring or other peer-mediated interventions, prereferral strategies, cooperative learning, and models such as ALEM. All of these have been shown to benefit some children under some circumstances. Reviews of empirical findings do not, however, support the contention that implementing these interventions, singly or in combination, provides appropriate education for all children with disabilities in regular classrooms (e.g., Bryan & Bryan, 1988; Fuchs & Fuchs, 1988; Hallahan, et al., 1988; Lloyd, Crowley, Kohler, & Strain, 1988). In short, if conclusions are to be based on empirical evidence, then proponents of restructuring have so far not built a convincing case for their views; claims that integrated

programs are known to work appear to be at least as exaggerated as claims that current programs do not work (cf. Oakland & Cunningham, 1990). It might be noted, furthermore, that the programs most frequently attacked by REI proponents as having been shown to be ineffective, i.e., pull-out programs for children with learning disabilities (cf. Gartner & Lipsky, 1989; Wang et al., 1989), are currently the most integrated models of special education (Harris, 1989).

THE REI IN SOCIOPOLITICAL CONTEXT

Given the mixed evidence regarding the success of special education as currently structured and as proposed by advocates of restructuring, how does one account for REI rhetoric? My contention is that the REI did not develop ex-nihilo, nor was it constructed by non-dominant sociopolitical forces during the past decade. Rather, the REI reflects the zeitgeist of the 1980s; it is, in large measure, the dominant sociopolitical philosophy of the 1980s applied to public schooling.

Attempts to reform education must be seen in their historical and contemporary contexts. The political, economic, and social forces that affect all functions of government, including public elementary and secondary education, must be considered if reform proposals are to be understood. In fact, understanding why specific reforms of education are proposed requires examination of the assumptions guiding the restructuring of other government agencies and programs. The effects of these assumptions on policy development in other agencies and programs--and ultimately the effects on the citizens they are intended to serve--may then provide a basis for prediction of the probable effects on public education, should parallel reforms be implemented in schools.

Public education is primarily a trailer, not a leader in political, economic, and social change. That is, public education is a fundamentally conservative institution, reflecting rather than leading broad social reform. It reflects the basic values of society and represents an adopted social agenda; it does not set the agenda for social change (cf. Cuban, 1988; Sizer, 1985). Cuban (1988) describes two levels of change: First-order change makes what already exists work better; second-order change is alteration in the fundamental ways in which organizations are put together--"new goals, structures, and roles that transform familiar ways of doing things into new ways of solving persistent problems" (p. 342). He notes further that if second-order change is to occur "*basic social and political changes would need to occur outside of schools*" (p. 344).

Thus a decade after the first inauguration of Ronald Reagan and George Bush, public education became a candidate for restructuring along the lines already laid down in other social systems by the Reagan-Bush administration. Two points are critical in understanding this restructuring and its implications for education: (a) the social and political changes occurring in the 1980s were what Cuban calls first-order changes, not changes that altered the fundamental purposes of schools; (b) many of the changes reduced or eliminated benefits to powerless, vulnerable individuals and groups and widened the gap between haves and have-nots in our society. If we become aware of the dangers inherent in the assumptions that have guided the restructuring of other social agencies during the Reagan-Bush era, we may yet avert for special education the shambles that have been made of other programs designed to serve constituencies of disadvantaged and powerless people.

A decade ago the U. S. made a dramatic sociopolitical turn to the right. Restructuring became a key word in discourse about government and social change

throughout the world. In the U. S., restructuring entailed turning away from government programs designed to protect individuals from the ravages of social and economic power. President Reagan came to office following a period of several decades of expansion of social programs; the general public, many government officials, and some social scientists had become disenchanted with government's social welfare programs (cf. Palmer & Sawhill, 1982). As Mayer (1989) noted, "It has become the fashion to see government as incapable of getting things done--if not at the root of many problems" (p. 5). During the Carter administration, the country had fallen into what some called a period of malaise. In the late 1970s the country was ripe for change, and the shift in political philosophy was reflected in more than the election of a conservative Republican president--both parties became more conservative.

The fact that some proposals for changes in education and other social programs received bipartisan support during the 1980s does not necessarily compel the conclusion that these proposals were not part of a conservative agenda; the rightward shift of most voters and politicians was part of the Reagan phenomenon and the weltanschauung of the 1980s. The dismantling of social programs in the 1980s was led by the Reagan administration, but it was abetted by both Democrats and Republicans. Describing the shameful decline in nutrition programs during the 1980s, a leading nutritionist noted that "Both parties must share the blame for the 1980s as they can share the praise for the 1970s" (Mayer, 1989, p. 3).

The Reagan-Bush administration's approach to government and problems of social welfare may have been advantageous to the majority of Americans in the 1980s, particularly to the most advantaged, but it was decidedly disadvantageous to the significant minority of our citizens who were already disadvantaged (cf. Bawden & Levy, 1982; Minarik, 1988; Peterson, 1988). I believe that widespread implementation of the REI would not only be consistent with the Reagan-Bush approach to problems of social welfare but lead to outcomes for children who have serious difficulties in school that parallel the disasters in health care, maternal and child care, nutrition, housing, and employment now so apparent among the significant and growing underclass of Americans (cf. Baumeister, Kupstas, & Klindworth, 1990; Kozol, 1990; Mayer, 1989).

The Reagan-Bush administration was guided in its restructuring of federal programs by key assumptions regarding the role of government. These assumptions not only reshaped federal programs but became the basis for restructuring many state social welfare programs as well. Consequently, federal initiatives to alter programs and regulations affected social programs at all levels of government. Education is the last program of government to become a target for restructuring based on politically conservative notions of social management. I shall comment on three of these assumptions guiding restructuring of social programs in the Reagan era and offer my perspective on the implications for restructuring special education.

Assumption 1: Programs designed to help the disadvantaged are not working and must be restructured. During the Reagan era, programs of federal assistance to disadvantaged individuals were drastically scaled back under suppositions that these programs failed to address real problems, that they made people increasingly dependent on government assistance, and that state and local governments as well as volunteer organizations and philanthropic individuals were the proper loci of efforts to resolve social problems (Peterson, 1982; Palmer & Sawhill, 1982). Loss of public confidence that social assistance programs were worthwhile was not necessarily based on evidence of their failure; exaggeration of the problems of welfare fraud and loafers contributed to the perception that programs were not working. Many programs were cast as failures primarily because more individuals were enrolled in them and they were becoming more expensive. For example, in 1968 two million people received food stamps. By 1971, this number had grown to 11 million. Nutrition programs fell victim to the belief that if they were working the number of persons benefiting from them should be declining, not increasing. Between 1981 and 1984, $12 billion was cut from government food programs (Mayer, 1989).

The charge that special education as an enterprise has failed (e.g., Gartner & Lipsky, 1989; National Center on Education and the Economy, 1989; Reynolds, 1989; Wang et al., 1988) is remarkably consistent with the scathing commentary on social welfare programs that became part of our cultural heritage during the Reagan era. Special education programs, as well as other programs of social assistance, are vulnerable to the popular notion that if they are expanding without eliminating the problem they are not working.

The decline in federal support for social programs has not been offset by increases in state and local funding. Indeed, decreased federal funding for categorical programs encouraged cuts in state spending for those programs as well (Inman, 1985). One result of disinvestment in social programs has been an increase in the underclass of American citizens and a soaring number of children at risk for a variety of developmental disabilities (cf. Baumeister et al., 1990). If programs of federal assistance do not work, their diminution or absence clearly works even less well for those in need. I surmise that restructuring special education along lines consistent with what has already occurred in other social programs will not have a salutary effect on the lives of children.

Assumption 2: Too many people are considered disadvantaged--programs have grown too large and generous. One set of policy changes under the Reagan-Bush administration involved narrower targeting of benefits to individuals--tightening eligibility requirements under the assumption that people were qualifying too easily for assistance programs. If we must have the program, this assumption suggested, then let us make certain that it is a safety net for true hardship cases, being watchful not to provide benefits for marginal cases. For example, "These changes typically confine income-related assistance programs to the poorest recipients and those whom society generally does not expect to work (the 'truly needy')" (Palmer & Sawhill, 1982, p. 17). Thus, more limited deductions for child care, greater restrictions on earned income in the AFDC (Aid to Families with Dependent Children) Program, tighter income eligibility restrictions in school lunch and food stamp programs, lower income limits and higher required contributions for housing assistance, and a variety of other measures designed to rescind federal social programs were implemented. These changes contributed to the growing number of American children experiencing deprivation and needing a variety of social services.

In the sociopolitical context of such changes in federal policy, it is not surprising that President Reagan's primary appointee in special education stated, "Recent studies suggest that a significant percentage of the children served in the special learning disability category are not handicapped" (Will, 1984, p. 13, no references cited). Others expressed the opinion that two-thirds of the children enrolled in special education have relatively minor problems, most or all of which could be addressed by general education (Wang et al., 1988). As compensatory education and other social welfare programs were reduced, however, the need of more children for special education became greater. This might have been predictable. The surprise is not the need for service to more children under various special education categories, including learning disabilities; it is that advocates for children with disabilities should decry the increase in children so served (e.g., Gartner & Lipsky, 1989, p. 9) in an era of greatly reduced social services of other kinds. Wolch (1985) describes how the service-dependent poor are diverted--misassigned to services or require additional services--when the social programs for which they had been eligible are no longer accessible. I see growth in special education as a logical consequence of reduction of other social services to families and children, resulting in increased risk factors (cf. Baumeister et al., 1990). Tightening eligibility requirements for special education in the face of increasing poverty and other social factors heightening the incidence of children's disabilities--for example, by making "judgmentally" handicapped children (Reynolds, Wang, & Walberg, 1987) ineligible--would, I believe, add insult to injury.

Assumption 3: Federal regulation is unnecessary or even hurtful--control should be returned to states and localities, and regulations should emphasize performance rather than monitoring. Under the assumption that federal regulation stifles creative solutions, prevents local decision makers from making common sense judgments, and wastes resources, a variety of government agencies and programs were deregulated (Eads & Fix, 1982). Deregulation of the airlines and the savings and loan industry, for example, was accomplished; deregulation of education was only partially implemented. A major aspect of deregulation was combining federal assistance programs into block grants, giving states, localities, and private entities more discretion in spending and operating programs. The consequences of deregulation have been unfavorable to many citizens, particularly those least fortunate. In education, deregulation and block funding have resulted in declining funds for projects and services intended to ensure equity; programs for disadvantaged students have sustained substantial cuts (cf. Peterson, 1988; O'Neill & Simms, 1982; Verstegen & Clark, 1988). Disadvantaged children do not seem to benefit from the withdrawal of protective federal regulations.

States and localities were assumed by the Reagan-Bush administration to be more responsive to local needs and able to make better use of all their resources if left unhampered by federal regulations. In addition to this philosophy of local control the Reagan-Bush administration held the assumption that return of authority to states and localities would weaken advocacy groups that lobby for domestic social programs. President Reagan was quoted as saying,

> It's far easier for people to come to Washington to get their social programs. It would be a hell of a lot tougher if we diffuse them and send them back to the states. All their friends and connections are in Washington. (Peterson, 1982, p. 169)

Finally, the Reagan-Bush approach to regulation is to minimize federal intrusiveness:

> Accordingly, it prefers the operation of market-like regulatory mechanisms and supports regulatory techniques that provide regulated parties with maximum flexibility--such as mandating standards of performance (e.g., levels of pollutants) rather than ways of achieving them. (Eads & Fix, 1982, p. 132)

Nevertheless, in areas of social assistance in which it perceived fraud and abuse to be major problems--AFDC and Food Stamps, for example--the Reagan administration imposed strict regulatory standards (Eads & Fix, 1982).

In my view, the proposals for restructuring advanced by Gartner and Lipsky (1989), Wang et al. (1988), the National Center on Education and the Economy (1989), and other advocates of the REI are remarkably consistent with the Reagan-Bush approach to regulation and funding of other social programs. I see no reason to believe that deregulating special education, combining funds for special education with a variety of compensatory programs, and rewarding achievement outcomes rather than monitoring compliance will serve children with disabilities better than the current structures. As O'Neill and Simms (1982) noted,

> Consolidation of handicapped programs may improve program efficiency. However, the consolidation will not necessarily lead to administrative cost reductions that are sufficient to offset the budgetary reductions. Since federal aid to the handicapped only covers a small part of the total cost of educating this group, the states argue that budget cuts, in the absence of legislative mandates, are imposing additional costs that they should not have to bear. (p. 342)

Regulatory relief and legislative change appear to be central to the restructuring sought by REI proponents. But, as Murnane (1985) has noted in the case of Title I (now Chapter I under consolidation legislation), local schools tend to treat consolidated funding as general revenue, and the funds intended for disadvantaged children tend to be spent elsewhere in school budgets to permit tax relief or benefits to all students. "The first ten years of experience with Title I demonstrated both the difficulty of targeting aid to disadvantaged children and the success of the regulations in achieving that goal" (Murnane, 1985, p. 130). It is unfortunate that a decade after its full implementation and without its ever having been funded at a level approximating the original federal limit, the Education for All Handicapped Children Act (EHCA) is under attack as one of many compensatory programs that "carve kids into separate pieces and make it difficult to build initiatives that work for the student" (National Center on Education and the Economy, 1989, p. 18).

ALTERNATIVES TO THE REI

Although some of the suggestions of REI advocates are unassailable (Who can argue against the improvement of education for all children, the improvement of general as well as special education, better relationships between regular and special teachers, greater coordination of service agencies and programs, or education in the least restrictive environment?), REI proponents have exaggerated both the failures of present structures and the advantages of their proposed restructuring. The alternative to the REI is not necessarily the status quo; restructuring can occur within a framework of realities and protections for handicapped children. I suggest that we begin by recognizing and predicating our action on at least four such realities. First, without fundamental realignment of social structures outside the schools, we are necessarily dealing with first-order change--how to make what we have work better (cf. Cuban, 1988). We need to use the structure of EHCA to better advantage for students who have special needs. Second, many students not now identified as handicapped have great difficulty in school and need the individualized decision making prescribed by EHCA. These students' needs will not be met without a very substantial increase in resources allocated specifically to their education. Special education provides a model of appropriate individualization that is not predicated on categorization once basic entitlement is determined. Some or all of the entitlements of EHCA should be extended to these students (cf. Carnine & Kameenui, 1990; Gerber, 1989). Third, effective instruction for children who have special difficulty in school is sometimes different from that typically recommended by school reformers and appropriate for students with histories of school success (cf. Carnine & Kameenui, 1990), and these different instructional approaches cannot be used simultaneously with a given child or group of children. Therefore, separate instruction is sometimes necessary for some students. Fourth, the duality of general and special education has been exaggerated. Teachers appear to perceive the present arrangement of general and special education as a single or unitary system, not a dual system (Semmel, Abernathy, Butera, & Lesar, 1990). Moreover, public and private education, not regular and special education, are America's dual systems (cf. Peterson, 1988). Merging general and special education could reduce or eliminate public school service options that parents deem most appropriate for their handicapped children, encouraging the privatization of special education and leaving the well-off with alternatives, the poor with few or none.

REFERENCES

Baumeister, A. A., Kupstas, F., & Klindworth, L. M. (1990). New morbidity: Implications for prevention of children's disabilities. *Exceptionality, 1*, 1-16.

Bawden, L., & Levy, F. (1982). The economic well-being of families and individuals. In J. L. Palmer & I. V. Sawhill (Eds.), The Reagan experiment: An examination of economic and social policies under the Reagan administration (pp. 459-483). Washington, DC: Urban Institute Press.

Biklen, D., & Zollers, N. (1986). The focus of advocacy in the LD field. *Journal of Learning Disabilities, 19*, 579-586.

Bryan, J. H., & Bryan, T. H. (1988). Where's the beef? A review of published research on the Adaptive Learning Environment Model. *Learning Disabilities Focus, 4*(1), 9-14.

Carnine, D., & Kameenui, E. (1990). The regular education initiative and children with special needs: A false dilemma in the face of true problems. *Journal of Learning Disabilities, 23*, 141-144.

Cuban, L. (1988). A fundamental puzzle of school reform. *Phi Delta Kappan, 69*, 341-344.

Eads, G. C., & Fix, M. (1982). Regulatory policy. In J. L. Palmer & I. V. Sawhill (Eds.), *The Reagan experiment: An examination of economic and social policies under the Reagan administration* (pp. 129-153). Washington, DC: Urban Institute Press.

Epstein, J. L. (1988). Effective schools or effective students: Dealing with diversity. In R. Haskins & D. MacRae (Eds.), *Policies for America's public schools: Teachers, equity, and indicators* (pp. 89-126). Norwood, NJ: Ablex.

Fuchs, D., & Fuchs, L. S. (1988). An evaluation of the Adaptive Learning Environments Model. *Exceptional Children, 55*, 115-127.

Gartner, A., & Lipsky, D. K. (1989). *The yoke of special education: How to break it.* Rochester, NY: National Center on Education and the Economy.

Gerber, M. M. (1989, Autumn). The new "diversity" and special education: Are we going forward or starting again? *California Public Schools Forum, 3*, 19-31.

Hallahan, D. P., Kauffman, J. M., Lloyd, J. W., & McKinney, J. D. (Eds.) (1988). *Journal of Learning Disabilities, 21*(1) [special issue on the Regular Education Initiative].

Hallahan, D. P., Keller, C. E., McKinney, J. D., Lloyd, J. W., & Bryan, T. (1988). Examining the research base of the regular education initiative: Efficacy studies and the Adaptive Learning Environments Model. *Journal of Learning Disabilities, 21*, 29-35, 55.

Harris, L. (1989, June). *The ICD survey III: A report card on special education.* New York: Louis Harris & Associates.

Inman, R. P. (1985). Fiscal allocations in a federalist economy: Understanding the "new" federalism. In J. M. Quigley & D. L. Rubinfeld (Eds.), *American domestic priorities: An economic appraisal* (pp. 3-33). Berkeley, CA: University of California Press.

Kauffman, J. M. (1990, April). *What happens when special education works? Special education reform proposals in sociopolitical context.* Invited paper presented at the annual meeting of the American Educational Research Association, Special Education Special Interest Group, Boston.

Kozol, J. (1990, Winter/Spring). The new untouchables. *Newsweek Special Issue*, 48-53.

Lloyd, J. W., Crowley, E. P., Kohler, F. W., & Strain, P. S. (1988). Redefining the applied research agenda: Cooperative learning, prereferral, teacher consultation, and peer-mediated models. *Journal of Learning Disabilities, 21*, 43-52.

Marston, D. (1987-88). The effectiveness of special education: A time-series analysis of reading performance in regular and special education settings. *Journal of Special Education, 21*(4), 13-26.

Mayer, J. (1989, November). *Nutritional problems in the United States: Then and now.* Unpublished manuscript, Tufts University.

Minarik, J. J. (1988). Family incomes. In I. V. Sawhill (Ed.), *Challenge to leadership: Economic and social issues for the next decade* (pp. 33-66). Washington, DC: Urban Institute Press.

Murnane, R. J. (1985). An economist's look at federal and state education policies. In J. M. Quigley & D. L. Rubinfeld (Eds.), *American domestic priorities: An economic appraisal* (pp. 118-147). Berkeley, CA: University of California Press.

National Center on Education and the Economy. (1989). *To secure our future: The federal role in education.* Rochester, NY: Author.

Oakland, T., & Cunningham, J. L. (1990). Advocates for educational services for all children need improved research and conceptual bases. *School Psychology Quarterly, 5*, 66-77.

O'Connor, P. D., Stuck, G. B., & Wynne, M. D. (1979). Effects of short-term intervention resource-room program on task orientation and achievement. *Journal of Special Education, 13*, 375-385.

O'Neill, J. A., & Simms, M. C. (1982). Education. In J. L. Palmer & I. V. Sawhill (Eds.), *The Reagan experiment: An examination of economic and social policies under the Reagan administration* (pp. 329-359). Washington, DC: Urban Institute Press.

Palmer, J. L., & Sawhill, I. V. (1982). Perspectives on the Reagan experiment. In J. L. Palmer & I. V.

Sawhill (Eds.), *The Reagan experiment: An examination of economic and social policies under the Reagan administration* (pp. 1-28). Washington, DC: Urban Institute Press.

Peterson, G. E. (1982). The state and local sector. In J. L. Palmer & I. V. Sawhill (Eds.), *The Reagan experiment: An examination of economic and social policies under the Reagan administration* (pp. 157-217). Washington, DC: Urban Institute Press.

Peterson, P. E. (1988). Economic and political trends affecting education. In R. Haskins & D. MacRae (Eds.), *Policies for America's public schools: Teachers, equity, and indicators* (pp. 25-54). Norwood, NJ: Ablex.

Reynolds, M. C. (1989). An historical perspective: The delivery of special education to mildly disabled and at-risk students. *Remedial and Special Education, 10*(6), 7-11.

Reynolds, M. C., Wang, M. C., & Walberg, H. J. (1987). The necessary restructuring of special and regular education. *Exceptional Children, 53*, 391-398.

Robert Wood Johnson Foundation. (1988, December). *Serving handicapped children: A special report.* Princeton, NJ: Author.

Semmel, M. I., Abernathy, T. V., Butera, G., & Lesar, S. (1990). *Teacher perceptions of special education reform: An empirical study of the regular education initiative (REI).* Unpublished manuscript, University of California at Santa Barbara.

Singer, J. D. (1988). Should special education merge with regular education? *Educational Policy, 2,* 409-424.

Sizer, T. R. (1985). *Horace's compromise: The dilemma of the American high school* (updated ed.). Boston: Houghton Mifflin.

Verstegen, D. A., & Clark, D. L. (1988). The diminution in federal expenditures for education during the Reagan administration. *Phi Delta Kappan, 70,* 134-138.

Wang, M. C., Reynolds, M. C., & Walberg, H. J. (1988). Integrating the children of the second system. *Phi Delta Kappan, 70,* 248-251.

Wiederholt, J. L., & Chamberlain, S. P. (1989). A critical analysis of resource programs. *Remedial and Special Education, 10*(6), 15-37.

Will, M. C. (1984). Let us pause and reflect--but not too long. *Exceptional Children, 51,* 11-16.

Wolch, J. R. (1985). Commentary. In J. M. Quigley & D. L. Rubinfeld (Eds.), *American domestic priorities: An economic appraisal* (pp. 173-180). Berkeley, CA: University of California Press.

6

THE REI DEBATE: WHAT IF EVERYBODY IS RIGHT?

Frederick J. Weintraub
The Council for Exceptional Children

The authors of this section all present compelling argument and evidence to support their particular perspective on the degree to which students with disabilities should be educated in integrated settings. However, the issue about how to deliver appropriate educational services to 4.2 million students with disabilities is not as simply resolved as a debate where the winner is determined on the basis of which orators presented the most compelling case. In the world of education composed of millions of diverse students, professionals, parents and policy makers, truth is not as easily determined as it is in a debate or chapters of a book.

HISTORICAL PERSPECTIVE ON THE DEBATE

The recent controversy over the "Regular Education Initiative," proposed by former Assistant Secretary for Special Education and Rehabilitative Services Madeline Will (1985), is the most recent example of a long standing policy and professional disagreement over whether students with disabilities would be more appropriately educated in integrated settings and whether such students should be identified as having a disability.

In 1956, Arthur Hill, the former head of special education in the U.S. Office of Education, wrote:

A new cliche has appeared on the special education horizon. It now is smart to talk about an 'integrated program of special education.' Integration is a better term than 'segregation,' another cliche over which many bitter arguments went on in the past. It has a positive rather than a negative connotation. Nevertheless, it is merely a word, with many meanings and interpretations. Furthermore, it has become a type of nebulous ideal; an if-you-don't-have-it-you-don't-belong sort of thing.

Undoubtedly, many unrealistic and undesirable measures are being adopted in the name of 'integration.' In some places integration merely means the assignment of handicapped children to one or more class periods with unhandicapped children. Where this occurs the result easily may be the disintegration of children and their learning experiences, especially if the planning has not been undertaken carefully according to the needs of each child and the interests of the receiving classroom teachers. (p. 317)

Ten years later, the U.S. Office of Education proposed merging the federal program for preparing special educators into a more general program for preparing regular educators. They called for taking the following four steps:

(1)   Concentrate on the learning need, rather than on the handicap in educating children and therefore in the preparation of personnel.

(2)   Emphasize the underpinnings of learning and of teaching. Though the teaching process may be more complex with the handicapped, with some of the handicapped the ultimate objective remains the same for all children. (It is more complex to teach some so-called normal children than some handicapped.)

(3)   While increasing our knowledge of the education of the handicapped, we must help to modify "general" education so as to include in it some of that body of knowledge up to now the private stock of the special educator.

(4)   (And an inevitable sequitur)-- the establishment of a positive attitude toward integrating the education of the handicapped in the total school program, while still continuing to provide for special needs--more effectively. ("Hearings Before," 1966, pp. 119-120)

Congressman Hugh Carey, Chairman of the Ad Hoc Subcommittee on the Handicapped of the U. S. House of Representatives, which conducted extensive hearings on the proposal, in expressing his concern about the proposals potential impact on students with disabilities noted:

This word 'mainstream,' of course, is being so bruited about in so many connections now, political, economic, and otherwise, that I kind of hope that as the mainstream gets muddier from the union of so many new tributaries that they are not going to throw all these in the educational mainstream until we find out where the mainstream is going. ("Hearings Before," 1966, p. 122)

As a result of these hearing the Congress passed PL 89-750 establishing a Bureau for the Education of the Handicapped with responsibility for administering a number of specific programs directed at students with disabilities and special education personnel. The forerunner of what is now The Education of the Handicapped Act.

In 1974, Maynard Reynolds and Bruce Balow of the University of Minnesota appeared before the Select Subcommittee on Education of the U. S. House of Representatives to oppose H. R. 70 (what we now know as PL 94-142). The following statement from their testimony characterizes the basis of their opposition:

At a time when both special and regular educators are moving toward the integration of the two systems of education, this Bill would place a premium on the obverse of such efforts. The philosophy of normalization, which is widely accepted in Europe and has acquired an impressive number of adherents in the United States, would be ill-served by the Bill's emphasis on labels and categories of handicap. Furthermore, the Bill would withhold financial support from preventive services by special educators for incipient or early problematical cases. In sum, the basis of H. R. 70 appears to be the special education philosophy which was necessary a decade ago in order to expand the services to all children but which does not accord with the changes in philosophy which have occurred since then. (pp. 3-4)

PHILOSOPHICAL DIFFERENCES

The proponents of a fully integrated educational system argue a philosophic view that, because all children are diverse in their learning styles and needs, education should focus on creating a regular education system that can accommodate such diversity in all classrooms. They also contend that an inclusive educational environment would eliminate the need for disability determination or labeling, which they perceive to be stigmatic.

The opponents argue that the educational system is so complex, resistent to change and dependent on the abilities and attitudes of individual professionals that accomplishing such change is unrealistic and places students with disabilities at substantial risk. They are not defenders of the *status quo,* but see change in a more evolutionary context.

It is interesting to note that the integration debate has historically taken place almost exclusively within the special education community. There have been few regular educators who have advocated an inclusive system or who have even spoken out against such a system. The recent reports on educational reform, beginning with *A Nation at Risk* (National Commission on Excellence in Education, 1983), provide almost no recognition that students with disabilities comprise one-tenth of the children and youth in our schools, let alone discuss how their educational needs can best be addressed. Although some of the authors in this section suggest a hypothetical relationship between the current debate and larger social, political, and educational trends, there is little concrete evidence to support

this view. The *regular* education initiative was in reality a special education initiative, directed at *regular* education promoted by *special* educators, without the involvement or interest of regular educators. Thus, both sides in the debate share a common problem--regular education. One side--the inclusivists--seek to change it, but the other side--the realists--accept it, albeit regretfully, and work within its evolving nature. Both sides appear to have little influence on the larger educational community. For example, I question whether the current directions of school reform including higher graduation standards, more rigorous curricula, standardized outcome measures and testing, and fewer electives or curricular options reflect the influence of either side in the REI debate.

PREMISES OF INCLUSIVISTS AND REALISTS

In considering this debate, however, there are subtle, but important, issues that the reader should keep in mind. First, special education as a legally-based delivery system, has at its foundation the premise that, because of their unique educational needs, students with disabilities vary so greatly that the appropriate education for the child must be individually determined. Thus, Public Law 94-142 and all state laws and regulations require an elaborate set of procedures and protections for determining what is appropriate for an individual student. These policies empower the student's parents and professionals who know the student to determine, through a process of preparing an individualized educational program (IEP), what is appropriate.

The premise presumes that the parties involved have choices which they are free to make based upon what they believe to be the best interest of the student. Their view of "best" may or may not be shared by other professionals, advocates, or government agencies, and may be in direct conflict with what another lEP team determined to be best for a similar child. The inclusivists suggest that there is only one appropriate educational choice, thus challenging the fundamental legal premise of special education. The realists suggest that although the individualization process does not always result in the *best* professional decision, it is essential to maintain the process. Thus, there exists a conflict between those whose beliefs would dictate what is appropriate for a class or group of students and those who would rely on an individualized process approach for determining appropriateness.

Second, federal and state policies define special education as "specially designed instruction to meet the unique needs of the child." Handicapped children and youth are defined by these policies as having a disability and requiring special education. Thus, students must have a disability, a unique educational need and require specially designed instruction, before they are eligible for special education. ln addition, the regular educational system must first attempt to meet the child's needs through the use of "supplementary aids and services." Therefore, legally, only students who actually need special education and for whom the regular education system has demonstrated that it cannot provide appropriate service, are eligible for special education. If this logic is followed in practice, then only students who have a disability and are unable with assistance to benefit from regular education, are eligible for special education.

Third, for the past twenty years, persons with disabilities and their advocates have fought a battle to assure both their right to access to the opportunities of society and the special benefits they require to make such access meaningful. The recent passage and signing of The Americans with Disabilities Act is one more major step in this effort. This has and continues to be necessary because of historical and continuing patterns of discrimination against persons with disability in education, employment, housing, transportation and other sectors of society. For government to provide protections and special benefits to a class of people, it is necessary to define the members of the class and establish eligibility criteria. To be determined to have a disability not only entitles a student to certain special education rights, but also to a vast array of life-long rights. These rights and benefits are not available to persons without disabilities. For example, some students with disabilities are protected from being expelled from education, such a right is not shared by other students.

The inclusivists argue that many students with disabilities, notably those with mild disabilities, should not be labeled because such labeling invites stigma and discrimination. The realists counter that without identifying students as members of a protected class, there is no means to guarantee them the rights and benefits to which they are entitled. The inclusivists suggest that their world view would extend such rights and benefits to all persons. But, the realists argue that such a goal is not politically or economically feasible, at least at this time.

CONCLUSION

In examining this section and the rest of the book, the reader may legitimately conclude that the views of the inclusivists and the realists are not necessarily incompatible. The critical difference may be a difference in perspective on time. Reynolds and Gartner and Lipsky offer one dream of an educational environment that meets the needs of all students, a dream that is shared by many special educators. Kauffman and Hocutt, Martin, and McKinney question the viability of that vision in the context of today's realities, a view that is also shared by many special educators. In any profession, it is important to pursue views of the future actively, without being constrained by the realities of the present. Historically, this has been the strength of special education. However, it is equally important to be able to develop such views, without condemning the professionally acceptable practices of the present.

REFERENCES

Hearings before the Ad Hoc Subcommittee on the Handicapped of the Committee on Education and Labor. (1966). Washington, DC: U. S. House of Representatives.

Hill, A. (1956). A critical glance at special education *Exceptional Children, 22, 315-317, 344.*

National Commission on Excellence in Education. (1983) *A Nation at risk: The imperative for educational reform.* Washington, DC: U. S. Department of Education.

Reynolds, M., & Balow, B. (1974). *Statement before the Select Subcommittee on Education of the Committee on Education and Labor.* Washington, DC: U. S. House of Representatives.

Will, M. (1986). *Educating students with learning problems: A shared responsibility.* Washington DC: Office of Special Education and Rehabilitation Services, U. S. Department of Education.

PART II

7

BEHAVIOR DISORDERS AND THE SOCIAL CONTEXT OF REGULAR CLASS INTEGRATION: A CONCEPTUAL DILEMMA?

Hill M. Walker and Michael Bullis
University of Oregon

The purpose of this chapter is to examine critical issues relating to the education of students with behavior disorders (BD) within the context of schooling. Specifically, we examine the case for applying the regular education initiative (REI) to this student population as it has been discussed in the school reform literature.

We strongly believe that *each* student with a disability or handicapping condition should be educated in the least restrictive environment (LRE) that the student can reasonably accommodate *and* in which an appropriate educational program can be delivered. Our educational system must prepare each student in the best way possible to achieve at their maximum potential while in school and to negotiate the transition to adult life successfully. Accordingly, we are very much in favor of the eradication of ineffective professional practices, the empowerment of teachers, use of teacher assistance teams, and the development of powerful intervention procedures, resources and delivery systems that "push the envelope" of education, that is, create change(s) that will have the greatest positive impact achievable for each student.

However, we are not in favor of mainstreaming merely for the sake of mainstreaming. Nor do we believe that mere placement in the regular classroom is in any way equivalent to or synonymous with best practice when implemented in the absence of other critical considerations such as the design and delivery of an appropriate educational program. Courts have repeatedly ruled that PL 94-142 in no way compels school districts to place handicapped students in regular educational classrooms, but only in the least restrictive setting consistent with their needs and that of other students (Rose, 1988; Yell, 1989, 1990).

Empirical evidence overwhelmingly indicates that simply placing a student with a disability in a regular education environment can be an extremely punishing, frustrating, and negative experience *if* (a) the student is unprepared to deal with the minimal demands and performance requirements of the setting (Gersten, Walker, & Darch, 1988; Safran & Safran, 1985); (b) the student is perceived by the receiving teacher as not falling within the range of his or her standards of "teachability" (Gerber & Semmel, 1984; Kornblau & Keogh, 1980; Walker, 1986); and (c) the student does not possess the necessary skills and attributes to gain peer acceptance and develop satisfactory peer relations (Fox, 1989; Hollinger, 1987;

Gresham & Reschly, 1986; Sabornie, 1985; Sabornie & Kauffman, 1986). In such instances, the hope that the student will progress academically and benefit socially from mere placement in a regular classroom setting will likely not be realized; in fact, the opposite set of outcomes (lack of teacher acceptance, rejection by nonhandicapped peers, and academic failure with concomitant decrements in self-esteem) are far more likely.

Thus, it is our position that the REI, as articulated to date in the professional literature by school reform advocates (e.g., Biklen & Zollers, 1986; Gartner & Lipsky, 1987, 1989; Lilly, 1988; Lipsky & Gartner, 1987; Reynolds, Wang, & Walberg, 1987; Stainback & Stainback, 1984, 1985; Wang, Reynolds & Walberg, 1986, 1988), represents a case of both the overgeneralization of anticipated REI outcomes as well as unsubstantiated and false claims regarding the efficacy of current and past special education practices. About these proposals, we agree with Schumaker and Deshler (1987, p. 36): "The wholesale application of such proposals to both elementary and secondary schools without acknowledging key differences in organizational structures, curricula, and learner variables is a gross oversimplification of a complex problem." In addition, the calls by Fuchs, Fuchs, Fernstrom, and Hohm (in press) for the development and implementation of *responsible* social integration strategies and procedures should be heeded in the face of mounting pressures to dismantle traditional special education systems and to integrate handicapped students on a wholesale basis. The potential for abuses in this context are legion and their avoidance is of great import.

In our view, the REI has been inappropriately extended by its advocates from an initial focus on the perceived over-referral of students with learning disabilities and now includes the full range of students with handicaps spanning all levels of severity, including be-

havior disorders (Kauffman, 1989). This extension seems to have been initiated in the absence of a careful analysis of the behavioral and learning characteristics of students with behavior disorders and how these might interact with the behavioral ecology of regular classroom settings (Braaten, Kauffman, Braaten, Polsgrove & Nelson, 1988; Hollinger, 1987). Teacher and peer acceptance, for example, are extremely important determinants of classroom ecology and are critical arbiters of major changes initiated in either the organizational structure or student diversity of the regular classroom setting. Unfortunately, these factors have received scant attention in the REI and school reform literatures, yet they are both crucial to the ultimate success of any school reform efforts, and especially to the REI as it is currently constructed.

The remainder of this chapter presents a review and discussion of the REI and school reform that supports our basic position that the REI does not apply uniformly across handicapping conditions, and that for students with serious behavior disorders it creates particular problems. Specifically, the following issues and topics are addressed: (a) the REI as a professional movement, (b) the status of efforts to accommodate students with behavior disorders in public school settings, (c) the classification and attributes of school-related behavior disorders, (d) implications of the behavioral characteristics of BD students for implementation of the REI, (e) the role of the regular classroom teacher as a final arbiter of the REI, (f) the role of secondary and transition issues in impacting REI implementation, and (g) implications for the future.

THE REI AS A PROFESSIONAL MOVEMENT

We believe it important to examine the REI from an historical and philosophical perspective. The REI debate and the school reform movement's treatment of special education have closely replicated the generic model of scientific revolutions as described by Kuhn (1970). In this model, reformist pressures are expressed in the ongoing struggle between paradigms that compete intensely for hegemony within a specific area of scientific inquiry or practice. Strategy and tactics used by competing paradigms include denigration of the efficacy, value, social relevance, and impact of other paradigms while simultaneously extolling the virtues and attributes of the paradigm being advocated. If a given paradigm achieves hegemony, then its advocates are in a powerful position to influence legislation, establish policy and regulatory mechanisms, chart new directions and targets for innovation, and set standards of acceptable practice in a given field or specialty. Thus, the rewards for achieving paradigm hegemony are substantial and provide powerful motivation and justification for even the most extreme forms of reformist rhetoric and behavior.

Precision teaching, deinstitutionalization, social integration and mainstreaming, behavior modification, and direct instruction are all examples of paradigms that have achieved and (in some cases) relinquished varying degrees of dominant influence within the fields of special and regular education over the past two decades. They also illustrate the downside of the struggle among paradigms and the manner in which they play out over time. That is, winning paradigms inevitably produce a relatively large cadre of antagonists who generate continuing pressures for the promulgation and acceptance of alternative models of practice. Ultimately, such paradigms are weakened through a build up of strong pressures for change due to such factors as failure to achieve their stated claims, the costs associated with their implementation, and the quest for renewal and innovation. In this process they lose

much or all of their leadership status and influence if they are unwilling to embrace renewal and to make the necessary compromises with advocates of more powerful extant models or attractive new competing models. Sometimes, the essential features of the original paradigm are adapted and co-opted into new models and preserved in a revised form. For example, the curriculum based measurement approach bears this relationship to the original precision teaching model that was developed and aggressively promulgated in the late sixties and early seventies (Shinn, 1989).

From this perspective, it appears that advocates of the REI are heavily engaged in an intense struggle for hegemony with defenders of traditional special education practices. The ultimate outcome of this struggle cannot be predicted at present but a major paradigm shift does not appear in the offing. It is highly unlikely that traditional special education structures will be dismantled and a true merger of regular and special education realized in the foreseeable future. However, the field of special education appears to be quite open to experimentation with new service delivery models (e.g. collaborative consultation, teacher assistance teams, site-based management, and so forth) but not at the expense of denying its legitimacy as a field or of its right to exist.

We believe that the REI may ultimately prove to have more relevance to some handicapping conditions than others (e.g. learning disabilities as opposed to hearing impairments, visual impairments, or behavior disorders) and will be perceived as having achieved highly variable degrees of success in relation to students representing the broad range of handicapping conditions. In our view, it is also likely that behavior disordered students will be among those *least* affected by whatever enduring change(s) in professional practices, if any, are ultimately dictated by increased integration of atypical students.

REGULAR SCHOOL ACCOMMODA-TION OF BD STUDENTS

The public schools' record of effective-ly accommodating students with be-havior disorders (usually identified by schools as seriously emotionally dis-turbed or SED) is close to abysmal. If schools can be justifiably accused of the over-referral of students with learning disabilities, an equally strong case can be made regarding their neglect of students experiencing serious behavior disorders. As a general rule, school administrators and other school-based decision makers actively resist the referral, systematic evaluation, and certification of students experiencing serious problems in their so-cial-behavioral adjustment.

Grosenick and her associates (Grosenick & Huntze, 1983; Grosenick, George, & George, 1987) have conducted extensive surveys and analyses of program practices of public schools for behavior disordered students through their *Nation-al Needs Analysis Project in Behavior Dis-orders.* They estimate that approximately 750,000 eligible students in public school settings currently receive *no* specialized services whatever for their social-be-havioral adjustment problems.

Estimates of the proportion of the public school population that manifests serious behavior disorders range from 2% to approximately 30% with a 2% to 3% prevalence rate generally viewed as a con-servative estimate (Kauffman, 1987). Ex-pert testimony (Forness, 1989) and surveys of current school practices, how-ever, indicate that states vary consider-ably in the proportion of the total school population actually served. In a recent study of variables affecting the under-identification and under-service of the BD school population, Center and Obringer (1987) found that the range across all 50 states was from .03 to 3.09%. Haring (1987) found that the states in his sample certified and served approximate-ly .50 to .90 of 1 percent of the school age population in any given school year. Grosenick et al. found the average to be 1.13% in their national surveys where ad-ministrators were respondents. The Seventh Annual Report to congress on the Status of P.L. 94-142 implementation (U.S. D.O.E., 1985) cited a .91% prevalence rate of BD students identified and served. In the Tenth Annual Report (1988), barely 9% of the total hand-icapped population was classified as SED. Further, compared to other handicapping conditions (e.g., LD, speech impaired), the growth in numbers of this population served has been miniscule (see Gerber & Levine-Donnerstein, 1989). Given a low-end BD prevalence rate of 2% of the total school population, these studies indicate that substantially fewer than half the ac-tual number of eligible BD students are actually identified and served as behavior disordered.

It is unclear why this population is so seriously under-identified and under-served. Long (1983) argued that school districts that have low per-pupil expendi-tures, have a high minority population, fail to screen the school age population systematically for behavior disorders, and view the *seriously emotionally disturbed* label as stigmatizing, tend both to under-identify and to under-serve students manifesting these behavior patterns. However, in a subsequent study of high BD and low BD service districts, Center and Obringer (1987) were unable to repli-cate these findings.

We believe that the primary reasons for underidentifying students in this category are more likely related to such factors as these:

- School district decision makers are reluctant to certify as SED those students who have aversive, conduct disor-ders because they view them as willful troublemakers rather than as students who are hand-icapped by their behavior;

- PL 94-142 constraints about disciplinary practices and due process protections come into play with certification;

- The specter of huge costs associated with identification and certification that may involve external school agencies (residential programs, psychiatric services, hospitalization, etc.) haunts schools;

- School districts are insensitive to serious disorders such as depression, anxiety, peer neglect and rejection, and affective disturbances that often do not prompt teacher concern or ownership due to their low salience and non-disruptiveness;

- Controversy abounds about the subjectivity associated with *judgementally determined* handicapping conditions as opposed to those with obvious physical or cognitive bases; and

- The SED label is seen as stigmatizing and the PL 94-142 definition as vague.

Whatever the specific reasons, it is all too apparent that the number of students who manifest serious to severe behavior problems and who are in clear need of special educational and related services seems to be growing, but school administrators are increasingly pursuing legal bases for reducing or denying services to students who are handicapped by their behavior. This is particularly true if the behavior patterns of such students are perceived as disruptive or socially aversive, i.e. aggressive, oppositional, or antisocial (see Kelly, 1986; Slenkovitch, 1983; 1984).

Historically, BD students have been among the very last to be integrated back into the regular classroom due to their aversive behavioral characteristics (Sarason & Doris, 1978). Grosenick et al. (1987) note that, currently, school district intake procedures for BD students are far more well developed than program exit and transition procedures. In a powerful analysis of school district practices, Neel and Rutherford (1981) argue that if a student is regarded as socially maladjusted, she or he is likely to be exposed to control, containment, or punishment strategies whereas if the student is judged to be emotionally disturbed, therapeutic services are a more likely outcome and the student is viewed as a victim of her or his disorder. Walker et al. (1990), analyzed archival school records and found that students with acting out, disruptive behavior problems received proportionally fewer school-based special services than did students with internalizing behavior problems and deficits (e.g. social withdrawal, peer neglect, social skills problems, anxiety, depression).

Grosenick et al. (1987) found that although the school administrators in their sample generally believed their program practices were effective, there were no validated standards for the design and implementation of best practice procedures for BD students in public schools. In a study of public school programs for BD students, Noel (1982) found highly variable but generally low levels of program efficacy. This apparent lack of efficacy in some BD practices is indeed ironic given the long-term existence of some very effective program models for BD students that are empirically validated (see Hewett, 1968; Morgan & Jenson, 1988; O'Connor, Stuck, & Wyne, 1979; Quay, Werry, McQueen, & Sprague, 1966; Quay, Glavin, Annesley, & Werry, 1972; Walker & Buckley, 1972; 1974). Clearly, the available *instructional* (Brophy & Good, 1986) and *behavioral* technologies (Strain, Guralnick, & Walker, 1986; Morgan & Jenson, 1988) exist to support the design and implementation of highly effective, school-based program practices for the BD population. Yet these practices are often not in evidence within public school programs for BD students. Perhaps adequate incentives for the design and implementation of such models are not in place within many school systems. Too often, simple accommodation rather than substantive change and improvement are the primary goals of such programs.

It seems certain that many BD students would have moderate to extreme difficulty in meeting the minimum behavioral expectations and standards of most regular classrooms (Hersh & Walker, 1983; Kerr & Zigmond, 1986; Safran & Safran, 1984; Walker, 1986). Though behavioral consultation models, along with school-wide teacher assistance teams, have grown dramatically in the past decade, teachers are still very constrained in their ability to accommodate students with serious behavior disorders within the context of the regular classroom. BD students place intense pressures upon the teacher's management and instructional skills, often severely disrupt the classroom environment, and engage in aversive forms of social behavior (stealing, lying, cheating, defiance) that are frequently unacceptable to teachers. Students with this behavioral profile would literally overwhelm many regular teachers' ability to manage their behavior in a reasonably effective manner (Byrnes, 1990).

In summary, it is clear that most school districts have not developed and do not use an adequate continuum of services and placements for the BD student population (Grosenick et al., 1987). Such students tend to be assigned to specialized placements within or outside the public schools, suspended, placed on long-term home tutoring regimens, or accommodated within regular classrooms when such alternatives are not available.

However, in order to address adequately even the most basic needs of those BD students currently certified and served in public school programs, much greater attention needs to be given to implementing programs, procedures, and knowledge that have generally been available in this field. In our view, the specific setting(s) in which such intervention programs are implemented and service delivery occurs are far less important questions than their quality and overall impact in addressing the unserved social, academic, and behavioral deficits of this school population.

THE CLASSIFICATION AND ATTRIBUTES OF SCHOOL-RELATED BEHAVIOR DISORDERS

Upon entering the school setting, children are required to make two extremely critical social-behavioral adjustments termed respectively *adult- or teacher-related* and *peer-related* adjustment (Walker, McConnell, & Clarke, 1985). *Teacher-related* adjustment refers to meeting the behavioral demands and expectations of teachers within the context of instructional settings. *Peer-related* adjustment involves negotiating complex peer group dynamics and relations satisfactorily that occur primarily in free play settings such as recess. Both of these adjustments are of substantial importance to satisfactory achievement of the two major outcomes of schooling: academic achievement and social development. The long term implications of failure in either adjustment domain are extremely serious (Parker & Asher, 1987).

Figure 1 illustrates a model of interpersonal social-behavioral competence within school settings. This figure lists both *adaptive* and *maladaptive* behavioral correlates that are related to these two forms of adjustment and that are supported by empirical evidence reported in the literature. Positive and negative out-

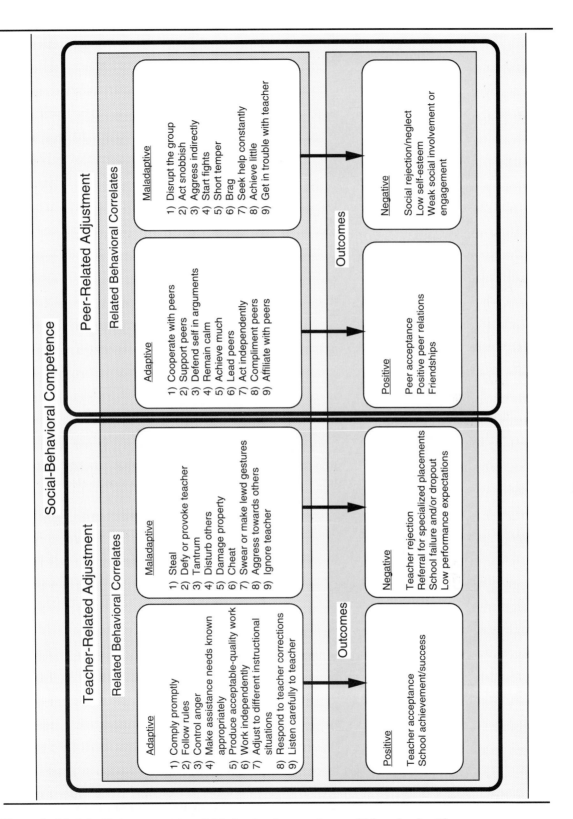

Figure 1: Model of interpersonal social-behavioral competence within school settings.

comes associated with them are also listed.

Students with behavior disorders often experience very serious failures in one or both of these critical adjustments. As noted, failure in one of them is very serious, failure in both, places a student at high risk for a host of negative developmental outcomes including low self-esteem, low achievement, peer rejection, juvenile delinquency, school dropout, mental health problems in adulthood and so forth (Kazdin, 1985; Parker & Asher, 1987). A host of classification schemes have been developed that purport to account for the behavioral characteristics that contribute to these forms of adjustment failure. In the next paragraphs, we discuss some of the more prominent schemes.

School personnel have been strongly influenced in their conceptualizations and assessments of behavior disorders by clinically derived, classification systems that have only limited relevance to the social-behavioral adjustment problems that students experience in the school setting (Walker & Fabre, 1987). The most influential of such clinical classifications are the DSM-III system of the American Psychiatric Association and the World Health Organization Classification System (Quay, 1986). These two systems are far more relevant to adult psychopathology than school adjustment problems and were not developed with school settings

BEHAVIOR PATTERNS

	Externalizing	Internalizing
Teacher-Related	• Acting out, noncompliant behavior • Teacher Defiance • Behavioral excesses • Low achievement • Disruption of classroom ecology • High probability of referral • Resistant to social influence tactics	• High levels of appropriate classroom behavior • Nonassertive behavior patterns • Problems with self • Performance deficits • Low achievement • Low probability of referral

Peer-Related	• Variable peer status
	  - some acceptance
	  - some rejection
	• Failure to use social skills that support positive peer interactions
	• High levels of social engagement
	• High levels of negative/aggressive social behavior
		• Neglected or rejected peer status
		• Low levels of participation in peer controlled activities
		• Social isolation and withdrawal
		• Low levels of negative social behavior

TYPES OF ADJUSTMENT

Figure 2: Interrelationships of bipolar behavior patterns and school adjustment types.

as a primary target referent (Achenbach, 1985).

The results of multivariate, statistical approaches to the classification of maladaptive behavior and the students who manifest such attributes have been much less evident in their influence on school professionals and their assessment practices in relation to the BD student population. This approach uses statistical techniques to isolate interrelated patterns of behavior. Its use dates from the 1940s and it has many advantages over clinically derived systems such as the DSM III, especially within school settings (Quay, 1986).

Over the past decade, broad support has developed for an empirically-derived, bipolar classification of behavior disorders that is particularly relevant to school adjustment. The bipolar dimensions of this classification system have been referred to as *conduct disorder* versus *personality disorder* and as *externalizing disorders* versus *internalizing disorders* (see Achenbach & Edelbrock, 1978; Ross, 1980). Evidence for the behavioral relevance of these two dimensions has been reported in the literature for populations ranging in age from preschool through adulthood. These dimensions together are inclusive of most of the behavior disorders and serious adjustment problems experienced by students in the school setting. *Externalizing* problems and disorders, for example, would include *conduct disorders, antisocial and aggressive behavior, hyperactivity*, and *oppositional behavior patterns.* Similarly, *internalizing* problems and disorders would include *social withdrawal, depression, phobias, anxiety disorders*, and *disturbances of affect.*

In addition, these behavioral dimensions are very useful in accounting for the two major types of social-behavioral adjustment failure occurring in the school setting, i.e., *teacher-related* and *peer-related* problems (Guralnick, 1986; Walker & Fabre, 1987; Walker, McConnell, &

Clarke, 1985). Figure 2 illustrates interrelationships between these behavioral dimensions and *teacher-related* versus *peer-related* forms of adjustment.

Students with externalizing behavior problems experience severe difficulty in their adjustment to the behavioral expectations and performance requirements of teachers who control instructional environments. In contrast, students with internalizing behavior problems experience very few problems in their rule-governed behavior in relation to teacher expectations; in fact, internalizers are often among the best behaved students in regular class settings. In terms of their peer relations, however, internalizers often experience severe forms of neglect and rejection or both, and are often isolated in free play settings. Externalizers have high levels of social engagement and participation within free play settings and do not appear to experience the same degree of peer rejection as do internalizers. In fact, some externalizers are rated by their peers as popular (see Parker & Asher, 1987; Quay, 1986; Ross, 1980; Walker et al., 1990).

Regular classroom teachers consistently assume responsibility for externalizing behavior problems but do not do so for internalizing problems (Brophy & Evertson, 1981; Gerber & Semmel, 1984). That is, teachers are very likely to assume responsibility for remediating or refering externalizing problem students but they tend not to do so for internalizers. In addition, problems in peer relations and social skills deficits are not rated by teachers as essential to a successful classroom adjustment (Hersh & Walker, 1983; Kerr & Zigmond, 1986). Internalizers are most vulnerable to serious problems in these two areas.

The externalizing versus internalizing dichotomy can also be used to examine the post-school, community adjustment experiences of BD adolescents and young adults. Externalizing, antisocial, aggressive behaviors are relatively stable from childhood to adulthood (Loeber, 1982; Olweus, 1979) and persons who exhibit them tend to be less successful in such general life endeavors as job tenure and status, marriage, child rearing, interpersonal relationships and so forth (Cowen, Pederson, Babigian, Izzo, & Trost, 1973; Huesmann, Eron, Lefkowitz, Walder, 1984; Janes, Hesselbrock, Myers, & Penniman, 1979; Mitchell & Rosa, 1981; Parker & Asher, 1987; Robins, 1978; Roff & Wirt, 1984).

Thus, empirically derived behavioral classification systems are available for describing and classifying the behavioral characteristics of the BD student population in both school and post-school settings. Such systems are very useful in judging the severity of behavior disorders, in making predictions about their likely progression, and in designing interventions for them (Quay, 1986). Their effective use, especially in the arena of systematic screening, has the potential to solve many of the problems of neglect and under-referral of the BD student population from regular education settings.

Thus far, we have discussed the REI, the way the educational system currently serves BD students, and the classification of the behavioral characteristics of these students. In the remainder of this chapter, three major factors affecting the REI are addressed. These are (a) implications of the characteristics of BD students for successful implementation of the REI, (b) the role of the regular classroom teacher as final arbiter of this process, and (c) secondary and transition issues.

BEHAVIORAL CHARACTERISTICS OF SED STUDENTS AND THE REI

BD students' behavioral characteristics make delivery of specialized intervention services within regular classrooms highly problematic. The social ecologies of regular classroom and playground settings are often hostile en-vironments for students with behavior disorders from both teacher and peer perspectives (Fox, 1989; Gresham & Reschly, 1986; Kauffman, Lloyd, & McGee, 1989; Sabornie & Kauffman, 1986; Walker, 1986). Delivering the complex interventions necessary to address the behavior problems of BD students in the regular classroom context can be extremely difficult and highly constrained. This difficulty is due in part to the structural characteristics of regular classrooms and teachers' reactions to the aversive characteristics of BD students (Braaten, Kauffman, Braaten, Polsgrove, & Nelson, 1988; Kauffman, Gerber & Semmel, 1988). Moreover, we believe these observations apply equally well to *externalizing* and *internalizing* behavior problems and disorders.

Historically, teacher attitudes toward mainstreaming have not been as positive as we would perhaps like (Larrivee & Cook, 1979; Ringlaben & Price, 1981). Further, recent research by Ritter (1989) confirms that regular teachers react especially negatively to the externalizing behavioral characteristics of students in their classes. Gersten, Walker, and Darch (1988) also reported that regular teachers have low tolerance levels for students' maladaptive classroom behavior. None of these findings bode well for the restructuring of special education for BD students as proposed by advocates of the REI.

Social-behavioral competence is a powerful mediator of success during transitions between school levels and from school to the community; and can actually function as a buffer against some of the stresses and adjustment pressures that accrue during this process (Dodge & Murphy, 1984). BD students are often particularly deficient in this domain and are thus especially vulnerable to transition failure. Social integration and transition strategies for this population need to be very carefully planned, implemented, and monitored. Unfortunately, mainstreaming efforts for BD students are not notably in evidence and are often very inadequate to the task when they are available (Fuchs et al., in press; Walker, 1984). Coleman, Pullis, and Minnett, (1987) concluded that *none* of the social goals of the mainstreaming movement have been realized to date. Similarly, Gresham (1982) reviewed evidence relating to the major social acceptance, social participation, and peer modelling assumptions that framed the passage of PL 94-142 and concluded that none were empirically supported.

Again, we wish to restate the point made at the beginning of this chapter: We believe handicapped individuals should access, to the maximum extent possible, the least restrictive environments available to them in both school and non-school settings. However, this goal should be tempered with the knowledge that integration strategies must be carefully planned and crafted so as to: (a) prepare the handicapped individual to succeed in that next less-restrictive environment, (b) prepare the receiving environment to adjust to or accommodate the behavioral differences of the target individual, and (c) monitor and manage the transition process effectively. If so, the intended outcomes of social integration are far more likely to be achieved.

THE REGULAR CLASSROOM TEACHER AS THE FINAL ARBITER OF THE REI

Historically, major innovations within the educational enterprise have been proposed by professionals who work outside the context of public schools and who are often based in universities (Davis, 1989). Practicing educators (teachers, administrators, special services personnel) ultimately dispose of such innovations through their acceptance, rejection or adaptation of them. If such innovations do not pass the test of teacher

acceptability, they do not usually survive or they survive in a form quite different from that originally envisioned by their developers. The REI and its proposed structural reforms of special and regular education are likely to follow this rule. Gerber and Semmel (1984) have provided a very powerful conceptual analysis of the ecology of schooling as it relates to this issue. In a now-classic paper, they argue that regular classroom teachers carry with them an image of the idealized teachable student and that all students are informally compared to this standard. Empirical support for this model of the teachable student and its role in the teacher referral process has been provided by Kornblau and Keogh (1980). Students who diverge too far from the teacher's standard of teachability become prime candidates for referral and targets of remediation efforts and specialized placements. BD students with externalizing behavior problems are perhaps most likely to be the objects of such teacher-initiated actions. Shinn, Tindal, and Spira (1987) partially replicated the Gerber and Semmel (1984) thesis by showing that teacher referrals are relatively free of bias and are highly accurate reflections of the academic performance profiles of those referred students showing high levels of deficit responding.

Thus, teachers use the referral process for a dual purpose: (a) to secure assistance for student deficits or excesses that they cannot or will not provide, and (b) to reduce the diversity or heterogeneity of the regular classroom setting, thus making it easier to manage and instruct. In this context, regular teachers have been most concerned about class size and classroom diversity in the school reform movement (Drahn, 1989). The REI has the potential to increase both of these dimensions dramatically within the regular classroom and to exacerbate the burdens already attendant upon overly stressed regular teachers who are not adequately supported or compensated for their current efforts. In addition, we are seeing increasing reports of school administrators and managers of child study teams harassing teachers into not making referrals and in some instances, simply denying them the opportunity of referring *any* students for periods of time. School reform is not an appropriate context for the use of such coercive tactics in the name of improved practices.

If current school reform efforts are to have even a reasonable chance of gaining the acceptance and cooperation of regular teachers, substantial increases in teacher assistance and support levels must be forthcoming. Given past practices, we are not optimistic that the necessary increase in resources will be allocated. If such reforms are implemented in the absence of these essential support levels, the disruption to the schooling process for all students and their teachers will likely be very damaging and will cast these reforms in a very controversial light. In our view, the ultimate success of any school reform initiative depends upon regular teachers' views of its effectiveness and cost efficiency, their perceptions of its social validity, and the extent to which it ameliorates or removes the instructional and management burdens introduced by substantially increased student diversity and class sizes (see Witt & Elliott, 1985).

SECONDARY AND TRANSITION ISSUES

Several recent studies on the school-to-community transition of adolescents certified as having BD and who also graduate, indicate they experience unemployment rates of around 30% to 50%. If employed, they tend to secure low paying, entry level jobs with a questionable future for advancement; and by and large, they do not enter postsecondary educational programs. Most are not served through community service agencies, such as departments of vocational

rehabilitation (Neel, Meadows, Levine, & Edgar, 1988; Kortering & Edgar, 1988; Wagner & Shaver, 1989). In a major follow-up study of the post-school status of behaviorally handicapped students, Wagner (1989) reported that this student population experiences massive school failure, and that 19% are arrested while still in school--a figure that rises to 43% within two years of leaving school! Moreover, it is clear that a high percentage of BD students drop out of school with minimal academic and functional abilities (Wagner & Shaver, 1989).

At the secondary level, the REI encounters three inter-related issues that make its implementation difficult. These are (a) the inherent structural differences between secondary and elementary schools, (b) the overlay and influence of the nature of vocational and transitional programming, and (c) access of handicapped students to traditional vocational education. Schumaker and Deshler (1987), in a thoughtful and provocative article on the implementation of the REI at the secondary level for students with learning disabilities (LD), identify problems with this attempt at school reform. As there are many academic similarities between students with BD and those with LD (Hallahan & Kaufman, 1977), it is reasonable to assume that Schumaker and Deshler's observations and conclusions would also apply to the BD student population. Three major barriers to the REI were discussed by Schumaker and Deshler in this context. First, there is a large gap between the skill levels of LD students and the setting demands of secondary classrooms (i.e., the differences between student abilities and content demands become pronounced in these later grades). Second, although it is possible to educate secondary students using small group, intensive instruction, the structure and goals of classes at this level rarely allow for these procedures to be used effectively. And, third, the inherent organization of secondary schools (eg., class schedules, curricula content, outside pressures) make it extremely unlikely that the REI can be implemented simply and efficiently at this level.

Interestingly, Schumaker and Deshler also noted that school reform movements have been historically resisted by teachers, especially those teachers in secondary schools. They present logical and research-based procedures that can be implemented to improve and change the secondary school setting, thus making it more accommodating for the LD student (e.g., creating a partnership between regular and special education, specifying clear roles for all involved parties, offering comprehensive nonacademic vocational and social skills services, altering academic instruction to fit the needs of low-achieving students, and acknowledging the difficulties and longterm nature of organizational change). However, these steps are not consistent with the REI and it seems clear that reform at the secondary level is, in fact, an entirely "different ball game."

The second major factor that must be addressed, at the secondary level, in relation to the appropriate and effective instruction of BD adolescents, relates to vocational and functional skill issues. From research reviewed in previous sections, we conclude that BD adolescents and young adults are very likely to experience problems working, maintaining positive social relationships, resisting antisocial acts, completing their secondary training, and accessing and continuing postsecondary education. Several investigations point to the extreme importance of job-related social skills for the job retention of BD young adults (Hursh & Kerns, 1988). These studies suggest a positive relationship between vocational preparation and school completion for at-risk youth (Bishop, 1989; Thornton & Zigmond, 1987, 1988) and document an important link between competitive work experience in high school and employment success after leaving public educa-

tion (Hasazi, Gordon, & Roe, 1985). It is apparent that considerable instruction at the secondary level for BD students should be focused on functional skill training in vocational and social areas, as this time period could be the last chance for BD students to acquire these crucial skills. Further, this instruction may be best offered in community work placements and settings that are not consonant with traditional classroom settings.

The third major REI barrier at the secondary level for BD students concerns access to traditional vocational education. Unfortunately, vocational education teachers and programs have been resistant to the inclusion of disabled youth into their programs (Halpern & Benz, 1986; Olympus Research Corporation, 1975). Presently there are few empirically derived and tested instructional materials for BD adolescents (Halpern & Benz, 1986); research on the functional training of BD adolescents is sparse; and there are few model programs to guide development efforts (Bullis & Gaylord-Ross, in press; Fink & Kokaska, 1983; Nelson & Kauffman, 1977). Moreover, we contend that the intervention focus should be on community-based preparation at the secondary level. The following quote illustrates this position (Nishioka-Evans & Fredericks, in press).

Certain skills can be practiced or role played in the classroom but they must eventually be generalized to community settings and demonstrated within "real" situations. For instance, one can practice a job interview in a classroom but one must actually demonstrate those skills in a *bona fide* job interview. Certainly the use of the calculator can best be taught in a classroom, but the use of a calculator to figure out the costs of items in stores, totaling the balance in a checkbook, or budgeting one's money must be eventually demonstrated in the "real" world. *There are no functional living skills, social skills, or vocational skills that can be adequately learned solely in a classroom environment.* Each must be practiced in the actual community or situation in which the skill is to be used.

In summary, the instructional demands at the secondary level, in terms of both content and method, as well as the structure of high schools, makes it difficult to believe that the REI can be implemented effectively in these grades as it is currently articulated. It is critical that education at this level be as pragmatic and functionally oriented as possible. Most students will need actual work experiences coupled with a solid basic education to maximize their chances of being successful in adult life.

IMPLICATIONS FOR THE FUTURE

We began this chpater with a description of how Kuhn's (1970) model of the structure of scientific revolutions applies to proposed reforms of regular and special education. Unless existing paradigms that represent current practice are open to renewal and the possibility of change, they are unlikely to retain their dominant status. Such is the case with special education as it is currently constructed.

Unfortunately, the REI proposes a radical restructuring of special education because it is perceived as ineffective, stigmatizing, oppressive, discriminatory, a means of suppressing the underclass, and so forth. Radical restructuring carries no guarantee that improvements in the efficacy or acceptance of either regular or special education will be achieved. In fact, the regular education enterprise seems already stressed to the breaking point in accommodating its current man-

date and expectations due to such factors as societal spillover problems (divorce, neglect, abuse), the changing demographics of the school population, negative attitudes toward schooling and so forth. The REI will severely exacerbate this situation. There are at least three possibilities in this context: *no change, improvement,* or *decline* in the efficacy of current practices and educational outcomes. It is very difficult, if not impossible, to predict future outcomes relating to which reform elements will be accepted and put into practice, and their ultimate effects.

Certainly, we have the means and (we hope) the will to accommodate greater numbers of mildly handicapped students within the regular classroom setting. Radical restructuring, however, is probably not the ultimate answer for students with behavior disorders and the professionals who serve them, nor is a continued rigid investment in the existing structure and delivery patterns for the majority of special education services. Clearly, a larger number of mildly handicapped students can and should access regular class settings *but* with adequate teacher and student assistance levels. Special education, especially in relation to students with BD, must be open to innovation and compromise and to building cooperative relationships with regular educators.

Reform efforts for this population, in particular, should aggressively focus on the improvement of program practices, regardless of the setting or context in which they are delivered. There is a powerful, empirically-derived knowledge base on the remediation of school-related behavior problems that is greatly underused in educating BD students and an emerging literature on transition strategies. We would be well served to concentrate our collective efforts on effectively implementing what we already know in relation to serving this population and on improving promising instructional and management practices for them.

NOTE

The authors are indebted to Bud Fredericks, Michael George, James Kauffman, and Judith Grosenick for critical reviews of earlier versions of this chapter.

REFERENCES

Achenbach, T. (1985). *Assessment and taxonomy of child and adolescent psychopathology.* Beverly Hills, CA: Sage.

Achenbach, T., & Edelbrock, C. (1978). The classification of child psychopathology: A review and analysis of empirical efforts. *Psychological Bulletin, 85,* 275-301.

Biklen, D., & Zollers, N. (1986). The focus of advocacy in the LD field. *Journal of Learning Disabilities, 19,* 579-586.

Bishop, J. (1989). *Vocational education for at-risk youth: How can it be made more effective?* Ithaca, NY: Cornell University.

Braaten, S., Kauffman, J., Braaten, B., Polsgrove, L., & Nelson, M. (1988). The regular education initiative: Patent medicine for behavioral disorders. *Exceptional Children, 55,* 21-28.

Brophy, J., & Good, T. (1986). Teacher and student achievement. In M. Wittrock (Ed.), *Handbook of research on teaching* (3rd ed., pp. 328-375). New York: McMillan.

Brophy, J., & Evertson, C. (1981). *Student characteristics and teaching.* Boston: Longman.

Bullis, M., & Gaylord-Ross, R. (in press). *Vocational and transition issues for seriously emotionally disturbed adolescents and young adults* [Series]. In R. Rutherford & L. Bullock (Eds.). Reston, VA: Council for Exceptional Children.

Byrnes, M. (1990). The regular education initiative debate: A view from the field. *Exceptional Children, 56,* 345-349.

Center, D., & Obringer, J. (1987). A search for variables affecting underidentification of behaviorally disordered students. *Behavioral Disorders, 12*(3), 169-175.

Coleman, J., Pullis, M., & Minnett, A. (1987). Studying mildly handicapped children's adjust-

ment to mainstreaming: A systemic approach. *Remedial and Special Education, 8*(6), 19-31.

Cowen, E., Pederson, A., Babigian, H., Izzo, L., & Trost, M. (1973). Long-term follow-up of early detected vulnerable children. *Journal of Consulting and Clinical Psychology, 41,* 438-446.

Davis, W. (1989). The regular education initiative debate: Its promises and problems. *Exceptional Children, 55*(5), 440-448.

Dodge, K., & Murphy, R. (1984). The assessment of social competence in adolescents. In P. Karoly & J. J. Steffen (Eds.), *Adolescent behavior disorders: Foundations and contemporary concerns* (Vol. 3, pp. 61-96). Lexington, MA: Lexington Books.

Drahn, K. E. (1989). The regular education initiative: Political obstacles to widening the mainstream. *Dissertation Abstracts International, 50*(09A). (University Microfilms No. 90-03, 309).

Fink, A., & Kokaska, C. (1983). *Career education for behavior disordered students.* Reston, VA: Council for Exceptional Children.

Forness, S. (1989). Testimony before the U.S. Senate subcommittee on the handicapped in support of reauthorization of the Education of the Handicapped Act. Washington, D.C.

Fox, C. (1989). Peer acceptance of learning disabled children in the regular classroom. *Exceptional Children, 56*(1), 50-60.

Fuchs, D., Fuchs, L., Fernstrom, P., & Hohm, M. (in press). Toward a responsible reintegration of behaviorally disordered students. *Behavioral Disorders.*

Gartner, A., & Lipsky, D. (1987). Beyond special education: Toward a quality system for all students. *Harvard Educational Review, 57,* 367-395.

Gartner, A., & Lipsky, D. (1989). *The yoke of special education: How to break it.* Rochester, NY: National Center on Education and the Economy.

Gerber, M., & Levine-Donnerstein, D. (1989). Educating all children: Ten years later. *Exceptional Children, 56,* 30-40.

Gerber, M. M., & Semmel, M. I. (1984). Teacher as imperfect test: Reconceptualizing the referral process. *Educational Psychologist, 19*(3), 137-148.

Gersten, R., Walker, H. M., & Darch, C. (1988). Relationship between teachers' effectiveness and their tolerance for handicapped students. *Exceptional Children, 54*(5), 433-438.

Gresham, F. (1982). Misguided mainstreaming: The case for social skills training with handicapped children. *Exceptional Children, 48*, 422-433.

Gresham, F., & Reschly, D. (1986). Social skill deficits and peer acceptance of mainstreamed learning disabled children. *Learning Disability Quarterly,9*, 23-32.

Grosenick, J., George, M., & George, N. (1987). A profile of school programs for the behaviorally disordered: Twenty years after Morse, Cutler and Fink. *Behavioral Disorders, 12*(3), 159-169.

Grosenick, J. K., & Huntze, S. L. (1983). *National needs analyis in behavioral disorders: Severe behavior disorders*. Columbia, MO: Department of Special Education, University of Missouri.

Guralnick, M. (1986). The peer relations of young handicapped and nonhandicapped children. In P. Strain, M. Guralnick, & H. Walker (Eds.), *Children's social behavior: Development, assessment and modification* (pp. 93-131). New York: Academic Press.

Hallahan, D., & Kauffman, J. (1977). Categories, labels, behavioral characteristics: ED, LD, and EMR reconsidered. *Journal of Special Education, 11*,139-149.

Halpern, A., & Benz, M. (1986). *Toward excellence in secondary special education*. Salem: Oregon Department of Education.

Haring, N. (Ed.). (1987). *Assessing and managing behavior disabilities*. Seattle, WA: University of Washington Press.

Hasazi, S. B., Gordon, L. R., & Roe, C. (1985). Factors associated with the employment status of handicapped youth exiting high school from 1979 to 1983. *Exceptional Children, 51*, 455-469.

Hersh, R. H., & Walker, H. M. (1983). Great expectations: Making schools effective for all students. *Policy Studies Review, 2*(Special # 1), 147-188.

Hewett, F. (1968). *The emotionally disturbed child in the classroom*. Boston: Allyn & Bacon.

Hollinger, J. (1987). Social skills for behaviorally disordered children as preparation for mainstreaming: Theory, practice and new directions. *Remedial and Special Education, 8*(4), 17-27.

Huesmann, L., Eron, L., Lefkowitz, M., & Walder, L. (1984). Stability of aggression overtime and generations. *Developmental Psychology, 20*, 1120-1134.

Hursh, N., & Kerns, A. (1988). *Vocational evaluation in special education*. Boston: College-Hill.

Janes, C., Hesselbrock, V., Myers, D. G., & Penniman, J. (1979). Problem boys in young adulthood: Teacher's ratings and twelve-year follow-up. *Journal of Youth and Adolescence, 8*, 453-472.

Kauffman, J. (1987). Foreword. In N. G. Haring (Ed.), *Assesing and managing behavior disabilities*. Seattle: University of Washington Press.

Kauffman, J. (1989). *Characteristics of behavior disorders of children and youth* (4th ed.). Columbus, OH: Merrill.

Kauffman, J. M., Gerber, M. M., & Semmel, M. I. (1988). Arguable assumptions underlying the regular education initiative. *Journal of Learning Disabilities,21*,6-11.

Kauffman, J. M., Lloyd, J. W., & McGee, K. A. (1989). Adaptive and maladaptive behavior: Teachers' attitudes and their technical assistance needs. *Journal of Special Education, 23*, 185-201.

Kazdin, A. E. (1985). *Treatment of antisocial in behavior children and adolescents*. Chicago, Ill: Dorsey Press.

Kelly, E. (1986). *Issues, procedures and criteria in discriminating SED from conduct disordered students*. Presentation at the annual meeting of the Oregon Association of School Psychology, Lincoln City, Oregon.

Kerr, M., & Zigmond, N. (1986). What do high school teachers want? A study of expectations and standards. *Education and Treatment of Children, 9*(3), 239-249.

Kornblau, B., & Keogh, B. (1980). Teachers' perceptions and educational decisions. *Journal for Teaching and Learning, 1*,87-101.

Kortering A,. & Edgar, E. (1988). Vocational rehabilitation and special education: A need for cooperation. *Rehabilitation Counseling Bulletin, 31*,178-184.

Kuhn, T. (1970). *The structure of scientific revolutions* (2nd ed.). Chicago: University of Chicago Press.

Larrivee, B., & Cook, L. (1979). Mainstreaming: A study of the variables affecting teacher attitude. *Journal of Special Education, 13*, 315-124.

Lilly, S. (1988). The regular education initiative: A force for change in general and special education. *Education and Training in Mental Retardation, 23*, 253-260.

Lipsky, D., & Gartner, A. (1987). Capable of achievement and worthy of respect: Education for handicapped students as if they were full-fledged human beings. *Exceptional Children, 54*, 69-74.

Loeber, R. (1982). The stability of antisocial and delinquent child behavior: A review. *Child Development, 53*, 1431-1446.

Long, K. (1983). Emotionally disturbed children as the undetected and underserved public school population: Reasons and recommendations. *Behavioral Disorders, 9*, 46-54.

Mitchell, S., & Rosa, P. (1981). Boyhood behavior problems as precursors of criminality: A fifteen-year follow-up. *Journal of Child Psychology and Psychiatry, 22*, 19-33.

Morgan, D., & Jenson, W. (1988). *Teaching behaviorally disordered students: Preferred practices.* Columbus, OH: Charles Merrill.

Neel, R., Meadows, N., Levine, P., & Edgar, E. (1988). What happens after special education: A statewide follow-up study of secondary students who have behavioral disorders. *Behavioral Disorders, 13*, 209-216.

Neel, R., & Rutherford, R. (1981). Exclusion of the socially maladjusted from services under P.L. 94-142: Why? What should be done about it? In F. Wood (Ed.), *Perspectives for a new decade: Educators' responsibilities for seriously disturbed and behaviorally disordered children and youth.* Reston, VA: Council for Exceptional Children Publications.

Nelson, C. M., & Kauffman, J. (1977). Educational programming for secondary school age delinquent and maladjusted pupils. *Behavior Disorders, 2*, 102-113.

Nishioka-Evans, V., & Fredericks, H. D. Bud. (in press). Functional curriculum. In E. Cipani (Ed.), *Emotional disturbance.* Palo Alto, CA: Mayfield.

Noel, M. (1982). Public school programs for the emotionally disturbed: An overview. In M. Noel & N. Haring (Eds.), *Progress or change: Issues in educating the emotionally disturbed* (Vol. 2, pp. 1-28). Seattle: University of Washington Press.

O'Connor, P., Stuck, G., & Wyne, M. (1979). Effects of a short term intervention resource room program on task orientation and achievement. *Journal of Special Education, 13*, 375-385.

Olweus, D. (1979). Stability of aggressive reaction patterns in males: A review. *Psychological Bulletin, 86*, 852-875.

Olympus Research Corporation. (1975). *An assessment of vocational education programs for the handicapped.* Salt Lake City: Author.

Parker, J., & Asher, S. (1987). Peer relations and later personal adjustment: Are low-accepted children at risk? *Psychological Bulletin, 102*, 357-389.

Quay, H. (1986). Classification. In H. Quay & J. Werry (Eds), *Psychopathological disorders of childhood* (pp. 1-35). New York: Wiley & Sons.

Quay, H., Glavin, J., Annesley, F., & Werry, J. (1972). The modification of problem behavior and academic achievement in a resource room. *Journal of School Psychology, 10*, 187-198.

Quay, H., Werry, J., McQueen, M., & Sprague, R. (1966). Remediation of the conduct problem child in the special class setting. *Exceptional Children, 32*, 509-515.

Reynolds, M., Wang, M., & Walberg, H.J. (1987). The necessary restructuring of special and regular education. *Exceptional Children, 53*, 391-398.

Ringlaben, R., & Price, J. (1981). Regular classroom teachers' perceptions of mainstreaming effects. *Exceptional Children, 47*, 302-304.

Ritter, D. (1989). Teachers' perceptions of problem behavior in general and special education. *Exceptional Children, 55*, 559-565.

Robins, L. N. (1978). Study childhood predictors of adult antisocial behavior: Replications from longitudinal studies. *Psychological Medicine, 8*, 611-622.

Roff, J., & Wirt, R. (1984). Childhood aggression and social adjustment as antecedents of delinquency. *Journal of Abnormal Child Psychology, 12*, 111-126.

Rose, T. (1988). Current disciplinary practices with handicapped students: Suspensions and expulsions. *Exceptional Children, 55*, 230-240.

Ross, A. (1980). *Psychological disorders of children: A behavioral approach to theory, research and therapy* (2nd ed.). New York: McGraw-Hill.

Sabornie, E. (1985). Social mainstreaming of handicapped students: Facing an unpleasant reality. *Remedial and Special Education, 6*(2), 12-16.

Sabornie, E., & Kauffman, J. (1986). Social acceptance of learning disabled adolescents. *Learning Disability Quarterly,9*, 55-60.

Safran, S., & Safran, J. (1984). Elementary teachers' tolerance of problem behaviors. *Elementary School Journal, 85*, 247-253.

Safran, S., & Safran, J. (1985). Classroom context and teachers' perceptions of problem behaviors. *Journal of Educational Psychology, 77*, 20-28.

Sarason, S., & Doris, J. (1978). Mainstreaming: Dilemmas, opposition, opportunities. In M.C. Reynolds (Ed.), *Futures of education for exceptional children: Emerging structures*. Reston, VA: Council for Exceptional Children.

Schumaker, J. B., & Deshler, D. (1987). Implementing the Regular Education Initiative in Secondary Schools - A different ball game. *Journal of Learning Disabilities, 21*, 36-42.

Shinn, M. (1989). *Curriculum-based measurement: Assessing special children*. New York: Guilford.

Shinn, M., Tindal, G., & Spira, D. (1987). Special education referrals as an index of teacher tolerance: Are teachers imperfect tests? *Exceptional Children, 54*, 32-40.

Slenkovitch, J. (1983). *P.L. 94-142 as applied to DSM III diagnoses: An analysis of DSM III diagnoses vis-a-vis special education law* Cupertino, CA: Kinghorn.

Slenkovitch, J. (1984). *Understanding special education law. (Vol. 1). Cupertino, CA : Kinghorn.*

Stainback, W., & Stainback, S. (1984). A rationale for the merger of special and regular education. *Exceptional Children, 51*, 102-111.

Stainback, S., & Stainback, W. (1985). The merger of special and regular education: Can it be done? A response to Lieberman and Mesinger. *Exceptional Children, 51*, 517-521.

Strain, P., Guralnick, M., & Walker, H. M. (Eds.). (1986). *Children's social behavior: Development, assessment, and modification.* New York: Academic Press.

Thornton, H., & Zigmond, N. (1987). *Predictors of dropout and unemployment among LD high school youth: The holding power of secondary vocational education for LD students*. Pittsburgh, PA: University of Pittsburgh.

Thornton, H., & Zigmond, N. (1988). Secondary vocational training for LD students and its relationship to school completion status and post school outcomes. *Illinois Schools Journal, 67*(2), 37-54.

U.S.D.O.E. (1985). *Seventh annual report to Congress on the implementation of the Education of the Handicapped Act*. Washington, DC: U.S. Office of Special Education Programs.

U.S.D.O.E. (1988). *Tenth annual report to Congress on the implementation of the Education of the Handicapped Act*. Washington, DC: U.S. Office of Special Education Programs.

Wagner, M. (1989). *The national longitudinal transition study*. Palo Alto, CA: Stanford Research Institute.

Wagner, M., & Shaver, D. (1989). *Educational programs and achievements of secondary special education students: Findings from the National Longitudinal Transition Study*. Menlo Park, CA: SRI International.

Walker, H. M. (1984). The Social Behavior Survival program (SBS): A systematic approach to the integration of handicapped children into less restrictive settings. *Education and Treatment of Children, 6*(4), 421-441.

Walker, H. M. (1986). The Assessments for Integration into Mainstream Settings (AIMS) assessment system: Rationale, instruments, procedures, and outcomes. *Journal of Clinical Child Psychology, 15*(1), 55-63.

Walker, H. M., & Buckley, N. (1972). Programming generalization and maintenance of treatment effects across time and across settings. *Journal of Applied Behavior Analysis, 5*, 209-224.

Walker, H. M., & Buckley, N. (1974). *Token reinforcement techniques: Classroom applications for the hard to teach child*. Eugene, OR: E-B Press.

Walker, H. M., & Fabre, T. R. (1987). Assessment of behavior disorders in the school setting: Issues, problems and strategies revisited. In N. G. Haring (Ed.), *Assessing and managing behavior disabilities* (pp. 198-243). Seattle: University of Washington.

Walker, H. M., McConnell, S. R., & Clarke, J. Y. (1985). Social skills training in school settings: A model for the social integration of handicapped children into less restrictive settings. In R. McMahon & R. D. Peters (Eds.), *Childhood disorders: Behavioral-developmental approaches* (pp. 140-168). New York: Brunner/Mazel.

Walker, H. M., Severson, H. H., Todis, B. J., Block-Pedego, A. E., Williams, G. J., & Haring, N. G. (1990). Systematic screening for behavior disorders (SSBD): Further validation, replication and normative data. *Remedial and Special Education, 11*(2), 32-46.

Wang, M., Reynolds, M., & Walberg, H. (1986). Rethinking special education. *Educational Leadership, 44*(1), 26-31.

Wang, M., Reynolds, M., & Walberg, H. (1988). *Handbook of special education research and practice (Vol. 3: Low incidence conditions).* New York: Pergamon Press.

Witt, J., & Elliott, S. (1985). Acceptability of classroom management strategies. In T. R. Kratochwill (Ed.), *Advances in school psychology* (Vol. 4, pp. 251-288). Hillsdale, NJ: Lawrence Erlbaum.

Yell, M. (1989). Honig versus Doe: The suspension and expulsion of handicapped students. *Exceptional Children, 56*(1), 60-70.

Yell, M. (1990). The use of corporal punishment, suspension, expulsion, and timeout with behavior disordered students in public schools: Legal considerations. *Behavior Disorders, 15*, 100-110.

8

MAINSTREAMING ACADEMICALLY HANDICAPPED CHILDREN IN URBAN SCHOOLS

Jay Gottlieb and Mark Alter
New York University

Barbara W. Gottlieb
Herbert H. Lehman College

Even a cursory review of literature regarding the history of special education reveals the heavy influence of legislation and judicial decisions on contemporary practices. This state of affairs did not occur by accident. Many inappropriate procedures prevailed prior to the passage of Public Law 94-142 (Education of All Handicapped Children Act, 1978), and that law was designed to prevent further abuses. Among the more glaring of these inappropriate practices-- at least as they involved judicial intervention--involved alleged discriminatory assessments which resulted in the identification of a disproportionate number of minority children as handicapped and their subsequent segregation in separate, often unequal, educational programs. Certainly other problems existed, such as the exclusion of many handicapped children from school, but these are not the focus of this chapter. We are concerned with the procedures used by school personnel to decide who is mainstreamed and what happens as a result. In our view these procedures should emanate from an assessment both of the pupil and the environ-

ment, and we therefore view assessment and mainstreaming to be closely intertwined.

Assessments in special education are conducted for two main reasons: (a) to determine whether a youngster is, in fact, handicapped and, if so, the appropriate classification for the child and (b); to identify the components of an appropriate education for the classified youngster, including but not limited to identifying the least restrictive environment. The Larry P. case (Larry P. v. Wilson Riles, 1971) made the legal and conceptual tie between assessment and placement. In his decision Judge Peckham spoke not only of the discriminatory nature of the testing practices that were used to classify minority children as educable mentally retarded (EMR), he also mentioned, on nine separate occasions, that placement in segregated special classes, which was almost inevitable once a child was found to be EMR, was a dead-end.

Historically, assessments of minority youngsters were often conducted as a vehicle to legitimize placement in self-contained environments. Because minority youngsters were shunted into segregated classes, usually for mentally retarded pupils, and because the courts viewed this as an abridgement of their civil rights, subsequent federal legislation was designed to prevent these abuses from recurring. Since the passage of PL 94-142 there has been a precipitous drop in the number of children classified as EMR, and a corresponding increase in the number of children, especially minority children (Tucker, 1980), classified as learning disabled.

Issues related to the appropriate classification of minority group pupils are national in scope and probably affect the vast majority of school districts in the country. However, we think that the higher proportion of minority group children in urban school districts makes the difficulties in providing an appropriate education for minority youngsters more salient than it is in suburban school districts. We also believe that for a variety of reasons research findings and practices that are in place in suburban or rural schools cannot easily be generalized to the urban scene.

Differences between urban school districts and suburban or rural districts are numerous. Cities typically have both very rich and very poor people living in them. Many affluent people send their children to private schools and many middle-class people send their children to parochial schools. But the children of poor people, who are most often ethnic minorities, attend public schools. Thus, the composition of the urban public schools tends to be segregated both economically and ethnically. Teacher turnover tends to be more problematic in urban schools. Compounding the problem of the greater need for special services in urban school districts is the fact that various state reimbursement formuli often operate to the detriment of urban school districts, which are more heavily underfunded than their neighboring, more affluent, suburban districts (Ascher, 1989). As an example, New York City has 36% of the state's

pupils but receives only 32% of available state aid for schools (New York_Times, 1990). There is thus a combination of greater need among pupils attending urban public schools and proportionately fewer resources available to serve the need.

PERSPECTIVE

This chapter is concerned with the sometimes unique issues that relate to the identification and mainstreaming of academically handicapped children in special education programs in urban school districts. Before we address the issues of identification and mainstream placement we elaborate our perspective on academic handicap and on mainstreaming.

Educable Mental Retardation and Learning Disabilities--The Academic Handicaps

It has been traditional in special education to regard both children with mental retardation (EMR) and children with learning disabilities (LD) as mildly or academically handicapped. Earlier we briefly alluded to the fact that there has been a substantial reduction in children classified as EMR and a corresponding increase in children classified as LD. MacMillan, Meyers, and Morrison (1980) pointed out some antecedents and consequences of this transformation and indicated the difficulty in interpreting and synthesizing research findings from literature that employed EMR subjects at different time periods. MacMillan et al. illustrated that many children classified as EMR during the 1970's would be classified as LD today. Today EMR and LD children often overlap to some degree.

But the problem of differential diagnosis is even more complex than whether a child should be classified as LD or EMR, and this complexity is more frequently evident in urban than in suburban or rural schools and could directly influence mainstreaming decisions. The origin of the problems of identification and placement stems from the high incidence of misbehavior teachers report among children whom they refer for evaluation and who are subsequently classified as academically handicapped.

The special education literature often distinguishes between academically handicapped youngsters and behaviorally handicapped children, as if the two groups are separate. Many times they are not. It is often difficult to separate children having academic and behavioral handicaps, and it is especially difficult to do so in urban school districts where the workload for child study teams is often overwhelming with too many youngsters to be evaluated and too little time available to do it.

According to referring teachers, 34% of children who are classified as academically handicapped in urban districts also misbehave--at times severely--and 74% of those who are classified as behaviorally handicapped also have academic difficulties (Gottlieb, 1985). Many of these children are classified as handicapped and placed in special education because there are insufficient alternative programs or services of demonstrable quality to provide more intensive instructional or management interventions than the classroom teacher can ordinarily provide.

Similar circumstances exist today in the classification of many minority children as LD as existed a decade ago in the classification of minority children as EMR: Many are misclassified. A result may be that misclassified children develop an acquired handicap, that is, they emulate handicapped children in such ways as chronically poor achievement, low self-esteem, and misbehavior, and they receive an inappropriate education both in self-contained classes and in mainstream classes.

Mainstreaming

We consider mainstreaming to be the process of developing a special education *instructional* program for academic or social purposes (or both) designed to accommodate a handicapped youngster in a regular education classroom for some part of the school day. We distinguish between mainstreaming and integration, which we consider to be synonymous with *placement* of handicapped children in classes with non-handicapped peers, without a defined instructional program accompanying the placement. There can be no mainstreaming without integration; there can certainly be integration without mainstreaming. In the absence of a description of the general education classroom we believe it is impossible to determine whether placement in that classroom is in fact the least restrictive, or is even appropriate. There is a third term that is often used in conjunction with mainstreaming: the least restrictive environment. We define least restrictive as that enviornment which imposes the fewest restrictions on a child's cognitive, emotional, and/or social development, regardless of the physical location of that environment. We are aware of our idiosyncratic definition for the term Least Restrictive Environment (LRE). However, the Federal requirement that handicapped children are to be placed in the least restrictive environment that is *appropriate* makes that definition extremely difficult to implement in actual practice. As we indicate elsewhere in this chapter, in the absence of information about the general education classroom in which handicapped children are being proposed for placement we maintain it is virtually impossible to determine whether a placement is appropriate. For many urban children, but certainly not all, the least restrictive environment is a general education classroom.

HANDICAPPED CHILDREN IN URBAN SCHOOL DISTRICTS

A prerequisite for interpreting and understanding programs in special education is to become acquainted with the population being served. Not until we know who is handicapped can we evaluate pupils' progress in the vast array of special education programs and services to which they are exposed. In order to describe handicapped children in general and mainstreamed handicapped children in particular, and to describe difficulties in developing mainstream programs in urban schools, we very briefly review existing literature and present unpublished data obtained from several studies we conducted in urban districts between 1985 and 1989 (e.g., Gottlieb, 1985). We begin by examining three sequential steps in the process of identifying children as handicapped: referral, evaluation, and placement.

Why Children are Referred to Special Education

Urban special educators often believe that the majority of children who are referred for a multi-disciplinary evaluation are referred because they misbehave in the general education classroom. This is an incorrect belief, although a substantial percentage of children are indeed referred for behavioral reasons. Data from two large urban school districts suggest that the majority of children are referred for evaluation for academic reasons. In one urban district where 758 records were sampled, 55% of the referrals were made exclusively for academic reasons, 35% were referred for a combination of academic and behavioral reasons, and 10% were referred exclusively for behavioral reasons. In the second district, 50% of the 201 referrals we sampled were exclusively for academics, 25% were for a combination of academic and behavioral reasons, and the remaining 25% were solely for behavioral reasons. Taken together, the data from both school districts indicate that the majority (75%-90%) of children are referred for academic reasons, but that about half (45% and 50% in the two urban districts) are also referred because they are perceived as having behavioral difficulties.

These data may be contrasted with data obtained from a primarily upper middle-class small neighboring suburban school district where 78% of the 85 referred pupils' records reviewed showed that they were referred exclusively for academic reasons, 14% for a combination of academic and behavioral reasons, and 8% exclusively for behavioral reasons. That is, in this suburban district only 22% of the pupils were referred for behavioral reasons. Thus, there are substantial similarities and substantial differences in the reasons for referrals in urban and suburban districts. In both types of districts, the overwhelming majority of children were referred because teachers perceived that they lacked academic skills. In the urban districts, however, the lack of academic skills among the referred children is far more likely than in the suburban district, to be accompanied by behavioral problems a difference that has substantial importance for mainstreaming practices.

It is insufficient to focus on the reason for referral without knowing who gets referred. Gender and ethnic disparities have long been of concern to special educators, and we were sensitive to these concerns in our prior research. The common finding that boys are over-represented in special education classes is mirrored in referrals for evaluation. Boys are referred about twice as often as girls (68% versus 32%). Ethnic disparities that have historically plagued special education and resulted in numerous legal challenges to prevailing practices are not mirrored in overall referral distributions, however. White children who comprised approximately 23% of the school-wide population in one urban district comprised about 21% of the referrals. Black youngsters who comprised 39% of the population comprised exactly 39% of the referrals in our sample. The greatest disparities existed for Hispanic youngsters who comprised 35% of the population but represented 40% of the referrals, many for language-related problems. Overall, referrals by ethnicity of pupils are not widely discrepant from the ethnic census of the school district, with the possible exception of referrals for Hispanic children.

The lack of overall disproportion in referrals is masked by differences in patterns of referral rates between teachers and parents (Gottlieb, Gottlieb, & Trongone, 1990). The rate of referral for white parents is roughly twice that of minority parents. Conversely, the rate of teacher referrals is substantially higher for minority children than for white children.

There is, also, ethnic disproportion in the percentage of children placed in special education programs, with the greatest disproportion occurring for black pupils who are classified as emotionally disturbed. The percentage of black pupils who were classified as ED exceeded their percentage in the school population by over 16% (Beattie, 1985). Black pupils were also overrepresented in the LD category by 7% and in the EMR category by 9%. Hispanic youngsters were only overrepresented in the category of language-impaired. White youngsters were underrepresented in special education by 6%-8%, depending upon the particular category of handicap. In sum, special classes tend to be heavily weighted with male minority children, almost half of whom are perceived as having behavior problems.

Referred Children in Urban Schools: What is Evaluated and What is Not

We have also examined the tests administered to referred students. Children who are referred for special education placement are administered an exhaustive battery of psychological and educational tests. The school psychologist administers a Wechseler Intelligence Scale for Children-Revised (WISC-R), a Bender Motor Gestalt Test, and a projective test of one kind or another. In addition, a Wide Range Achievement Test is very frequently administered by the psychologist. The major variability in a psychologists' assessment battery is in the administration of a Rorschach, which is given to children who are referred for behavioral reasons almost twice as frequently as it is given to children who are not referred for misbehavior.

The consistency of the psychologists' test battery contrasts markedly with the wide range of educational tests administered by special education members of child study teams. Special educators administered an average of seven tests, most often the Peabody Individual Achievement Test, Peabody Picture Vocabulary Test, Detroit Test of Learning Aptitude, Beery Test of Visual Motor Integration, and Key Math. A wealth of additional tests was administered to smaller percentages of children, with the specific tests not apparently related to the reason for the referral. Each team appeared to use its own preferred tests independent of the child's presenting problem.

Thus, a referred child was administered an average of at least 11 tests, 4 by the psychologist and 7 by the special educator, and a profile of the child's strengths and weaknesses was developed. From this profile an appropriate education must be developed.

One of the defining features of an appropriate education for a handicapped pupil is the determination of the least restrictive environment in which that youngster can function. Conventional wisdom indicates that there is a negative correlation between amount of time in a general educational classroom and degree of restrictiveness a child is thought to experience: the more time spent in that placement the less restrictive the placement. Moreover, placement in a neighborhood school is less restrictive than placement in a school away from home. The reality is that because there is often not a full range of special education offerings in a single school building, many handicapped children are forced to attend school out of their immediate neighborhood in order to receive appropriate special education.

Before a mainstreaming determination can be made, at least a minimum of information should be collected on the nature and characteristics of the general education classroom into which the child is scheduled to be placed. Such information should include a knowledge of the teacher's tolerance for and ability to cater to academic and behavioral diversity, the curriculum being used, class size, grouping practices, if any, that are employed, the achievement level of the classmates, and the level of academic demand imposed by the teacher. This information could be gathered by formal observation, interviews, questionnaires, and any other techniques that are appropriate. Further, we believe this information should be reviewed and discussed in a planning meeting and presented for the parent's informed consideration.

In small school districts, members of child study teams are usually aware of the range of special education offerings in all schools within the district, and they have some familiarity with a substantial number of classes and teachers in the district. Therefore, regardless of whether there is any formal mention made of teacher char-

acteristics or of classroom composition in the evaluation of the youngster--information that is often not required by state regulation--there is reasonable expectation that whenever feasible this information is incorporated into placement and mainstreaming decisions and is at least minimally appropriate regardless of the school the youngster must attend.

In urban areas, on the other hand, school districts are often enormous and child study team members seldom, if ever, know the configuration of educational offerings in all schools within the district. It is not unusual for child study team members to have never seen some of the schools within their district or know where the schools are located. At best they know the special education programs and have marginal knowledge of the general education teachers and programs of the schools within which they work. Obviously, they seldom know the teacher or the general education classroom configuration in other schools. If a child requires placement in another school building, it is virtually certain that the characteristics of the general education classes were not reviewed prior to a mainstreaming recommendation.

The current structure of the evaluation process in large school systems mainly, and in smaller ones to a lesser extent, concentrates disproportionately on the assessment of a youngster and far less on an evaluation of the mainstream environment in which the special education is to be delivered. Because mainstreaming decisions logically *must* involve some knowledge of environmental concerns--concerns which are known to affect the quality of mainstreaming and its impact on pupils (Kaufman, Agard, & Semmel, 1986)--decisions based on limited or no data about the receiving class are as likely as not to be appropriate. Unless we become aware of qualities in the general education class uniquely tailored to the handicapped child's needs, that youngster in all likelihood will exhibit the same general level of academic skill that was responsible for the initial referral but with a more pernicious effect; now the teacher will condone it because the child is called handicapped. In our view this does not augur well for an appropriate education.

Just as the child study team must be aware of the educational features of a receiving classroom, there is also an obvious need for the general education teacher to be knowledgeable about the youngster, specifically about the content of the mainstreamed pupil's IEP, including goals, objectives, learning styles, and most importantly the expected goals of the mainstream placement. In interviews we conducted over the past 8-10 years in several urban school systems, far fewer than 10% of general education teachers who had mainstreamed children enrolled in their classes had more than a perfunctory knowledge of the handicapped child's IEP. None had ever participated in any formal multi-disciplinary conference having to do with the special education child. Additionally, the majority of teachers never had even seen the IEP, and a substantial percentage did not know what an IEP was. How can we seriously maintain that a regular class placement is appropriate when the child study teams know little about the general education class, and the general education teacher knows little about the mainstreamed special education pupil?

Characteristics of Special Education Pupils

On average, pupils who were referred and found eligible for special education had standardized group reading achievement test scores that placed them at the 29th percentile (SD = 15), and there were no significant differences in standardized reading achievement scores when children who were referred exclusively for academics were compared to children who were referred for behavioral reasons, with or without accompanying academic reasons. The full-scale IQ of the referred group was approximately 90, and there were no significant differences in IQ score in relation to the reason children were referred.

The majority of referred pupils were classified as learning disabled. The major distinction was whether the youngsters with LD were recommended for a resource room placement or for placement in a self-contained class, a distinction which is actually an LRE decision and not a classification decision. In our larger urban sample 33.8% of the referred pupils were subsequently classified as LD and placed in resource rooms, 31.4% were placed in self-contained classes for pupils with LD, 20.4% in self-contained classes for pupils with emotional disturbances, and 14.3% were found ineligible to receive special education services. Almost 20% of the pupils who were recommended for placement in self-contained classes for children with LD had IQs that by state regulation would render them eligible for placement in classes for EMRs. These children were seldom administered tests of adaptive behavior, and classification as EMR was evidently not seriously considered. Also, 80% of the pupils classified as LD and placed in self-contained classes had IQs less than 90, a score that is sometimes considered the lower bound for normalcy.

Means and standard deviations for full-scale IQ and reading achievement scores for children recommended for differing classifications have been reported by Kastner and Gottlieb (in press). From these data, 67% of the children can be successfully classified into a particular handicapping category on the basis of a full-scale IQ and other information that is available prior to the actual evaluation, specifically information regarding gender, race, teacher's reason for referral, and the score from a standardized reading achievement test that is administered annually to all children in the school district. Moreover, we were able to predict successfully the classification of 75.8% of children who were classified as learning disabled and placed in resource rooms using only information that was available prior to any member of the child study team administering a single test of any kind, including an intelligence test.

Finally, and in our view quite important, the data reported by Kastner and Gottlieb show that the major defining characteristics of urban children who are classified as learning disabled and placed in self-contained classes are: **They have low IQs** (corresponding to approximately the 12th percentile) **and depressed reading scores** (averaging at the 20th percentile). Other definitional considerations that so often appear in the literature are of negligible importance. For example, the discrepancy between ability and achievement is such that actual achievement scores often surpass predicted scores in reading, not the other way around as definitions of LD imply. Moreover, there is no more intra-test WISC-R scatter among children classified as LD than can be found among children classified as emotionally disturbed or non-handicapped (Gottlieb, 1985). Finally, mention is seldom made of suspected neurological impairment. There is, however, about a 9.25 point discrepancy between verbal and performance IQ scores (SD= 12), with the latter being higher (Mean Verbal IQ = 77.9; Perfromance IQ = 87.1).

Who is Placed in Special Education?

In urban school districts, the classification of a child as handicapped is invariably followed by placement in a special education program. Only about 3% of parents challenged the child study team's classification of a child. The classification of emotionally handicapped was most frequently contested by parents. And of the 3% that were disputed, almost all were placed in special education programs, although not necessarily in the programs that the child study team thought was most appropriate.

Characteristics of Handicapped Children who are Mainstreamed

If few data are typically collected regarding the nature of the general education classroom, how do urban schools decide who is to be mainstreamed and where they are to go? Simply stated, we do not know. We do know, however, that pupils who are in self-contained classes for children with LD and who are mainstreamed do not have significantly higher standardized reading or math test scores than pupils who are in self-contained classes for LD children, but who are not mainstreamed. In one of our studies, a random sample of LD pupils who were mainstreamed (N = 166) had a mean reading percentile score of 20, but LD pupils who were not mainstreamed (N = 439) had a mean percentile score of 18. The corresponding scores for math for the identical sample were 10.7 and 9.2, for the mainstreamed and non-mainstreamed groups, respectively.

Designing Mainstream Programs--Logical and Research Considerations

One of the often overlooked and obvious aspects of any discussion of mainstreaming is the fact that virtually all mildly handicapped pupils who were placed in special education began their school career in general education classes. Only when the children demonstrated to their classroom teachers that they were unable to succeed were they referred, evaluated, declared eligible, and placed in special education. Our data indicate that inner-city teachers are not randomly or capriciously referring children. Most children who are referred for evaluations are substantially behind academically. For any of many reasons, teachers maintain that these children are not likely to progress much in regular education. Therefore, if we are to mainstream these children in such fashion that they *are* likely to progress in a general education it is incumbent upon us to develop programs and services that will support the youngster to a level that is satisfactory to the classroom teacher. Logically, it is insufficient to accept as the standard of success the same level of academic and behavioral performance that was responsible for the initial referral. We must strive for improved performance. Unfortunately, our research programs and our resulting conclusions are not typically enunciated with this criterion in mind.

Two of the interesting aspects of the literature on the effectiveness of mainstreaming are the way that the research questions are framed and the wide diversity of findings that emerge from these studies. Our contention is that in large part, the way the research is conducted influences the findings and conclusions that emerge.

Framing the Research Questions

When mainstreaming is studied from an experimental or quasi-experimental perspective, the research question most frequently addressed is whether the experimental mainstream program yields better academic achievement, social-emotional adjustment, or classroom behavior than the control self-contained class. The research question that is seldom posed is whether the mainstreamed children function at a level that is within the range of proficiency that the general education classroom teacher believes acceptable for the child to progress adequately and remain in the class. In the absence of information about this level of progress, the mainstream program should not be declared successful regardless of whether the child performs as well as in a self-contained class. Alternative services, programs, and placements have to be developed so the youngster can progress satisfactorily.

Another issue of concern in research on mainstreaming that we have not seen addressed pertains to threats to the internal validity of the research. We are referring specifically to the outcome criteria that we employ, which invariably influence the nature and direction of conclusions we draw. There is an enduring belief that mainstreaming is the preferred alternative, and that because of legal mandates it is incumbent upon special educators to create a mainstream placement that is effective for academically handicapped pupils. Our research is designed such that the mainstreamed children constitute the experimental group who receive the overwhelming portion of the investigators' intellectual rigor as well as the investigators' human and fiscal resources. The control group, the segregated children, receive what they ordinarily would receive were no research program in place. Under such circumstances--when investigators' involvement typically leans heavily towards integrated placements--the research data have indicated either no difference between experimental and control groups, or differences favoring experimental groups, as we shall soon indicate. Would similar outcomes have emerged if the segregated-class control group received the bulk of our attention and resources? Can we construct self-contained placements that are superior to integrated placements on a set of predefined dimensions? If we can, are mainstreamed environments still the preferred placement?

Diversity of Findings

The literature on mainstreaming academically handicapped pupils is diverse, and has been well reviewed on several occasions in recent years. For example, one major early review indicated that mainstreaming is not any more effective than self-contained classes for promoting social and/or academic achievement gains (Semmel, Gottlieb, & Robinson, 1979), but another review concluded that mainstreaming does yield more positive outcomes for handicapped children (Madden & Slavin, 1983). The conflicting findings are easy to reconcile, however. The earlier review by Semmel et al. which concluded that mainstreaming and segregated placement produced similar outcomes relied on studies in which the mainstreaming program represented little more than placing a child in a general education classroom, or integration in our terms. These studies may have had an innovative special education component, but the general education portion of the children's educational program, that is, the mainstream component, was *status quo*. The later review by Madden and Slavin which concluded that mainstreaming was more effective than self-contained placements relied more heavily on studies in which the general education classroom had an active instructional program that was designed to accommodate handicapped learners, that is, the authors relied on studies of mainstreaming. Gradually, the literature has shifted from research on mainstreaming as placement (integration) to research on mainstreaming as an instructional program. We briefly review both sets of literature, focusing primarily on those studies that were conducted in urban schools.

Research on Integration--Placement in General Education Classes

Research on mainstreaming as placement has been of two general varieties. One set of studies has primarily examined outcomes that accrue to handicapped children. The second type of study examined classroom processes that occur in mainstream and self-contained placements, at times relating these processes to child outcomes variables. Most often, the classroom process variables focused on teachers' instructional behavior, either the amount of time allotted to instruction or the instructional behavior the teacher engages in with handicapped and non-handicapped learners. The emphasis on teacher's behavior in the research litera-

ture reflects the recognition that teachers play an important role in determining the ultimate success of mainstreaming efforts.

OUTCOME STUDIES. Comparisons of outcomes accruing to children with mental retardation in special classes and regular education classes have been available for close to sixty years, beginning with Bennett's (1932) study. A series of 10 studies conducted in this country have compared EMR children enrolled in regular classes to EMR children enrolled self-contained classes. This body of research is collectively referred to as the efficacy studies. Results of these studies were fairly evenly split with some finding superior achievement in regular classes and others finding no achievement differences. These studies were critically reviewed by Kirk (1964), and more recently by Corman and Gottlieb (1978), and Madden and Slavin (1983).

A uniform characteristic of the efficacy research is that none of the EMR children in the regular education programs had been enrolled in special education classes. More contemporary research on mainstreaming typically compares children who had already been classified as handicapped but are placed in different educational settings. Two studies in this line were able to assign pupils randomly to experimental and control treatments, the lack of which was a critical flaw in all but one (Goldstein, Moss, & Jordon, 1965) of the earlier research studies.

Budoff and Gottlieb (1976) reported one study of the relative benefits of mainstreaming and self-contained placements on academically handicapped pupils. In that study 31 EMR students between the ages of 93 and 168 months were randomly assigned either to a self-contained class or to full-time mainstreaming with support from a remedial learning center for about 40 minutes daily, five days a week. The study was conducted in a small urban school district, where the percentage of minority children was relatively low. The mean IQ of both groups was about 70. Results of the study indicated that there were no statistically significant achievement differences between the two groups at the conclusion of the first year. The mainstreamed students, however, reported more positive attitudes toward school.

Calhoun and Elliot (1977) reported on the academic achievement of 50 black EMR children who had been randomly assigned either to self-contained classes or to regular education classes. Results over a three-year period indicated a progressively widening gap favoring regular education placement. We note that the regular education program was individualized and not the typical curriculum approach most often encountered in regular education classes; the modifications to the regular class curriculum may have had a pronounced effect on the positive findings.

Academic outcomes were not the sole concern of research on mainstreaming. Studies have also focused on the social outcomes of mainstreaming, and many of these have been reviewed earlier (Semmel et al., 1979; Madden & Slavin, 1983). That literature has consistently indicated that mainstreamed youngsters occupy an inferior status in the social hierarchy of the peer group (e.g., Goodman, Gottlieb, & Harrison, 1972). A smaller literature indicates that mainstreamed academically handicapped youngsters behave in a more prosocial manner than segregated peers (Gampel, Gottlieb, & Harrison, 1974).

PROCESS STUDIES--INSTRUCTING HANDICAPPED CHILDREN IN THE MAINSTREAM. Mainstreaming as placement in regular education has not only focused on benefits that accrue to children as a consequence of that placement. Other studies have investigated the general education classroom processes that were associated with academic and social benefits to handicapped children.

One of the first and by far the most intensive efforts to understand how teachers instruct mainstreamed handicapped learners was initiated by Project PRIME (Programmed Re-entry into Mainstream Education) (Kaufman et al., 1986). Data for this study were collected in 1971 but not published until 1986. This research consisted of in-depth testing and classroom observations of 373 children with educable mental retardation selected from among 43 school districts in the state of Texas. Included were both urban school districts and suburban and rural districts. Data for the different settings were not separated. Comparisons were made between teachers' instructional behavior in mainstreamed classes and in self-contained special classes.

Although the Project PRIME data analysis was voluminous and does not lend itself to simple summary, we highlight several major findings:

- First and foremost, the academic progress of EMR pupils was influenced by the educational environment they experienced. Teacher characteristics, socioemotional climate, and instructional operations affected the academic status of EMR pupils. This study demonstrated clearly, and on a large and representative sample, that the nature of schooling makes a marked impact on the academic status of EMR learners. By contrast, peer characteristics were the major contributors to the academic status of nonhandicapped learners. In our view these data reinforce our earlier comments regarding the need to assess the classroom environment into which a child with handicaps is scheduled to be mainstreamed before mainstreaming actually occurs.

• The nature of the classroom also had a marked affect on the social competence of EMR pupils, although social acceptance and social behavior were affected by different factors. A substantial amount of variance both in social acceptance and social rejection (23-28%) was also accounted for by variations in the classroom environment.

Research on mainstream classroom processes conducted subsequent to Project PRIME has consisted primarily of small-scale studies, most frequently on children with LD, and may or may not have been conducted in urban school districts. Much of the research subsequent to PRIME investigated a limited number of variables, with the child's degree of task involvement and the total frequency of interactions with the teacher being the main focuses of interest (Bryan & Wheeler, 1972; Forness & Esveldt, 1975; Richey & McKinney, 1978). Results of these studies were consistent in demonstrating that children with LD are less task involved, but the studies were less consistent in their findings regarding frequency of interactions. Although the majority of research indicated that children with LD interacted more than nonhandicapped peers (e.g., Forness & Esveldt, 1975), other studies revealed no significant differences (Richey & McKinney, 1978).

We initiated a series of studies on the classroom processes occurring during mainstreaming of LD youngsters in inner-city elementary schools. Our initial studies, like the majority of others which examined the processes of mainstreaming, focused on LD children whose special education was delivered in a resource room. The remainder of the school day was spent in the general education classroom. One of the hallmarks of general education classes in inner-city schools is that many children in any given classroom read below grade level. The gap between mainstreamed handicapped children and other children is often relatively modest. Given the modest and at times non-existent achievement gap between children with and without handicaps in the general education classroom, we anticipated that teachers would not treat the former appreciably different than the latter. Our research was designed with this general hypothesis in mind.

A total of 59 LD and 59 control group children in elementary schools formed the sample of our first study of teacher-student interactions with mainstreamed children (Alves & Gottlieb, 1986). Results of the analyses on teachers' instructional interactions indicated teachers differentiated handicapped from nonhandicapped pupils by the frequency with which the two groups were provided with Academic Questions, Extended Feedback, and Total Amount of Interactions. Handicapped children received more total teacher interaction, but academic questions and extended feedback were addressed more frequently to the nonhandicapped learners. Thus, our findings supported previous research in indicating that handicapped children receive more interactions from teachers. But the data also indicated that the interactions that they experience are primarily procedural, not academic.

A major limitation of the preceding study was that the differences in teacher-student interactions toward handicapped and non-handicapped children could not be attributed directly to the handicapped status of the mainstreamed students. It is equally possible that the reason teachers provided fewer academic interactions to the handicapped children was that they were low-achievers. In other words, handicapped status and achievement level were confounded in the study.

We conducted a second study in an urban school district to determine whether it was the handicapped status of the mainstreamed children or their achievement level that was responsible for the way that teachers interacted with them (Parker, Gottlieb, Gottlieb, Davis, & Kunzweiller, 1989). Three groups of elementary school children were selected for the second study: 31 average-achievers reading on or above grade level, 31 low-achievers functioning one or more years below grade level, and 31 mainstreamed handicapped children. All 93 children were members of minority groups, with the majority being black.

In each classroom, three children were observed, one low-achiever, one average achiever, and one mainstreamed handicapped child. Observations were conducted for 9 30-minute sessions, a total of four and one-half hours of observations in each classroom. As before, observations were made on academic questioning, extended feedback, and total amount of interactions. There were significant differences in the total amount of interaction, academic questions, and extended feedback that the three groups of children received. The results indicate that low-achievers have fewer total interactions, are asked fewer academic questions, and are given less feedback than the other two groups.

These results indicate that the low-achieving status of children, and not the fact that they are labeled as handicapped, contributes to teachers' interaction patterns. Mainstreamed children are not treated differently, i.e., with less academic demand, than other children in class who are not low-achievers.

The data are different from several other studies that found that handicapped children receive more teacher interactions, but of a procedural nature. We did not observe that mainstreamed handicapped children received more interactions from the teacher. Again, it may be that teachers provide more procedural interactions when they perceive the children to be low-achievers who may not be able to keep up with the academic demand of the class.

Perhaps the most interesting finding was that the identified handicapped children were seldom the lowest achieving children in the general education classroom. In fact, we observed 38 classrooms in one of our studies, and in only one classroom was the identified LD youngster the lowest achiever. This was balanced by the fact that another LD pupil was the highest achiever in his classroom. Overall, within their classes the mainstreamed LD youngsters tended to be in the second quartile in tested standardized achievement.

How important is teacher instructional style on children's academic achievement? Is there a significant correlation between children's pre- and post-test standardized achievement scores and the extent to which they received academic questions or extended feedback? Correlation coefficients were computed among reading achievement scores, extent of academic questions, and extent of extended feedback that children received. The coefficient between achievement and academic questioning for all 93 children in the Parker et al. (1989) sample was .25 (p .01), and the corresponding coefficient between achievement and extended feedback was .37 (p .001). Therefore, both academic questions and extended feedback relate significantly to children's achievement scores at the end of the school year.

Thus, even in the absence of educational approaches designed to accommodate handicapped learners in general education classrooms, the diversity created by teachers' everyday instructional styles has a differential impact on the pupils. Whether the research is large in scope (PRIME) or much smaller in scope (those we described in the previous paragraphs), the data indicate that classroom environments are important, they matter, and consequently, they are worthy of assessment prior to the decision to mainstream. Information derived from the study of classroom processes can mark a beginning in identifying a long-sought goal in special education: defining an appropriate placement in the mainstream for handicapped learners. But, mainstreaming may be implemented even more effectively if we adopt a more comprehensive approach to service delivery, an approach that transcends teachers' instructional styles and incorporates grouping practices, instructional methodologies, curriculum adaptation, and the use of peers as agents of instruction.

Mainstreaming as Educational Programming

Previous research reviewed here examined mainstream programs in which the primary consideration was placement in less restrictive settings. Obviously, if mainstreaming is to succeed it must be conceptualized far more elaborately than mere placement. Two major approaches to instructional design have been reported in the literature as ways to accommodate handicapped learners full-time in the mainstream: ALEM, the Adaptive Learning Environments Model (Wang, Peverly, & Randolph, 1984) and Team Assisted Individualization (TAI) (Slavin, 1984). Because TAI is discussed elsewhere in this volume and because it has not been reported on a sample of urban handicapped children (Slavin, personal communication), we will focus our comments on ALEM.

ALEM is a full-time mainstreaming model combining elements of individualized prescriptive instruction with aspects of informal education. The model itself is based on guiding principles, one of which is that the general education classroom teacher is the primary instructor for all handicapped and nonhandicapped children, and that the special education teacher consults with the classroom teacher and provides direct instruction to handicapped children in the mainstream. Children work in small groups, large groups, and at times individually, and progress from activity to activity at their own pace. ALEM focuses on academic achievement and self-management skills for all students, including handicapped students.

A large-scale implementation of ALEM was carried out in a large urban school system during the 1982-1983 school year. Twenty-six classrooms located in five school buildings were selected as sites. EMR, LD, and ED handicapped youngsters were enrolled in the program. Three general classes of measures were obtained: degree of implementation, classroom process outcomes, and student achievement and attitudinal outcomes.

With respect to student outcomes, the achievement data indicated that the handicapped children who participated in the ALEM classes made slightly more than one year of gains in both reading and math. Although this study did not directly employ a control group, the achievement gains were higher than those made by other, comparable, handicapped children in their traditional self-contained classroom settings. Not reported, however, were the mean gains made by the different classifications of handicapped children. Because pupils classified as EMR in this school district function considerably lower than those classified as LD or ED, it is possible that only the latter two groups benefitted from ALEM, but not the former.

The ALEM research was subjected to criticism on methodological grounds from Fuchs and Fuchs (1988). Many of these criticisms appear to be justified. However, from the vantage point of several observations of ALEM classrooms made by the first author of this chapter at the data collection sites reported on by Wang et al. (1984), he has no doubt that ALEM represented a quantum improvement over the classes that the special education youngsters would have attended had ALEM not been available. Several hours of nonscientific visual observation during the winter and spring of the school year revealed that the handicapped youngsters participated fully in the general education classroom routines, and that the admittedly self-selected principals, teachers, and pupils were enthusiastic about the program. We are also aware that the school administrators in the districts involved were highly supportive of ALEM. In conversations one of us (JG) had with a building principal during the writing of this chapter, seven years after ALEM was removed from his school, the principal raved that both he and the parents of handicapped and nonhandicapped children who had participated in ALEM seven years ago still saw the socialization benefits that accrued to their children. The principal's comments were spontaneous and unsolicited. ALEM was removed from the schools only because peculiarities in the state's special education funding formula would have resulted in the local school system losing millions of dollars in state aid had the program been retained and expanded. Overall, ALEM offers at least some hope that with proper training and support, an innovative mainstreaming program can be implemented in inner city schools and can represent a substantial improvement over existing self-contained programs for handicapped learners, under certain conditions. The fact that a program may be legitimately subject to criticism on methodological grounds does not mean that it is ineffective, it means only that we do not as yet know whether it is as effective as the program developers maintain.

Our cautiously positive view of ALEM does not imply, however, that we believe it is a valuable vehicle to mainstream very large numbers of handicapped children in urban schools at this time. Recall that ALEM was implemented in schools under experimental conditions where all participants, from principals to pupils, volunteered. It is not at all certain that ALEM could be or would be equally well implemented and produce equally positive results in districts where the superintendent is not actively seeking changes in the way special education is delivered, where building principals harbor no disenchantment with self-contained classes, where general education teachers are reticent about instructing handicapped pupils, or where the pupils are not preselected by school administrators on the basis of their perceptions that the targeted pupils represent a group who are most apt to benefit from a mainstream program. It is premature to maintain that on the basis of data reported by Wang et al. (1984), we now have the means to offer all, or even most, handicapped children full-time programming in general education classrooms. But in our view it should certainly not be dismissed as ineffective. We believe such a contention is a severe disservice.

SUMMARY

The data on mainstreaming are quite clear. Beneficial results on behalf of handicapped children are possible when effective programming is in place and when a variety of steps are taken by the school district to increase the chances for success. In the absence of effective programming, such as when mainstreaming is simply equated with placement with non-handicapped children for academic or non-academic activities, the data are equally clear-cut that mainstreaming does not promote positive academic or social gains among handicapped pupils.

In urban school districts several factors militate against successful mainstreaming practices. First, as we indicated earlier, neither federal nor state regulation requires in-depth study of the mainstream educational environment into which the handicapped child is to be placed. Given the importance of teachers and peers on the academic and social performance of handicapped youngsters this omission is serious. How can we decide whether a placement is appropriate or is not restrictive if we know virtually nothing about that environment?

Second, we also indicated earlier that in urban districts a substantial portion of children who are referred for special education evaluation, and who are subsequently found eligible and placed in special education programs, are referred for behavioral reasons (45-50%). Behaviorally impaired children are the least desirable candidates for mainstreaming from the general education teacher's perspective. In fact, in a dissertation on mainstreaming (Adler, 1990) 60% of mainstreamed ED children who had been mainstreamed in September were removed from the mainstream by November, when data collection began. Corresponding data for LD children revealed fewer than 10% were removed. In the study by Adler the investigator had no control over which children were placed in the mainstream nor which were removed from the mainstream.

Will mainstream programs be effective when they are mandated for everyone rather than being introduced to a receptive school audience? Recall that ALEM was put in place in a willing school district. Data were reported from a study where the school board and superintendent were supportive, where the superintendent selected building principals who had good management and educational leadership skills, where principals selected teachers who were likely to make the program work, and where pupils were selected because they were right for the program. Moreover, the individual who developed the program was personally involved in it, invested the bulk of her fiscal and intellectual resources nurturing and refining it, and reported the results of the evaluative studies regarding its effectiveness. This is not stated as a criticism; this is the way we typically conduct our business.

ALEM was successful because the investigator was concerned about the educational program and because there was general recognition that the program was most likely to succeed in schools where the principals were effective leaders and in classes having effective teachers. Which part of federal or state law demands that we so closely scrutinize the principals and teachers who control and who define the educational context of the mainstream?

Further, we must not lose sight of the fact that there is a major bank of data substantially missing in the special education empirical literature, data that are absolutely essential before widespread implementation is undertaken. We desperately need demonstration programs, on a large-scale, using non-volunteers, implemented by school administrators with only minimal assistance from the programs' developers, and evaluated by independent individuals who are not affiliated with the program developer or the school district. Only when demonstration programs are evaluated can we have confidence that large-scale implementation of innovative programming is warranted.

Finally, we must constantly recall that critics of segregated special education maintain that handicapped children can be accommodated in general education classes. If that were true, the vast majority would not have been referred, evaluated, found eligible, and placed in special education in the first place. Dissatisfaction with special education--and there are indeed many legitimate grounds for dissatisfaction--in no way implies that the general education systems can successfully absorb the bulk of handicapped youngsters. Those children who failed there once are likely to fail there again. And although there are programs that show considerable promise for profitably accommodating handicapped youngsters in regular education classes, studies of them were conducted under circumstances that may not reflect the everyday realities of schools, especially in urban districts. To the extent that the positive findings are replicable under less ideal circumstances, the programs may indeed supplant self-contained classes. To date, however, we do not know whether the programs can deliver the required results under common everyday circumstances.

REFERENCES

Adler, S. H. (1990). *Student status, classroom behavior, ability level, and gender as salient for differences in teacher student interactions.* Unpublished doctoral dissertation, New York University.

Alves, A., & Gottlieb, J. (1986). Teacher interactions with mainstreamed handicapped students and their nonhandicapped peers. *Learning Disability Quarterly, 9*, 77-83.

Ascher, C. (1989). *Urban school finance: The quest for equal educational opportunity.* Alexandria, VA: National School Board Association. (ERIC/CUE Digest Number 55, ED 311 147)

Beattie, R. I. (1985). *Special education: A call for quality.* Final report to Mayor Edward I. Koch of the Commission on Special Education.

Bennett, A. (1932). *A comparative study of subnormal children in the elementary grades.* New York: Teachers College, Bureau of Publications.

Bryan, T., & Wheeler, R. (1972). Perception of learning disabled children: The eye of the observer. *Journal of Learning Disabilities, 5*, 484-488.

Budoff, M., & Gottlieb, J. (1976). Special class EMR children mainstreamed: A study of an aptitude (learning potential) X treatment interaction. *American Journal of Mental Deficiency, 81*, 1-11.

Calhoun, G., & Elliott, R. (1977). Self-concept and academic achievement of educable retarded and emotionally disturbed pupils. *Exceptional Children, 44*, 379-380.

Corman, L., & Gottlieb, J. (1978). Mainstreaming mentally retarded children. A review of research. In N. R. Ellis (Ed.), *International review of research*

in mental retardation (Vol 9, pp. 251-275). New York: Academic Press.

Education of All Handicapped Children Act of 1975, 20 U.S.C. 1401 (1978).

Forness, S. R., & Esdvelt, K. (1975). Classroom behavior of children with learning disabilities. *Journal of Learning Disabilities, 8*, 382-385.

Fuchs, D., & Fuchs, L. S. (1988). Evaluation of the Adaptive Learning Environments Model. *Exceptional Children, 55*, 115-127.

Gampel, D. H., Gottlieb, J., & Harrison, R. H. (1974). Comparison of classroom behavior of special class EMR, integrated EMR, low IQ, and non-retarded children. *American Journal of Mental Deficiency, 79*, 527-535.

Goldstein, H., Moss, J., & Jordan, L. J. (1965). *The efficacy of special class training on the development of mentally retarded children* (U.S. Office of Education Cooperative Project, No. 619). Urbana: University of Illinois.

Goodman, H., Gottlieb, J., & Harrison R. H. (1972). Social acceptance of EMRs integrated into a nongraded elementary school. *American Journal of Mental Deficiency, 76*, 412-417.

Gottlieb, J. (1985). Report for the Mayor's Commission on Special Education on COH Practices in New York City. In R. I. Beattie (Chair) *Special Education: A Call for Quality.* New York City: Office of the Mayor.

Gottlieb, J., Gottlieb, B. W., & Trongone (1990). *Parent and teacher referrals for a psycho-educational evaluation.* Manuscript submitted for publication.

Kastner, J., & Gottlieb, J. (in press). Classification of children in urban special education: Importance of pre-assessment information and intelligence test scores. *Psychology in the Schools.*

Kaufman, M. J., Agard, J. A., & Semmel, M. I. (1986). *Mainstreaming: Learners and their environment.* Brookline, MA: Brookline Press.

Kirk, S. A. (1964). Research in education. In H. A. Stevens & R. Heber (Eds.) *Mental Retardation: A review of research* (pp. 57-99). Chicago: University of Chicago Press.

Larry P. v. Wilson Riles. (1971). Civil Action No. C-70-37 (N.D. Cal. 1971).

MacMillan, D. L., Meyers, D. L., & Morrison, G. M. (1980). System-identification of mildly mentally retarded children: Implications for interpreting and conducting research. *American Journal of Mental Retardation, 85*, 108-115.

Madden, N. A., & Slavin, R. E. (1983). Mainstreaming students with mild academic handicaps: Academic and social outcomes. *Review of Educational Research, 53*, 519-569.

New York Times, January 28, 1990, p. B2.

Parker, I. M., Gottlieb, J., Gottlieb, B. W., Davis, S., & Kunzweiller, C. (1989). Teacher behavior towards low achievers, average achievers, and mainstreamed minority group learning disabled children. *Learning Disabilities Research, 4*, 101-106.

Richey, D., & McKinney, J. (1978). Classroom behavioral styles of learning disabled children. *Journal of Learning Disabilities, 11*, 297-302.

Semmel, M. I., Gottlieb, J., & Robinson, N. (1979). Mainstreaming: Perspectives on educating handicapped children in the public schools. In D. Berliner (Ed.) *Review of Research in Education* (Vol. 7, pp. 223-279). Washington, D.C.: American Educational Research Association.

Slavin, R. E. (1984). Team Assisted Individualization: Cooperative learning and individualized instruction in the mainstreamed classroom. *Remedial and Special Education, 5*(6), 33-42.

Tucker, J. A. (1980). Ethnic proportions in classes for the learning disabled: Issues in non-biased assessment. *Journal of Special Education, 14*, 93-105.

Wang, M. C., Peverly, S., & Randolph, R. (1984). An investigation of the implementation and effects of a full-time mainstreaming program. *Remedial and Special Education, 5*(6), 21-32.

9

CHARACTERISTICS OF STUDENTS WITH LEARNING DISABILITIES: A SUMMARY OF THE EXTANT DATA BASE AND ITS IMPLICATIONS FOR EDUCATIONAL PROGRAMS

Tanis Bryan, Mary Bay, Norma Lopez-Reyna, and Mavis Donahue
University of Illinois at Chicago

Our purpose in writing this chapter is twofold. First, we begin by summarizing the extant data base that describes characteristics of children with learning disabilities (LD). If educational planning is to be responsive to the needs of children, it is mandatory to begin with an understanding of the educational problem. A review of the research on characteristics of students with learning disabilities should serve as a framework for proposals on how best to meet the educational needs of this population. Based on our knowledge of these characteristics, our second purpose is to identify critical aspects of educational programs that we think will move us closer to the goal of accommodating the needs of these students.

This may seem at odds with this text's focus upon the Regular Education Initiative (REI). We hold the REI to be a political-philosophical-economic-social issue whose proponents (a) are attempting to address the overwhelming numbers and needs of children for whom the educational system of America is failing, and (b) wish to broaden and guarantee the civil rights of children with special needs. We respect these goals and believe the proponents to be sincere in their efforts to promote the well being of children. In this chapter we are neither for nor against the REI; nor are we neutral. We are advocates of the position that students with learning disabilities are entitled to receive free and appropriate educational programs, with appropriateness defined on the basis of the child's needs rather than ideology.

As you read this chapter, you will note that we recognize and point out the limitations of the extant data base, in general, and the degree to which it informs and limits our decisions about educational planning, in particular. These shortcomings underscore the complexity of the problem and reflect the short history of research on learning disabilities.

DEFINITIONS

A reasonable place to start to catalog the characteristics of students with learning disabilities is with the various definitions of learning disabilities. Historically, one of the first definitions, published in 1966, described children with minimal brain dysfunction. The term minimal brain dysfunction was deemed unacceptable because there was no technology to link learning problems to parts or functions of the brain. The 1966 definition was thus replaced by the 1969 definition which carefully eliminated any direct reference to brain dysfunction. The 1969 definition, subsequently used in 1975 in PL 94-142 states:

> Children with learning disabilities exhibit a disorder in one or more of the basic psychological processes involved in understanding or using spoken or written language. These may be manifested in disorders of listening, thinking, talking, reading, writing, spelling, or arithmetic. They include conditions which have been referred to as perceptual handicaps, brain injury, minimal brain dysfunction, dyslexia, developmental aphasia, etc. They do not include learning problems which are due primarily to visual, hearing, or motor handicaps, to mental retardation, emotional disturbance, or to environmental disadvantage. (Elementary and Secondary Amendments of 1969)

Since 1975 there have been three major efforts to revise the definition. Although it is unlikely that federal legislation will be amended using these more recent definitions, the revisions inform us about professional and parental consensus regarding the nature of learning disabilities. Because the three revisions incorporate similar changes, our comments regarding the changes follow presentation of the revisions.

In 1981 the National Joint Committee for Learning Disabilities (NJCLD), a committee of representatives from six organizations involved with learning disabilities, developed this definition:

> Learning disabilities is a generic term that refers to a heterogeneous group of disorders manifested by significant difficulties in the acquisition and use of listening, speaking, reading, writing, reasoning or mathematical abilities. These disorders are intrinsic to the individual and presumed to be due to central nervous system dysfunction. Even though a learning disability may occur concomitantly with other handicapping conditions (e.g., sensory impairment, mental retardation, social and emotional disturbances) or environmental influences (e.g., cultural differences, insufficient/inappropriate instruction, psychogenic factors), it is not the direct result of these conditions or influences. (Meyers & Hammill, 1982, p. 6)

The Association for Children and Adults with Learning Disabilities (ACLD)(now known as the Learning Disabilities Association of America, LDAA) took issue with the NJCLD definition and developed its own:

> Specific Learning Disabilities is a chronic condition of presumed neurological origin which selectively interferes with the development, integration, and/or demonstration of verbal and/or nonverbal abilities. Specific Learning Disabilities exists as a distinct handicapping condition in the presence of average to superior intelligence, adequate sensory motor systems, and adequate learning opportunities. The condition varies in its manifestations and in degree of severity. Throughout life the condition can affect self-esteem, educa-

tion, vocation, socialization, and/or daily living activities. (Special Education Today, 1985, p. 1)

The third definition is the product of the Interagency Committee on Learning Disabilities, a committee with representatives from each of the National Institutes of Health that was mandated by the Congress to develop a research agenda for learning disabilities for the 1990s. As part of its work, the committee submitted this definition:

Learning Disabilities is a generic term that refers to a heterogeneous group of disorders manifested by significant difficulties in the acquisition and use of listening, speaking, reading, writing, reasoning, or mathematical abilities, or of social skills. These disorders are intrinsic to the individual and presumed to be due to central nervous system dysfunction. Even though a learning disability may occur concomitantly with other handicapping conditions (e.g., sensory impairment, mental retardation, social and emotional disturbance), with socioenvironmental influences (e.g., cultural differences, insufficient or inappropriate instruction, psychogenic factors), and especially with attention deficit disorder, all of which may cause learning problems, a learning disability is not the direct result of those conditions or influences. (Kavanagh & Truss, 1988, p. 550)

The revised definitions make significant changes in the 1975 definition by (a) describing learning disabilities as a generic group of heterogeneous problems, (b) linking learning disabilities to central nervous system dysfunction, and (c) including social problems as characteristics of learning disabilities. The

revisions also are notable for changes not made; although the changes are significant, the revised definitions are not radically different from the 1969/1975 definition. We believe it is safe to say that the definition war has reached an armistice; there appears to be professional and parental acceptance not only of the fact of learning disabilities but also considerable agreement as to the concept of learning disabilities.

Within the field of learning disabilities, the war of the next decade is likely to be concerned with the operationalization of the terms used in the definition and the translation of diagnoses into effective practice. Within special education the war will continue to rage over how best to meet the needs of mushrooming numbers of underachieving youngsters. In the meantime, let us consider the evidence about the characteristics of persons with learning disabilities as specified in the definitions and how these manifest themselves in areas of academic achievement.

CHARACTERISTICS OF STUDENTS WITH LEARNING DISABILITIES

Central Nervous System Dysfunction

The roots of this field are firmly planted in the notion that people with learning disabilities have dysfunctions in the central nervous system (CNS). These roots, submerged in the 1969/1975 definition, re-emerged strongly in each of the recent revisions. Since the 1969/1975 definition excluded references to CNS dysfunction because there was no technology that allowed us to link learning problems with brain processes, we must ask what evidence do we now have to support the notion that children with LD manifest "presumed central nervous system dysfunction." Hynd and Semrud-Clikeman (1989) recently published an extensive review of research that used recently developed methods to study brain processing and anatomy. The results suggest that in the brains of dyslexics there are physical features that may be associated with language delay and handedness and other architectural signs of anomalies. However, there is little direct evidence to document a relationship between deviations in brain morphology and dyslexia because the research suffers from methodological deficiencies, particularly regarding the diagnosis of dyslexia, appraisal of handedness and neurolinguistic deficits, and a failure to produce evidence that this pattern of involvement is unique to the dyslexic syndrome.

In the absence of a technology to link the brain and learning, we ask why professionals and parents included references to CNS dysfunction in the revisions of the definition. We suspect that the intent was to distinguish between students with learning disabilities and other low-achieving students. A second reason might be to encourage research (and funding) on the links between the brain and behavior. The goal of identifying physiological antecedents to learning problems is not new (see for example, the history of research in mental retardation). The mandate for research that was generated by the Interagency Committee includes the need for federal funding to support research on brain-learning-behavior linkages. The extent to which such research will be useful in the designing of educational programs for LD students is not yet known.

Psychological Processing Deficits

The 1969/1975 definition states that learning disabilities reflect a "disorder in one or more of the basic psychological processes involved in understanding or using spoken or written language...manifested in disorders of thinking, listening, talking," etc. (Elementary and Secondary Amendments of 1969). There is considerable controversy in the area of learning disabilities research as to whether poor performance by LD students on learning tasks reflects attention deficits, poor memory, lack of appropriate learning strategies, deficient language skills or combinations of these factors (Torgesen & Houck, 1980; Vellutino, Steger, DeSetto, & Phillips, 1975). Given that a major portion of the research in learning disabilities centers around information processing deficits in attention, memory, and language, our discussion focuses on these topics.

ATTENTION. Research on attention problems comes from two very different sources: laboratory studies and teachers' ratings. Laboratory studies have assessed the three components of attention: the orienting response (coming to attention), vigilance (paying attention across time), and selective attention (attending to only some parts of a situation). The results of these studies found no differences on attention in the orienting response or coming to attention (Dykman, Ackerman, Holcomb, & Boudreau, 1983), but that students with learning disabilities differ from nondisabled students on measures of vigilance (i.e., paying attention across time); this appears to be characteristic of LD students who are also hyperactive (Anderson, Holcomb, & Doyle, 1973; Doyle, Anderson, & Holcomb, 1976). Studies of selective attention (Hallahan & Reeve, 1980) and impulsivity (Keogh & Margolis, 1976) have found that children with learning disabilities may be two to three years behind nondisabled children on central learning tasks (attending to the relevant and ignoring the irrelevant features of a stimulus array) and are more impulsive. Research addressed to learning-disabled students' "meta-attention," their thoughts about attention, has found that children with learning disabilities were less skilled than nondisabled students at noting the situational conditions that facilitate attention (Loper, Hallahan, & Ianna, 1982). The evidence based on laboratory measures has found no evidence for problems in orienting, but some evidence for deficits in vigilance, selective attention, and meta-cognition.

The greatest support for the notion that students with learning disabilities have problems in paying attention comes from teachers' ratings and observations of classroom behavior. Using such measures, McKinney and colleagues found that students with learning disabilities are rated as less task-oriented, more distractible and more introverted, and they are observed to be more off-task and less attentive than normally achieving peers (McKinney, McClure, & Feagans, 1982; Richey & McKinney, 1978). Based on these results, McKinney developed a system to categorize children based on measures of intellectual ability, achievement, and classroom behavior. Four subtypes of learning-disabled children were identified. Three of the four categories involve some dimension of attention, be it poor task orientation or distractibility.

The importance of attention can be seen in a follow-up of students with learning disabilities across a three-year period. McKinney and Speece (1986) found that children with attention problems and children with problem behaviors in first and second grades showed poorer achievement in later grades compared to children who did not present atypical behaviors and those who were withdrawn. Children with attention deficits and problem behaviors were the most variable subtype but, when they changed groups, they changed to another atypical subtype, not to a normal subtype. These groups showed the least favorable academic progress even though the children in this study received resource room services one hour each day, four days a week.

Attention problems clearly play a significant role in teacher referrals for special education services. Cooper and Farran (1988) found that aberrant work-related behaviors (disorganization and distractibility) placed kindergartners at 12 times greater risk for referral than normally behaving classmates. This research was extended by Cooper and Speece (1987) to relate behavioral categories to learning environments. Conducted with first grade teachers and children, their analysis found that poor work-related skills were associated with referral except when combined with low verbal IQ. Poor reading achievement was not associated with referral except when it was accompanied by poor work related skills.

Further support for the role of attention in referral was found in a series of studies to identify teachers' reasons for referring children for special education services. Bryan, Bay, Shelden, and Simon (1990) asked teachers to view a videotape of classroom instruction and tell what they were thinking and noticing about children whom they had earlier identified as being at-risk for referral. Overwhelmingly the teachers responded that the at-risk children were not attending, not responsive, and not involved in the instructional activity. Teachers noted both subtle and not-so-subtle student behaviors that signified loss of attention. Teachers' reflections seldom focused on specific deficits in a skill or content area; rather, they described several behaviors that they interpreted as a lack of attention to ongoing instructional activities.

We should note that other studies have failed to find support for the attentional-deficit hypothesis. Samuels and Miller (1985) used laboratory and classroom measures of attention and found no evidence that children with learning disabilities have attentional problems. Similarly, Bay and Bryan (1990) found no differences in measures of on-task behavior between at-risk students and average achievers. It is not clear why the laboratory study results are inconsistent. With regard to classroom studies, we suggest that the term attention is being used by teachers as a generic term to describe a host of behaviors associated with disengagement from instructional procedures.

MEMORY. Memory is a psychological process that has been hypothesized to play an important role in affecting learning disabilities. Bauer (1987) provides several examples of how students with learning disabilities differ from normally achieving students (NA) on various forms of memory. First, LD students use less effective, elaborative encoding processes. The amount of information recalled by LD students decreases more rapidly as the delay between presentation and recall increases. When subjects were allowed to present information that is to be learned at their own pace, the LD students presented a word list for a shorter time than NA students and required more trials to criterion. The greater study time used by the NA students was due to their spending more time in elaborative encoding and this in turn resulted in fewer trials to criterion.

Research that examined the use of rehearsal finds that LD students tend to use single-item rehearsal, whereas the nondisabled subjects use cumulative rehearsal which is associated with higher recall. Learning-disabled and nondisabled students demonstrate awareness of single-item rehearsal, but the LD students show less awareness of cumulative rehearsal, categorizing, subjective organization, and forming associations. The LD students are aware that studying for a longer time may be necessary but they do not apply this knowledge and do not actually study longer. For instance, when required to read text until they thought they knew the material, the LD subjects were less likely to use control processes and recalled less than nondisabled subjects. The LD subjects were aware that they did not use adequate control processes. Noteworthy is the fact that these performance differences did not appear to be a function of motivation. Incentives may improve the performance of LD and nondisabled children who do not have memory problems, but they do not influence the recall of children who have short-term

memory deficiencies as evidenced by their below normal performance on digit span measures (Torgesen & Houck, 1980). In sum, there is support for characterizing students with learning disabilities as having problems in memory processes in general and, more specifically, in the appropriate application of these processes.

In response to such research findings, there have been efforts to subcategorize types of memory problems. For example, Swanson (1988) has used factor analyses to sort out different subcategories of children with LD according to their performance on different types of memory tasks. Using three tasks to test children's ability to access information from long-term memory, and to process it, the results identified eight subgroups. Across memory measures the LD subjects did more poorly than the nondisabled subjects on recall of targeted words in elaborated and base sentences, monitoring of resources during elaborative encoding (selective attention) and monitoring of resources during high-effort encoding (recall insertion scores). All subgroups of LD subjects were inferior to nondisabled readers in accessing structural resources on demanding tasks. Individual differences in recall were related to: (a) sufficient amount of structural resources for task demands (e.g., word knowledge), (b) sufficient momentary supply of central processing capacity, and (c) sufficient "allocation policy" (e.g., selective attention) of limited resources.

LANGUAGE. The role of oral language deficits in reading and learning disabilities has been recognized since the onset of the field, and each proposed definition has acknowledged this emphasis. In fact, the 1969 definition explicitly describes learning disabilities as a language disorder. Ironically, this definition was in some ways before its time, in that it was formulated in the absence of a research literature that could explicate the nature of the relations between oral language and learning difficulties.

However, the rapid expansion of research on oral language development with LD students during the last 20 years provides much support to the fact that the 1969 definition's emphasis on oral language disorders was not misplaced. A sizeable body of research now indicates that, as a group, LD children are less skilled than normal achievers on a wide variety of phonological, semantic, syntactic, and communicative tasks (see Donahue, 1987, for a review). Furthermore, efforts to delineate subgroups of LD children have found that the largest single subgroup can be characterized as language-impaired and usually constitutes over half of the LD sample (e.g., Feagans & Appelbaum, 1986; Lyon & Watson, 1981; Satz & Morris, 1980).

For example, there is accumulating evidence that LD students have basic deficits in effective processing of the phonological structure of spoken language, as manifested by difficulty in encoding phonological information in working memory, speech sound production, and speech sound segmentation (see Catts, 1989, for a review). It has been argued that these phonological processing deficits are primarily responsible for LD students' well-documented problems in vocabulary knowledge and rapid word retrieval, as well as the comprehension and production of syntactic and morphological structures (e.g., Mann, Cowin, & Schoenheimer, 1989).

Equally important to those of us concerned about instructional and curricular design, language researchers have begun the task of identifying which aspects of oral language development are related to specific academic and social skills. For example, there is now compelling evidence of a causal link between phonological processing skills (especially speech sound segmentation) and reading ability in word recognition as well as reading comprehension (e.g., Ball & Blach-

man, 1990; Bradley & Bryant, 1985; Stanovich, 1988; Wagner & Torgesen, 1987). Similarly, difficulty in rapid word retrieval is predictive of later decoding and comprehension problems in reading (e.g., Wolf & Obregon, 1989). Furthermore, LD children's ability to re-tell a story in first grade was found, not only to be related to reading comprehension three years later, but to be a much better predictor than IQ (Feagans & Short, 1984).

It seems reasonable to hypothesize that these oral language deficits also influence the ability of children with LD to form satisfying social relationships. Although no research studies directly test this hypothesis, there is now available a body of literature reflecting the conceptual shift from a dominant focus on syntactic and semantic growth to a broader consideration of how children learn to communicate effectively with others. For example, children with LD have been found to be less skilled than nondisabled children in adapting messages and narratives to their listeners' perspective, in conveying referential information and repairing communicative breakdowns, and in engaging in conversational turn-taking. At this point, the interactions among LD children's syntactic-semantic problems, social-cognitive deficits, and self-perceptions, and their cumulative impact on communicative performance remain unspecified (Donahue, 1987). However, it seems likely that identifying where and how linguistic, social, and communicative domains intersect is critical to understanding how to enable children with LD to make social and academic progress in mainstream classrooms.

SUMMARY. The results of the research on attention, memory, and language are important for several reasons. First, there is now strong evidence that children exhibiting inappropriate behaviors (i.e., children in kindergarten and first grade who are described by teachers as lacking attention and not being task-oriented) are very likely to experience increasing problems in behavior and academic achievement. Second, teachers do not refer children simply on the basis of poor reading achievement, rather they are responding to a group of behaviors called lack of attention for want of a better term. The research on memory and information processing show that although children can be subcategorized there are generic problems across subcategories such as speed of recoding and elaborative encoding that have direct bearing on academic achievement. Finally, the frequency and variety of LD children's oral language difficulties and the degree to which they are implicated in academic and social development suggests that more careful assessment is needed. Clearly, a consideration of language domains must be included in the design of effective interventions.

Social Problems

There is an abundance of evidence indicating that persons with learning disabilities are at-risk for problems in the social domain. There is considerable evidence that peers, teachers and parents rate children with LD as less socially skilled than nondisabled children (Gresham & Elliott, 1984). This research does not tell why students with learning disabilities are less likely to be accepted than their peers; nor does it tell whether there is a relationship between LD students' academic achievement and social status or between their perceived social needs, social status, and academic achievement. Nonetheless, because the importance of peer relationships in social and intellectual domains has been well documented (Asher, 1983), there is sufficient reason for parents and professionals to include social problems as a characteristic of learning disabilities in recent definitions.

Various aspects of LD persons' social problems have been studied. These include problems related to beliefs about the self (i.e., self-concept, self-esteem, self-efficacy) and problems related to getting along with others. Feelings and beliefs about the self are important because they mediate the decisions we make for ourselves in cognitive, social, and emotional domains. That is, children's responsiveness to instruction, their willingness to persevere when learning becomes difficult, and their responses to failure have been found to be related to these beliefs. There is abundant evidence that persons with LD are more likely to develop maladaptive notions about themselves. Although low self-concepts may be associated with specific academic content areas, these feelings become more broadly defined and the less frequent experiences of success do not easily alter these beliefs.

In addition to problems in acquiring adaptive self beliefs, students with LD are at-risk for problems in their social relationships. Problems in the social interactive domain may reflect the learning disability itself (e.g., a language deficit) or may result from social experiences (e.g., being socially isolated or rejected). We suggest that although interpersonal social problems can manifest themselves in various ways, the basic core of the problem has to do with social problem solving or social cognition; i.e., the cognitive behavioral process by which the individual discovers or identifies the most effective means for coping with problematic situations that are encountered in daily living (D'Zurilla & Nezu, 1980).

Social cognition has been assessed using several methodologies, and the results of the research have consistently found that students with LD are likely to perform more poorly than their nondisabled classmates. For instance, Stone and LaGreca (1984) found judges gave lower global ratings of social competence to students with LD than comparison students on a role playing measure of making friends in a new school. Schumaker, Hazel, Sherman, and Sheldon (1982) found high school students with LD to be less skilled than classmates on social problem solving skills needed in work-related situations. Weiss (1984) found that when presented with televised scenarios of children's play behaviors, students with LD were more likely to interpret ambiguous behaviors as having hostile meanings. In a role-play study of strategies that adolescents use to resist peer pressure to engage in illegal acts, Pearl, Bryan, and Herzog (in press) found junior high and secondary students with LD to differ from their nondisabled classmates in their expectations for how peers might exert pressure to participate, in their explanations for why individuals would refuse to participate, and in the anticipated affect of how participants might feel. In sum, there is accumulating evidence that students with LD differ from nondisabled students in their social cognitive performance. It is striking that many of these studies have been conducted with adolescents with LD, thus demonstrating the continuation of social cognitive differences into adolescence.

Academic Deficits

As problems in reading, mathematics, or writing are likely to be evident in most children identified as LD, we turn our attention to these three academic areas and present a brief overview of characteristics that are frequently observed in children with LD.

READING. The problems of a large portion of children who have been identified as LD can be traced to their difficulty in learning how to read. Reading requires the development and integration of the complex processes involved in word recognition and comprehension. Considering the complexity of the reading task, it is not surprising that learning to read becomes a challenge for many LD students.

Based on what we know about LD students' psychological processing deficits, it is understandable that the primary reason for referral for special education services is deficient reading. Less-skilled readers and children with LD exhibit breakdowns in linguistic awareness at the phonemic level (Catts, 1989) and in retrieving names with speed and accuracy (Denckla & Rudel, 1976; Wiig, Semel, & Nystrom, 1982). However, less-skilled readers are able to use context cues as efficiently as skilled readers if their word recognition is at a comparable level of accuracy and speed (Stanovich, Cunningham, & Feeman, 1984). Consistent with previously cited research, students with LD demonstrate deficient metacognitive and linguistic abilities that are necessary for efficient reading comprehension. For example, it has been documented that these students tend to approach text in a relatively passive manner; i.e., they do not monitor the extent to which they are acquiring meaning from the text which they are reading (Stanovich, 1986).

MATHEMATICS. Even though deficiencies in reading are more likely to be noticed than deficiencies in math, McLeod and Armstrong (1982) found that many LD students have significant discrepancies in math and one-fourth of LD students are identified because of their primary disability in math. Because the acquisition of quantitative concepts, and their application, figure prominently in the school curriculum, this presents still another problem for the student with LD.

Even though systematic description and analysis of LD students' math skills is remarkably limited, increasingly, data are accumulating that suggest some children with LD exhibit breakdowns in their ability to acquire and process information related to quantitative concepts and relations. For example, Russell and Ginsburg (1984) have documented LD children's deficits in knowledge of basic facts. Pellegrino and Goldman (1987) suggest that many children experience difficulty in comprehending and executing complex procedures such as multicolumn addition and subtraction. Furthermore, less-than-expert performance is generally characterized as slow and prone to error.

WRITING. Although the area of writing has not received major attention until recent years, it has been evident for quite some time that students with LD are deficient in composition skills when compared to their normally achieving peers. Until recently, the emphasis of research was primarily on comparing the written products on such measures as spelling, punctuation, vocabulary, and thematic maturity (Poteet, 1978; Poplin, Gray, Larsen, Banikowski, & Mehring, 1980; Moran, 1981). Current writing research is focused on the process of composing, and LD students have been found to be deficient in areas such as idea generation, text organization, and monitoring of the writing process (the metacognitive knowledge). Writing involves planning (idea generation, goal setting, organizing), drafting (transcribing, utilizing appropriate spelling, punctuation, spacing, etc.), and editing (revising for coherence, compliance with original goals, checking on needs of the reader, etc.). All of these subprocesses need to occur, not in progression, but simultaneously. Thus, what Flower and Hayes (1980) have described as a "juggling of constraints" which occur within the limits of the individual's short-term memory is particularly difficult for the LD student.

Novice writers and students with LD demonstrate difficulties in areas such as idea generation, text structure, and metacognitive control of the writing process. Researchers have observed that they tend to write in an associative fashion, reflecting generation of ideas as

they write (Scardamalia & Bereiter, 1986; Thomas, Englert, & Gregg, 1987). Thus, though each sentence may be related to the previous one, their writing may reflect production with no overall goals of the topic or the order of the whole text, often resulting in incoherent text. Students with LD have also been noted to have difficulties related to text structure. That is, in addition to having difficulty categorizing ideas into sets of related ideas (Englert, Raphael, & Anderson, 1986) they differ from normally achieving students in their ability to produce text that conforms to the conventional text structures such as inclusion of setting, problem, and outcome (e.g., Nodine, Barenbaum, & Newcomer, 1985). Finally, LD students demonstrate less ability to monitor the writing subprocesses involved in the pre-writing, transcribing, and editing components of producing text and tend to be more dependent on external control such as teachers (Englert et al., 1986) and peers (Lopez-Reyna, 1989).

SUMMARY. In this section we have briefly summarized three of the major academic deficits of children with LD. We have shown that children demonstrate learning difficulties at every stage of acquisition of basic academic skills. Space prohibits a more extensive description of these academic problems, but it should be noted that problems in psychological processing (attention, memory, language) and basic academic skills (reading, writing, arithmetic) are likely to spill over into academic content areas (e.g., science, social studies).

IMPLICATIONS FOR THE DESIGN OF EDUCATIONAL PROGRAMS

Thus far we have summarized the extant data base that describes children with LD. The various components of the LD definition were used to guide our selection of topics: central nervous system dysfunctioning, psychological processing deficits, social problems, and academic difficulties. The description of LD students provided by this summary is useful in considering the type of educational program that is necessary to accommodate the LD student's emotional, social, and academic needs.

In the remainder of this chapter, we identify what we consider to be critical aspects of an educational program for LD students based on the research describing the characteristics of this population. We believe that conceptualizing the structure and design of educational programs based on children's characteristics must take into account the demands of the general education curriculum, the demands of the typical classroom environment, as well as the expectations of parents and others interested in the education of children. Considering the complexity of the task and the degree to which educating children with LD represents a challenge to both special and general educators, we think that contemplating the nature of educational programs based on the available research is a good place to begin.

Our discussion is organized around three aspects of program design common to practitioners: assessment, curriculum content, and instruction. Moreover, the discussion is nested in a continual consideration of the emotional, social, and academic needs of children with learning disabilities.

Assessment

We have conceptualized and defined learning disabilities as a processing dysfunction. Data indicate that children with LD have information processing deficits, yet we have no adequate measures of such processes. It is clear that educational programs for these students must include procedures that inform educators of the approach the student uses when confronted with a learning task. Such infor-

mation would be useful, particularly in making decisions about curriculum content and instructional approach. Of course, assessment procedures must continue to measure the extent to which a student attains a particular body of knowledge as well as the acquisition of specific skills. Currently, we have many static measures of intelligence and achievement that provide information along these domains. But, evaluative procedures that assess the degree to which the student has attained knowledge of a particular strategy or set of strategies and can monitor the use of such techniques are also needed.

Curriculum-based assessment (CBA) is a new term for an old method, defined simply as "A procedure for determining the instructional needs of a student based upon the student's ongoing performance within existing course content" (Gickling & Havertape, 1981). Suggesting that children often develop inappropriate behaviors in response to their academic frustrations and that these lead to referral for special education services, Tucker (1985) offers CBA as the key to determining appropriate levels and types of instruction.

Unlike standardized test scores that do not provide information that links directly to instruction, CBA data are collected directly from the students' performance within their existing course content. Because assessment is ongoing, data can be used to make decisions about levels of instruction and about the appropriateness of particular types of instruction. CBA incorporates a variety of informal assessment procedures such as classroom quizzes, informal inventories, and observation for the collection of progress data as well as the use of diagnostic probes to measure the appropriateness of a particular instructional strategy. The latter are typically one-time measures, but the former are collected frequently. The usefulness of CBA for monitoring student progress and for modifying instruction based on student performance has been well documented (e.g., Deno & Fuchs, 1988; Fuchs, 1986; Fuchs, Deno, & Mirkin, 1984).

Dynamic assessment is used to obtain a clearer understanding of the operation of basic psychological *processes* involved in problem solving in contrast to standardized tests that provide a static measure of the *product,* i.e., the answer (Campione & Brown, 1985). Dynamic assessment is based on the notion that some children may not have acquired information or skills being assessed, but may be able to do so readily if given the opportunity or with minimal prompting. In dynamic assessment the child is tested with a series of graded prompts to establish how much and what type of instruction the child needs to obtain a specified goal. In one approach to dynamic assessment, the examiner begins with global hints on how to solve a problem and adds more specific clues if the child is unsuccessful. The sequence of hints initially provides tangentially related or orienting information, leaving unstated several components of an efficient problem solving strategy that are systematically added in later prompts. Another approach involves administering tests according to standard procedures but upon completion, providing direct instruction in methods of solving the problems, and then re-testing to assess the child's ability to apply newly learned strategies. Still another approach involves a combination of error analysis and children's verbalizations (in response to instructions to "think aloud") by which the examiner attempts to evaluate directly a set of target processes. Dynamic assessment is based on the idea that assessment results need to be updated continuously as the student begins to acquire skills within a domain and the evaluator refines the diagnosis to reflect the most current information of the individual child's competence.

Given the myriad learning profiles exhibited by children with LD, the use of dynamic assessment holds great promise. As interest grows, methods may be developed to assess a student's performance at various stages of knowledge acquisition across curricular domains, providing critical information for tailoring instructional interventions.

Curriculum Content

The research summarized thus far suggests several directions for curriculum content, or *what* LD children should learn in school. In addition to the traditional areas of study, we think that children with learning disabilities must receive instruction in two other critical areas.

As presented previously, empirical evidence indicates that children with LD exhibit specific breakdowns in their ability to process information, and suggests that they have not learned how to learn. Currently, a great deal of attention is being directed to teaching students with LD to be more strategic in their learning by teaching them specific strategies that makes them more active participants in the learning process.

An example of this approach, Reciprocal Teaching, developed by Palincsar and Brown (1984) has attracted much attention. In this method, the goal is to improve students' reading comprehension by making students actively engaged in the learning process and by instructing them in specific strategies that they can use to comprehend the text material. Initially, teacher and students work together with the teacher doing most of the work. The teacher and students take turns leading a dialogue about the text, generating summaries and making predictions, and clarifying misleading or complex sections of the text. The teacher first models the key strategies of summarizing (reviewing a passage orally), questioning (making up questions about the main idea), clarifying, and predicting. Following this phase, the teacher encourages the children to lead the dialogue and gives the students guidance and feedback on their performances.

The effectiveness of incorporating instruction in specific reading comprehension strategies was compared to that of a teaching method in which the children were taught how to answer implicit and explicit questions by referring to the text (Palincsar & Brown, 1984). The evaluation of the reciprocal teaching and information-location approach was based on daily tests in which students answered questions after reading a new passage. Reciprocal teaching led to dramatic improvement, with five of six students soon performing at levels equivalent to those of normal seventh-graders. Retesting eight weeks later found that students in the reciprocal teaching group were still performing significantly better than they had prior to the training.

Another example of strategy instruction is directed toward the needs of adolescents with LD. Based on the notion that students can be taught learning strategies, a group of researchers has designed the Learning Strategies Curriculum. Rather than teaching students specific curriculum content, the learning strategies are techniques, principles, or rules that enable a student to learn, to solve problems, and to complete tasks independently in academic as well as in non-academic settings (Deshler & Schumaker, 1984). Divided into three strands, the strategies help students to acquire information from written materials, identify and store important information, and express themselves through writing. The method of teaching these strategies consists of several steps including pretesting, presentating and modeling the strategy, involving the student in practice with corrective feedback, and guiding the student through a series of generalization steps (Deshler & Schumaker, 1986). Based on several years of multiple-baseline design studies, it appears that these strategies are quite effective in teaching the use of learning strategies to handicapped adolescents (Clark, Deshler, Schumaker, & Alley,

1984; Schumaker, Deshler, Alley, & Warner, 1983).

Strategy instruction is an important curricular area for this population of children. As students with LD acquire a repertoire of strategies, they gain control over their ability to approach a learning task. Through the acquisition of strategies, the effect of information processing deficits seems to be minimized.

A second curricular area crucial to the education of children with LD focuses on increased awareness and understanding of social situations, plus the behaviors needed to interact effectively with peers and adults. Again, based on the evidence pertaining to LD children's and adolescents' social problems, it appears that a significant aspect of any educational program designed for LD children should include the identification and understanding of social dilemmas and the knowledge of behaviors needed to respond appropriately in these situations. This is an area that is quite new to the field of learning disabilities; hence, there are few studies that provide evidence of its utility.

One approach is to use cooperative goal structures to organize classroom instruction (see the chapter by Slavin and Stevens in this volume). A second approach is to integrate social problem solving skills into the reading curriculum. Williams and Ellsworth (1990) developed and tested an instructional program designed to teach adolescents with LD to make better personal decisions. The program, tested in resource rooms, presents students with schema-general questions for problem solving coupled with practice in generating problem-specific questions to reach appropriate decisions. Williams and Ellsworth presented problems in short narratives based on problems students must solve in their own lives and helped them to apply a schema to reach decisions.

Finally, pioneering work was done by Hazel, Schumaker, and Sheldon-Wildgen

(1982) in their efforts to help youth with LD. Hazel et al. provided a training program for delinquent, LD, and nondisabled adolescents in which participants enacted various scenarios involving important social skills such as resisting peer pressure and negotiating conflict. The researchers reported that all groups showed improvement. Unfortunately, no control or comparison group was employed. Nonetheless, this study has served to stimulate others who are concerned with developing social skills programs for students with LD.

Expanding the traditional curriculum to include knowledge of strategies and social functioning are two critical aspects of designing educational programs for LD students. In addition, the manner in which students are taught must be considered in relation to the characteristics of the students. Instruction on *how* the students should be taught is presented next.

Instruction

As discussed previously, LD children's beliefs about the causes of their successes and failures are critical to the manner in which they approach a learning task. There is compelling evidence to show the benefits of integrating into instructional strategies our knowledge of children's beliefs (Borkowski, Weyhing, & Carr, 1988). First, as discussed earlier, we know that children with LD often report that they lack ability. To encourage children to believe they are smart, Dweck (1986) has suggested we change our (and teachers') notions about the nature of intelligence from a static characteristic that cannot change to a dynamic characteristic that does change. The message to be communicated to children is that the more you learn, the smarter you get, regardless of how long it takes or how hard you have to work. Children are more likely to persevere when dynamic rather than static expectations are built into instruction. Our suggestion is that teachers

create environments wherein children believe that intelligence is a dynamic characteristic, that they get smarter as they learn new information. But how do teachers create such an environment? We think this can be accomplished in several ways.

First, in the process of instructing students with LD, teachers must provide continual corrective feedback. Corrective feedback differs from positive and negative feedback in that it does more than indicate whether a response is accurate, it expands on the student's response and provides guidance for acquiring additional knowledge and specific skills. It also communicates to children teachers' expectations that they can and will succeed. Studies with low-achieving populations, indicate the usefulness of corrective feedback in teaching basic skills in reading and math (Rosenshine & Stevens, 1986). However being corrective is not enough. In addition, the feedback needs to be subtle and not focused on comparisons with other children in the classroom. Although social comparisons take place all the time, and everywhere, teachers can minimize social comparisons by noting the ways in which the following occur: grouping of children for instruction, communicating of children's grades, and asking of questions (Good, Grouws, & Edmeier, 1983).

In addition to being constructive and subtle, the feedback given to students needs to encourage adaptive attributions by linking a positive statement about one's performance with a specific learning strategy. Borkowski et al. (1988) demonstrated the power of this approach in research that tested the impact of attribution training and strategy training on children's reading comprehension. In the attribution training conditions children were taught to respond to failure by saying, "I need to try and use the strategy" and to respond to success by saying, "I tried hard, used the strategy, and did well." The notion is that even though children come to a task with long-standing maladaptive attributions, these attributions can be changed if they acquire new skills and if the new skill acquisition is accompanied by adaptive interpretations of this learning. Students who received attribution training plus strategy training in this study showed about a 50% improvement in summarizing paragraphs compared to a 15% improvement shown by children who received only strategy training.

Finally, we think that it is critical that teachers model adaptive attributions in the classroom. As simple and straightforward as such statements might seem to be, it is important to recognize that teachers do not use adaptive attribution statements in the normal course of instruction. In a recent study, teachers were presented rationales and models for making such statements to students considered at-risk or LD (Bryan & Bryan, personal communication, October 15, 1989). The presentation of a videotaped model of these behaviors however, did not induce teachers to make such statements in their responses to children; indeed, a classroom observational posttest found teachers did not make a single attributional statement. Why teachers did not adopt the strategy and how we can encourage them to do so remain to be determined.

CONCLUSION

There is a new theory in science called "chaos" which is based on the notion that chaos in nature is normal, and the absence of chaos signals pathology. An example of this theory is brain waves which are normal when they appear chaotic but pathological when flat or regular. If chaos is normal, then the field of learning disabilities is normal. In the 20 years since the term learning disabilities came into common use, the field has been in a constant state of tumult and change. For most of the twenty years the major source of chaos was the definition of learning disabilities. The dispute over the definition, however, seems to have been set aside recently, and there seems to be considerable public consensus about the definition, at least in terms of how to diagnose the presence of LD. The major source of contention today revolves around issues of service delivery: how best to educate students with learning disabilities.

Our knowledge of the characteristics of children with LD leads to several specific suggestions for service delivery, that is, for the structure and content of educational programs that will meet the needs of these students. Broadly speaking, our ideas suggest changes in assessment and evaluative procedures, curricular content, teachers' beliefs (in particular, beliefs about intelligence), and teachers' behaviors. Clearly, our suggestions are not meant to be exhaustive; the data describing children with LD suggest many other features that should be considered when designing programs for this group of students.

What does seem clear to us is that such changes will not be accomplished easily. Such techniques as using pull-out programs that provide specialized instruction, reducing the teacher-pupil ratio so children can receive more individualized attention, modifying the general education curriculum, and combinations of these, probably will not suffice. Nor will such changes be accomplished if the focus is solely on changing teachers' attitudes and educating them in the processes necessary for collaborative consultation. Rather, such changes require a reconceptualization of the structure and content of educational programs for children with LD. We believe that *this* is the challenge to the educational community. We recognize that embedded in the notion of reconceptualization are issues such as: Who will educate these children and, to what extent will they be educated with nonhandicapped youngsters? These issues, however, are peripheral to the task. What is central is a careful consideration of program content, structure, and method of instruction. And, such considerations must attend to the academic, social, and emotional growth of the children.

Considering the complexity of the task, it makes sense that all professionals be involved: those who have expertise in classroom organization, management, and instruction; those who understand the unique needs of children with LD; those who possess knowledge about curriculum content and how to assess the degree to which children have attained that content; and, of course, those who have knowledge about children's emotional and social growth and development. Through a team effort, we hope to maximize the likelihood that students with learning disabilities can emerge from their school experiences with the knowledge and skills necessary to live independently, with positive feelings about themselves, and with optimistic views about their abilities to do well in adult endeavors.

REFERENCES

Anderson, R. P., Halcomb, C. G., & Doyle, R. B. (1973). The measurement of attentional deficits. *Exceptional Children, 39*, 534-539.

Asher, S. R. (1983). Social competence and peer status: Recent advances and future directions. *Child Development, 54*, 1427-1434.

Ball, E. W., & Blachman, V. (1990). *Does phoneme awareness training in kindergarten make a difference?* Manuscript submitted for publication.

Bauer, R. H. (1987). Control processes as a way of understanding, diagnosing, and remediating learning disabilities. *Advances in Learning and Behavioral Disabilities*, Suppl. 2, 41-81.

Bay, M., & Bryan, T. (1990). *Differentiating groups of students on critical classroom factors as a means for advancing our understanding of the referral decision.* Manuscript submitted for publication.

Borkowski, J. G., Weyhing, R. S., & Carr, M. (1988). Effects of attributional retraining on strategy-based reading comprehension in learning-disabled students. *Journal of Educational Psychology, 80*, 46-53.

Bradley, H., & Bryant, P. (1985). *Rhyme and reason in reading and spelling.* Ann Arbor: University of Michigan Press.

Bryan, T., Bay, M., Shelden, C., & Simon, J. (1990). Teachers' and at-risk students' stimulated recall of instruction. *Exceptionality, 1*, 167-179.

Campione, J. C., & Brown, A. L. (1985). *Dynamic assessment: One approach and some initial data.* Preparation of this manuscript and the research reported therein were supported by Grants HD-05951, HD--6864, and HD-15808 from the National Institute of Child Health and Human Development.

Catts, H. (1989). Phonological processing deficits and reading disabilities. In A. Kamhi & H. Catts (Eds.), *Reading disabilities: A developmental language perspective* (pp. 101-132). San Diego, CA: College Hill Press.

Clark, F. L., Deshler, D. D., Schumaker, J. B., & Alley, G. R. (1984). Visual imagery and self-questioning: Strategies to improve comprehension of written materials. *Journal of Learning Disabilities, 17*, 145-149.

Cooper, D. H., & Farran, D. C. (1988). Behavioral risk factors in kindergarten. *Early Childhood Quarterly, 3*, 1-19.

Cooper, D. H., & Speece, D. L. (1987, August). *A novel methodology for the study of children at risk for school failure.* Paper presented at the American Educational Research Association Conference, Washington, D.C.

Denckla, M., & Rudel, R. (1976). Rapid automatized naming (RAN): Dyslexia differentiated from other learning disabilities. *Neuropsychologia, 14*, 471-478.

Deno, S. L., & Fuchs, L. S. (1988). Developing curriculum-based measurement systems for data-based special education problem solving. In E. L. Meyen, G. A. Vergason, & R. J. Whelan (Eds.), *Effective instructional strategies for exceptional children* (pp. 481-504). Denver: Love.

Deshler, D. D., & Schumaker, J. B. (1984). *Strategies instruction: A new way to teach.* Salt Lake City: Worldwide Media, Inc.

Deshler, D. D., & Schumaker, J. B. (1986). Learning strategies: An instructional alternative for low achieving adolescents. *Exceptional Children, 52*, 583-589.

Donahue, M. (1987). Interactions between linguistic and pragmatic development in learning disabled children: Three views of the state of the union. In S. Rosenberg (Ed.), *Advances in applied psycholinguistics*(Vol. 1, pp. 126-179). Cambridge: Cambridge University Press.

Doyle, R. B., Anderson, R. P., & Holcomb, C. G. (1976). WISC and WISC-R profiles of learning disabled children: A review. *Learning Disability Quarterly,9,* 48-54.

Dweck, C. S. (1986). Motivational processes affecting learning. *American Psychologist,41,* 1040-1048.

Dykman, R. A., Ackerman, P. T., Holcomb, M. A., & Boudreau, B. A. (1983). Physiological manifestations of learning disability. *Journal of Learning Disabilities,16,* 46-53.

D'Zurilla, T. J., & Nezu, A. (1980). A study of the generation-of-alternatives process in social problem solving. *Cognitive Therapy Research, 4,* 67-72.

Elementary and Secondary Education Amendments. (1970, April). U.S.C., PL 91-230, Sec. 2, 84 Stat.121.

Englert, C. S., Raphael, T. E., & Anderson, L. M. (1986, October). *Metacognitive knowledge and writing skills of upper elementary and students with special needs: Extensions of text structure research.* Paper presented at the National Reading Conference, Austin, Texas.

Feagans, L., & Appelbaum, M. (1986). Validation of language subtypes in learning disabled children. *Journal of Educational Psychology, 78,* 358-364.

Feagans, L., & Short, E. (1984). Developmental differences in the comprehension of narratives by reading disabled and normally achieving children. *Child Development, 55,* 1727-1736.

Flower, L., & Hayes, J. R. (1980). The dynamics of composing: Making plans and juggling constraints. In L. W. Gregg & E. R. Steinberg (Eds.), *Cognitive processes in writing* (pp. 31-50). Hillsdale, NJ: Erlbaum.

Fuchs, L. S. (1986). Monitoring progress among mildly handicapped pupils: Review of current practice and research. *Remedial and Special Education, 7*(5), 5-12.

Fuchs, L. S., Deno, S. L., & Mirkin, P. K. (1984). The effects of frequent curriculum-based measurement and evaluation on pedagogy, student achievement, and student awareness of learning. *American Educational Research Journal, 21*, 449-460.

Gickling, E. E., & Havertape, J. (1981). Curriculum-based assessment. In J. A. Tucker (Ed.), *Non-test-based assessment: A training module* (pp. CBAU1-CBAU3). Minneapolis: National School of Psychology Inservice Training Network, University of Minnesota.

Good, T. L., Grouws, D. A., & Edmeier, H. (1983). *Active mathematics teaching.* New York: Longman.

Gresham, F. M., & Elliott, S. N. (1984). Assessment and classification of children's social skills: A review of methods and issues. *School Psychology Review, 13,* 292-301.

Hallahan, D. R., & Reeve, R. E. (1980). Selective attention and distractibility. In B. K. Keogh (Ed.), *Advances in special education* (Vol. 1, pp. 141-181). Greenwich, CN: JAI Press.

Hazel, J. S., Schumaker, J. B., & Sheldon-Wildgen, J. (1982). Application of a group training program in social skills and problem solving skills to learning disabled and non-learning disabled youth. *Learning Disability Quarterly,5,* 398-408.

Hynd, G. W., & Semrud-Clikeman, M. (1989). Dyslexia and brain morphology. *Psychological Bulletin, 106,* 447-482.

Jorm, A., & Share, D. (1983). Phonological recoding and reading acquisition. *Applied Psycholinguistics,4,* 103-147.

Kavanagh, J. F., & Truss, T. J. (1988). *Learning disabilities: Proceedings of a national conference* (pp. 345-354). Parkton, MD: York Press.

Keogh, B. K., & Margolis, J. (1976). Learn to labor and to wait: Attentional problems of children with learning disorders. *Journal of Learning Disabilities,9,* 276-286.

Loper, A. B., Hallahan, D. P., & Ianna, S. O. (1982). Meta-attention in learning disabled and normal children. *Learning Disability Quarterly, 5,* 29-36.

Lopez-Reyna, N. (1989). *Comparison of writing instructional approaches on microcomputer-based collaborative writing by learning disabled, linguistic minority and non-minority junior high school students.* Unpublished doctoral dissertation, University of California, Santa Barbara.

Lyon, R. & Watson, B. (1981). Empirically derived subgroups of learning disabled readers: Diagnostic characteristics. *Journal of Learning Disabilities, 14,* 256-261.

Mann, V., Cowin, E., & Schoenheimer, J. (1989). Phonological processing language comprehension and reading ability. *Journal of Learning Disabilities, 22,* 76-89.

McKinney, J. D., McClure, S., & Feagans, L. (1982). Classroom behavior of learning disabled children. *Learning Disability Quarterly, 5,* 45-52.

McKinney, J. D., & Speece, D. L. (1986). Academic consequences and longitudinal stability of behavioral subtypes of learning disabled children. *Journal of Educational Psychology, 78,* 365-372.

McLeod, T. M., & Armstrong, S. W. (1982). Learning disabilities in mathematics-skill deficits and remedial approaches at the intermediate and secondary level. *Learning Disability Quarterly, 5,* 305-311.

Meyers, P. I., & Hammill, D. D. (1982). *Learning disabilities.* Austin, Tex: Pro-Ed.

Moran, M. R. (1981). Performance of learning disabled and low achieving secondary students on formal features of a paragraph-writing task. *Learning Disability Quarterly, 4,* 271-280.

National Joint Committee for Learning Disabilities (NJCLD), (1981). *Issues on definition.* Towson, MD: The Orton Dyslexia Society.

Nodine, B. F., Barenbaum, E., & Newcomber, P. (1985). Story composition by learning disabled, reading disabled, and normal children. *Learning Disability Quarterly, 8,* 167-181.

Palinscar, A. M. S., & Brown, A. L. (1984). Reciprocal teaching of comprehension-fostering and monitoring activities. *Cognition and Instruction, 1,* 117-175.

Pearl, R., Bryan, T., & Herzog, A. (in press). Resisting or acquiescing to peer pressure to engage in misconduct: Adolescents expectations of probable consequence. *Journal of Youth and Adolescence.*

Pellegrino, J. W., & Goldman, S. R. (1987). Information processing and elementary mathematics. *Journal of Learning Disabilities, 20,* 23-32.

Poplin, M. S., Gray, R., Larsen, S., Banikowski, A., & Mehring, T. (1980). A comparison of components of written expression abilities in learning disabled and non-learning disabled students at three grade levels. *Learning Disability Quarterly, 3*(4), 46-53.

Poteet, J. A. (1978). *Characteristics of written expression of learning disabled and non-learning disabled elementary school students* (ERIC Document ED 159-830). Muncie, IN: Ball State University.

Richey, D. D., & McKinney, J. D. (1978). Classroom behavioral styles of learning disabled children. *Journal of Learning Disabilities, 11,* 297-302

Rosenshine, B., & Stevens, R. (1986). Teaching functions. In M. Wittrock (Ed.), *Handbook of research on teaching* (3rd ed, pp. 376-391). New York: MacMillan.

Russell, R. L., & Ginsburg, H. P. (1984). Cognitive analysis of children's mathematical difficulties. *Cognition and Instruction, 1,* 217-244.

Samuels, S. J., & Miller, N. L. (1985). Failure to find attention differences between learning disabled and normal children on classroom and laboratory tasks. *Exceptional Children, 51,* 358-375.

Satz, P., & Morris, R. (1980). Learning disability subtypes: A review. In F. Pirozzolo & M. Wittrock (Eds.), *Neuropsychological and cognitive processes in reading* (pp. 109-141). New York: Academic Press.

Scardamalia, M., & Bereiter, C. (1986). Research on written composition. In M. C. Wittrock (Ed.), *Handbook of research on teaching* (pp. 778-803). New York: MacMillan.

Schumaker, J. B., Deshler, D. D., Alley, G. R., & Warner, M. M. (1983). Toward the development of an intervention model for learning disabled adolescents. *Exceptional Education Quarterly, 3*(4), 45-50.

Schumaker, J., Hazel, J. S., Sherman, J. A., & Sheldon, M. (1982). Social skill performances of learning disabled, non-learning disabled, and delinquent adolescents. *Learning Disability Quarterly, 5,* 388-397.

Special Education Today. (1985). 2, 1.

Stanovich, K. (1986). Cognitive processes and the reading problems of learning-disabled children: Evaluating the assumption of specificity. In F. Torgesen & B. Wong (Ed.), *Psychological and educational perspectives on learning disabilities* (pp. 87-131). New York: Academic Press.

Stanovich, K. E. (1988). Explaining the differences between the dyslexic and the garden-variety poor reader: The phonological-core variable-difference model. *Journal of Learning Disabilities, 21,* 590-604.

Stanovich, K., Cunningham, A., & Feeman, D. (1984). The relationship between early reading acquisition and word decoding with and without context: A longitudinal study of first-grade children. *Journal of Educational Psychology, 76,* 668-677.

Stone, W. L., & LaGreca, A. M. (1984). Comprehension of nonverbal communication: A reexamination of the social competencies of learning-disabled children. *Journal of Abnormal Child Psychology, 12,* 505-518.

Swanson, H. L. (1988). Memory subtypes in learning disabled readers. *Learning Disability Quarterly, 11,* 342-357.

Thomas, C. C., Englert, C. S., & Gregg, S. (1987). An analysis of errors and strategies in the expository writing of learning disabled students. *Remedial and Special Education, 8,* 21-30.

Torgesen, J., & Houck, G. (1980). Processing deficiencies in learning disabled children who perform poorly on the digit span task. *Journal of Educational Psychology, 72,* 141-160.

Tucker, J. A. (1985). Curriculum-based assessments: An introduction. *Exceptional Children, 52,* 199-204.

Vellutino, F. R., Steger, J. A., DeSetto, L., & Phillips, F. (1975). Immediate and delayed recognition of visual stimuli. *Journal of Experimental Child Psychology, 19,* 223-232.

Wagner, R., & Torgesen, J. (1987). The nature of phonological processing and its causal role in the acquisition of reading skills. *Psychological Bulletin, 101,* 192-212.

Weiss, E., (1984). Learning disabled children's understanding of social interactions of peers. *Journal of Learning Disabilities, 17,* 612-615.

Wiig, E., Semel, E., & Nystrom, L. (1982). Comparison of rapid naming in language learning-disabled and academically achieving 8-year-olds. *Language, Speech, and Hearing Services in Schools, 13,* 11-23.

Williams, J. P., & Ellsworth, N. J. (1990). *Teaching learning-disabled adolescents to think critically using a problem-solving schema.* Portion of an unpublished doctoral dissertation submitted to Teachers College, Columbia University by N. J. Ellsworth, conducted under the direction of J. P. Williams, Sponsor, and Jeannette Fleischner.

Wolf, M., & Obregon, M. (April 1989). *88 children in search of a name: A 5-year investigation of rate, word retrieval, and vocabulary in reading development and dyslexia.* Paper presented at the Society for Research in Child Development Convention, Kansas City, MO.

10

SCHOOLS ARE FOR ALL KIDS: THE IMPORTANCE OF INTEGRATION FOR STUDENTS WITH SEVERE DISABILITIES AND THEIR PEERS

Martha E. Snell

University of Virginia

The statutory language of the Act, its legislative history, and the case law construing it, mandate that all handicapped children, regardless of the severity of their handicap, are entitled to a public education. The district court erred in requiring a benefit/eligibility test as a prerequisite to implicating the Act. School districts cannot avoid the provisions of the Act by returning to the practices that were widespread prior to the Act's passage, and which indeed were the impetus for the Act's passage, of unilaterally excluding certain handicapped children from a public education on the ground that they are uneducable.

The law explicitly recognizes that education for the severely handicapped is to be broadly defined, to include not only traditional academic skills, but also basic functional life skills, and that educational methodologies in these areas are not static, but are constantly evolving and improving. It is the school district's responsibility to avail itself of these new approaches in providing an education program geared to each child's needs. (*Timothy W. v. Rochester School District*, 1989, p. 50)

In November, 1989, the Supreme Court refused to reconsider New Hampshire's request that this ruling from the U. S. Court of Appeals for the First Circuit, be over turned. Their refusal without comment to reopen the *Timothy W.* case reaffirms the Education of the Handicapped Act (EHA; Education of All Handicapped Children Act of 1975) and the decision from the lower court:

- Schools cannot select which students with disabilities they will serve and which students they will not serve;

- Educational curricula for students with severe disabilities need to focus on individually determined functional skills pertinent to the person's current and future life;

- Educational methods for this group of students must reflect current best practices.

The *Timothy W.* decision is powerful and uncompromised. But the battle for the right to a public school education for **all** students was one that many thought had been won in the 1970s. Despite the outcome of *Timothy W.*, many parents and professionals were dismayed that the educability battle was reopened in 1989. Other issues such as nonaversive approaches to severe behavior problems and integrating students having severe disabilities with their peers, already occupied researchers in the field. Serious study of these issues clearly depended on accepting that all students could learn and were entitled to an individualized educational program (IEP).

This book focuses on the meaning of integration for students with disabilities. Integration is now viewed by most professionals in the field and by an increasing number of parents as an essential educational methodology which has evolved logically from earlier practices. As stated in the *Timothy W.* decision, school districts must avail themselves of these new and improved approaches. This chapter describes what integrated programs for students with severe disabilities should look like and why integration is an essential element of an appropriate program.

THE LEAST RESTRICTIVE ENVIRONMENT REQUIREMENT AND ITS IMPACT ON INTEGRATION

In the statute of PL 94-142 that sets forth the requirement for the least restrictive environment (LRE), the original value Congress placed on integration for all students becomes evident:

To the maximum extent appropriate, handicapped children, including children in public or private institutions or other care facilities, are educated with children who are not handicapped, and that special classes, separate schooling, or other removal of handicapped children from regular educational environment occurs only when the nature or severity of the handicap is such that education in the regular classes with the use of supplementary aids and services cannot be achieved satisfactorily. (20 U.S.C. 1415[5][B])

Despite the preference Congress expressed for education in the regular educational environment, the meaning of the LRE principle remains imprecise (Taylor, 1988). Originally, LRE was used by Reynolds (1962) and Deno (1970) to describe a continuum of educational placements ranging from least restrictive (more normalized, less segregated, and least intensive services) to most restrictive (less normalized, more segregated, and more intensive services). (Refer to the top half of Figure 1). Despite this broad interpretation of LRE, the field generally has endorsed the LRE principle to support placement of most students with disabilities in the most integrated or normalized setting possible (Taylor, 1988; Turnbull, 1986). However, special education typically has developed its services for students with severe disabilities to fit the LRE continuum model because federal regulations mandated that "a continuum of alternative placements [be] available to meet the needs of handicapped children for special education and related services" (Federal Register, 1977, p. 42497).

Particularly for students with severe disabilities, who typically require more services than other students with milder disabilities, this traditional definition of the LRE continuum has interfered with placement in integrated settings. Taylor (1988) describes seven pitfalls of the LRE principle:

- Restrictive environments are legitimatized;

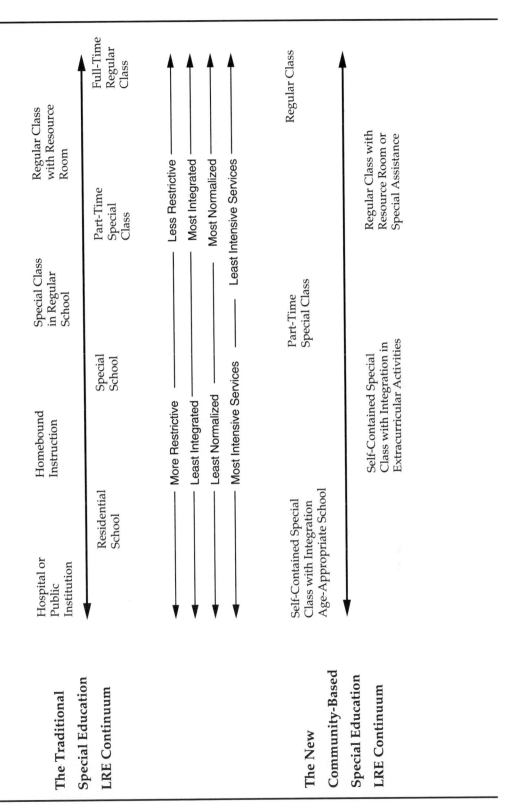

Figure 1: The traditional and new LRE continua in education. (Adapted from Taylor, 1988, pp. 43, 49 with permission.)

- Integration and segregation are confused with intensity of services;

- The LRE principle assumes pupils must be ready for less restrictive environments;

- Professional judgement determines restrictiveness of a setting and thus, placement in integrated settings is not viewed as a right that all students have;

- The LRE principle supports the restriction of an individual's basic rights to freedom and community participation;

- It assumes that people with disabilities should move to less restrictive environments as they grow and change, though this may be disruptive to the individual's stability; and

- It emphasizes locations and buildings rather than servies or specific supports that enable one to function in integrated settings.

To many it seems quite plausible that the combined influence of the LRE principle and widespread ignorance about the education of people with severe disabilities led many school divisions in the 1970s and 80s to construct separate school facilities or centers for these students (Brady, McDougall, & Dennis, 1989; Taylor, 1988). These separate school programs were often cooperative efforts between districts or regional programs developed to allow several districts to pool funds for shared separate educational programs serving low-incidence students with severe disabilities (e.g., BOCES in New York, intermediate school districts in Michigan). These students typically had one or more of the disability labels: moderate, severe, or profound mental retardation, multiple handicaps, autism, or deaf-blindness. However, a small fraction of students with severe disabilities (often students with autism) have been served in private residential programs, often outside of the state where they live, with the public school system paying the educational costs.

Data reported by Danielson and Bellamy (1989) indicate that the use of segregated facilities for educating school-aged students with any type of disability in the United States has remained fairly stable from 1976 until 1986. In the current *10th Report to Congress on the Implementation of EHA* (U.S. Department of Education, 1988), average placement statistics show that 26% of students with disabilities are placed in regular classes, 41% are served in resource rooms, 24.9% are served in separate classes within a regular education building, 3.8% are placed in separate day schools, 1.6% in private separate day school facilities, 1% in public residential facilities, 0.4% in private residential facilities, 0.3% in correctional facilities, and 0.8% in hospital or home-bound placements. Danielson and Bellamy's analysis of the same data for 1986 showed high state-to-state variability in the use of separate classes and segregated facilities which they felt suggested "that some states have been more successful than others in providing services in regular settings that were seen as appropriate by local decision makers" (p. 452) and "factors in addition to the characteristics of students are determinants of individual educational placements, and that the decision-making power vested in the IEP process has not been sufficient to overcome these factors" (p. 453).

The 1988 federal report also described placement by handicapping condition. The category of students labeled mentally retarded (mild to profound mental retardation) probably includes most students referred to as having severe disabilities. This category had the lowest national average for being placed in regular classes (3%) and in resource rooms (25%); by contrast, students with learning disabilities averaged 77% in regular classes or resource rooms! Nationally, 56% of students labeled mentally retarded are placed in separate classrooms. The statistics for students labeled as having deaf-blindness and multiple handicaps often overlaps with this group and a high percentage of these students also are placed in very restrictive settings. Lipsky and Gartner (1989) analyzed the 1987 federal data and found that placement of persons labeled as mentally retarded in regular education had the widest range of all categories across states (5% to 87% in regular classes), supporting Danielson and Bellamy's (1989) finding of high state-to-state variability. Especially concerning persons with the label of mental retardation, it appears that where one lives is a more decisive factor to the restrictiveness of the placement than is the disability itself.

In the *Tenth Annual Report to the Congress* (U.S. Department of Education, 1988), these state-by-state placement differences were discussed along with the most common noncompliance problems found in state monitoring visits. The report included some disturbing conclusions about states that were monitored: (a) "virtually every state monitored had significant problems meeting LRE requirements"; (b) states lack "procedures to ensure that the removal of handicapped children from the regular educational environment is justified"; and (c) states revealed a substantial amount of evidence as to whether "LRE is even considered before a placement is made," instead states tend to place by disability label or for "administrative convenience" rather than by following the mandate for the least restrictive environment (p. 178).

WHY IS INTEGRATION IMPORTANT FOR STUDENTS WITH SEVERE DISABILITIES, THEIR PEERS, AND OTHERS?

About 1% of the population of school students have severe disabilities and this group is estimated as comprising 10% of all students identified as needing special education in a school district (Sailor et al., 1989). Students with severe disabilities typically include school-aged persons labeled as having "severe or profound mental retardation" and who also may have sensory, movement, or emotional disabilities. The Association for Persons with Severe Handicaps (TASH) defines this group as including:

> [I]ndividuals of all ages who require extensive ongoing support in more that one major life activity in order to participate in integrated community settings and to enjoy a quality of life that is available to citizens with fewer or no disabilities. Support may be required for life activities such as mobility, communication, self-care, and learning as necessary for independent living, employment, and self-sufficiency. (TASH, 1989, p. 30)

Numerous reasons have been detailed for accepting the new, community-based version of LRE in special education (refer to the bottom half of Figure 1) and for integrating students having severe disabilities in age-appropriate schools and community settings (Hanline & Halvorsen, 1988; Lipsky & Gartner, 1989; McDonnell & Hardman, 1989; Meyer, Peck, & Brown, 1991; Sailor et al., 1989; Snell, 1988a; Snell & Eichner, 1989; Stainback, Stainback, & Forest, 1989). Probably the three most important and reciprocal benefits from integration, which also have fairly consistent support in research, are (a) the development of social skills in students with severe disabilities across all school age groups, (b) the improvements in the attitudes that nondisabled peers have for their peers with disabilities, and (c) the development of positive relationships and friendships between peers as a result of integration. Conversely, without planned, structured, and ongoing integration activities, appropriate social behavior will not be learned by students with severe disabilities nor will their nondisabled peers have positive attitudes toward them or meaningful relationships with them.

Authors often note that students with severe disabilities in integrated schools have age-appropriate role models for communication, social behavior, and dress; are more frequently motivated in learning activities when working alongside nondisabled peers; can encounter and learn to respond to realistic performance expectations present in schools and society; and have more chances to learn in natural contexts which will generalize to future integrated jobs and life in the community. Furthermore, some relationships that develop in integrated settings will continue and will serve as natural supports in and outside of school for these children and adolescents and later as adults in their jobs and in the community. For parents, educators in general, and nondisabled peers, benefits of integration that frequently are reported include: (a) improved expectations for, and attitudes toward, students with disabilities; (b) enhanced competence of parents of children with disabilities at facing parenting due to being better informed and from having a positive base of experience; (c) enriched capability of taxpayers and voters to address legislation influencing persons with disabilities in a more sensible way; and (d) an appreciation of the human diversity and individual differences in achievement that are a part of life.

INTEGRATED PROGRAMMING FOR STUDENTS WITH SEVERE DIS-ABILITIES: WHAT DOES IT MEAN?

Currently, among researchers and practitioners of integrated programs serving students with severe disabilities there is a general consensus that the concept of integrated schools is essential to an appropriate education and that the exceptions to the practice of integration are very rare (e.g., Lipsky & Gartner, 1989). Snell and Eichner (1989) discuss some of the conditions or problems that may require exclusion from integrated schooling; they emphasize that the varying competence of the receiving school cannot justify exclusion, nor can educational reasons be justified, especially in light of the *Timothy W.* decision. However, in rare cases, there may be medical or behavioral problems present in any student that require temporary exclusion from integrated schooling: (a) the presence of highly contagious diseases such as impetigo or chicken pox, (b) seriously assaultive behavior present even after program improvements are made by trained staff, and (c) students who are dependent on constant medical attention or nonportable life support equipment and thus can not leave the hospital or their home. However, any exclusion from regular school settings needs to be "time-defined and regularly revised" warn Snell and Eichner (1989, p. 122), because history has shown that some students who formerly were excluded from integrated schools are now included due to advances in educational and medical technology [e.g., the success of nonaversive methods to reduce seriously aggressive behavior (Durand & Kishi, 1987) and the impact of clean intermittent catheterization on students with myelomeningocele (Turnbull, 1986)].

Integrated programs for this group of students **do not** simply require that these students are educated in the regular school where nondisabled students also attend. Although this has been the primary goal of educators battling for integration in the 1980s, geographic integration alone does not guarantee the desired outcomes (Brown et al., 1989a; Sailor et al., 1989). Integration should yield enough contact between peers with disabilities and those without that modeling, meaningful interactions, and friendships can occur. Integration effects appear to be multiplied when they involve a students' existing supports (i.e., family, neighborhood, and community). Thus, many who have studied or implemented integration with this group of learners over the past decade agree that a variety of programmatic criteria are required for students to achieve the desired outcomes of integration (Biklen, 1985; Brown et al., 1987; Sailor et al., 1989; Snell & Eichner, 1989; Voeltz, 1984). Although the research support for standards to judge integration success is not uniformly developed, I shall describe the criteria separately along with the existing support for each criterion.

Home School Location

The program should be located at the student's home school or the school that the student would attend if not disabled (Brown et al., 1989a; Thousand, Fox, Reid, Godek, & Williams, 1986). The rationale for using home school placement rests on the failure of existing integration approaches that cluster students with disabilities and on the benefits of using a nearby school. Many traditionally integrated school programs have employed a clustered school approach, whereby enough students to comprise a class (4 to 8 students) would be bused to a single school and served in a homogeneous special education classroom by a teacher who usually has some specialized training (Brown et al., 1989a). Homogeneous special classrooms refer to those serving a group with one special education label (e.g., learning disabilities, severe and profound mental retardation, trainable mentally retardation, etc.) in contrast to a heterogeneous group of students that includes student who have different special labels and that may include students without special education labels. Traditionally, it has been believed that the more narrowly defined the special education group the better, based on the assumption that services and methods would be similar. However, homogeneous classrooms, particularly when the members have severe disabilities, are far from homogeneous.

Practice has shown that the cluster school approach and homogeneous grouping cause many problems. These approaches, for example, may result in an imbalance in the natural proportion of students with disabilities in a school to those without disabilities which, in turn, has been blamed for poor integration outcomes (Brown et al., 1989a). To obtain a group of students with severe disabilities requires drawing from an area larger than a neighborhood and sometimes larger than a school district in rural areas. Thus, students in districts using these approaches have long bus rides and less time for instruction; long distances also prohibit involvement in extra-curricular school activities. Parents have long rides for school visits. Students do not attend the same school as their brothers or sisters, or as their neighbors of a similar age, thus removing natural supports. Acquaintances and friendships that develop are less likely to grow and last because of the distance. Finally, community-based instruction, now accepted as a best practice for students with severe disabilities, may fail to yield skill generalization because the student is not in his or her own community.

One domain of continuing research and debate among educators and researchers in the area of severe disabilities is where the integrated student should be based for his or her educational program: in the special class, in the regular class with same age peers, in the community, or in a combination of these settings. If one accepts the rationale for placement in the student's home school, then in most less populated locations, placement will require that some educational time be spent in the regular classroom with support. I shall discuss how such support can be given to the student and to the regular educator in a later section on implementation.

Comprehensive Nature of the School

Sailor et al. (1989) define the comprehensive local school as the school a student would attend if he or she did not have disabilities and that also "can meet the educational service needs of all its prospective students, regardless of their individual characteristics and regardless of how diverse, extensive, or costly their special services requirements" (p. 3). Students with severe disabilities require services far beyond the ordinary. The student's need for attending a local school should not be pitted against the student's equally important need for services.

As some have feared in the past, integration does not have to mean that needed services are lost. The *Roncker v. Walter* (1983) decision gave clear support to the provision of related services in integrated settings over the same services provided in segregated school settings, even when less expensive and more efficient. The costs of exporting related services from a segregated school setting to one that is integrated "do not necessarily justify placing a student in a segregated setting" (Brady et al., 1989, p. 47). Educators studying the provision of related services to students with severe disabilities who are integrated have found that speech, occupational, and physical therapy services can be provided more cost-efficiently (Piuma, 1989) and more effectively in integrated school programs

than in segregated school programs (Frassinelli, Superior, & Meyers, 1983; Giangreco, 1986; Giangreco, York, & Rainforth, 1989; Rainforth & York, 1987).

Sailor and his colleagues (1989) discuss the specialized instructional unit, that they identify as one of the services a student with severe disabilities is likely to need in the local school. In contrast to special class, this term indicates the need for "some permeability in membership or placement," that students will require over their school career. The specialized instructional unit for students with severe disabilities is not limited to related services and includes functional skill instruction with a specially trained teacher or assistant, transitional plan development and implementation during the student's high school years, as well as program development and teacher consultation from speech therapists, occupational and physical therapists, and others. Consistent with the home school requirement, instruction would occur in a variety of settings identified as relevant for that student: special class, library, cafeteria, regular class, community, or job site.

Central or Age-Appropriate Location in the School

The program or specialized instructional unit needs either to be near or part of the classroom the student would be assigned to if not disabled. Practice has shown that when a class is isolated in a trailer or a special wing or is located next to a class of younger or older students without disabilities, the students with severe disabilities have fewer interactions or fewer appropriate peer interactions than they do when more centrally placed or placed near or with their nondisabled peers (Brinker, 1985; Condon, York, Heal, & Fortschneider, 1986; Voeltz, 1980). When students with disabilities are placed with persons who are not of similar chronological age, the interactions and modeling will not be age appropriate and is less desirable (Cole, Vandercook, & Rynders, 1987). Conversely, a lack of similarity in interests, dress, and behavior between persons with disabilities and their non-disabled peers has been shown to influence negatively the expectations and attitudes nondisabled persons have for people with severe disabilities (Bak & Siperstein, 1987; Bates, Morrow, Pancsofar, & Sedlak, 1984).

A good school location is necessary but not adequate. Although physical integration is an essential part of integrated programs, proximity alone cannot be viewed as a guarantee for increased positive interactions between persons with severe disabilities and their peers (Cole, Meyer, Vandercook, & McQuarter, 1986; Strain, 1984; Voeltz, 1984). If students with severe disabilities are to be a meaningful part of the student body of a school, several school characteristics have been identified as being critical (Meyer, Eichinger, & Park-Lee, 1987; Sailor et al., 1989; Stainback et al., 1989).

The first among these practices concerns a school philosophy which supports the belief that all students have abilities, can learn, and can make contributions (Bogdan & Biklen, 1985). This effective school philosophy can permeate school policy and practices in ways that appear to facilitate integration of learners with disabilities (Hahn, 1989; Lezotte, 1989). Principals can be instructional leaders who influence an entire school body. When they have high standards for **all** students and teachers, they communicate a commitment to excellence that can transcend special categories of learners. However, when principals are opposed to mainstreaming or integration or see it as the business of special education, its success at best is limited and at worst is doomed (Bodgan & Biklen, 1985; Robson, 1981).

A second essential practice is that school policy that guides programs for nondisabled students does not differ radically from school policy that guides programs for students who have disabilities. For example, the school calendars and the arrival and dismissal times for students with disabilities should not be different from those for nondisabled students in the same district. Attendance at school sport activities or assemblies and the use of the cafeteria, the playground, the library, and other school resources should not be differentiated because of the presence of a disability. Although the use of a wheelchair may necessitate an accessible bus or assistance from peers and the presence of students with behavioral needs may require a bus aide, schools should strive to extend integration into their transportation system as well (Sailor et al., 1989).

Third, positive peer interactions and friendships are valued as being important to all students. Researchers have demonstrated the importance of and instruction and scheduling to improvements in social interactions between nondisabled peers and students having severe disabilities. These approaches have taken many forms, such as programs in disability awareness, buddy systems, special friendships, peer tutors, and circles of friends. Documented outcomes of these programs have included increases in positive reciprocal interactions, cooperative and appropriate play, positive attitudes in nondisabled peers, skill acquisition and generalization by students with disabilities in peer tutor programs, and the development of mutual friendships (cf., Brinker & Thorpe, 1986; Strain, 1983).

Individual Schools in a District Generally Reflect the Community's Natural Proportion of Disability

In any given school about 1% of the students have severe disabilities, and other students requiring special services typically do not exceed 15% of the school population. The clustered school system in which a small number of schools serve an entire district's or several districts' population of students with disabilities is viewed as nonconducive to successful integration in that school (Brown et al., 1989a). There appear to be limits to how much diversity beyond the expected proportion an environment can absorb without adverse effects. By contrast, in schools without students having special needs, nondisabled students are more likely to have unfavorable attitudes towards persons with disabilities due to their lack of experience (Brinker, 1985; Voeltz, 1980). At least one exception has been suggested to the general principle of integration of **all** students with disabilities according to natural proportion. Sailor and his colleagues (1989), along with some educators of students who are deaf, feel that students with deafness who use manual communication systems have unique needs to gather in clusters for part of the day or week with others who are deaf to communicate.

WHAT ARE THE BARRIERS TO INTEGRATION?

Statistics presented earlier on integrated programs for students with severe disabilities portray a dismal and inconsistent record. In a few isolated states like Iowa, Oregon, Vermont, and Hawaii hardly any students are segregated in separate schools; and in more cities such as San Francisco and Madison, Wisconsin, and in many more school districts, integrated schooling is widely available to all students with severe disabilities. In many of these places, change efforts have been concentrated and supported with state or federal funds; though in Iowa, these change efforts are uniquely a result of a state commitment to integration and **not** associated with special federal project money (S. Maurer, personal communication, October, 1989). The statistics indicating the prevalence of segregating

practices for students with severe disabilities have been associated with several complex barriers to integration (Brady et al., 1989; Gartner & Lipsky, 1987; Landau, 1987; Latham, 1987; McDonnell & Hardman, 1989; Peck, Hayden, Wandschneider, Peterson, & Richarz, 1989; Snell & Eichner, 1989):

- Courts have not consistently defined the LRE requirement;

- Federal and state enforcement agencies have not enforced LRE, despite EHA compliance monitoring in states by the Federal level;

- School districts have avoided making changes unless required to do so; thus, they continue to run dual programs in special education and regular education which foster many disincentives to integration;

- Implementers at the state and local school levels have resisted efforts to integrate all students;

- Policy makers have feared that integration of students with severe disabilities will not be cost-effective, when in fact studies have shown it to be quite cost-effective in both short and long-term analyses (Piuma, 1989);

- Universities have not addressed the rationale for integration or inclusive education and methods for implementing integration as they train new teachers and administrators, both in regular and special education; and

- The model settings where integration is working (especially home school models using regular class placement) are still too few; those that exist have not been visible to many.

Most leaders in special education of persons with severe disabilities support the restructuring of education, or inclusive education, as being central to further improvements in school integration (e.g., Biklen, 1985; Lipsky & Gartner, 1989; Sailor et al., 1989; Stainback et al., 1989). This recommendation is consistent with recent calls for the restructuring of schools to promote effective education. In September, 1989, President Bush met with all the states' Governors and the Cabinet for a Summit on Education in America. With regard to the topic of this chapter, several conclusions of this Summit are pertinent: (a) "the urgent need for flexibility in using Federal funds," and (b) the commitment to restructuring schools to include decentralization of authority or school-based management (Jeffersonian Compact, 1989, p. 22).

In the Jeffersonian Compact (1989), a statement resulting from the summit, one of the several examples of flexibility in the use of Federal funds was the practice of using waivers to permit students qualifying for special education to return to regular classes with extra support. Decentralization of authority or site-based management, one aspect of restructured schools, would mean many changes. The Compact mentioned that decentralization would mean greater choice for parents and students, greater authority for and accountability by teachers and principals, and an instructional program designed for all students to accomplish work skills. This last change is consistent with earlier changes in the Vocational Act mandating supported employment and transition planning for students with severe disabilities who are moving from school to work.

Thus, regardless of the type or severity of the disability, public schools must pro-

vide appropriate educational programs; the law is unequivocal in this mandate. There are no exceptions. The Summit results suggest strongly that our schools need some repairs including several specifically named which would support the basic position of this chapter:

- Students belong in their home school, regardless of their disability;

- Students with special needs will still require individualized educational support, those with severe disabilities will require continuing support; and

- School-based management is consistent with the idea that students with special needs attend the school they would attend if they did not have special needs (their home school), and that the principal would organize the program to meet the diverse and individualized needs of all students.

WHAT STRATEGIES HAVE WORKED TO BUILD INTEGRATED PROGRAMS?

There are numerous research and implementation reports that can guide schools wishing to move students with severe disabilities from separate educational programs and integrate them into regular schools. This section will summarize the general principles of these strategies and cite selected supportive references.

- Integration is facilitated when: it is supported by top school administrators; it is preceded by district-wide planning involving parents, teachers, and students (special and regular education), along with key community members; districts recruit building principals as leaders in implementation; it is implemented system-wide; total program quality is addressed, not just integration; there are plans for the promotion of interactions between peers, not just physical proximity; and when the goals of integration include movement into each student's age-appropriate neighborhood school (McDonnell & Hardman, 1989; Sailor et al., 1989; Snell & Eichner, 1989).

• School staff and parents involved in planning should learn about and possibly visit other school programs where quality integrated programs are in operation: "seeing is believing" (Snell & Eichner, 1989).

• Horizontal interactions (people of the same role communicating with each other) should be used to explain the rationale and logistics of integration to parents, teachers, and administrators (Sailor et al., 1989).

• Integration plans need to have mechanisms for evaluation along the way including consumer satisfaction and methods for regular (initially, even day-to-day) problem-solving at the school level by a school site team (McDonnell & Hardman, 1989; Sailor et al., 1989).

• Planning needs to be comprehensive and dynamic, addressing issues of transportation, staff inservice, school plant changes, staff supervision, related services changes, instructional staff changes, and support and

information sharing with parents, teachers, and students (Sailor et al., 1989).

• Staff and students need to be prepared for the implementation of integration which typically has included disability awareness programs, training staff and nondisabled students in methods to promote positive interactions, and an active system for sharing information prior to and concurrent with integration (Sailor et al., 1989).

• Disability awareness strategies **and** methods to create interaction opportunities that are appropriate to the age-group need to be implemented on a continuing basis with a systematic reduction in teacher intrusiveness over time. These methods include:

A. Organized interaction groupings such as play groups, peer tutoring, special friends, or club activities during and after school (e.g., Chin-Perez et al., 1986; Kohl, Moses, & Stettner-Eaton, 1983; Knapczyk, Johnson, & McDermott, 1983; Voeltz, 1980, 1982);

B. Less structured interactions occurring at play or through schedule changes (e.g., Haring Lovinger, 1989; Odom, Hoyson, Jamieson, & Strain, 1985; Sasso & Rude, 1987);

C. Integrated periods planned through IEP objectives (Hunt, Goetz, & Anderson, 1986; Peck, Killen, & Baumgart, 1989);

D. Organized peer support through circles of friends or use of the McGill Action Planning System (Forest & Lusthaus, 1989; Strully & Strully, 1989; Vandercook, York, & Forest, 1989).

WHAT ASPECTS OF INTEGRATION NEED CLARIFICATION AND MORE STUDY?

Today's largest area of disagreement concerns where students with severe disabilities, once in the regular school, will spend their time: regular education, special education, community-based instruction, or some combination of each for what age (Brown et al., 1989b; Snell, 1988b). Will instruction in the context of regular education mean that community-based instruction away from the school be sacrificed (Snell, 1988b)? How far can mainstreaming into regular education be extended and still meet the needs of all students? Can **supported education** (through the provision of supplementary aids, services, and staff and student support) be provided in the context of the regular classroom to students having disabilities so that integrated programs can be achieved satisfactorily for all students and staff (Sailor, 1991; Taylor, 1988)? What support models, alone or in combination, work best in which settings (e.g., Sailor et al., 1989; Thousand et al., 1986; Vandercook et al., 1989)? These questions will be the focal points of integration research in the 1990s, because research in the field of severe disabilities typically has moved beyond simply documenting the value of integration.

Over the past 15 years, I have thought and read much about integration; as is true of others, I have also written, testified, and worked for the integration of persons with severe disabilities. Integration used to mean deinstitutionalization, but now integration for school-aged persons with severe disabilities extends rightfully to the benefits of receiving an education in one's home school alongside nondisabled peers. I find that the more

active my role has become in making integrated school programs happen, the more convinced I have become that the principle of integration is well worth the enormous effort it takes. My convictions about the value of students with severe disabilities receiving instruction alongside their peers and attending their home school have been powerfully influenced by seeing the actual outcomes of these approaches. "Seeing is believing" continues to be one of the most successful strategies for promoting changes in integration and has been a major factor in the evolution of my thinking about integration.

REFERENCES

Bak, J. J., & Siperstein, G. N. (1987). Similarity as a factor affecting change in children's attitudes toward mentally retarded peers. *American Journal of Mental Deficiency, 91*, 524-531.

Bates, P., Morrow, S. A., Pancsofar, E., & Sedlak, R. (1984). The effects of functional vs. nonfunctional activities on attitudes/expectations of non-handicapped college students: What they see is what we get. *The Journal of the Association for Persons with Severe Handicaps, 9*, 73-78.

Biklen, D. (Ed.). (1985). *Achieving the complete school: Strategies for effective mainstreaming.* New York: Teacher's College Press.

Bogdan, R., & Biklen, D. (1985). The principal's role in mainstreaming. In D. Biklen, (Ed.), *Achieving the complete school: Strategies for effective mainstreaming* (pp. 30-51). New York: Teacher's College Press.

Brady, M. P., McDougall, D., & Dennis, H. F. (1989). The schools, the courts, and the integration of students with severe handicaps. *The Journal of Special Education, 23*, 43-58.

Brinker, R. P. (1985). Interactions between severely mentally retarded students and other students in integrated and segregated public school settings. *American Journal of Mental Deficiency, 91*, 150-150.

Brinker, R. P., & Thorpe, M. E. (1986). Features of integrated educational ecologies that predict social behavior among severely mentally retarded and nonretarded students. *American Journal of Mental Deficiency, 91*, 150-159.

Brown, L., Rogan, P., Shiraga, B., Zanella Albright, K., Kessler, K., Bryson, F., VanDeventer, P., & Loomis, P. (1987). A vocational follow-up evaluation of the 1984 to 1986 Madison Metropolitan School district graduates with severe intellectual disabilities. *Monograph of The Association for Persons with Severe Handicaps, 2*(2).

Brown, L., Long, E., Udvari-Solner, A., Davis, L., VanDeventer, P., Ahlgren, C., Johnson, F., Gruenewald, L., & Jorgensen, J. (1989a). The home school: Why students with severe intellectual disabilities must attend the schools of their brothers, sisters, friends, and neighbors. *The Journal of the Association for Persons with Severe Handicaps, 14*, 1-7.

Brown, L., Long, E., Udvari-Solner, A., Schwartz, P., VanDeventer, P., Ahlgren, C., Johnson, F., Gruenewald, L., & Jorgensen, J. (1989b). Should students with severe intellectual disabilities be based in regular or special education classrooms in home schools? *The Journal of the Association for Persons with Severe Handicaps, 14*, 8-12.

Chin-Perez, G., Hartman, D., Sook Park, H., Sacks, S., Wershing, A., & Gaylord-Ross, R. (1986). Maximizing social contact for secondary students with severe handicaps. *The Journal of the Association for Persons with Severe Handicaps, 11*, 118-124.

Cole, D. A., Meyer, L. M., Vandercook, T., & McQuarter, R. J. (1986). Interactions between peers with and without severe handicaps: The dynamics of teacher intervention. *American Journal of Mental Deficiency, 91*, 160-169.

Cole, D., Vandercook, T., & Rynders, J. (1987). Dyadic interactions between children with and without mental retardation: Effects of age discrepancy. *American Journal of Mental Retardation, 92*, 194-202.

Condon, M. E., York, R., Heal, L. W., & Fortschneider, J. (1986). Acceptance of severely handicapped students by nonhandicapped peers. *The Association for Persons with Severe Handicaps, 11*, 216-219.

Danielson, L. C., & Bellamy, G. T. (1989). State variation in placement of children with handicaps in segregated environments. *Exceptional Children, 55*, 448-455.

Deno, E. (1970). Special education as developmental capital. *Exceptional Children, 37*, 229-237.

Durand, M., & Kishi, G. (1987). Reducing severe behavior problems among persons with dual sensory impairments: An evaluation of a technical assistance model. *The Journal of the Association for Persons with Severe Handicaps, 12*, 2-10.

Education of All Handicapped Children Act of 1975, 20 U.S.C. 1401 (1978)

Federal Register. (1977, August 23). Education of Handicapped Children: Implementation of Part B of the Education of the Handicapped Act, *42*(163), Part II, 42474-42518.

Forest, M., & Lusthaus, E. (1989). Promoting educational equality for all students. In S. Stainback, W. Stainback, & M. Forest (Eds.), *Educating all students in the mainstream of regular education* (pp. 43-57). Baltimore: Paul H. Brooks.

Frassinelli, L., Superior, K., & Meyers, J. (1983 November). A consultation model for speech and language intervention. *American Speech and Hearing Association (ASHA) Newsletter*, pp. 25-30.

Gartner, A., & Lipsky, D. K. (1987). Beyond special education: Toward a quality system for all students. *Harvard Educational Review, 57*, 367-395.

Giangreco, M. (1986). Effects of integrated therapy: A pilot study. *The Journal of the Association for Persons with Severe Handicaps, 11*, 205-208.

Giangreco, M., York, J., & Rainforth, B. (1989). Providing related services to learners with severe handicaps in educational settings: Pursuing the least restrictive option. *Pediatric Physical Therapy, 1*(2), 55-63.

Hahn, H. (1989). The politics of special education. In D. K. Lipsky & A. Gartner (Eds.), *Beyond separate education: Quality education for all* (pp. 225-241). Baltimore: Paul H. Brookes.

Hanline, M., & Halvorsen, A. (1988). Parent perceptions of the integration transition process: Overcoming artificial barriers. *Exceptional Children, 55*, 487-492.

Haring, T. G., & Lovinger, L. (1989). Promoting social interactions through teaching generalized play initiation responses to preschool children with autism. *The Journal of the Association for Persons with Severe Handicaps, 4*, 58-67.

Hunt, P., Goetz, L., & Anderson, J. (1986). The quality of IEP objectives associated with placement of integrated versus segregated school sites. *The Journal of the Association for Persons with Severe Handicaps, 11*, 125-130.

Jeffersonian Compact. (1989, October 1). *The New York Times*, Section 4, pp. 1, 22.

Kohl, F. L., Moses, L. G., & Stettner-Eaton, B. A. (1983). The results of teaching fifth and sixth graders to be instructional trainers with students who are severely handicapped. *The Journal of the Association for Persons with Severe Handicaps, 8,* 32-40.

Knapczyk, D. P., Johnson, W. A., & McDermott, G. (1983). A comparison of the effects of teacher and peer supervision on work performance and on-task behavior. *The Journal of the Association for Persons with Severe Handicaps, 8,* 41-48.

Landau, J. (1987, May). *Out of the mainstream: Education of disabled youth in Massachusetts.* Boston: Massachusetts Advocacy Center.

Latham, G. (1987). Mainstreaming: A victim of disincentives. *Principal, 67,* 33-35.

Lezotte, L. W. (1989). School improvement based on the effective schools research. In D. K. Lipsky & A. Gartner (Eds.), *Beyond separate education: Quality education for all* (pp. 25-37). Baltimore: Paul H. Brookes.

Lipsky, D.K., & Gartner, A. (Eds.). (1989). *Beyond separate education: Quality education for all.* Baltimore: Paul H. Brookes.

McDonnell, A. P., & Hardman, M. L. (1989). The desegregation of America's special schools: Strategies for change. *The Journal of the Association for Persons with Severe Handicaps, 14,* 68-74.

Meyer, L. H., Eichinger, J., & Park-Lee, S. (1987). A validation of program quality indicators in educational services for students with severe disabilities. *The Journal of the Association for Persons with Severe Handicaps, 12,* 251-263.

Meyer, L. H., Peck, C., & Brown, L. (Eds.). (1991). *Critical issues in the lives of persons with severe disabilities.* Baltimore: Paul H. Brookes.

Odom, S., Hoyson, M., Jamieson, B., & Strain, P. S. (1985). Increasing handicapped preschoolers' peer social interactions: Cross-setting and component analysis. *Journal of Applied Behavior Analysis, 18,* 3-16.

Peck, C. A., Hayden, L., Wandschneider, M., Peterson, K., & Richarz, S. (1989). Development of integrated preschools: A qualitative inquiry into sources of resistance among parents, administrators, and teachers. *Journal of Early Intervention, 13,* 353-364.

Peck, C. A., Killen, C. C., & Baumgart, D. (1989). Increasing implementation of special education instruction in mainstream preschools: Direct and generalized effects of nondirective consultation. *Journal of Applied Behavior Analysis, 22,* 197-210.

Piuma, M. F. (1989, October). *Benefits and costs of integrating students with severe disabilities into regular public school programs: A study summary of money well spent.* Unpublished manuscript, Department of Special Education, San Francisco State University, San Fransisco, CA.

Rainforth, B., & York, J. (1987). Integrating related services in community instruction. *The Journal of the Association for Persons with Severe Handicaps, 12,* 190-198.

Robson, D. L. (1981). Administering educational services for the handicapped: Role expectations. *Exceptional Children, 47,* 377-378.

Reynolds, M. (1962). A framework for considering some issues in special education. *Exceptional Children, 28,* 367-370.

Roncker v. Walter, 700 F.2d 1058-1063 (6th Cir. 1983). Sailor, W. (1991). Community school: An essay. In L. Meyer, C. Peck, & L. Brown (Eds.), *Critical issues in the lives of people with severe disabilities* (pp. 379-385). Baltimore: Paul H. Brookes.

Sailor, W., Anderson, J. L., Halvorsen, A. T., Doering, K., Filler, J., & Goetz, L. (1989). *The comprehensive local school: Regular education for all students with disabilities.* Baltimore: Paul H. Brookes.

Sasso, G. M., & Rude, H. A. (1987). Unprogrammed effects of training high-status peers to interact with severely handicapped children. *Journal of Applied Behavior Analysis, 20,* 35-44.

Snell, M. E. (1988a). Curriculum and methodology for individuals with severe disabilities. *Education and Training in Mental Retardation, 23,* 302-314.

Snell, M. E. (1988b). Gartner and Lipsky's "Beyond special education: Toward a quality system for all students," Messages for TASH. *The Journal of the Association for Persons with Severe Handicaps, 13,* 137-140.

Snell, M. E., & Eichner, S. J. (1989). Integration for students with profound disabilities. In F. Brown, D. H. Lehr (Eds.), *Persons with profound disabilities: Issues and practices,* (pp. 109-138). Baltimore: Paul H. Brookes.

Stainback, W., Stainback, S., & Forest, M. (1989). *Educating all students in the mainstream of regular education.* Baltimore: Paul H. Brookes.

Strain, P. S. (1983). Identification of social skill curriculum targets for severely handicapped children in mainstream preschools. *Applied Research in Mental Retardation, 4*, 369-382.

Strain, P. S. (1984). Social interactions of handicapped preschoolers in developmentally integrated and segregated settings: A study of generalization effects. In T. Field (Ed.), *Friendships between normally developing and handicapped children* (pp. 187-208). Norwood, NJ: Aldex.

Strully, J. L., & Strully, C. F. (1989). Friendships as an educational goal. In W. Stainback, S. Stainback, & M. Forest (Eds.), *Educating all students in the mainstream of regular education* (pp. 59-68). Baltimore: Paul H. Brookes.

Taylor, S. J. (1988). Caught in the continuum: A critical analysis of the principle of the least restrictive environment. *The Journal of the Association for Persons with Severe Handicaps, 13*, 41-53.

Tenth annual report to Congress on the implementation of the Education of the Handicapped Act. (1988). Washington, DC: Department of Education.

The Association for Persons with Severe Handicaps. (1989, May). *TASH resolutions and policy statements.* (Available from TASH, 7010 Roosevelt Way, NE, Seattle, WA, 98115).

Thousand, J. S., Fox, T. J., Reid, R., Godek, J., & Williams, W. (September, 1986). *The Homecoming Model: Educating students who present intensive educational challenges within regular educational environments.* Unpublished manuscript, University of Vermont, Center for Developmental Disabilities, Burlington, VT.

Timothy W. v. Rochester School District, 875 F.2d 954 (1989).

Turnbull, H. R., III. (1986). Appropriate education and Rowley. *Exceptional Children, 52*, 347-352.

Turnbull, H. R., with Ellis, J. W., Boggs, E. M., Brookes, P. O., & Biklen, D. P. (Eds.). (1981). *Least restrictive alternatives: Principles and practices.* Washington, D.C.: American Association on Mental Deficiency.

United States Department of Education. (1987). *Tenth Annual Report to Congress on the implementation of P. L. 94-142.*

Vandercook, T., York, J., & Forest, M. (1989). The McGill Action Planning System (MAPS): A strategy for building the vision. *The Journal of the Association for Persons with Severe Handicaps, 14*, 205-215.

Voeltz, L. M. (1980). Children's attitudes toward handicapped peers. *American Journal of Mental Deficiency, 84*, 455-464.

Voeltz, L. M. (1982). Effects of structured interactions with severely handicapped peers on children's attitudes. *American Journal of Mental Deficiency, 86*, 380-390.

Voeltz, L. M. (1984). Program and curriculum innovations to prepare children for integration. In N. Certo, N. Haring, & R. York (Eds.), *Public school integration of severely handicapped students: Rational, issues, and progressive alternatives* (pp. 155-183). Baltimore: Paul H. Brookes.

11

THE REI DEBATE: A TIME FOR SYSTEMATIC RESEARCH AGENDAS

Deborah Deutsch Smith
Diane Shaner Bassett
University of New Mexico

Since 1983, debate surrounding the General or Regular Education Initiative (REI) has brought some special educators together and divided others. Camps of parents and professionals have developed differing positions about what should comprise the education offered to children with disabilities. In some cases, battle lines have been drawn; in other cases, healthy dialogues, pilot programs, and research projects are being initiated. Regardless of the level of heat and emotionality that these debates cause, the content of communication centers on how two concepts presented in the Education for All Handicapped Childrens Act (EHA) should be interpreted. These two concepts--Least Restrictive Environment (LRE) and Free Appropriate Public Education (FAPE)--are at the heart of agreements and disagreements regarding where children with disabilities should be educated and what that education should encompass.

It would be helpful to spend a few moments describing these two concepts-- LRE and FAPE--to bring the reasons for disagreements into clearer focus. Within the context of the Regular Education Initiative debates, LRE is frequently used synonymously with the terms *mainstreaming* and *integration*. For many parents and

professionals, LRE has come to mean placement exclusively in the regular education setting. LRE and FAPE are concepts that professionals are seeking to define and operationalize. For some (Biklen & Zollers, 1986; Gartner & Lipsky, 1987; Lilly, 1988; Reynolds, Wang, & Walberg, 1987; Stainback & Stainback, 1984; Wang & Birch, 1984; Wang, Reynolds & Walberg, 1987; Will, 1986), FAPE can only occur in one setting: the regular education classroom. For others (Anderegg & Vergason, 1988; Baker & Zigmond, 1990; Bryan, Bay, Lopez-Reyna, & Donahue, 1991; Fuchs & Fuchs, 1988; Hallahan, Kauffman, Lloyd, & McKinney, 1988; Hallahan, Keller, McKinney, Lloyd, & Bryan, 1988; Schumaker & Deshler, 1988; Walker & Bullis, 1991), FAPE raises questions about the most appropriate curriculum content and instructional methods, regardless of placement. We believe that LRE and FAPE cannot, and should not, be operationalized singularly, and must be left to broad interpretation. Although special educators seem to be perpetually looking for *the* single answer, *the* one best educational methodology, and *the* cure for a particular disability, we believe that the authors of EHA purposively and correctly created ambiguity when they set forth the concepts of LRE and FAPE so that educational programs could be individually tailored to the unique needs of each child.

SOME PURPOSES OF LRE AND FAPE

A review of the legislative history of PL 94-142 (EHA) serves to illuminate the ambiguity that does and should exist when LRE and FAPE are balanced and evaluated for individual children. The debates chronicled in the Congressional Record of 1975 present us with portraits of dedicated legislators, civil rights activists, special education professionals, and parents determined to provide broad educational rights and sweeping reforms for all children with disabilities. The intent of EHA was kept broad to allow for states' and school districts' individual interpretation and application of fiscal and program considerations. Most importantly, however, EHA, as it was developed, allows for interpretation of LRE and FAPE to be accorded on an individual basis to each of the millions of children with disabilities. It is this individual application, predicated on a broad conceptualization of the law, that renders EHA its ultimate strength.

EHA has been called the Parents' Bill of Rights (Richmond, 1983). In many ways, it was patterned after the U.S. Bill of Rights, which was conceived and written to allow for alteration and interpretation through social change. The fact that the U.S. Bill of Rights still survives as a hallmark of a dynamic constitutional government reflects the power of its simple message: Rights of individuals have ultimate precedence over the power of government. Concepts associated with human rights cannot survive the test of time if they are defined or applied too narrowly. Laws, rules, and regulations must be flexible to allow for societal change, growth, and even stagnation. If concepts and rights are to prevail, they

must stand solidly apart from actual application of statutory enforcement. They must have a life of their own.

LRE and FAPE are two such concepts that mandate broad interpretation and require flexibility so that services can be properly provided to a diverse population comprised of individuals with different strengths and needs. These concepts also were designed to work in tandem: to provide a balance between placement and policy, individuals' needs, and program availability. To assign a singular definition or interpretation to either of these terms strips them of their ultimate power. For example, to define LRE as placement exclusively in the regular education classroom would not allow for the flexibility necessary to match available programs with the needs of an individual child. It would not allow for the delivery of a curriculum that is incompatible or inappropriate with the regular education system (e.g., social skills, community-based instruction, life skills, mobility training, and sign language). LRE and FAPE must be allowed to guide us in creating an array of options, based on individuals' needs, which can be operationalized by legislators and practitioners alike.

DEBATES CAN BE A SIGN OF A DYNAMIC FIELD

Special education is not a static profession but a dynamic entity that is constantly looking for new solutions to old problems. For over 150 years, special educators have questioned their own approved and commonly adopted educational practices. They have studied the efficacy of programs offered throughout this century (Bennett, 1932; Blatt, 1958; Cowen, 1938; Goldstein, Jordon, & Moss, 1962; Pertsch, 1936). Across this period of time, the field has undergone tremendous changes, systematically redefining its populations, and continually conducting research to develop new and improved instructional methods and service delivery systems. Throughout our history, professionals have challenged the status quo and, usually, the outcome is an improved educational system. For example, a debate about relative emphasis on teaching goals raged in the field of learning disabilities for years. Many professionals adhered to the notion that emphasis on training students' perceptual skills would lead to improved academic performance. In fact, this might well have been the most commonly applied remedial strategy of the time. Other professionals felt that academic skills (e.g., reading) would improve only when children received direct instruction. Instead of focusing on the process or the manner in which children input information, these professionals emphasized the importance of the child's ability to document what the student had learned. The debate tore the field apart, but was resolved through research, analysis, and synthesis (Hammill & Larsen, 1973). The resulting field looks at student performance as a measure of progress, an array of innovative teaching tactics (e.g., learning strategies), and a new generation of research on motivation, learning style, and thinking skills. Debates, then, might be viewed as part of an evolutionary process that has resulted in a stronger field and improved educational practice.

Some professionals (Davis, 1989; Vergason & Anderegg, 1989; Walker & Bullis, 1991) argue that the REI debate is incomplete, because it has not engaged the full community of educators who will be affected by the reforms proposed by REI advocates. Discussions about REI have been held, almost exclusively, within the field of special education. The forum for such discussions must be broadened to include parents and regular educators at all levels. In a recent study, Ysseldyke, Thurlow, Wotruba, and Nania (1990) surveyed approximately 200 regular education teachers about the issues surrounding integration of students with handicaps into their classes. Results of their survey indicated that regular classroom teachers do little to change their instructional methods for students with handicaps who are mainstreamed into their classes. Secondary teachers instruct more mainstreamed students than do elementary teachers, and also do so with fewer assisting personnel. According to Ysseldyke and his colleagues, the data suggest that regular education teachers either do not see a way to change or are unable to alter their classroom environments to accommodate mainstreamed students. These data lead us to believe that much work, training, and collaboration need to occur before even our modest expectations of mainstreaming can be achieved.

Of course, numerous demonstration and pilot programs are being tested, and students with a wide range of disabilities are being integrated into regular education settings. The success of some of these projects has led selected professionals to believe that integration, even with some of our most difficult youngsters, can be successfully accomplished. For example, some researchers (Gottlieb, Alter, & Gottlieb, 1991; Wang & Birch, 1984; Wang, Peverly, & Randolf, 1984) report that teachers and administrators in three studies who participated in the ALEM Project strongly support the benefits of full integration. Snell (1991) also cites positive outcomes of educating youngsters with severe disabilities in regular education classrooms. However, as noted by others (Fuchs & Fuchs, 1988; Bryan & Bryan, 1988), these pilot programs are limited in number, and have been conducted under experimental conditions by parents, students, and school personnel who volunteered to participate. In these projects, the teachers and students were the recipients of intensive assistance from other professionals. In addition, select and singular groups of youngsters with handicaps were included (e.g., only the severely handicapped or only the mildly handicapped). As a field, we have not yet tested how well one regular classroom environment can educate children who have very different handicaps (hearing impairments, visual impairments, learning disabilities, severe emotional disturbance, or language disorders). In other words, we do not know how diverse or homogeneous a group of children must be for a proper education to be accorded appropriate to all of them.

Clearly, many questions remain to be answered about the dynamics that make integrated programs viable. For example, what incentives, implied and explicit, are necessary for regular education teachers to desire the composition of their student population to be more diverse and less homogeneous? How many students with disabilities can a regular education environment tolerate? How many different professionals can realistically and successfully collaborate in one setting? Does the integration of students with handicaps affect the achievement gains of the regular education students? Are some school settings more suitable for integration than others? For example, can regular education teachers in sparsely populated areas handle students with severe disabilities without support from specialists when there are not sufficient numbers of these children in a particular class or school to afford a specialist per student?

The answers to these questions will not be found between the covers of professional special education journals. They will not be found when the only professionals arguing these points are special educators trained in the principles of individualization and remediation. They will not be found when regular educators--the professional population who will be the most affected--are unaware that questions even exist about who should educate children with special needs and where that education should be delivered. And, answers to these important questions will certainly not be found until debates can be supplanted by discussions and dialogues.

Debates can and should evolve to discussions so collaboration and problem solving can be attempted, for integration cannot be one right answer, one right placement, or one right curriculum. Neither can it come from one profession or one level of expertise. Discussions from every strata of both regular and special education must provide the basis from which to conduct high-quality, conclusive research to determine which placements and which practices work for which students. The cry for more interchange and more research are neither recent (Deshler & Schumaker, 1986; and see Bryan et al., 1991; Walker & Bullis, 1991), nor uniformly implemented. Perhaps importantly, the determination of what an appropriate education should comprise cannot be achieved until we ascertain what the goals should be for students identified as having special needs.

WHAT IS AN APPROPRIATE EDUCATION?

Although the concepts of LRE and FAPE are interrelated, most of the discussion about REI has centered on the concept of LRE. Professionals have spent considerable energy and effort discussing issues surrounding placement. For example, Snell (1991) suggested that all related services needed by children with disabilities can be brought to the regular education classroom. Rather than placement alone, we believe the issue needing careful attention from researchers and practitioners is what should comprise the educational content presented to youngsters with various educational needs. In other words, the concept of FAPE must receive systematic study.

Researchers (Edgar, 1987) have begun to question the relevance of the curriculum offered to students with different disabilities. For example, some professionals and advocates who work with students who are deaf adamantly state that a regular classroom placement is the most restrictive for children who are deaf (Commission of the Education of the Deaf, 1988). Lane (1988) believes that disagreements about where these students should be educated pit special education professionals against their consumers (the deaf community): "The hearing leadership of special education has maintained that the local school offers the least restrictive environment for deaf education; deaf people themselves think it is the most restrictive" (p. 9). Lane argues that the paternalistic attitude of well-meaning educators prevents people who are deaf from the right to choose their own educational options, language, and culture; for choice to exist requires that numerous educational options be available. Lane's argument leads us to believe that an array of educational options needs to be available for all students with special needs, so that these individuals and their families have a choice and can balance LRE and FAPE according to the goals they have for themselves.

Other rationales also exist for a diversity of curricular and instructional options. Professionals working with individuals with severe and profound handicaps have been experimenting with community-based instruction, and find that the curriculum (what is taught) is more meaningful and learning generalizes to real life situations better when instruction is provided outside of the school setting (Falvey, 1989; Wehman & Hill, 1982; Wilcox & Bellamy, 1982). Similarly, others (Hasazi & Cobb, 1988; Hasazi, Salembier, & Finck, 1983; Larson, 1981) feel that students with mild disabilities profit more from training in real job settings than classroom situations. Despite these data, curricular options are not available in each school district for students with various educational needs. As a field, special education has neither studied nor implemented an array of curricula or how to match individuals to curricular options. We believe what is needed are systematic lines of inquiry resulting in sequenced instructional objectives, product development, and evaluation techniques.

Defining the components of an appropriate education is not an easy task. In part, it requires a determination of the goals for the children we serve. Edgar's (1987) work might bring us closer to setting such goals. His data and observations indicate that special education students are not very successful as adults, which may be due to their excessively high dropout rates. According to the U.S. Department of Education's 12th Annual Report to Congress (1990) only 53% of students with disabilities graduated from high school with either a diploma or a certificate. Zigmond and Thornton (1985) report that about 54% of students with learning disabilities who start ninth grade quit before graduation. Students who do not quit frequently cut classes and are unprepared when they do attend (deBettencourt & Zigmond, 1990). If great numbers of students with handicaps are not actively involved in their education or are leaving school before graduation, perhaps they are telling us that our curriculum and program offerings are not relevant or meaningful. If one goal for these students is to complete high school, it would behoove educators to ask these and former students--our ultimate consumers--what curricula should contain (Davis, 1989). Numerous follow-up studies (Edgar, 1987; Lovett, Haring, & Smith, 1990; Scuccimarra & Speece, 1990) indicate that even students with mild disabilities are under-employed or unemployed. Many young adults with learning disabilities continue to live with their parents. Is a goal of maintaining these students in regular education classes appropriate? As professionals, we need to concentrate our efforts to bring FAPE more clearly into focus. It is only then that the balance between LRE and FAPE can be determined and evaluated.

A NEW VISION OF A SPECIAL EDUCA-TION ARRAY

The authors of the preceding chapters offer rationales for an array of special education services. Bryan et al. (1991) assert that educational programs must take into account curricular and environmental demands as well as the expectations of parents and others. In their review of mainstreaming research, Gottlieb et al. (1991) found that the educational environment was more influential on students with disabilities academic success than on their non-handicapped peers' success. They advocate further research to establish assessment procedures to analyze the classroom environment where students with handicaps are to be integrated. Walker and Bullis (1991) argue against a radical restructuring of special education and point to the need for solid basic education coupled with functional skills for students with behavior problems. Others (Keogh, 1988; Semmel & Gerber, 1988; Schumaker & Deshler, 1988; Wiederholt, 1989) also call for a new perspective for special education with a multitude of service delivery options, instructional methods, and curriculur targets available. What is needed is an array that is not linear or sequential but a dynamic interchange and flow of services, personnel, and programs.

The authors of the chapters presented in this section represent different fields within special education. Despite their different orientations, several common themes emerge that point to a new direction for discussion about effective practices, both in regular and special classrooms. These themes reflect many special educators' awareness of the real pitfalls of education for students with handicaps, regardless of placement. They realize that effective education cannot be based on placement alone, but must work in concert with effective teachers, teaching strategies, related service personnel, and curricula. A great number of models have been developed over the years to describe the variety of services required by children with disabilities. Probably the most well known is the Cascade of Services Model (Deno, 1970). The Deno model is linear and sequential, showing a conceptualization of services from the most restrictive (residential center schools) to the least restrictive (regular education classroom). The model moves hierarchically from mild to severe disabilities, with mild disabilities paralleled with least restrictive environments and students with severe disabilities relegated to more restrictive placements. In another way to illustrate the wide range of services that children with special needs require, Smith and Luckasson (in press) shows a more fluid approach (see Figure 1).

The diagram developed by Smith and Luckasson attempts to illustrate the holistic nature of services required by individual children with special needs. The central focus of the model is the individual, around which the determinants of the least restrictive environment must be considered. A constellation of services, personnel, and placement issues must revolve around each individual. Each determinant is accorded equal importance to the delivery of appropriate services for each child. For example, a child with a severe handicap may not be automatically placed on a continuum that has traditionally been more restrictive. Rather, placement becomes just one consideration in providing an appropriate education. So, too, the considerations for a child with mild handicaps must include the intensity and duration of services which may or may not be in the regular classroom. This model helps us see that external service options cannot work without consideration of the individual as the focal point.

Few special educators argue against integration. It is a desired goal, and one which, if effective, can enhance the chances of eventual independent living. However, the terms mainstreaming and integration are misleading if they speak to placement only. In this text, Bryan et al. (1991), Walker and Bullis (1991), and Gottlieb et al. (1991) all address the importance and effectiveness of data-based curricula, and believe it is critical to the success of many educational programs. They also emphasize the importance of other factors: teacher attitudes toward students with handicaps, class size, and grouping practices. Their points were made about specific categories of exceptional learners, but also apply across many groups of people with handicaps. For example, Bryan and her colleagues make a strong case for considering the social-emotional climate of a classroom, as well as the instructional patterns evidenced by individual instructors. They call for a fundamental change in teacher attitudes and--more importantly--a reconceptualization of program content, including structure and method of instruction. Based on current research on the characteristics of students with learn-

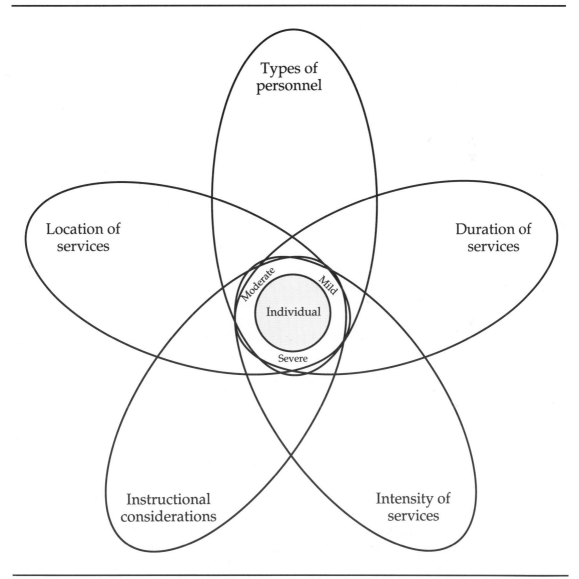

Figure 1: Considerations for individualized determination of LRE.

ing disabilities they emphasize that specific changes in assessment, evaluation, curriculum, and teacher behaviors must be evidenced in regular classrooms before they will truly provide appropriate placements for these students. Nearly all the authors call for a more in-depth examination of what really happens in regular classrooms--especially those without the benefit of exemplary teachers, curricula, or support systems. Are all classrooms and their teachers prepared to accept the wide variety of learners that true integration will bring?

A variety of educational options available to children with special needs must be created. These options will most likely vary by locale, educational context, and individual child. Special education has evolved into different subsets of specializations for a reason: Different kinds of handicapping conditions warrant different educational delivery options. For example, it might be easier to integrate a student with profound handicaps (with an aide) than a student with severe behavior disorders or even a student with moderate learning disabilities. Students with visual impairments might well be served in a regular education class and receive mobility and life-skills training through specialized center services. Conversely, students who are hearing impaired may require an environment which can educate them with intensive communication options. A residential placement may be a more appropriate option for some of these students. Individual determination of service, educational, and placement options is imperative.

The context of public education raises global issues which can influence the integration of students with handicaps into regular education settings. For example, the description of the urban schools presented in this text by Gottlieb and his colleagues (1991), as well as other data regarding our nation and its city schools, casts some light on American public education now and in the near future. For example, over 50% of the school children of five states and the District of Columbia are members of minority groups; four other states also have a composition of more than 40% from minority backgrounds (MIT, 1990). In the Los Angeles Unified Schools in 1989, 80% of children came from ethnic backgrounds other than Anglo, which is a substantial change in student demographics since the implementation of a desegregation plan (R. Rueda, personal communication, May 21, 1990). The so-called "White Flight" has left this and other public school systems with a majority of nontraditional students to serve.

Perhaps regular education also needs to entertain the concept of an array of services that will better meet the needs of an increasingly diverse and pluralistic population. If the urban schools of New York are truly comprised of children who are poor, members of minority groups, at risk, and low achievers, the integration of children with mild disabilities takes on an entirely different notion. Perhaps the best educational approach for all children in such urban settings is to adopt a special education model. In these cases, we might observe a *Special Education Initiative* for regular education classes. Under this scheme, groups of targeted students, assessed individually for strengths and needs, would work together on both basic skills and strategic interventions. Some of these effective practices would include placing children in groups according to their entry levels (Gersten & Woodard, 1987), teaching to mastery (Lovitt, 1984), emphasis on oral language skills (Marvin, 1989), self-control skills (Lloyd & Landrum, 1990), story mapping (Idol, 1987), reciprocal teaching (Palinscar & Brown, 1983), learning strategies (Deshler & Schumaker, 1986) and direct instruction (Englemann, 1977). Thus, the regular class placement becomes an opportunity for all students to be placed within a true array of curricular and service options. Therefore, depending on composition and educational needs of the members of the regular education student body, integration plans should vary.

A CALL FOR A SYSTEMATIC RESEARCH AGENDA

We are not presumptuous enough to set a research agenda for either the entire field of special education or for each category of exceptionalities our field serves. It is for professionals, advocates, parents, and perhaps the children themselves, who represent each group of handicapping conditions, to arrive at the specific topics requiring the serious attention of researchers. As we have advocated an array of services, we also advocate an array of research investigations that centers on groups of children with different educational goals and needs. So, it is for professionals who represent each exceptionality to devise a systematic line of research about what should comprise appropriate educational programs for each group of learners. Once appropriate educational arrays are defined, developed, and implemented, the issues surrounding LRE can be better articulated.

Regardless of the direction that specific research agendas take, we hope that some of the following questions will be addressed:

• What is a "typical" regular education classroom? Are there sets of variables to which we can ascribe the label "regular education?" Do these variables change by setting: urban, suburban, and rural?

• What are the specific differences between elementary, midschool, and high school regular education classrooms? What are the differences in setting demands? How must students adjust to meet these demands?

• What cultural and linguistic variables must be taken into consideration when integrating students with special needs into regular class settings?

• What are attitudes of regular educators about the integration of students with special needs? What kinds of additional training will they need to provide an appropriate education for all students? What kind of administrative support is necessary to accomplish this goal?

• What, ultimately, should be the goals for students with special needs? Is it important that they graduate with diplomas? Should the acquisition of vocational skills be a priority? Where do goals relating to social skills fit into the curriculum?

• What are the key components to effective social integration of students with special needs? Under what conditions is social integration best achieved?

• How do students with special needs feel about the education they are receiving? Which placements and services do they prefer? What are high school graduates' and school leavers' reflections on the quality and type of education they received?

• Which curricula and instructional methods seem to be the most effective when dealing with a wide range of students in a regular classroom? Have these curricula been used in a variety of contexts with a variety of learners? Are they appropriate for urban and rural populations? Are they easily adaptable by teachers and supportable by administrators? Are they cost effective?

- How do we best measure and evaluate teachers, programs, training, and placements in a holistic manner to arrive at appropriate, individual determination of services?

- How can we balance the push for academic excellence with the realities of the abilities of our students? Can we demonstrate effective education for all students without being necessarily dependent on achievement scores as the only measurable evidence of success?

We believe that when the above questions are answered, a fine array of educational services can be crystallized. We hope that our field can truly meet the goals set forth in EHA by providing the best education possible in the least restrictive environment for each child with a special need.

REFERENCES

Anderegg, M. L., & Vergason, G. A. (1988). An analysis of one of the cornerstones of the Regular Education Initiative. *Focus on Exceptional Children, 20*(8), 1-7.

Baker, J. M., & Zigmond, N. (1990). Are regular education classes equipped to accommodate students with learning disabilities? *Exceptional Children, 56*, 515-526.

Bennett, A. (1932). *A comparative study of subnormal children in the elementary grades.* New York:

Teachers College, Columbia University, Bureau of Publications.

Biklen, D., & Zollers, N. (1986). The focus of advocacy on the LD field. *Journal of Learning Disabilities, 19*, 579-586.

Blatt, B. (1958). The physical, personality, and academic status of children who are mentally retarded attending special classes as compared with children who are mentally retarded attending regular classes. *American Journal of Mental Deficiency, 62*, 810-818.

Bryan, T., Bay, N., Lopez-Reyna, N., & Donahue, M. (1991). Characteristics of students with learning disabilities: A summary of the extant database and its implications for educational programs. In J. W. Lloyd, N. N. Singh, & A. C. Repp, Eds.), *The regular education initiative: Alternative perspectives on concepts, issues, and methods* (pp. 113-131). Sycamore, IL: Sycamore.

Bryan, J. H., & Bryan, T. H. (1988). Where's the beef? A review of published research on the Adaptive Learning Environments Model. *Learning Disabilities Focus, 4*(1), 9-14.

Commission of the Education of the Deaf. (1988). *Toward quality: Education of the Deaf.* Washington, DC: Government Printing Office.

Cowen, P. A. (1938). Special class vs. grade groups for subnormal pupils. *School and Society, 48*, 27-28.

Davis, W. E. (1989). The Regular Education Initiative debate: Its promises and problems. *Exceptional Children, 55*(5), 440-446.

deBettencourt, L. U., & Zigmond, N. (1990). The learning disabled secondary school dropout: What teachers should know. What teachers can do. *Teacher Education and Special Education, 13*(1), 17-20.

Deno, E. (1970). Special education as developmental capital. *Exceptional Children, 37*, 229-237.

Deshler, D. D., & Schumaker, J. B. (1986). Learning strategies: An instructional alternative for low-achieving adolescents. *Exceptional Children, 52*, 583-590.

Edgar, E. (1987). Secondary programs in special education: Are many of them justifiable? *Exceptional Children, 53*, 555-561.

Englemann, S. E. (1977). Sequencing cognitive and academic tasks. In R. D. Kneedler and S. G. Tarver (Eds.), *Changing perspectives in special education* (pp. 46-61). Columbus, OH: Charles E. Merrill.

Falvey, A. (1989). *Community based curriculum: Instructional strategies for students with severe handicaps* (2nd ed.). Baltimore: Paul H. Brookes Publishing.

Fuchs, D., & Fuchs, L. (1988). Evaluation of the Adaptive Learning Environments Model. *Exceptional Children, 55*, 115-127.

Gartner, A., & Lipsky, D. K. (1987). Beyond special education: Toward a quality system for all students. *Harvard Educational Review, 57*, 367-395.

Gersten, R., & Woodward, J. (1987). *Integrating minority handicapped students into regular classes: A staff development emphasis.* OSERS Research Project.

Goldstein, H., Jordan, L., & Moss, J. W. (1962). *Early school development of low IQ children: A study of special class placement.* U.S. Office of Education Cooperative Research Program. (Project SAE 8204, Interim Report). Urbana, IL: University of Illinois, Institute for Research of Exceptional Children.

Gottlieb, J., Alter, M., & Gottlieb, B. W. (1991). Mainstreaming academically handicapped children in urban schools. In J. W. Lloyd, N. N. Singh, & A. C. Repp (Eds.), *The regular education initiative: Alternative perspectives on concepts, issues, and models* (pp. 95-112). Dekalb, IL: Sycamore.

Hallahan, D., Kauffman, J., Lloyd, J., & McKinney, J. (1988). Introduction to the series: Questions about the Regular Education Initiative. *Journal of Learning Disabilities, 21*, 3-5.

Hallahan, D., Keller, C., McKinney, J., Lloyd, J., & Bryan, T. (1988). Examining the research base of the Regular Education Initiative: Efficacay studies and the Adaptive Learning Environments Model. *Journal of Learning Disabilities, 21*, 29-35.

Hammill, D. D., & Larsen, S. C. (1973). The effectiveness of psycholinguistic training. Exceptional Children, 41, 5-14.

Hasazi, S. B., & Cobb, R. B. (1988). Vocational education of persons with mild handicaps. In R. Gaylord-Ross, Vocational education for persons with handicaps. Mountain View, CA: Mayfield Publishing Co.

Hasazi, S. B., Salembier, G., & Finck, K. (1983). Directions for the 80's: Vocational preparation for secondary mildly handicapped students. *Teaching Exceptional Children, 15*, 206-209.

Idol, L. (1987). Group story mapping: A comprehensive strategy for both skilled and unskilled readers. *Journal of Learning Disabilities, 20*, 196-205.

Keogh, B. (1988). Perspectives on the Regular Education Initiative. *Learning Disabilities Focus, 4*(1), 3-5.

Lane, H. (1988). Is there a "Psychology of the Deaf?" *Exceptional Children, 55*, 7-19.

Larson, C. (1981). *EBCE State of Iowa dissemination model for BD and LD students.* Fort Dodge: Iowa Central Community College.

Lilly, S. (1988). The Regular Education Initiative: A force for change in general and special education. *Education and Training in Mental Retardation, 23*(4), 253-260.

Lloyd, J. W., & Landrum, T. J. (1990). Self-recording of attention to task: Treatment components and generalization of effects. In T. E. Scruggs & B. Y. L. Wong (Eds.), *Intervention research in learning disabilities* (pp. 235-262). New York: Springer-Verlag.

Lovett, D. L., Haring, K. A., & Smith, D. D. (1990). A follow-up study of recent special education graduates of learning disabilities programs. *Journal of Learning Disabilities, 23*, 108-113.

Lovitt, T. C. (1984). *Tactics for teaching.* Columbus, OH: Charles E. Merrill Publishing Company.

Marvin, C. A. (1989). Language and learning. In D. D. Smith, (Ed.), *Teaching students with learning and behavior problems* (pp. 147-181). Englewood Cliffs, NJ: Prentice-Hall.

MIT. (1990). *Education that works: An action plan for the education of minorities.* Cambridge, MA: Massachusetts Institute of Technology, Quality Education for Minorities Project.

Palinscar, A. S., & Brown, A. L. (1988). *Reciprocal teaching of comprehension-monitoring activities* (Contract No. 400-76-0116). Cambridge, MA: National Institute of Child Health & Human Development.

Pertsch, C. F. (1936). *A comparative study of the progress of subnormal pupils in the grades and in special classes.* New York: Teachers College, Columbia University, Bureau of Publications.

Reynolds, M., Wang, M., & Walberg, H. (1987). The necessary restructuring of special and regular education. *Exceptional Children, 53*, 391-398.

Richmond, J. B. (1983). An evaluation of the effectiveness of P. L. 94-142. *Exceptional Parent, 13*(4), 13-18.

Scuccimarra, D. J., & Speece, D. L. (1990). Employment outcomes and social integration of students with mild handicaps: The quality of life two years after high school. *Journal of Learning Disabilities, 23,* 213-219.

Schumaker, J. B., & Deshler, D. D. (1988). Implementing the Regular Education Initiative in secondary schools: A different ball game. *Journal of Learning Disabilities, 21,* 36-42.

Semmel, M. I., & Gerber, M. M. (1988). *The future of special education research.* A report of proceedings of the National Inquiry Study Group on development of a research agenda for the future of education for students with special needs. Santa Barbara: University of California.

Smith, D. D., & Luckasson, R. L. (in press). *Special Education.* Englewood Cliffs, NJ: Prentice-Hall.

Snell, M. E. (1991). Schools are for all kids: The importance of integration for students with severe disabilities and their peers. In J. W. Lloyd, A. C. Repp, & N. N. Singh (Eds.), *The regular education initiative: Alternative perspectives on concepts, issues, and models* (pp. 133-148). Sycamore, IL: Sycamore.

Stainback, W., & Stainback, S. (1984). A rationale for the merger of special and regular education. *Exceptional Children, 51,* 102-111.

United States Department of Education (1990). *Twelfth annual report to Congress on the implementation of the Education of the Handicapped Act.* Washington, DC: U.S. Government Printing Office.

Vergason, G., & Anderegg, M. (1989). *The rest of the story: an answer to the "Regular Education Initiative: A force for change in general and special education."* Unpublished manuscript.

Walker, H., & Bullis, M. (1991). Behavior disorders and the social context of regular class integrations:

A conceptual dilemma? In J. W. Lloyd, N. N. Singh, A. C. Repp (Eds.), *The regular education initiative: Alternative perspectives on concepts, issues, and models* (pp. 75-93). Sycamore, IL: Sycamore.

Wang, M., & Birch, J. (1984). Effective special education in regular classes. *Exceptional Children, 50,* 391-398.

Wang, M., Peverly, S., & Randolf, R. (1984). An investigation of the implementation and effects of a full-time mainstreaming program. *Remedial and Special Education, 5*(6), 21-32.

Wang, M., Reynolds, M., & Walberg, H. (1987, April). *State of the art and future directions of research, practice, and policy related to the education of students with special needs.* Paper presented at the American Educational Research Association, Washington, DC.

Wehman, P., & Hill, J. (1982). Preparing severely handicapped youth for less restrictive environments. *Journal of the Association for the Severely Handicapped, 7*(1), 33-39.

Wiederholt, J. L. (1989). Restructuring special education services: The past, the present, the future. *Learning Disability Quarterly, 12,* 181-191.

Wilcox, B. & Bellamy, G. T. (1982). *Design of high school programs for severely handicapped students.* Baltimore: Paul Brookes Publishing Co.

Will, M. (1986). *Educating children with learning problems: A shared responsibility.* A report to the secretary. Washington, DC: U.S. Department of Education.

Ysseldyke, J. E., Thurlow, M. L., Wotruba, J. W., & Nania, P. A. (1990). Instructional arrangements: Perceptions from general education. *Teaching Exceptional Children, 22*(4), 4-9.

Zigmond, N., & Thornton, H. S. (1985). Follow-up of post-secondary aged LD graduates and dropouts. *Learning Disabilities Research, 1*(1), 50-55.

PART III

12

INCREASING THE AMOUNT AND QUALITY OF LEARNING THROUGH DIRECT INSTRUCTION: IMPLICATIONS FOR MATHEMATICS

Douglas Carnine
University of Oregon

Concern over student performance in mathematics is growing. In international comparisons, we consistently rank near the bottom. Even when we devote many years of attention to a topic, such as fractions, the results are disappointing. In France, fractions are not introduced until the equivalent of our seventh grade. At the end of that year, French students clearly outperform U.S. students. Only one-third of the seventh-grade-age U.S. students can add fractions such as 1/2 and 1/3.

The situation for students with learning disabilities is even more dismal. In one large study, 8- and 9-year-olds identified as having learning disabilities were found to perform at about the first grade level in math calculations and applications, while 16- and 17-year-old students identified similarly scored at about the fifth grade level (Cawley & Miller, 1989). What proficiency such students exhibit is usually restricted to calculations, rather than analysis or problem solving (Algozzine, O'Shea, Crews, & Stoddard, 1987).

Serving atypical students in general education classrooms requires effective instruction in that setting, whether the subject is math, reading, science, or social studies. Two central, school-related variables that influence achievement in general education classrooms are how subject-matter content is organized in curricular material, and how teachers interact with their students. In math, the importance of curricular material is indicated by correlations of .7 to .8 between topic emphasis observed in classrooms and found in the math texts used in those classrooms. However, most widely-used math texts do not appear to be designed with below-average students in mind (e.g., Kameenui & Griffin, 1989). Thus, the way concepts are explained and integrated probably contribute to the confusion experienced by many students.

The other classroom variable has to do with how much interactive teaching takes place. As Baker and Zigmond (1990) reported in their observational study of a low-income urban school "students spent at least one-third of instructional time on activities such as waiting for teacher directions, getting and putting away materials, and lining up and moving to new activities. ....There was almost no interactive instruction or student talk in reading and math classes" (p. 525). For general education classrooms to successfully accommodate a full range of student abilities, change seems needed in both the organization of textbook content and in the way time is used.

RESEARCH ON DIRECT INSTRUCTION

An ideal solution to these problems would be a combination of curricular material and teaching methods that could boost the performance of both mainstream and special-needs students (learning disabled, chapter 1, bilingual). One candidate is the Direct Instruction system. In a major national study (Stebbins, St. Pierre, Proper, Anderson, & Cerva, 1977), economically disadvantaged and handicapped students who participated in Direct Instruction in kindergarten through third grade performed as well as their more advantaged peers. In that study, the Direct Instruction system was also compared with other educational approaches (Gersten & Carnine, 1984). The other approaches ranged from Piagetian-derived to open-classroom models, psychodynamic approaches, and several models based on discovery learning. The third graders in over a dozen Direct Instruction school districts scored at the 48 percentile on the math section of the Metropolitan Achievement Test. The mean percentile for all the other approaches (except for that of the University of Kansas) *was below the 20th percentile*. A confirmation of these findings came from interviews with parents conducted by the Huron Institute (Haney, 1977). Parents of students in Direct Instruction felt their children were getting a better education than did parents of students in any other approaches. Moreover, Direction Instruction students' scores were also highest on measures of self-esteem, responsibility for success in school, and responsibility for failure in school.

Out of the thousands of students included in the study, 321 students were not economically disadvantaged. These students scored well above the third-grade level in mathematics (Gersten & Carnine, 1984); their grade-equivalent scores were:

- 4.3 in problem number solving (the 75th percentile)

- 4.4 in concepts (the 68th percentile)

- 4.8 in computation (the 83rd percentile)

In a related finding, Gersten, Becker, Heiry, and White (1984) reported that although students entering Direct Instruction with relatively low IQ's scored lower on entry level mathematics tests than did students who entered with higher IQ's, both groups gained at least one grade-equivalent unit per year (see Figure 1). Also, students who entered Direct Instruction with an IQ of over 111 did not, as a group, experience regression toward the mean, which would be expected.

Other research has focused exclusively on special education students who received Direct Instruction. White (1988) conducted a meta analysis of experimental studies lasting a week or more with mildly, moderately, and severely handicapped students. Of the 25 studies identified, no outcome measures significantly favored the comparison treatment; 53% of the outcome measures significantly favored the Direction Instruction treatment. The mean effect size was .84 standard deviation units.

These summative findings are complemented by the formative results reported by Haynes and Jenkins (1986). They compared special education instruction in an urban district and in a Direct Instruction suburban district:

The suburban sample showed lower proportions of academic other, out of room, off-task, individual seatwork, one-to-one instruction, and interactions with teachers. They showed higher proportions of small group instruction, cognitive instruction, and direct reading. The suburban sample spent nearly three times more minutes daily in academic activities than did the urban sample (24 vs. 8.5). (p. 175)

TWO MAJOR COMPONENTS OF DIRECTINSTRUCTION

The process variables studied by Haynes and Jenkins (1986) relate to only one of the two major components of the Direct Instruction system; effective teaching methods. These effective teaching behaviors were first given prominence by Rosenshine (1976), after he analyzed a large body of educational research to determine which instructional practices were consistently associated with higher academic achievement scores. He noted that such scores are demonstrated when teachers observe the following practices:

- Devote substantial time to active instruction.

- Break complex skills and concepts into small, easy-to-understand steps and systematically teach in a step-to-step fashion.

- Provide immediate feedback to students about the accuracy of their work.

- Conduct much of the instruction in small groups to allow for frequent student-teacher interactions.

Many reviews of effective teaching practices have been published since 1976; one recent one used the phrase Critical Instructional Factors (Christenson, Ysseldyke, & Thurlow, 1989) to describe similar procedures.

The Direct Instruction system that originated in 1968 with the federal pro-

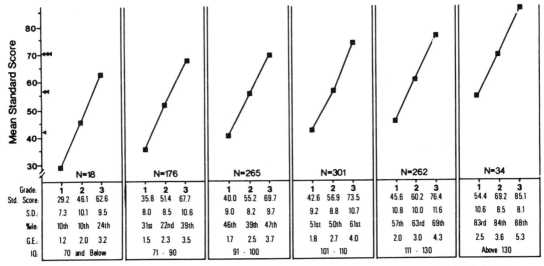

Figure 1: Total mathematics score on the Metropolitan Achievement Test showing longitudinal progress by IQ block for children who entered direct instruction model sites at kindergarten (N = 1056). (From "entry IQ and yearly academic growth of children in direct instruction programs: A longitudinal study of low SES children" by R. Gersten, W. Becker, T. Heiry, and W. White, 1984, *Educational Evaluation and Policy Analysis*, 6, (2) 109-121. Copyright 1984 by American Educational Research Association. Reprinted by permission.

gram, Follow Through, incorporated most of these practices. However, there was a second component of even greater importance, analyses of subject area content and the resulting curricular material. These analyses are explicated in detail in *Theory of Instruction* (Engelmann & Carnine, 1982) and, more recently, have been related to research on the brain's basic operation of noting samenesses (Carnine, 1990). Thus, Direct Instruction comprises both a set of teacher practices and curricular analyses that manifest themselves in instructional programs.

The instruction takes the form of frequent interchanges between the teacher and the students. To ensure that what is intended is delivered, daily lessons are designed in script form, showing the teacher what to do and what to say during these interchanges. Although the use of scripted lesson plans has been criticized as restricting the teacher's initiative and creativity, some important values derive from the use of scripts. One goal is designing disseminable procedures for improving instruction. Scripts permit the use of explicitly pretested examples and explanations. (The procedures that govern the creation of instructional examples and explanations are discussed later.) The teacher knows that if the students have the prerequisite skills, the teaching sequence will work. The teacher does not have to spend time experimenting with various possible illustrations, choosing appropriate language, and analyzing possible teaching sequences.

Scripted lessons also facilitate the effective use of direct observation. A staff developer observing the behavior of a student receiving Direct Instruction is able to focus on a narrow range of critical instructional variables that are likely to have a significant impact on student performance. In addition, a variety of direct observation instruments have been developed (Gersten, Carnine, Zoref, & Cronin, 1986) specifically to facilitate the collection of data on both teacher and student behavior during the course of Direct Instruction.

The next section illustrates how Direct Instruction points out important connections in mathematics. Math educators understandably value the integration of concepts to illustrate important connections (Lindquist, 1984; Trafton, 1984; & Steen, 1989). The illustrations from primary grade mathematics range from basic math facts to problem solving (analyzing word problems). These examples are fairly detailed because they bring to life the heart of the Direct Instruction system; the analysis of the curriculum. This second major component is usually overlooked because of the greater prominence obtained by the effective teaching practices, as articulated by Rosenshine (1976), Christenson et al. (1989), and others. However, effective teaching practices are only part of an overall solution. The ways in which topics are analyzed and then explained are equally important. The following discussion of facts illustrates how cognitively simple content can be conceptually integrated and taught efficiently. The greater complexity of word problems is reflected in the explanation of how this content can be conceptually integrated and explicitly taught, to the benefit of both special education and above-average students.

ILLUSTRATIONS OF DIRECT INSTRUCTION CURRICULUM ANALYSIS

Basic Facts

Basic facts as families. Addition and subtraction facts are usually treated as 200 discrete sets of three numbers to be memorized. An alternative organizational structure to teaching facts is to teach them as members of families. This structure prompts important relationships between addition and subtraction, as well as reduces the number of sets to be memorized from 200 to 55. From these 55 number families, all 200 addition and subtraction facts can be quickly derived. The 55 number families appear in Figure 2.

Number families are written on an arrow so that they can be transformed into both addition and subtraction statements.

For example, in the number family

$$6 \qquad 9 \longrightarrow 15$$

6 and 9 are treated as "small numbers" and 15 is treated as a "big number." Four facts can be derived from this family. Each of two addition facts starts with one of the small numbers and adds the other small number to produce the big number: $6 + 9 = 15$ and $9 + 6 = 15$. The subtraction facts begin with the big number and subtract one of the small numbers, yielding the other small number: $15 - 6 = 9$ and $15 - 9 = 6$. Students who memorize 55 number families know how to deduce all 200 facts: 45 of the 55 families yield 4 facts (2 addition and 2 subtraction), which account for 180 facts. Each of the 10 families on the diagonal in Figure 2, such as theses families

$$1 \qquad 1 \longrightarrow 2 \qquad 2 \qquad 2 \longrightarrow 4 \qquad 3 \qquad 3 \longrightarrow 6$$

yields two facts (e.g., $1 + 1 = 2$ and $2 - 1 = 1$; $2 + 2 = 4$ and $4 - 2 = 2$; etc.). 180 facts + 20 facts = 200 facts. Memorizing 55 families is easier and less time consuming than memorizing 200 facts. Teaching the fact number families

Figure content (number family table):

```
1→2(1,1)  1→3(1,2)  1→4(1,3)  1→5(1,4)  1→6(1,5)  1→7(1,6)  1→8(1,7)  1→9(1,8)  1→10(1,9)  1→11(1,10)

2→4(2,2)  2→5(2,3)  2→6(2,4)  2→7(2,5)  2→8(2,6)  2→9(2,7)  2→10(2,8)  2→11(2,9)  2→12(2,10)

3→6(3,3)  3→7(3,4)  3→8(3,5)  3→9(3,6)  3→10(3,7)  3→11(3,8)  3→12(3,9)  3→13(3,10)

4→8(4,4)  4→9(4,5)  4→10(4,6)  4→11(4,7)  4→12(4,8)  4→13(4,9)  4→14(4,10)

5→10(5,5)  5→11(5,6)  5→12(5,7)  5→13(5,8)  5→14(5,9)  5→15(5,10)

6→12(6,6)  6→13(6,7)  6→14(6,8)  6→15(6,9)  6→16(6,10)

7→14(7,7)  7→15(7,8)  7→16(7,9)  7→17(7,10)

8→16(8,8)  8→17(8,9)  8→18(8,10)

9→18(9,9)  9→19(9,10)

10→20(10,10)
```

Figure 2: Addition and subtraction number family table.

also promotes the integration of the concepts of addition and subtraction.

The counting relationships among facts. More can be done to help students learn facts than just reducing the memory load from 200 sets of numbers to 55. Additional teaching of counting relationships between facts eases the learning of these 55 sets. For example, number families with a 1 are fairly easy to learn, because the big number is the next number when counting in order. For example, 8 is the big number after 7 when counting by 1: $1 + 7 = 8$. Similarly, 9 is the big number after 8 when counting by 1: $1 + 8 = 9$. The big numbers in the top row of Figure 2 are simply the counting numbers 2, 3, 4, 5, 6, 7, 8, 9, 10, 11.

Facts with 2 as a small number are closely related to facts with the number 1 as a small number. This pattern is reflected in these corresponding addition facts:

$$\begin{array}{c} \overline{}\,1 + 6 = 7\,\overline{} \\ +1 \qquad\qquad +1 \\ \rightarrow 2 + 6 = 8\,\leftarrow \end{array}$$

This relationship is repeated for every pair of families. The increment from 1 to 2 equals the increment from 7 to 8 (and from 8 to 9, from 9 to 10, and so forth):

$$\begin{array}{c} \overline{}\,1 + 7 = 8\,\overline{} \\ +1 \qquad\qquad +1 \\ \rightarrow 2 + 7 = 9\,\leftarrow \end{array}$$

This relationship helps students learn to go from the easier facts with a 1 to facts with a 2; if $\underline{1} + 6 = \underline{7}$, then $\underline{2} + 6 = \underline{8}$.

Another example of counting relationships among facts can be seen in the relationship between facts with 10 as a small number and the difficult group of facts that have 9 as a small number. Addition facts that contain the number 10 as a small number are easy to remember because the digits in the answer come from the digits in the added numbers. For example, in the problem $3 + 10 = [\ ]$, the digits for the answer appear in the added numbers $\underline{3} + 10 = 1\underline{3}$. The answer 13 is composed of one ten and three ones.

The simplicity of facts with a 10 can help students with the more difficult group of facts, with a 9. For example, the family of 3, 10, 13 in the last column of Figure 2 has the corresponding family of 3, 9, 12 in the preceding column. The two corresponding addition facts for these families are:

9 is one less than 10

$$3 + 9 = 12 \qquad 3 + 10 = 13$$

so 12 is one less than 13

This relationship applies to every pair of problems:

9 is one less than 10

$$4 + 9 = \Box \qquad 4 + 10 = 14$$

so $\Box$ is one less than 14

So, when students see any addition problems with a 9, such as $7 + 9$, they can think of the easy corresponding fact ($7 + 10 = 17$) and come up with the answer to $7 + 9 = \Box$, which is one less than 17.

$$7 + 10 = 17 \quad \text{so } 7 + 9 = \boxed{16}$$

For research on the relationship between counting strategies and fact acquisition, see Carnine and Stein (1981), Carpenter and Moser (1983), and Thornton (1978).

Problem Solving

The most prevalent and frustrating math application exercise in primary-grade math programs is word problems (Kameenui & Griffin, 1989). The frustration stems largely from an inability of mathematics educators to devise explicit strategies that special-needs students can learn and successfully apply. A consequence of this frustration is the avoidance of any but the most rudimentary type of addition and subtraction word problems in textbooks (Peterson, Fennema, & Carpenter, 1989). Peterson et al. recommend that students be prepared to handle the variations of the four basic types of word problems: *join, separate, compare*, and *part/part-whole* (part/part-whole refers to classification: *Cats* and *dogs* would be the parts and *pets* would be the whole). The following analysis illustrates explicit strategies that students can successfully apply to this full range of problems.

An explicit strategy should prepare students to see the total structure of a problem and *not* just rely on specific key words. For example, the word "more" appears in many joining problems calling for addition; for example:

Juan had 7 marbles. He won 5 *more*. How many marbles does he have now?

But the word also appears in a significant number of comparison problems that call for subtraction:

Jill had 614 dollars. Tom had 829 dollars. How much *more* money did Tom have?

Students who think the word *more* always represents joining and calls for addition have a superficial understanding of problem solving, at best. Clearly, they could not be expected to answer these problems correctly.

The strategy illustrated next is aimed at teaching students to see the relationship between the situation described in a story problem and the concept of a number family composed of two small numbers (e.g., 5 + 4) and a larger number (e.g., 9). Number families are useful because they provide a map that can be used to diagram

the various types of word problems. The number family map in turn leads to setting up the addition or subtraction calculation. The strategy teaches students not to make quick judgments because of the presence of a particular word such as *more*. The strategy has students work in two stages. The students first graphically represent the situation described in the word problem; second they determine how to write the number problem. The strategy will be illustrated with joining and separating problems, then comparison problems, and finally part/part-whole problems.

Joining and separating problems. In the following word problem about Marco, special-needs students are likely to add 57 and 112 because the problem says that Marco earned more dollars. The students assume that because it is a joining problem, they should carry out the operation for joining by adding the numbers that are given. However, adding 57 and 112 does not lead to the correct answer.

Marco's mother will give him some money for a school trip. But he has to earn 57 more dollars. He needs 112 dollars. How much money will his mother give him?

To prevent this confusion, teachers explain how to represent the joining situation described in the word problem. This representation takes the form of a diagram based on the number family analysis. In joining problems such as the one about Marco earning more, the numbers that are joined or added are the small numbers. The total, in this case the number of dollars Marco needs, is the big number. As students have learned from working with number families, the two small values go on top of the arrow and the big number, which is the sum in this example, goes at the end of the arrow:

After students represent the situation with a number family, they are ready to apply what they have learned about the relationships between addition and subtraction to compute the answer. For example when the unknown in a number family is a small number, such as is the case with the number family in the Marco problem, the number family can be translated into a subtraction problem. The big number, 112, is the first number in the subtraction problem. The small number that is given, 57, is then subtracted from the big number, 112 - 57 = ☐, to produce the other small number: 112 - 57 = 55.

In short, students learn first to represent the joining situation described by the word problem and, second, to decide how to compute the answer based on the relationship between addition and subtraction. For example, if both small numbers are given in a problem, they are written above the arrow.

```
32        89
———————————→   ☐
```

The students would then add the small numbers to figure out the big number.

Comparison problems. In comparison problems, the comparison can be information given in a problem (e.g, Marco sold 57 fewer subscriptions than Lui) or the unknown asked about in a problem (e.g,. How much heavier was Mary?). Because of the words "sold fewer" in the following problem, many special-needs students will subtract.

> Marco sold 57 fewer magazine subscriptions than Lui. Marco sold 112 subscriptions. How many subscriptions did Lui sell?

Again, students can use number families to keep from getting confused. The first step is to represent the problem using a number family; students must identify the two values being compared in

the problem as either both small numbers or a small number and the big number. The students are shown a simple way to do this: They find the sentence that tells about the comparison and read it without the number that tells how many more or how many less. For example, students are taught to read the first sentence without the 57: "Marco sold fewer subscriptions than Lui." Because Marco sold fewer subscriptions, Marco is represented by a small number. By default, Lui is the big number. The students write M for Marco and L for Lui:

```
        M
———————————→   L
```

The word problem also has a number that gives the difference between Marco and Lui. That number is always a small number. Marco sold 57 fewer, so 57 is the other small number:

```
57        M
———————————→   L
```

The students next read the rest of the problem. The problem asks about Lui and gives a number for Marco, so the students draw a box around L and cross out Marco and write 112:

```
57        M̶  112
———————————→   [L]
```

Because the problem states both small numbers, the students write an addition problem:

```
   57
+112
```

The answer tells how many magazine subscriptions Lui sold.

Part/part-whole problems. Part/part-whole problems can be thought of as classification problems. To work part/part-whole problems, students need to understand the relationships among the classes named in a problem. For example, cats and dogs are members of the class pets; or as in the following problem, magazine subscriptions and newspaper subscriptions are members of the inclusive ("bigger") class, subscriptions. As in the earlier examples, special-needs students are likely to miss the problem by adding the numbers, because of the verb "get."

> Maria has to get 112 magazine and newspaper subscriptions. She is sure she can get 57 magazine subscriptions. How many newspaper subscriptions does she have to get?

To represent this situation with a number family, students treat subscriptions, the *big* class, as the *big* number. The names for the subordinate classes go in the places for the "small" numbers, on top of the number family arrow:

magazine   newspaper
————————————————→ subscriptions

The students cross out the words that have number values and draw a box around the word the problem asks about:

57
~~magazine~~   [newspaper]   112
————————————————→ ~~subscriptions~~

The students know the big number, 112; so they subtract: 112 - 57 = ☐. The answer gives the number for newspaper subscriptions. For research on teaching students explicit strategies to solve word problems, see Darch, Carnine, and Gersten (1984), Gleason, Carnine, and Boriero (in press), and Moore and Carnine (1989).

Number families are also useful for application problems beyond the primary-grades. Consider this problem:

Lui and Marco have agreed to sell subscriptions and boxes of candy to raise money for a school trip. They have to sell 115 subscriptions and 181 boxes of candy. Marco started early. When he finished he had sold 57 subscriptions and 90 boxes of candy. He claimed he sold his share of subscriptions. Has he? What's the total number of subscriptions and boxes of candy that Lui has to sell?

To solve this problem, students are taught to construct another type of map, a table such as this:

	Marco	Lui	Totals
Subscriptions	57		115
Candy	90		181
Totals			

To answer the first question about subscriptions, the students put the values from the top row of the table in a number family:

57   ☐
————————————————→ 115

They know the big number, so they subtract: 115 - 57 = ☐. Lui has to sell 58 subscriptions. So Marco has sold his fair share; he's sold 57.

Answering the second question-- "What's the total number of subscriptions and boxes of candy that Lui has to sell?"--requires students to handle problems with two unknowns: the number of boxes of candy and the total. Students are taught that before they can solve for the total, they must first solve for the number of boxes of candy. To do this, they draw a diagram for the values in the second row:

90   ☐
————————————————→ 181,

then write the subtraction problem, 181 - 90 = ☐, and figure out the answer, 91. The students now know two small numbers, the number of subscriptions (58) and the number of boxes of candy (91) Lui has to sell. To find the total Lui must sell (the "big" class), the students add the 58 subscriptions and 91 boxes of candy.

Teaching students the number family analysis for word problems is not easy. However, the analysis gives both the teacher and the students an explicit, manageable way to solve fairly difficult problems. The value of a specific strategy stands in stark contrast to what is offered as teaching in the most widely accepted math basal in 1990. The following quotes represent all the suggestions to the teacher for introducing new types of word problems in that basal:

- "Ask students if each problem describes a joining situation, a removing situation, or a comparing situation."

- "For each problem, ask students to explain their choice of a computation method."

- "Have student read all problems before actually solving any of them. Ask which problems require finding an estimated product."

CONCLUSION

Note that direct instruction teaching practices--frequent questions, small steps, constructive feedback, active monitoring, sufficient time, and so forth--could be applied to a very conventional analysis of facts and word problems. For the comparatively simple domain of facts, the outcome would be fairly reasonable. Students would memorize 200 addition and subtraction facts as unrelated pieces of information in an inefficient manner, but the students would be successful. For the more complex domain of problem solving, direct instruction teaching practices are not enough (Moore & Carnine, 1989). In fact, when students are being

taught to analyze word problems in a conventional manner, such as read, analyze, plan and solve, the lack of conceptually integrated instruction can lead to frustration. Darch, Carnine, and Gersten (1984) found that instructional practices, such as frequent assessment with extra instruction, were not beneficial and possibly harmful.

The apparent dilemma is whether to make important relationships explicit for average and below-average students, and possibly "hold back" the above-average students. A key assumption of this dilemma is that explicit, conceptually integrated instruction, such as found in Direct Instruction, is inappropriate for higher-order skills with above-average students (Peterson, 1979). Some recent research reviews indicate that this is not the case, at least for problem solving in computer science (Dalley & Linn, 1985), for learning to design scientific experiments (Ross, 1988), and for developing logical and analogical reasoning (Grossen & Carnine, 1989). It might be more accurate to say that careful, explicit instruction with above-average students is not as important for *less* cognitively complex pursuits. For below-average students, explicit, conceptually integrated instruction is fairly important at all levels of cognitive complexity. The hypothesized relationships are displayed in Figure 3.

The basis for the hypothesized relationships lies in the findings from the recent brain research cited earlier (Carnine, 1990); the noting of samenesses. With less complex content, students who are facile, intuitive learners (i.e., above-average students) note important connections fairly readily. Less capable students benefit from explicit instruction that points out these important connections.

For more complex content, research suggests that carefully integrated, explicit instruction benefits students from a full range of abilities. What is less clear is how explicit instruction on less complex content affects above-average students and how the differing amounts of practice required by students of varying ability can best be accommodated in a classroom.

An even larger problem is how to bridge the gap between typical educational practices and those implied by a system such as Direct Instruction. In Direct Instruction much more time is devoted to interactive teaching. Even though scripts are provided, interactive teaching is quite demanding and the scripts are constraining. Moreover, the interactions are governed, in nature and amount, by the performance of the students. Thus, the teacher is continually deciding (a) how to relate what students have learned to any current confusions, and (b) how much demonstration and guided practice to provide, given the typical spread of student abilities. Doing this well requires great professional as well as technical expertise.

In addition, the use of scripts symbolizes a major barrier to the adoption of Direct Instruction; its high degree of structure and teacher-centered philosophy. Many educators favor more child-centered and indirect approaches. These educators feel that the scripted lessons and extensive practice and assessment are unnecessary, at best. On the other hand, less able students seem to suffer when instruction is not sufficiently explicit. This belief is expressed by Delpit (1988) in her *Harvard Education Review* article:

> If such explicitness is not provided to students, what it feels like to people who are old enough to judge is that there are secrets being kept, that time is being wasted, that the teacher is abdicating his or her duty to teach. (p. 287)

The pressure to serve special-needs students effectively is growing, in part because our public schools are becoming more diverse. Mainstreaming is one cause. The other is changing demographics. In five states and the District of Columbia, 50% or more of the students are minority. In five other states, 40% of the students are minority. In 20 years, more than half the U.S. students will be minorities, which means there will no longer be a majority made up of any single group. Public schools, particularly in our cities, are being challenged to improve, yet with changing demographics and mainstream-

Importance of Direct Instruction

		Great		Moderate		Slight
Cognitive	High	SE	BA	A	AA	
Complexity						
of Task To						
Be Learned	Low	SE		BA	A	AA

Figure 3: Relationship between importance of direct instruction and and cognitive complexity for above Average (AA), Average (A), Below Average (BA), and Special Education (SE) students.

ing, maintaining current levels of achievement will be difficult. The only hope for public schools is genuine reform of the curriculum materials and the ways in which teachers and students spend their time. Lack of coordination between reform of the curriculum and teacher practices yields fragmented change that will not adequately serve special-needs students. Intensive, coordinated reform is the only honest option.

REFERENCES

Algozzine, B., O'Shea, D. J., Crews, W. B., & Stoddard, K. (1987). Analysis of mathematics competence of learning disabled adolescents. *Journal of Special Education, 21*, 97-107.

Baker, J., & Zigmond, N. (1990). Are regular education classes equipped to accommodate students with learning disabilities? *Exceptional Children, 56*, 515-526.

Carnine, D. (1990). New research on the brain: Implications for instruction. *Phi Delta Kappan, 71*, 372-377.

Carnine, D. W., & Stein, M. (1981). Organizational strategies and practice procedures for teaching basic facts. *Journal of Research in Mathematics Education, 12*, 65-69.

Carpenter, T. P., & Moser, J. M. (1983). The acquisition of addition and subtraction concepts. In R. Lesh & M. Landau (Eds.), *Acquisition of mathematics concepts and processes* (pp. 7-44). New York: Academic Press.

Cawley, J. F., & Miller, J. H. (1989). Cross-sectional comparisons of the mathematical performance of children with learning disabilities: Are we on the right track toward comprehensive programming? *Journal of Learning Disabilities, 22*, 250-254, 259.

Christenson, S., Ysseldyke, J., & Thurlow, M. (1989). Critical instructional factors for students with mild handicaps: An integrative review. *Remedial and Special Education, 10*, 21-31.

Dalley, J., & Linn, M. C. (1985). The demands and requirements of computer programming: A literature review. *Journal of Educational Computing Research, 2*, 253.

Darch, C., Carnine, D., & Gersten, R. (1984). Explicit instruction in mathematics problem solving. *Journal of Educational Research, 77*, 350-359.

Delpit, L. D. (1988). The silenced dialogue: Power and pedagogy in educating other people's children. *Harvard Education Review, 58*, 280-298.

Engelmann, S., & Carnine, D. (1982). *Theory of instruction.* New York: Irvington.

Gersten, R., Becker, W., Heiry, T., & White, W. (1984). Entry IQ and yearly academic growth of children in Direct Instruction programs: A longitudinal study of low SES children. *Educational Evaluation and Policy Analysis, 6*, 109-121.

Gersten, R., & Carnine, D. (1984). Direct Instruction mathematics: A longitudinal evaluation of low SES elementary students. *Elementary School Journal, 84*, 395-407.

Gersten, R., Carnine, D., Zoref, L., & Cronin, D. (1986). A multifaceted study of change in seven inner city schools. *Elementary School Journal, 86*, 257-276.

Gleason, M., Carnine, D., & Boriero, D. (in press). Improving CAI effectiveness with attention to instructional design in teaching story problems to mildly handicapped students. *Journal of Special Education Technology.*

Grossen, B., & Carnine, D. (1989). *Review of empirical evaluations of interventions for teaching logical and analogical reasoning.* Unpublished manuscript. Eugene: University of Oregon.

Haney, W. (1977). *Reanalysis of Follow Through parent and teacher data.* Boston: Huron Institute.

Haynes, M. C., & Jenkins, J. R. (1986). Reading instruction in special education resource rooms. *American Educational Research Journal, 23*, 161-190.

Kameenui, E., & Griffin, C. (1989). The national crisis in verbal problem solving in mathematics: A proposal for examining the role of basal mathematics programs. *Elementary School Journal, 89*, 575-593.

Lindquist, M. M. (1984). The elementary school mathematics curriculum: Issues for today. *Elementary School Journal, 84*, 595-609.

Moore, L., & Carnine, D. (1989). Evaluating curriculum design in the context of active teaching. *Remedial and Special Education, 10*, 28-37.

Peterson, P. L. (1979). Direct Instruction: Effective for what and for whom? *Educational Leadership, 37*, 46-48.

Peterson, P. L., Fennema, E., & Carpenter, T. (1989). Using knowledge of how students think about mathematics. *Educational Leadership, 46*(4), 42-46.

Rosenhine, B. (1976). Recent research on teaching behavior and student achievement. *Journal of Teacher Education, 27*, 61-64.

Ross, J. (1988). Controlling variables: A meta-analysis of training studies. *Review of Educational Research, 58*, 405-437.

Stebbins, L. B., St. Pierre, R. G., Proper, E. C., Anderson, R. B., & Cerva, T. R. (1977). *Education as experimentation: A planned variation model.* Vols. 4A, 4C. *An evaluation of Follow Through.* Cambridge, MA: Author.

Steen, L. (1989, September). Teaching mathematics for tomorrow's world. *Educational Leadership*, pp. 18-22.

Thornton, C. A. (1978). Emphasizing thinking strategies in basic fact instruction. *Journal for Research in Mathematics Education, 9*, 214-227.

Trafton, P. R. (1984). Toward more effective, efficient instruction in mathematics. *Elementary School Journal, 84*, 515-527.

White, W. A. T. (1988). A meta-analysis of the effects of Direct Instruction in special education. *Education and Treatment of Children, 11*, 364-374.

13

COOPERATIVE LEARNING AND MAINSTREAMING

Robert E. Slavin and Robert J. Stevens
Johns Hopkins University

Cooperative learning methods are instructional techniques in which students work in heterogeneous learning teams to help one another learn academic material (Slavin, 1983a, 1990). From its inception, one of the most important applications of cooperative learning has been to assist in mainstreaming students with academic handicaps (see Madden & Slavin, 1983a, 1983b; Johnson & Johnson, 1980). Using cooperative learning to facilitate mainstreaming may involve team teaching between regular and special education teachers, but it always involves handicapped and nonhandicapped students working together in small groups.

There are many reasons for using cooperative learning to facilitate mainstreaming. First, mainstreamed academically handicapped students tend to be poorly accepted by their nonhandicapped classmates (e.g., Bruininks, 1978). Cooperative learning activities, in which all students can make a meaningful contribution to the success of a group, offer a means of increasing friendships and acceptance among handicapped and nonhandicapped students (Madden & Slavin, 1983a; Stevens, Slavin, & Farnish, 1989). Cooperative methods have been found to increase friendships and peer acceptance in general (Slavin, 1990) and more specifically to improve race rela-

tions (Slavin, 1985a), so the extension to improvement of the acceptance of mainstreamed students can be expected. In particular, participation in cooperative groups helps academically handicapped students to blend in with classroom activities and social structure. Many observers have noted the difficulty of picking out the mainstreamed students in a cooperative learning classroom. The theoretical basis for expecting that cooperative learning will improve acceptance of mainstreamed academically handicapped students is similar to the basis for cooperative learning effects on race relations. Positive relationships between mainstreamed and nonhandicapped students are expected to arise when they are working together toward a common goal, because the task-related efforts of each student benefit the group and make each group member valued by the group, and because the interactive setting allows nonhandicapped students to get to know their handicapped group-mates as individuals rather than as members of a low-status group--special education students (see Slavin, 1985a, 1990).

In addition, there is good reason to believe that the structure of the traditional classroom contributes to the expression of negative affect toward low-performing students. Students in almost all classrooms compete with one another for acceptable grades and other rewards (Johnson & Johnson, 1987; Slavin, 1990). Only a few, those who do *better* than the others, will receive A's. The academically handicapped child, who is on the losing end of the competition more frequently than on the winning side, is often a target for expression of the negative feelings found to be generated in competitive situations (Ames, Ames, & Felker, 1977). If the classroom is changed so that cooperation rather than competition is emphasized and so that academically handicapped students can make a meaningful contribution to the success of a cooperative group, acceptance of such students seems likely to increase.

The rationale for expecting positive effects of cooperative learning on the achievement of mainstreamed academically handicapped students is similar to that for other students. In essence, cooperative learning is expected to enhance student achievement because it increases motivation to learn (because peers support learning), because students can provide explanations to one another within the proximal zone of development of their peers, because students learn by teaching others, and because students can provide one-to-one assessment and assistance tailored to each others' unique needs (Slavin, 1990). However, it is important to note that cooperative learning has only been successful in enhancing student achievement when it incorporates two elements: group goals and individual accountability (Slavin, 1983b, 1990). That is, students must receive rewards or recognition based on the success of their group, and this success must depend on the individual learning of all group members. Most often, this means that group scores are based on the average of all group members on quizzes or other assessments that students take without the help of their groupmates.

There is one additional rationale that applies to a few cooperative learning methods. Mainstreaming academically handicapped students inherently increases heterogeneity of the class. In very heterogeneous classes, there is a strong rationale for some sort of individualization, yet research on individualized instruction has not generally supported this approach (Fuchs & Fuchs, 1988; Horak, 1981). Two of the cooperative learning methods, Cooperative Integrated Reading and Composition (CIRC) (Stevens, Madden, Slavin, & Farnish, 1987) and Team Assisted Individualization (Slavin, 1985b), allow for the use of both homogeneous and heterogeneous groupings to accommodate instruction to individual needs. Cooperative learning helps make this work by providing a structure in which students can help each other and can help manage activities and materials that free the teacher to teach.

WHAT IS COOPERATIVE LEARNING?

The cooperative learning methods that have been used and evaluated as means of mainstreaming academically handicapped students fall into two major categories. One category includes simple methods, such as the Johnsons' methods (Johnson & Johnson, 1987) and Student Teams Achievement Division, (STAD) (Slavin, 1986). The other category includes complex methods, such as CIRC and TAI. The simple methods use class-paced instruction and are generic, in the sense that they can be applied to virtually any content and to grades 2-12. The complex methods employ means of accommodating instruction to individual needs, incorporate specific curriculum materials, and are designed for use in particular subjects and grade levels. The following sections describe these approaches and the research done on them in mainstreamed classes.

Simple Cooperative Methods

Two major simple cooperative methods have been evaluated in mainstreamed classes, although there are also studies which used additional methods. The two major methods are as follows: *Student Teams-Achievement Divisions* and the *Johnsons' methods*. In this section we discuss each of these and describe research on them.

STUDENT TEAMS-ACHIEVEMENT DIVISIONS. In STAD (Slavin, 1986, 1990), students are assigned to four-member, heterogeneous learning teams. Academically handicapped students are distributed among the teams. STAD classes follow a regular cycle of activities. First, the teacher presents a lesson. The students have an opportunity to work together to help one another master the material, using problems, worksheets, or other study aids. Finally, the students are individually assessed on brief quizzes or other assessments. Students receive points based on the degree to which their quiz scores exceed those they have received previously, and these improvement points are averaged to form team scores. Teams meeting a high criterion are designated "Superteams" and receive fancy certificates. Those which meet a lower criterion can earn less fancy "Greatteam" certificates.

JOHNSONS' METHODS. Cooperative learning methods developed by David and Roger Johnson (1987) have also been studied with mainstreamed academically handicapped students. In these methods, students work in 4-5 member groups to complete a common assignment sheet. The groups are praised and rewarded, and often graded, on the basis of the quality of the group worksheet. Group members often take on roles within the group (such as "praiser" and "recorder"), and students are given training in social skills and discussion of group process.

RESEARCH ON SIMPLE METHODS. Two principal types of measures have been used to study the effects of cooperative learning on cross-handicap relations:

sociometric and observational. Many studies used sociometric friendship measures, such as "Who are your friends in this class?" and a few used sociometric rejection measures, such as "If you were going to be working on a project with other children, there might be some children you would *not* want to have in your group. Please name these children if there are any." Some of the Johnsons' studies used observational measures of cross-handicap interaction. In general, they provided a ten-minute free period at the end of class in which the frequency of cross-handicap interactions in experimental and control classes was observed.

One study of STAD (Madden & Slavin, 1983a) was conducted in mainstreamed classes. In this study, academically handicapped students received many fewer rejection choices in the STAD groups than in control groups. However, there were no differences on a sociometric "friends" measure.

The largest number of cooperative learning studies involving mainstreaming of academically handicapped students evaluated the effects of the Johnsons' procedures on cross-handicap relations. The results of the Johnsons' studies on acceptance of academically and emotionally handicapped students are mixed but generally positive. Cooper, Johnson, Johnson, and Wilderson (1980) found significantly more friendship choices of academically or emotionally handicapped students in a cooperative condition than in an individualistic one, but there were no differences between the cooperative and competitive conditions. Armstrong, Johnson, and Balow (1981) found no differences between cooperative and individualistic treatments on sociometric measures. However, they found positive effects on two peer-rating scales in which students rated one another from smart to dumb and from valuable to worthless; but, there was no separate analysis of ratings of the academically handicapped students.

One of the four studies that measured cross-handicap interaction during free time found significantly positive effects for the cooperative treatment (Johnson & Johnson, 1981a), and one study (Johnson & Johnson, 1982) found marginally significant positive effects. The remaining two studies (Johnson & Johnson, 1981b; Johnson and Johnson, 1983) found no differences. The Johnson and Johnson (1981b) study used a measure in which students were assigned to new groups and asked to play a structured game. The researchers wished to determine whether a tendency toward cross-handicap interaction would transfer to a new setting and task but found no significant differences. Finally, Johnson and Johnson (1981b) found more cross-handicap acceptance as work partners among students in a cooperative condition than among students in an individualistic one, but they did not state whether they found positive effects both for acceptance of handicapped students by their peers and for acceptance of nonhandicapped students by handicapped classmates.

The earliest and largest of the cooperative learning field experiments to study the effects of cooperation in heterogeneous groups on acceptance of academically handicapped students was conducted by Ballard, Corman, Gottlieb, and Kaufman (1977). In this study, thirty-seven classes in grades three to five were randomly assigned to cooperative or control conditions (twenty-five experimental, twelve control). One educable mentally retarded student was in each class. In the cooperative classes students were assigned to four to six member heterogeneous groups; one group in each class contained the EMR student. Group members worked together to plan, produce and present a multimedia project. Students were instructed to break their task into subtasks to be performed by each group member. The results indicated the EMRs in the experimental groups were better accepted

by their classmates than were control EMRs. There were no differences in sociometric rejections.

Complex Cooperative Learning Methods

In simple forms of cooperative learning, teachers are given staff development in general methods which apply to any curriculum. Without exception, these generic models use class-paced instruction; that is, there is minimal adaptation of the pace and level of instruction to individual needs. Also, since generic cooperative learning methods do not change curriculum or other features of classroom organization and instruction, they do not get at many of the fundamental problems of educational practice.

Fundamental change in schools does not come about through staff development workshops. It comes about (if it ever does occur) through comprehensive changes in curriculum and school and classroom organization, which may be closely tied to changes in instructional methods. When schools undertake comprehensive reform, they are unlikely to do so by grafting innovation teaching methods onto existing curricula; rather, they are likely to seek methods that accomplish the primary goal of schooling, transmission of curriculum to students (see Slavin, Madden, & Stevens, 1989/90).

Since 1980, we and our colleagues at Johns Hopkins University have been developing and evaluating complex, comprehensive cooperative learning approaches to the three major curriculum areas in the elementary school curriculum: reading, writing, and mathematics. More recently, we have begun working to integrate our comprehensive approaches within the same elementary schools and to apply principles of cooperative learning throughout the school, among teachers and administrators as well as students, with an emphasis on mainstreaming and collaboration between regular and special education teachers. The remainder of this chapter describes these comprehensive models and the cooperative elementary school, and summarizes research on each.

TEAM ASSISTED INDIVIDUALIZATION

The first complex comprehensive cooperative learning model we developed and researched was Team Assisted Individualization (TAI) - Mathematics (Slavin, Leavey, & Madden, 1986), a program which combines cooperative learning with individualized instruction to meet the needs of diverse classrooms (Slavin, 1985b).

TAI was developed for several reasons. First, we hoped that TAI would provide a means of combining the motivational power and peer assistance of cooperative learning with an individualized instructional program capable of giving all students materials appropriate to their levels of skill in mathematics and allowing them to proceed through these materials at their own rates. Second, TAI was developed to combine programmed instruction with cooperative learning by turning most of the management functions (e.g., scoring answers, locating and filing materials, keeping records, assigning new work) over to the students themselves, and free the teacher to teach individuals and small, homogeneous teaching groups. Last, TAI was developed as a means of producing the well-documented social effects characteristic of cooperative learning (Slavin, 1990) while meeting diverse needs. The principal concern was with mainstreaming. We saw mainstreaming of academically handicapped students in mathematics as limited by a feeling on the part of regular-class teachers that they were unprepared to accommodate the instructional needs of these students (see Gickling & Theobald, 1975). Further,

studies of attitudes toward academically handicapped students consistently find that these students are not well accepted by their non-handicapped classmates (see Gottlieb & Leyser, 1981). Because cooperative learning methods have had positive effects on social relations of all kinds, and specifically on relationships between handicapped and non-handicapped students, we felt that the best possible mathematics program for the mainstreamed classroom, or indeed for any classroom containing a heterogeneous group of students would be one that combined cooperative learning with individualized instruction (see Madden & Slavin, 1983b).

Principal Features of TAI

TAI is primarily designed for grades 3-6, but has also been used at higher grade levels. It is almost always used without aides, volunteers, or other assistance. The principal elements of TAI are as follows (adapted from Slavin et al., 1986):

TEAMS. Students are assigned to four- to five-member teams. Each team consists of a mix of high, average, and low achievers, boys and girls, and students of any ethnic groups in the class. Every eight weeks students are reassigned to new teams.

PLACEMENT TEST. Students are pretested at the beginning of the program on mathematics operations. They are placed at the appropriate point in the individualized program based on their performance on the placement test.

CURRICULUM MATERIALS. Following instruction from the teacher (see "Teaching Groups," in a subsequent section), students work in their teams on self-instructional curriculum materials covering addition, subtraction, multiplication, division, numeration, decimals, fractions, word problems, statistics, and algebra. Word problems are emphasized throughout the materials. The units are in the form of books. Each unit has subparts including guides, practice pages, formative and unit tests, and answer sheets.

TEACHING GROUPS. Every day, the teacher teaches lessons to small groups of students drawn from the heterogeneous teams that are at the same point in the curriculum. Teachers use specific concept lessons provided as part of the program. The purpose of these sessions is to introduce major concepts to the students. Teachers make extensive use of manipulatives, diagrams, and demonstrations. The lessons are designed to help students understand the connection between the mathematics they are doing and familiar, real-life problems. While the teacher works with a teaching group, the other students continue to work in their teams on their self-instructional units. This direct instruction to teaching groups is made possible by the fact that students take responsibility for almost all checking, materials handling, and routing.

TEAM STUDY METHOD. Following the placement test, the students are given a starting place in the sequence of mathematics units. They work on their units in their teams, using the steps shown in Table 1.

TEAM SCORES AND TEAM RECOGNITION. At the end of each week, the teacher computes a team score. This score is based on the average number of units covered by each team member and the accuracy of the unit tests. Criteria are established for team performance. A high criterion is set for a team to be a "superteam," a moderate criterion is established for a team to be a "greatteam," and a minimum criterion is set for a team to be a "goodteam." The teams meeting the "superteam" and "greatteam" criteria receive attractive certificates.

FACTS TESTS. Twice each week, the students are given three-minute facts tests (usually multiplication or division facts). The students are given fact sheets to study at home to prepare for these tests.

WHOLE-CLASS UNITS. After every three weeks, the teacher stops the individualized program and spends a week teaching lessons to the entire class covering such skills as geometry, measurement, sets, and problem solving strategies.

Research on TAI

Seven field experiments have been conducted to evaluate the effects of TAI on student achievement, attitudes, and behavior (see Slavin, 1984, 1985b). TAI was also evaluated as part of the Cooperative School project described later. Academic achievement outcomes were assessed in six of the seven studies. In five of these, TAI students significantly exceeded control students in math computations. Similar effects were found for concepts and applications in only one of the four studies in which this variable was assessed. In the five studies in which the treatment effects for Computations were statistically significant, they were also quite large; on average, TAI classes gained twice as many grade equivalents as did control students. Effects of TAI were equally positive for high, average, and low achievers, and for academically handicapped as well as non-handicapped students.

Two general attitude scales were used in four of the studies, Liking of Math Class and Self-Concept in Math. Statistically significant effects favoring TAI were found for Liking of Math Class in three of these. For Self-Concept in Math, positive effects were found in two of the four studies. In no case did means for these variables favor a control treatment.

In two of the studies, teachers were asked to rate a subset of their students (all academically handicapped students plus six randomly selected non-handicapped students) on six scales: Classroom Behavior, Self-Confidence Behavior, Friendship Behavior, and Negative Peer Behavior (e.g., fighting) (Slavin, Madden, & Leavey, 1984). In one study statistically significant effects favoring TAI students were found on all four scales. The second study replicated these findings for Self-Confidence and Friendship behaviors, but not for the other two scales.

One principal impetus for the development of TAI was to meet the instructional needs of academically handicapped students in the context of the regular class, while providing these students with the cooperative experiences found in earlier research to improve the acceptance of academically handicapped students by their nonhandicapped classmates (see Madden & Slavin, 1983a). Effects of TAI on academically handicapped students have been positive on several dimensions. No achievement differences for the academically handicapped subsample were found in an eight-week pilot study, but significant and strong achievement effects were found in a 24 week experiment, where academically handicapped students gained 52% of a grade equivalent more in computations than did their control counterparts (Slavin, et al., 1984). In the pilot study, academically handicapped students in TAI gained more than control students in sociometric choices as "best friends" or as "o.k." They were also rated much more positively than control students on all four behavior rating scales.

COOPERATIVE INTEGRATED READING AND COMPOSITION

Following the success of the TAI mathematics program, we turned our development efforts toward reading and writing and language arts, the subjects which, along with mathematics, constitute the core of the elementary school program. Because these subjects are very different from mathematics, our approach to applying cooperative learning

Table 1: Steps for Completing Units in TAI-M

- Students locate their units within their books and read the guide page, asking teammates or the teacher for help if necessary. Then, the students begin with the first skill practice page in their unit.

- Each student works the first four problems on his or her own skill practice page and then has a teammate check the answers against an answer sheet printed upside-down at the back of each student book. If all four are correct, the student may go on to the next skill practice page. If any are incorrect, the student must try the next four problems, and so on, until he or she gets one block of four problems correct. If they run into difficulties at this stage, the students are encouraged to ask for help within their teams before asking the teacher for help.

- When a student gets four in a row on the last skill practice page, he or she takes Formative Test A, a 10-item quiz that resembles the last skill practice page. Students work alone on the test until they are finished. A teammate scores the formative test. If the student gets 8 or more of the 10 problems correct, the teammate signs the student's paper to indicate that the student is certified by the team to take the unit test. If the student does not get 8 correct (this is rare), the teacher is called in to respond to any problems the student is having. The teacher would diagnose the student's problem, briefly reteach the skill, and then may ask the student to work again on certain skill practice items. The student then takes Formative Test B, a second 10-item test comparable in content and difficulty to Formative Test A.

- When a student passes Formative Test A or B, her or she takes the test paper to a student monitor from a different team to get the appropriate unit test. The student then completes the unit test, and the monitor scores it. Two different students serve as monitors each day. If the student gets at least 12 items correct (out of 15), the monitor posts the score on the student's Team Summary Sheet. Otherwise, the test is given to the teacher, who meets with the student to diagnose and remediate the student's problems. Again, because students have already shown mastery on the skill practice pages and formative tests, it is very rare that they fail a unit test.

to reading and writing was very different from our approach to mathematics. For one thing, reading, writing and language arts subsume a set of subskills which each demand different approaches. For example, optimal procedures for teaching reading comprehension or vocabulary would certainly be different from those for teaching decoding, spelling, writing, or language mechanics.

The program we ultimately developed and researched is called Cooperative Integrated Reading and Composition, (CIRC) (Madden, Slavin, & Stevens, 1986; Slavin, Stevens, and Madden, 1988). The overall development plan focused on using cooperative learning as a vehicle by which to introduce practices identified in recent research on reading and writing into routine classroom practice, and to embed cooperative learning within the fabric of the elementary reading and writing program. The major elements of CIRC are presented in the following section.

Principal Features of CIRC

The CIRC program consists of three principal elements: Basal-related activities, direct instruction in reading comprehension, and integrated language arts and writing. In all of these activities, students work in heterogeneous learning teams. All activities follow a cycle that involves teacher presentation, team practice, peer pre-assessment, additional practice, and testing.

READING GROUPS. Students are assigned to two or three reading groups according to their reading levels, as determined by their teachers.

TEAMS. Students are assigned to pairs (or triads) within their reading groups. The pairs are then assigned to teams composed of partnerships from two different reading groups. For example, a team might be composed of two students from the top reading group and two from the low group. Mainstreamed academically handicapped and remedial reading (e.g., Chapter I) students are distributed among the teams.

Many of the activities within the teams are done in pairs, while others involve the whole team; even during pair activities, however, the other pair is available for assistance and encouragement. Most of the time, the teams work independently of the teacher, while the teacher either teaches reading groups drawn from the various teams or works with individuals.

Students' scores on all quizzes, compositions, and book reports are aggregated to form a team score. Teams that have an average of 90% on all activities in a given week are designated "Superteams" and receive attractive certificates; those that have an average of 80-90% are designated "Greatteams" and receive less elaborate certificates.

BASAL-RELATED-ACTIVITIES. Students use their regular basal readers. Basal stories are introduced and discussed in teacher-led reading groups that meet for approximately 20 minutes each day. During these sessions, teachers set a purpose for reading, introduce new vocabulary, review old vocabulary, discuss the story after students have read it, and so on. Presentation methods for each segment of the lesson are structured. For example, teachers are taught to use a vocabulary presentation procedure that requires a demonstration of understanding of word meaning by each individual, a review of methods of word attack, repetitive oral reading of vocabulary to achieve automaticity, and use of the meanings of the vocabulary words to help introduce the content of the story. Story discussions are structured to emphasize such skills as making and supporting predictions about the story and understanding major structural components of the story (e.g., problem and solution in a narrative).

After stories are introduced, students are given a series of activities to do in their teams when they are not working with the teacher in a reading group. The sequence of activities is shown in Table 2.

PARTNER CHECKING. After students complete each of the activities listed in Table 2, their partners initial a student assignment form indicating that they have completed and achieved criterion on that task. Students are given daily expectations as to the number of activities to be completed, but they can go at their own rate and complete the activities earlier if they wish, creating additional time for independent reading (subsequent section).

TESTS. At the end of three class periods, students are given a comprehension test on the story, are asked to write meaningful sentences for each vocabulary word, and are asked to read the word list aloud to the teacher. Students are not permitted to help one another on these tests.

The test scores and evaluations of the story related writing are major components of students' weekly team scores.

DIRECT INSTRUCTION IN READING COMPREHENSION. One day each week, students receive direct instruction from the teacher in reading comprehension skills such as identifying main ideas, drawing conclusions, and comparing and contrasting ideas. A special step-by-step curriculum was designed for this purpose. After each lesson, students work on reading comprehension worksheets or games as a whole team, first gaining consensus on one set of worksheet items, then practicing independently, assessing one another's work, and discussing any remaining problems on a second set of items.

INDEPENDENT READING. Every evening, students are asked to read a trade book of their choice for at least twenty minutes. Parents initial forms in-

Table 2: Sequence of Activities in CIRC

- *Partner Reading*: Students read the story silently first, and then take turns reading the story aloud with their partners, alternating readers after each paragraph. As their partner reads, the listener follows along and corrects any errors the reader makes.

- *Story Structure and Story Related Writing*: Students are given questions related to each narrative story emphasizing the story grammar. Halfway through the story, they are instructed to stop reading and to identify the characters, the setting, and the problem in the story, and to predict how the problem will be resolved. At the end of the story students respond to the story as a whole and write a brief composition on a topic related to the story (for example, they might be asked to write a different ending to the story).

- *Words Out Loud*: Students are given a list of new or difficult words used in the story that they must be able to read correctly in any order without hesitating or stumbling. These words are presented by the teacher in the reading group, and then students practice their lists with their partners or other teammates until they can read them smoothly.

- *Word Meaning*: Students are given a list of story words that are new in their speaking vocabularies and asked to look them up in a dictionary, paraphrase the definition, and write a sentence for each that shows the meaning of the word (i.e. "An octopus grabbed the swimmer with its eight long legs," not "I saw an octopus.")

- *Story Retell*: After reading the story and discussing it in their reading groups, students summarize the main points of the story to their partners. The partners have a list of essential story elements that they use to check the completeness of the story summaries.

- *Spelling*: Students pretest one another on a list of spelling words each week, and then work over the course of the week to help one another master the list. Students use a "disappearing list" strategy in which they make new lists of missed words after each assessment until the list disappears; then, they can go back to the full list, repeating the process as many times as necessary.

dicating that students have read for the required time, and students contribute points to their teams if they submit a completed form each week. Students complete at least one book report every two weeks, for which they also receive team points. Independent reading and book reports replace all other homework in reading and language arts. If students complete their basal-related activities or other activities early, they may also read their independent reading books in class.

INTEGRATED LANGUAGE ARTS AND WRITING. During language arts periods, teachers use a language arts and writing curriculum especially developed for the project. Students work on language arts in the same teams as in reading. During three one-hour sessions each week, students participate in a writer's workshop (Calkins, 1983; Graves, 1983), writing at their own pace on topics of their choice. Teachers present 10-minute mini-lessons at the beginning of each period on writing process, style, or mechanics, for example brainstorming for topics, conducting a peer conference revision on eliminating run-on sentences, or using quotations. Students spend the main part of the period planning, drafting, revising, editing, and publishing their writing. Informal and formal peer and teacher conferences are held during this time. Ten minutes at the end of the hour are reserved for sharing and "celebration" of student writing. Teacher-directed lessons on specific aspects of writing, such as organizing a narrative or a descriptive paragraph, using specific sensory words in a description, and insuring noun-verb agreement, are conducted during two periods each week, and students practice and master these skills in their teams.

INVOLVEMENT OF SPECIAL EDUCATION RESOURCE TEACHERS AND READING TEACHERS. One key concern in the design of the CIRC program was to integrate fully the activities of special education resource teachers and remedial reading teachers with those of the regular classroom teachers. This integration was done differently in the two evaluations of the full CIRC program. In the twelve-week pilot study (Madden, Stevens, & Slavin, 1986), resource and remedial reading teachers removed students from their reading classes for part or all of the reading period, and implemented the CIRC program in separate areas. However, in a 24-week full-scale evaluation (Stevens et al., 1987; Madden et. al., 1986), the schools involved scheduled resource and remedial reading pullouts at times other than reading or language arts and writing periods. Special and remedial reading teachers attended the CIRC training sessions but did not use CIRC methods or materials in their pullout programs, except that they occasionally helped students with problems they were encountering in the CIRC program being used in the regular class.

Research on CIRC

Two studies have evaluated the impact of the full CIRC program. CIRC has also been evaluated as part of the Cooperative School project described later. The first study (Madden, et al., 1986) evaluated the full CIRC program over a twelve-week period. Overall, the effects of the CIRC program on student achievement were quite positive. After adjusting for pretests, analyses of variance using class means on the California Achievement Test indicated that students in the CIRC classes gained significantly more (30% to 36% of a grade equivalent more) than control students in reading comprehension and reading vocabulary, 52% of a grade equivalent more in language expression, and 72% of a grade equivalent more in spelling. Only in language mechanics were experimental-control differences not significant, and even here, the CIRC students gained a quarter of a grade equivalent more than control students. On writing samples CIRC students significantly out-performed control students on ratings of organization, with an effect size of more than half of an individual-level standard deviation.

Tests for interactions with pretest levels indicated that the effects of CIRC were equal for students at all levels of prior achievement, high, average, and low. However, probably because of the small samples involved, effects computed separately for special education and remedial reading students were not statistically significant in this study (Madden et al., 1986).

The second study (Stevens et al., 1987) was designed to evaluate the CIRC program in third- and fourth-grade classes over a full school year, incorporating changes suggested by the experience of the pilot study. In addition to refinements in methods and materials, Study 2 changed the program for special education and remedial reading students. In Study 1 these students were pulled out of class (as usual) during reading times and experienced part or all of their exposure to the CIRC procedures in the pull-out class (this was not our preference, but was an accommodation to school district policies). In Study 2, special education and remedial students were left in the regular class, and were either pulled out for corrective instruction at other times or were not given additional instruction.

For the total samples involved, the results of Study 2 were even more positive than those of Study 1. On California Achievement Test reading comprehension, language expression, and language mechanics scales, class-level analyses of variance indicated that CIRC students gained significantly more than control students, averaging gains of almost two-thirds of a grade equivalent more than control students. Differences of twenty percent of a grade equivalent on reading vocabulary were not significant, however. On writing samples, CIRC students again out-performed control on organization, ideas, and mechanics ratings, but in this case the class-level analyses indicated significant differences only on ratings of ideas. Study 2 added informal reading inventories as measures of students' oral reading skills. CIRC students scored significantly higher than control students on word recognition, word analysis, fluency, error rate, and grade placement measures of the Durrell Informal Reading Inventory with effect sizes ranging from 44% to 64% of a standard deviation. As in Study 1, tests for interactions indicated that the CIRC program produced equal gains for students initially high, average, and low in reading skills.

Probably because of the longer duration and the fact that students were not pulled out of their reading classes, effects of the CIRC program on the reading achievement of special education and remedial reading students were much more positive than in Study 1. Mainstreamed special education students gained 1.92 grade equivalents more than special control students in reading comprehension and 1.44 grade equivalents more in reading vocabulary. Both of these differences were statistically significant. Students also achieved significantly more in CIRC than in traditional methods on measures of reading comprehension, language expression, and language mechanics, with experimental-control differences ranging from 66% to 80% of a grade equivalent. On the informal reading inventory scales, students in the lowest third of their classes gained as much as 1.38 deviations more than control students in oral reading fluency, and made other outstanding gains in word recognition, word analysis, and overall placement.

THE COOPERATIVE SCHOOL

The development and successful evaluation of the comprehensive TAI and CIRC models has created an exciting new possibility. With cooperative learning programs capable of being used all year in the 3 R's, it is now possible to design an elementary school program based upon a radical principle: Students, teachers, and administrators can work *cooperatively* to make the school a better place for working and learning. Recently, we have begun working with a small number of schools toward a vision of a *cooperative elementary school*, an organizational plan in which cooperative activities take place at the school level as well as at the classroom level (see Slavin, 1987).

Features of the Cooperative School

Each school working toward this vision is proceeding differently, and there may be many ways to structure a cooperative school. However, the major components of the plan we are currently pursuing are as follows.

- *Cooperative Learning in the Classroom.* Clearly, cooperative elementary schools would have cooperative learning methods in use in most classrooms and in more than one subject. Students and teachers should feel that the idea that students can help one another learn is not just applied on occasion but is a fundamental principle of classroom organization. Students should see one another as resources for learning, and there should be a school-wide norm that every student's learning is everyone's responsibility, that every student's success is everyone's success.

- *Integration of Special Education and Remedial Services with the Regular Program.* In the cooperative elementary school, special education and Chapter 1 teachers should team teach with regular teachers, integrating their students in teams with non-handicapped students and contributing their expertise in adapting instruction to individual needs to the class as a whole. If we take seriously the idea that all students are responsible for one another, this goes as much for students with learning problems as for anyone else.

- *Peer Coaching.* In the cooperative elementary school, teachers should be responsible for helping one another to use cooperative learning methods and to implement other improvements in instructional practice. Peer coaching (Joyce, Hersh, & Mc-Kibbin, 1983) is perfectly adapted to the philosophy of the cooperative school.

- *Cooperative Planning.* Cooperative activities among teachers should not be restricted to peer coaching. In addition, teachers should be given time to plan goals and strategies together, to prepare common libraries of instructional materials, and to make decisions about cooperative activities involving more than one class.

- *Building-Level Steering Committee.* In the cooperative elementary school, a steering committee composed of the principal, teacher representatives from each grade, representatives of other teaching staff (e.g., special education, Chapter 1, aides), and one or more parent representatives should discuss the progress the school is making toward its instructional goals and recommend changes in school policies and practices designed to achieve these goals.

- *Cooperation With Parents and Community Members*. The cooperative school should invite the participation of parents and of members of the community in which the school is located. Development of a community sense that children's success in school is everyone's responsibility is an important goal of the cooperative school.

Research on the Cooperative School

The Cooperative School project was designed as a two-year implementation to provide sufficient time to implement all of the components described. The instructional components were phased in during the first year so the teachers and students could master the processes of one program before they attempted the next program. After the first year, TAI and CIRC were fully implemented in two schools, as were the building-steering-committee and peer-coaching components. Special education and remedial education were largely integrated with regular education, but in some instances scheduling still required that some students be pulled out of their regular classes for instruction.

We conducted an interim evaluation after the first year of implementation comparing two Cooperative Schools to two matched control schools. The initial results were positive and significant. After adjusting for pretests, analyses of variance using California Achievement Test (CAT) data indicated Cooperative School students gained significantly more (10% to 60% of a grade equivalent more) than control students in reading vocabulary and reading comprehension. Similarly, students in the Cooperative School outperformed control students in math computation (14% to 100% of a grade equivalent higher). However, data on the math applications subtest indicated no significant differences.

These significant achievement effects were equal for students of all levels of initial achievement. Separate analyses relating to the academically handicapped students indicated that they had significantly higher achievement (10% to 100% of a grade equivalent higher) than their matched peers in reading vocabulary and reading comprehension. Technical problems made it impossible to examine mathematics achievement for the academically handicapped sample.

Students in the Cooperative School and control schools were also compared using a sociometric measure asking them to list their friends in the class. There were no significant premeasure differences on the number of friends listed. Posttest comparisons found that students in the Cooperative School listed significantly more friends (25% more) than did students in the control schools. Academically handicapped students were 30% more likely to be selected as friends by their classmates than were similar students in the control schools. The results of these sociometric measures confirm the impact found in previous cooperative learning studies cited above. Not only are peer relations in cooperative learning schools better than those in traditional schools, but mildly handicapped students are more socially accepted by their peers as well.

The research on comprehensive cooperative learning models and our initial experience with the cooperative elementary school program has convinced us that cooperative learning can become the basis for fundamental restructuring of the elementary program. The classroom can be successfully organized to meet a wide range of needs within the regular classroom setting with special services provided there rather than in separate pullouts. The comprehensive cooperative learning models work because they engage all students in working with one another to ensure the success of all, and they work because they treat all students as "special," in the sense that students' individual needs can be met through flexible use of both homogeneous and heterogeneous groupings. If we are to take the principle of mainstreaming seriously, we must work to make the regular classroom better able to accommodate a wide range of student needs. Cooperative learning methods provide one means of accomplishing this goal.

NOTE

Preparation of this chapter was supported by a grant from the Office of Educational Research and Improvement (No. OERI-R117-R90002) and the Office of Special Education and Rehabilitative Services (No. G-87-30141), U.S. Department of Education. However, any opinions expressed are ours, and do not represent Department of Education policy.

REFERENCES

Ames, C., Ames, R., & Felker, D. (1977). Effects of competitive reward structure and valence of outcome on children's achievement attributions. *Journal of Educational Psychology, 69*, 1-8.

Armstrong, B., Johnson, D. W., & Balow, B. (1981). Effects of cooperative vs. individualistic learning experiences on interpersonal attraction between learning-disabled and normal progress elementary school students. *Contemporary Educational Psychology,6,*102-190.

Ballard, M., Corman, L., Gottlieb, J., & Kaufman, M. (1977). Improving the social status of mainstreamed retarded children. *Journal of Educational Psychology, 69,*605-611.

Bruininks, V. L. (1978). Peer status and personality characteristics of learning disabled students. *Journal of Learning Disabilities, 11,*29-34.

Calkins, L. M. (1983). *Lessons from a child: On the teaching and learning of writing.* Exeter, NH: Heinemann.

Cooper, L., Johnson, D. W., Johnson, R., & Wilderson, F. (1980). Effects of cooperative, competitive, and individualistic experiences on interpersonal attraction among heterogeneous peer. *Journal of Social Psychology, 111*, 243-252.

Fuchs, D., & Fuchs, L. S. (1988). Evaluation of the Adaptive Learning Environments Model. *Exceptional Children, 55,*116-127.

Gickling, E., & Theobold, J. (1975). Mainstreaming: Affect or effect. *Journal of Special Education, 9,*317-328.

Gottlieb, J., & Leyser, Y. (1981). Friendship between mentally retarded and nonretarded children. In S. Asher & J. Gottman (Eds.), *The development of children's friendships* (pp. 150-181). Cambridge: Cambridge University Press.

Graves, D. (1983). *Writing: Teachers and children at work.* Exeter, NH: Heinemann.

Horak, V. M. (1981). A meta-analysis of research findings on individualized instruction in mathematics. *Journal of Educational Research, 74*, 249-253.

Johnson, D. W., & Johnson, R. T. (1980). Integrating handicapped children into the mainstream. *Exceptional Children, 47,*90-98.

Johnson, R. T., & Johnson, D. W. (1981a). Building friendships between handicapped students: Effects of cooperative and individualistic instruction. *American Educational Research Journal, 18,*415-424.

Johnson, D. W., & Johnson, R. T. (1981b). The integration of the handicapped into the regular classroom: Effects of cooperative and individualistic instruction. *Contemporary Educational Psychology,6*, 344-353.

Johnson, R. T., & Johnson, D. W. (1982). Effects of cooperative and competitive learning experiences on interpersonal attraction between handicapped and nonhandicapped students. *Journal of Social Psychology,166,*211-219.

Johnson, R. T., & Johnson, D. W. (1983). Effects of cooperative, competitive, and individualistic learning experiences on social development. *Exceptional Children, 49,*323-330.

Johnson, D. W., & Johnson, R. T. (1987). *Learning together and alone* (2nd ed.). Englewood Cliffs, NJ: Prentice-Hall.

Joyce, B. R., Hersh, R. H., & McKibbin, M. (1983). *The structure of school improvement*. New York: Longman.

Madden, N. A., & Slavin, R. E. (1983a). Effects of cooperative learning on the social acceptance of mainstreamed academically handicapped students. *Journal of Special Education, 17*, 171-182.

Madden, N. A., & Slavin, R. E. (1983b). Mainstreaming students with mild academic handicaps: Academic and social outcomes. *Review of Educational Research, 53*, 519-569.

Madden, N. A., Slavin, R. E., & Stevens, R. J. (1986). *Cooperative integrated reading and composition: Teacher's manual*. Baltimore, MD: Johns Hopkins University, Center for Research on Elementary and Middle Schools.

Madden, N. A., Stevens, R. J., & Slavin, R. E. (1986). *Reading instruction in the mainstream: A cooperative learning approach* (Tech. Rep. No. 5). Baltimore, MD: Center for Research on Elementary and Middle Schools, Johns Hopkins University.

Slavin, R. E. (1983a). *Cooperative learning*. New York: Longman.

Slavin, R. E. (1983b). When does cooperative learning increase student achievement? *Psychological Bulletin, 94*, 429-445.

Slavin, R. E. (1984). Team Assisted Individualization: Cooperative learning and individualized instruction in the mainstreamed classroom. *Remedial and Special Education, 5*(6), 33-42.

Slavin, R. E. (1985a). Cooperative learning: Applying contact theory in desegregated schools. *Journal of Social Issues, 41*(3), 45-62.

Slavin, R. E. (1985b). Team Assisted Individualization: Combining cooperative learning and individualized instruction in mathematics. In R. E. Slavin, S. Sharan, S. Kagan, R. Hertz-Lazarowitz, C. Webb, & R. Schmuck (Eds.), *Learning to cooperate, cooperating to learn* (pp. 177-209). New York: Plenum.

Slavin, R. E. (1986). *Using student team learning* (3rd ed.). Baltimore, MD: Center for Research on Elementary and Middle Schools, Johns Hopkins University.

Slavin, R. E. (1987). Cooperative learning and the cooperative school. *Educational Leadership, 45*(3), 7-13.

Slavin, R. E. (1990). *Cooperative learning: Theory, research and practice*. Englewood NJ: Prentice-hall.

Slavin, R. E., Leavey, M. B., & Madden, N. A. (1986). *Team accelerated instruction - mathematics*. Watertown, MA: Mastery Education Corporation.

Slavin, R. E., Madden, N. A., & Leavey, M. B. (1984). Effects of cooperative learning and individualized instruction on mainstreamed students. *Exceptional Children, 50*, 434-443.

Slavin, R. E., Madden, N. A., & Stevens, R. J. (1989/90). Cooperative learning models for the 3 R's. *Educational Leadership, 47*(4), 22-28.

Slavin, R. E., Stevens, R. J., & Madden, N. A. (1988). Accommodating student diversity in reading and writing instruction: A cooperative learning approach. *Remedial and Special Education, 9*(1), 60-66.

Stevens, R. J., Madden, N. A., Slavin, R. E., & Farnish, A. M. (1987). Cooperative integrated reading and composition: Two field experiments. *Reading Research Quarterly, 22*, 433-454.

Stevens, R. J., Slavin, R. E., & Farnish, A. M. (March, 1989). *The cooperative elementary school: Year 1 interim report*. Baltimore, MD: Center for Research on Elementary and Middle Schools, Johns Hopkins University.

14

BEHAVIORAL CONSULTATION IN EDUCATIONAL SETTINGS

Susan M. Sheridan
University of Utah

Thomas R. Kratochwill
University of Wisconsin-Madison

All children can learn. Schools have a responsibility to teach them, and school personnel and parents should work together to assure every child a free and appropriate education in a positive social environment. . . Necessary support services should be provided within general education, eliminating the need to classify children as handicapped in order to receive these services. (National Association of School Psychologists [NASP]/National Coalition of Advocates for Students [NCAS], 1985; p. 2).

This position statement, advanced by a joint task force that investigated current practices of assessment, placement, and education of "special needs children," exemplifies the sentiment of many psychologists and educators today. It arose as professionals recognized the limitations of the current public school service delivery system and became actively involved in reconceptualizing the way in which educational services can be provided to *all* children in the least restrictive setting.

This position statement represents one view of how children should receive educational services. It is one perspective among many that represent what is commonly called "The Regular Education Initiative," that calls for radical reform in services to special needs children, some of which involve the integration of special and general education. Our purpose here is not to review the pros and cons about diverse policies [in addition to the perspective offered in this text the reader is referred to Kauffman (1989) and a mini-series by Rosenfield (1990) that review the issues]. Rather, our goal is to describe how school psychological services can be used to provide free, appropriate educational services to all children more efficiently. Indeed, our perspective necessitates reconsideration of the typical existing psychological service delivery system. Specifically, we will outline how *behavioral consultation* may provide a vehicle for quality educational services to children.

Under the current educational system, students who experience problems in the classroom are often referred for multidisciplinary psychoeducational assessments, and the *expected* outcome of referral is placement in a special education program. However, several problems have been noted with this process. It is very time-consuming, requires coordination of efforts from many professionals, and is typically implemented with the sole purpose of determining eligibility for placement. Current practices are both inconsistent and unreliable (Algozzine & Ysseldyke, 1981; Christenson, Ysseldyke, & Algozzine, 1982; Epps, Ysseldyke, & Algozzine, 1983; Ysseldyke, Algozzine, & Epps, 1983; Ysseldyke, Algozzine, Richey, & Graden, 1982). And the typical outcome of the referral-assessment process is usually predictable--once referred, there is a high probability that a student will be tested (92% nationally) and placed in special education (73%) (Algozzine, Christenson, & Ysseldyke, 1982). Whether this is due to a "search for pathology" (Sarason & Doris, 1979) or other unidentified factors is unknown, but it now seems clear that these practices may lead to overidentification of students for special education. However, overidentification of students does not imply that quality education is compromised, or that special education is an inappropriate option for all students. Indeed, severity of the handicapping condition, and capabilities within the district to provide necessary adaptive and augmentative resources are important factors to consider in determining appropriateness of special or regular education placement on an individual basis.

A second problem with the present model of service-delivery relates to its functional utility. Results from traditional assessments (i.e., IQ and achievement) do little to clarify learning problems, suggest functional or instructional recommendations, provide information on baseline performance, or identify areas of student competence. Furthermore, when students are found ineligible for special educational services, "teachers often are left without any useful suggestions, and

students often do not receive alternative classroom interventions" (Graden, Casey, & Christenson, 1985; p. 378). Thus, although these students are experiencing problems, their special needs may be left unmet.

Based on these and other problems, it seems clear that psychologists and educators must redirect energies and resources to provide appropriate educational services to all students in the least restrictive educational setting. Of course, this setting may be a regular classroom, special classroom, or a combination of regular and special classrooms. The increasing interest in the provision of indirect services offers promising efforts in providing services in all settings, but continues to suffer from a lack of systematic procedural guidelines to facilitate implementation. Several states are adopting programs (e.g., prereferral intervention, teacher-assistance teams, and building-level support teams) designed to expand instructional options for all students in the least restrictive setting, however many of the programs have not been thoroughly conceptualized, and they do not adequately address the issues necessary for effective implementation (Zins, Curtis, Graden & Ponti, 1988). Behavioral consultation provides a conceptually and empirically sound framework for organizing, delivering, and evaluating services, and expanding options for all students within their educational settings, regardless of whether this is a regular or special education classroom.

OVERVIEW OF CONSULTATION

Consultation is an indirect form of service delivery that involves the problem-solving efforts of two or more people to clarify a student's needs, and develop, implement, and evaluate appropriate strategies for intervention. There are several theoretical models of consultation. West and Idol (1987) identified 10 distinct models that differed in terms of theoretical underpinnings, procedural details, responsibilities of participants, and goals of consultation. A detailed discussion of these models is beyond the scope of this chapter; interested readers are referred to the original or representative sources (see Table 1), or to West and Idol (1987) for a review. We focus the remainder of the chapter on the behavioral consultation model.

Consultation is an effective form of intervention in applied settings (Mannino & Shore, 1975; Medway & Updyke, 1985). Mannino and Shore (1975) found that 69% of the studies they reviewed showed positive change at the consultee, client, or system level. Medway (1979) noted that 76% of the investigations reported at least one or more positive effects from consultation interventions. Behavioral consultation was considered especially effective. Several more recent case studies and small case experimental designs also have illustrated the effectiveness of behavioral consultation in effecting client change (Pray, Kramer, & Lindskog, 1986; Sheridan, Kratochwill, & Elliott, 1990). Because of its indirect influence, problem-solving emphasis, and empirical support, behavioral consultation appears to be a particularly viable mechanism for providing services to all students in educational environments.

Characteristics of Behavioral Consultation

As traditionally conceived, behavioral consultation involves indirect services to

Table 1: Various Consultation Models and Representative Sources

Consultation Model	Source
Mental Health	Caplan (1970)
	Meyers, Parsons, & Martin (1979)
Behavioral	Bergan (1977)
	Bergan & Kratochwill (1990)
	Kratochwill & Bergan (1990)
Organizational	Schmuck & Runkel (1972)
Process	Schein (1969)
Collaborative	Idol, Paolucci-Newcomb, & Nevin (1986)

a client (e.g., child) who is served through a consultee (e.g., parent, teacher), by a consultant (e.g., psychologist, special education teacher, social worker) (Bergan & Kratochwill, 1990; Kratochwill & Bergan, 1990). Behavioral consultation is considered to be a particularly desirable model of indirect service-delivery in educational settings for several reasons. First, behavioral consultation assumes the provision of *indirect* services; that is, a consultant works with a consultee who provides direct services to a child. This model of service delivery may provide a broader impact on the consultee and client than other forms of direct service. Second, behavioral consultants use a *problem-solving* approach for the treatment of academic and social difficulties. As such, the emphasis is on a functional analysis of presenting problems, and is consistent with the current trend toward linking assessment to treatment. Third, behavioral consultation implies a *collegial relationship* between the consultant and consultee. Although the consultant controls the verbal process of consultation, each of these individuals is considered to have special expertise that can be applied to facilitate problem resolution.

Roles of Participants in Consultation

Participants in behavioral consultation include the consultant, consultee, and client. Each participant has his or her own unique role and responsibilities that can contribute to a positive outcome in consultation. It is the *consultant's* responsibility to (a) understand the stages in the consultation process (i.e., problem identification, problem analysis, treatment implementation, and treatment evaluation) and guide the consultee through these stages; (b) provide pertinent information and make resources available to the consultee; and (c) ensure that the consultee provides services that will benefit the client.

The *consultee* also has specific roles in consultation. First and foremost, the consultee must engage as an active participant throughout the entire consultation process, because the consultee's active involvement (i.e., "taking ownership") for problem definition, treatment selection, and problem-resolution will enhance treatment integrity and consumer satisfaction. The consultee is also responsible for describing a specific problem to the consultant. This initial problem specification may or may not be the target of consultation; it is through skillful dialogue with the consultant that a target problem is identified precisely. The consultee has an additional requirement of working directly with the client (i.e., implementing the treatment program). Thus, he or she is in a position to evaluate the feasibility, practicality, and general acceptability of the intervention. Because effectiveness of consultation is based on the assumption that the intervention was implemented with integrity (i.e., as designed), the consultant and consultee share the responsibility of continued communication and revision of the treatment program when it is not producing its desired effects.

The *client's* primary role in behavioral consultation is to participate in the treatment program and change in the direction of the goals established during consultation. Depending on various client-related factors (e.g., age, level of intellectual functioning, severity of problems), the client may participate to varying degrees in establishing the goals of consultation and in designing and implementing plans to produce goal attainment. In general, the client should be included in these important components of consultation whenever possible.

Goals of Behavioral Consultation

The principal goal of behavioral consultation is to produce change in client behavior. Changes may be desired in a variety of social, emotional, and educational domains, and consultation can help effect these changes in a structured, effective manner. However, it is important to recognize that the child is part of an ecological setting. As such, identified problems occur in the context of classroom, teacher, and instructional variables, and in their interaction with student variables. Thus, consultation interventions often focus on changing more than the client's behavior, extending to changing the ecology as well (Gettinger, 1988).

Changes in the consultee are also targeted in behavioral consultation. Goals associated with consultee change may include modification of individual knowledge or skills, or change in the consultee's confidence and ability to address client needs positively (Kratochwill & Bergan, 1990). Furthermore, a change in the consultee may be beneficial for clients who are not directly involved in consultation through generalization of the consultee's skills to a broader range of children.

Goals of behavioral consultation may also focus on producing change in the organization in which the client and consultee function (e.g., school). Organizational goals typically involve communication or problem-solving. Communication goals are concerned with the effectiveness of communication among different components of an organization (e.g., communication between teachers, between a teacher and a principal). Problem-solving goals involve improving the ability of individuals (e.g., teachers) to identify and solve problems, and to implement problem-solving strategies with integrity. Skill-based in-services and workshops, designed to help consultees develop practical problem-solving strategies and techniques are at least two vehicles through which consultants can address the problem-solving goals of an organization.

In addition to client and consultee change, goals in consultation focus on preventing problems. As a pre-referral intervention model, consultation can prevent inappropriate placements in special education (Graden et al., 1985). Likewise, future student problems may be prevented by increasing the skill and knowledge of regular classroom teachers to intervene effectively with diverse groups of students.

Stages of Consultative Problem-Solving

Work by Bergan, Kratochwill, and their associates (Bergan, 1977; Bergan & Kratochwill, 1990; Kratochwill & Bergan, 1990) provides a structure and operational format by which consultants can guide their practice. The process of behavioral consultation is typically described as occurring in four general stages (i.e., problem identification, problem analysis, treatment implementation, and treatment evaluation). These stages are procedurally operationalized through a series of standardized behavioral interviews. In general, *problem identification* involves specification of the problem or problems to be targeted in consultation; *problem analysis* explores the problem through evaluation of baseline data, identifies the variables that might facilitate problem solution, and suggests a plan in an attempt to solve the problem; *treatment implementation* involves implementation of the plan designed during problem analysis; and *treatment evaluation* is undertaken to determine the extent of plan effectiveness. Table 2 outlines specific behavioral objectives in Problem Identification, Problem Analysis, and Treatment Evaluation Interviews.

The *problem identification* stage of behavioral consultation is designed to specify the problems presented during consultation. The steps in the process eventually result in the (a) identification of a specific target problem, (b) designation of the goal or goals to be achieved through consultation, (c) measurement of current client performance, and (d) assessment of the discrepancy between current and desired client performance. The problem identification process is initiated by means of a Problem Identification Interview (PII). The major objectives for this interview include goal specification, assessment, and various procedural considerations.

The *problem analysis* stage of behavioral consultation is conducted when data collected during problem identification indicate the existence of a target problem(s). Problem analysis occurs in two broad phases. The first phase involves an analysis of factors that might lead to problem solution (the analysis phase); the second involves the development of plans to remediate the problem (the plan design phase). Thus, the consultant helps the consultee to identify factors that

Table 2: Stages and Objectives in Behavioral Consultation

I. Problem Identification
    A. Define the problem(s) in behavioral terms.
    B. Provide a tentative identification of antecedent, situation, and consequent conditions.
    C. Provide a tentative strength of the behavior (e.g., frequency or severity).
    D. Establish a procedure for collection of baseline data including sampling plan, and what, how and by whom it is to be recorded.

II. Problem Analysis
    A. Evaluate and obtain agreement on the sufficiency and adequacy of baseline data.
    B. Conduct a tentative functional analysis (i.e., discuss antecedent, consequent, and sequential conditions).
    C. Discuss and reach agreement on a goal for behavior change.
    D. Design an intervention plan including specification of conditions to be changed and the practical guidelines regarding treatment implementation.
    E. Reaffirm record-keeping procedures.

III. Treatment Implementation
    A. Determine whether the consultee has the necessary skills to implement the plan effectively.
    B. Monitor the data collection procedures and determine whether the plan is proceeding as designed.
    C. Determine whether any early changes or revisions in the treatment plan are necessary.

IV. Treatment Evaluation
    A. Determine whether the goals of consultation have been obtained.
    B. Evaluate the effectiveness of the treatment plan.
    C. Discuss strategies and tactics regarding the continuation, modification, or termination of the treatment plan.
    D. Schedule additional interviews if necessary, or terminate consultation.

might influence the attainment of problem solution, and to use those factors in designing a behavioral intervention to remediate the identified problem.

Problem analysis is implemented through a standardized Problem Analysis Interview (PAI). In this interview, the consultant and consultee decide on the existence of a problem that warrants attention. Conditions and skills are discussed that might influence the child's behavior. A plan is then designed by the consultant and consultee(s) to attempt problem solution. Specific objectives of this interview include problem validation, problem analysis, plan design, and procedural goals.

The third stage in consultative problem-solving is *treatment implementation*. During this stage, the plan designed in problem analysis is put into operation. The function of consultation during treatment implementation is to maximize the likelihood that the plan will produce desired outcomes. Although there is no formal interview during treatment implementation, there are several types of interactions that may occur between the consultant and consultee(s). These interactions include (a) brief contacts to monitor implementation, assist in plan revision, and schedule subsequent meetings; (b) observations to monitor child and consultee behaviors and to develop revisions in treatment implementation; and (c) training sessions, to develop skills in the individual(s) executing the treatment plan and increase treatment integrity.

After a treatment plan has been in effect for an adequate amount of time, the *treatment evaluation* stage of behavioral consultation is undertaken to determine whether the goals of consultation have been attained, whether the plan implemented has been effective, and if the treatment is acceptable to the consultee(s) and client. Treatment evaluation may indicate that consultation should be continued, terminated, or that a post-

implementation treatment plan (i.e., planning for generalization and maintenance) should be put into effect. An analysis of the acceptability of treatment may indicate that other procedures should be considered. The evaluation process involves the steps of evaluating goal attainment, evaluating plan effectiveness, and planning post-implementation activities. Treatment evaluation is initiated through the Treatment Evaluation Interview (TEI). In this interview, the consultant and consultee(s) determine whether goal attainment has been achieved. The need for further problem identification or analysis is discussed, and post-implementation plans are established to reduce the likelihood of problem recurrence.

ISSUES IN CONSULTATION RESEARCH AND PRACTICE

Acceptability of Consultation

Consultation represents an expansion and re-conceptualization of the roles and relationships of psychologists and other special service providers in education. However, the acceptability of this expanded model of service-delivery has not been documented empirically. Treatment acceptability may have a direct relationship to the clinical utility of an intervention, including consultation. Witt and Elliott (1982) identified three factors that may limit the acceptability (and hence, utilization) of effective interventions. Specifically, the need for extra personnel (e.g., classroom observers, teacher aides), additional resources and materials (e.g., concrete reinforcers or special instrumentation), and the need to devote an excessive amount of time to the intervention, inhibit treatment utilization. In a related study, Witt, Elliott, and Martens (1984) found that teacher time and skill, type of intervention (positive or negative), risk to the child, and effects on other children were among the factors that contributed to teachers' acceptability of an intervention.

To date, acceptability research has focused on the acceptability of specific interventions, with little or no emphasis given to the *process* of service-delivery (the process by which interventions are developed and recommended). Some hints on the opinions of regular education teachers toward consultation and the present service-delivery model of identification and placement have recently been provided by Coates (1989) who surveyed teachers in Iowa about their opinions of various features of the Regular Education Initiative (REI). Teachers were asked if they agreed or disagreed with a series of statements on the REI (see Table 3). The results indicated that there was general disagreement with the statements. Thus, in the sample of teachers there was "low acceptability" with many current beliefs about the REI. More specific to consultation, teachers indicated disagreement that even given additional consultative support, mildly handicapped students would have their educational needs met in the regular classroom.

In order to determine actual satisfaction with behavioral consultation, it is important to assess the degree to which behavioral consultation is accepted by consultees in real problem-solving interactions. However, virtually all our current research in this area is analogue in nature and falls considerably short of what is needed to understand the acceptability of treatments. Issues surrounding time and cost requirements, collection of behavioral data, and other practical and logistical factors should be investigated during the process of actual consultation. Methods of increasing acceptability and reducing barriers to implementation must then be developed.

In behavioral consultation research and practice, assessment of treatment acceptability should occur at several levels. First, the acceptability of the *process* of

treatment (i.e., consultation) should be assessed. Likewise, acceptability of the *content* of treatment (i.e., the behavioral intervention) is important. Both of these in isolation, and the interaction between the two, may influence treatment outcome. The *Behavior Intervention Rating Scale* (Von Brock & Elliott, 1987) is a 20-item questionnaire that can be used to quantitatively measure the degree to which both levels of intervention are acceptable to consultees. Table 4 depicts a revision of the original scale so that it would be helpful in assessing acceptability of consultation procedures.

A third level of treatment acceptability concerns the extent to which behavioral interventions are acceptable to clients (i.e., students). This can be assessed using the *Children's Intervention Rating Profile* (Witt & Elliott, 1985), a seven-item, one-factor scale that assesses students' acceptability of interventions.

Assessment of Target Behaviors

Identification of appropriate target behaviors is crucial in behavioral consultation. Bergan and Tombari (1976) found that problem identification was the primary determinant of consultation outcomes. Thus, careful and precise clarification of the presenting problem in consultation must be emphasized.

As currently practiced, assessment in consultation involves behavioral interviews between a psychologist and teacher, teacher observation of relevant target behaviors, and at times observation of the teacher and child by the consultant. There are several problems inherent in this approach. First, it may limit the range and type of target behaviors identified, and lead to an overly narrow behavioral scope (Kratochwill, 1985; Kratochwill, Sheridan, & Van Someren, 1988). Second, behavioral consultants traditionally analyze a given problem molecularly, without addressing the broader contexts within which it occurs (Martens & Witt,

Table 3: Teacher responses to survey items regarding the Regular Education Initiative

Item	Mean	SD
Financial resources currently allotted for mildly handicapped students could be preserved if such students are reintegrated into full-time regular education.	3.37	1.10
Identification of students for the purpose of providing special education strongly stigmatizes such students.	3.40	1.02
Given further preparation and training, I would be able to effectively meet the educational needs of those students currently served by the resource room program.	3.49	1.11
Stigmatization of mildly handicapped students would in a large part be eliminated by educating them entirely within the regular class.	3.61	1.07
Given extra training and support for teachers, class sizes could remain approximately the same if mildly handicapped students were served entirely through the regular class.	3.73	1.03
Given additional consultative type support, I would be able to meet the educational needs of mildly handicapped students in my class without the need for a resource room.	3.74	.99
The current system of evaluating and placing students in special programs represents a major barrier to the effective and efficient delivery of services to them and their families.	3.75	1.01
The skills needed to teach mildly handicapped and nonhandicapped students are essentially the same.	3.78	1.10
Currently, too many students are identified for special education.	3.82	.94
Given an effective set of techniques, it would be possible to both raise the achievement levels of the entire class, and meet the educational needs of learning disabled, mildly mentally handicapped, and slow learners entirely within the regular class.	3.85	1.04
Most children currently labeled learning disabled are not "truly" educationally handicapped.	3.87	1.00
Due process rights and Individualized Education Plans for mildly handicapped students can be preserved if current categories (i.,e., learning disabled, mental disability) are eliminated and such students are in the regular classroom full time.	3.87	.86
The current system of evaluating and placing students in special education puts too much blame on students themselves for their failure to achieve.	3.89	.94
Resource rooms are not an effective model for meeting the needs of mildly handicapped students.	4.00	.93
Identifying students for the purpose of providing special education is a discriminatory practice.	4.10	.80

Note (1 = strongly agree, 2 = agree, 3 = undecided, 4 = disagree, 5 = strongly disagree)

Source: Coates, R. D. (1989). The regular education initiative and opinions of regular classroom teachers. *Journal of Learning Disabilities*, 22, 532-536.

Table 4: Acceptability rating scale for consultation methods and procedures

Name: _____

BEHAVIOR INTERVENTION RATING SCALE

The purpose of this checklist is to assist in evaluating the consultation model used by the consultant. Please read the following items and indicate the degree to which you agree with each statement. A rating of 1 indicates strong disagreement, whereas a rating of 6 indicates strong agreement. Please answer each question. Thank you.

		strongly disagree	disagree	slightly disagree	slightly agree	agree	strongly agree
1.	This was an acceptable model of consultation for the identified problem.	1	2	3	4	5	6
2.	Most teachers/school psychologists would find this model of consultation appropriate for problems in addition to the one addressed.	1	2	3	4	5	6
3.	The consultation model was effective in changing the identified problem.	1	2	3	4	5	6
4.	I would suggest the use of this consultation model to other teachers.	1	2	3	4	5	6
5.	The child's behavior problem was severe enough to warrant use of this consultation model.	1	2	3	4	5	6
6.	Most teachers/school psychologists would find this model of consultation suitable for the behavior problem addressed.	1	2	3	4	5	6
7.	I would be willing to use this model of consultation in the classroom setting again.	1	2	3	4	5	6
8.	The consultation model did *not* result in negative side-effects for the child.	1	2	3	4	5	6
9.	This consultation model would be appropriate for a variety of children.	1	2	3	4	5	6
10.	This consultation model is consistent with those I have used in classroom settings.	1	2	3	4	5	6
11.	This model of consultation was a fair way to handle the child's problem behavior.	1	2	3	4	5	6
12.	This model of consultation was reasonable for the behavior problem addressed.	1	2	3	4	5	6
13.	I liked the procedures used in this model of consultation.	1	2	3	4	5	6
14.	This model of consultation was a good way to handle the identified behavior problem.	1	2	3	4	5	6

Table 4 continued

	strongly disagree	disagree	slightly disagree	slightly agree	agree	strongly agree
15. Overall, the consultation procedures were beneficial for the child.	1	2	3	4	5	6
16. The consultation procedures quickly improved the child's behavior.	1	2	3	4	5	6
17. The consultation procedures produced a lasting improvement in the child's behavior.	1	2	3	4	5	6
18. The consultation procedures improved the child's behavior to the point that it would not noticeably deviate from other classmates' behavior.	1	2	3	4	5	6
19. Soon after beginning consultation, a positive change in the problem behavior was noticed.	1	2	3	4	5	6
20. The child's behavior will remain at an improved level even after consultation is discontinued.	1	2	3	4	5	6
21. Using this model of consultation not only improved the child's behavior in the classroom, but also in other settings (e.g., other classrooms, home).	1	2	3	4	5	6
22. When comparing this child with a peer before and after consultation, the child's and the peer's behavior were more alike after consultation.	1	2	3	4	5	6
23. This model of consultation produced enough improvement in the child's behavior so the behavior no longer is a problem.	1	2	3	4	5	6
24. Other behaviors related to the problem behavior also are likely to be improved by the consultation procedures.	1	2	3	4	5	6

Adapted from: Von Brock, M. B., & Elliott, S. N. (1987). Influence of treatment effectiveness information on the acceptability of classroom interventions. *Journal of School Psychology, 25,* 131-144.

1988; Rogers-Warren & Warren, 1977). Relatedly, consultants often consider only those stimulus events that immediately precede and follow the target behavior. This ecological and temporal constriction can limit assessment and functional analyses of behavior (Cataldo, 1984).

Assessment in behavioral consultation should include the broader and more holistic context of a given problem, including ecological and setting events (Lentz & Shapiro, 1986). Setting events refer to temporally or contextually removed stimuli (or a chain of stimulus-response contingencies) that bear a functional relation to behavior (Wahler & Dumas, 1984; Wahler & Fox, 1981). The use of multi-source, multi-method assessment in behavioral consultation research and practice is desirable. Children, teachers, and classrooms are complex systems, and the integration of various measures is necessary to provide a comprehensive evaluation of the client's present status (Achenbach, McConaughy, & Howell, 1987; Kratochwill, 1985). A three-mode assessment framework (i.e., motor, cognitive, and physiological) to measure different problem domains, broaden the scope of potential target behaviors, and expand the understanding of a particular childhood disorder can be used in consultation. Direct and indirect assessment strategies (e.g., direct observations, permanent products, behavioral checklists, rating scales, and self-reports) are recommended to obtain important data across behavioral, temporal, and contextual bases (Kratochwill & Sheridan, 1990). Likewise, these measures provide important information in the assessment of the social validity (i.e., clinical meaningfulness) of behavioral outcomes.

Treatment Integrity

The relationship between treatment use and effectiveness is largely dependent upon the manner in which the treatment is implemented (i.e., treatment integrity). If integrity is high, the probability of effecting behavioral change may be increased (Elliott, 1986). The concept of treatment integrity can also be applied to the process of service-delivery (i.e., consultation), however this has not been a frequent practice in the consultation research literature.

Fuchs and Fuchs (1989) conducted a component analysis of the various stages of behavioral consultation which also served as an empirical investigation of the effects of differential levels of consultation integrity. However, the results of this study produced equivocal results. Although the more inclusive forms of behavioral consultation (including problem identification, problem analysis, strategy generation and implementation, and treatment evaluation) produced significant reductions in teachers' ratings of problem behaviors as compared to less inclusive forms of behavioral consultation procedures, direct observations of student behaviors at pre-intervention and post-intervention failed to corroborate this result.

In consultation research and practice, treatment integrity should be assessed on at least two levels: the integrity with which behavioral consultation services are provided, and the integrity with which behavioral interventions are implemented by treatment agents. Some methods that may prove helpful in assessment of treatment integrity include direct observations, self-monitoring, behavioral ratings, and interview analysis (Gresham, 1989).

Consultee Variables Contributing to Outcome

Recent research in consultation has identified teacher variables that appear to contribute to consultation outcome. Indeed, characteristics of the consultee are a major influence in the consultation process. In a review of consultee characteristics that have been found influential in the consultation process, Brown, Pryzwansky, and Schulte (1987) identified the following as especially important: consultee's expectations and preferences, experience, ethnic background, perception of consultants, perceived sense of control, and emotional state.

The "consultee as variable" is often overlooked as an important factor in consultation research and practice. According to Brown et al. (1987), "We need to consider what the consultee brings to the sessions, in terms of training for their role as well as cognitive and emotional characteristics, if consultation is to truly have an impact as a service delivery model" (p. 230). They suggest that consultee training can enhance consultee's knowledge regarding (a) when to request consultation, (b) methods of presenting the problem to facilitate problem solution, (c) what to expect from consultants, and (d) how to make their work style known to the consultant.

Kratochwill and Bergan (1990) identify the "collegial relationship" between a consultant and consultee as one of the defining characteristics of behavioral consultation. As such, the consultant and consultee are viewed as individuals, each with his or her own special expertise that can be brought to bear on the solution of problems. However, behavioral consultation training and research programs typically emphasize procedural details and principles of behavioral psychology, rather than the interpersonal and relationship issues in the consultative interaction. This is in contrast to some other models of consultation (e.g., mental health models), where consultant characteristics and variables have been studied empirically (see West & Idol, 1987 for a review).

The consultant-consultee relationship in behavioral consultation can affect intervention effectiveness and acceptability of consultation services. Among the several factors that may affect the consultative relationship are congruence among consultant and consultee theoretical orientations, expectancies of consultation, and personal characteristics and style. The consultant's use of therapeutic-like techniques (e.g., warmth, empathy, and genuineness), and the structure and directiveness provided by the consultant may also be important relationship factors.

The effect that each of these variables has on the behavioral consultation process and outcome is in need of empirical study. Data may be obtained through direct observations, expert evaluations, and self-monitoring techniques. The *Consultant Observational Assessment Form* (COAF; Curtis & Anderson, 1976) provides objective ratings on 21 dimensions of consultation behaviors (e.g., problem clarification, strategy generation, summarization) and interpersonal variables (e.g., empathy, support, interest). Reliability and validity of the COAF has been documented (M. J. Curtis, personal communication, October, 1989). Likewise, analysis of interview transcripts with a scale developed to assess consultee responses and resistance may address relationship issues empirically, as has been done in the parent training area (Chamberlain, Patterson, Reid, Kavanaugh, & Forgatch, 1984).

ADVANCES IN SCHOOL-BASED CONSULTATION

Conjoint Behavioral Consultation

The importance of involving parents in their child's education has been documented consistently (Hoover-Dempsey, Bassler, & Brissie, 1987). Apter (1982) reviewed the benefits of parent participation and concluded that their cooperation in school affairs may lead to high pupil achievement, better school attendance, better study habits, and fewer discipline problems. Likewise, parent involvement in education has been found to produce positive effects for parents and teachers

(Becher, 1986). Indeed, the more clearly home and school individuals can communicate and collaborate in their work with children, the greater the probability for success of interventions (Conoley, 1987).

Although the importance of including parents in education has been recognized repeatedly, few empirical studies are available that provide a systematic model of collaborative parent-teacher problem-solving. One form of home-school service delivery may be conceptualized through a behavioral consultation model. "Conjoint behavioral consultation" is offered as a viable, effective means by which positive, collaborative work relations between home and school individuals can be fostered in the best educational interests of children (Sheridan et al., 1990).

Research in behavioral consultation should be broadened to encompass a wider range of settings than has been traditionally true. Ideally, it would appear beneficial to acknowledge the interacting systems in a client's life (Apter & Conoley, 1984). As such, various individuals across settings may be included to provide important information related to a given client. The entire process of problem identification, problem analysis, plan implementation, and plan evaluation may be instituted with individuals across the significant settings in a child's life (i.e., home and school). This may assist in a comprehensive specification of a presenting problem. Continuous data collection across settings may help identify setting events that may be functionally related to, but temporally and contextually distal from the target behavior (Wahler & Fox, 1981). Likewise, consistent programming across settings may serve to enhance transfer and maintenance of consultation treatment effects (Drabman, Hammer, & Rosenbaum, 1979). Finally, engaging significant treatment agents across settings can help monitor the occurrence of behavioral contrast (Johnson, Bolstad, & Lobitz, 1976; Wahler, 1975) and be-

havioral side effects (Kazdin, 1982; Voeltz & Evans, 1982).

A structural model of conjoint behavioral consultation is depicted in Figure 1. In conjoint behavioral consultation, a collaborative home-school relationship is emphasized, with parents and teachers serving as joint consultees. The efficacy of conjoint behavioral consultation with parents and teachers of socially withdrawn children has been investigated with initial preliminary support (Sheridan et al., 1990). However, further research is needed to understand the strengths, limitations, and operative factors of this model more clearly (Sheridan, 1990).

Consultee Training

Perhaps the most salient potential barrier to effective implementation of a consultation model is lack of knowledge and common understanding about it's functions, objectives, and advantages. Indeed, a defining characteristic of all systems (including schools) is their resistance to change. This will be compounded when the individuals most directly involved (i.e., psychologists, teachers, and parents) have limited knowledge about the direction and purpose for change. Educating school personnel will likely be necessary in two broad domains: education regarding the consultation process, and education regarding behavioral management principles and procedures.

The manner in which consultants initially present themselves and the consultation process (i.e., roles, functions, and procedures) is often termed "entry into the system." This is a critical stage in forming consultation perceptions and relationships, and careful consideration must be given to the manner in which one introduces consultation to potential consultees. Initially, consultants should attend faculty meetings or initiate in-service sessions and workshops with teachers and administrators to (a) define the consultation role; (b) provide goals, objectives, and rationales for consultation (including how it can benefit students, teachers, and the school in general); (c) define role expectations and job descriptions; (d) review procedural details; (e) address questions and concerns; and (f) elicit suggestions and input from teachers and administrators regarding the importance of consultation in their school. The primary goals of early meetings are to open lines of communication between the consultant and potential consultees, and to specify clearly the goals and objectives of consultation. As with the individual case consultation process itself, if participants are actively engaged in early meetings, there is an increased prob-

ability that they will show more commitment to the successful implementation and outcome of consultation in their school.

Communication and education are ongoing events, and consultee training and education should not be perceived as single, isolated events (Curtis & Meyers, 1988). Brief in-services or periodic faculty meetings should be conducted throughout the school year to re-define consultation, clarify role or procedural ambiguities, and reiterate the advantages and benefits of consultation. Accountability data from successful cases in the school may further increase teacher's perceptions of the consultants effectiveness.

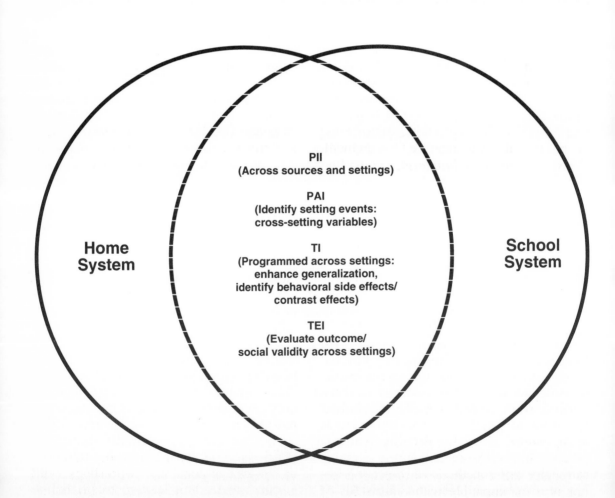

Figure 1: Structural model of conjoint behavioral consultation.

Most importantly, the consultant should present him- or herself as accessible to each potential consultee, and should be sincerely committed to the process of consultation.

A second area in consultee training regards training in various principles and procedures of behavior modification. Training teachers, parents, and other consultees in behavior management skills appears to be an important way to facilitate consultation (Kratochwill & Van Someren, 1985). Because the outcome of consultation depends in large part on the skills of the consultee in implementing the behavioral treatment plan with integrity, it is imperative that these be assessed and enhanced prior to implementation of an intervention. This can occur at two levels: large group training, and individual consultee training. In *large group training*, in-service meetings or workshops can be conducted to help consultees develop effective child management skills. Package approaches, including didactic instruction, modeling, role-playing, reinforcement, and feedback techniques have been found to be useful (Anderson & Kratochwill, 1988). At the *individual level*, a consultee can be trained to implement a specific behavioral program with a client. As with large group training, this can be facilitated through modeling, coaching, role-playing, reinforcement, and behavioral feedback.

CONCLUSIONS

In this chapter we presented behavioral consultation as a feasible, effective model of service-delivery in the provision of educational services to students in the least restrictive environment. However, consultation should not be considered a static model of service-delivery that can be used indiscriminately. It is not meant to replace other methods of direct service, nor is it incompatible with other roles of school psychologists and related school personnel. Rather, it can be considered on a continuum with other methods of service delivery, and represents an adjunct to the skill repertoire of special service providers (Graden et al., 1985).

The primary advantage of behavioral consultation is its preventive and remedial utility. However, there are several important considerations in the implementation of consultation services in applied settings. The success of consultation is largely dependent upon the degree to which the consultant effectively (a) gains sanction and support at all levels of the educational hierarchy, (b) defines roles and responsibilities of all participants, (c) presents a rationale for consultation services, (d) provides accountability data and evaluation criteria, and (e) maintains open lines of communication with all participants (Zins & Curtis, 1984). Likewise, the consultant's interpersonal skills, problem-solving skills, and content expertise are important skill areas that are essential to implementing a consultation model (Curtis & Meyers, 1988). Consultee variables, and the relationship between the consultant and consultee are also considered important.

This chapter opened with a consideration of the NASP/NCAS position statement regarding the provision of appropriate educational services for all children. Behavioral consultation occupies a central role in providing alternative service-delivery options. The success of these programs is measured not only by an evaluation of various options for atypical learners, but also by the ability of these students to function within the broadest possible environment.

NOTE

Preparation of this manuscript was supported in part by grants to the second author from the U.S. Department of Education, Office of Special Education and

Rehabilitative Services. The views expressed in the manuscript are solely those of the authors and do not reflect the views of the U.S. Department of Education.

REFERENCES

Achenbach, T. M., McConaughy, S. H., & Howell, C. T. (1987). Child/Adolescent behavioral and emotional problems: Implications of cross-informant correlations for situational specificity. *Psychological Bulletin, 101*, 213-232.

Algozzine, B., Christenson, S., & Ysseldyke, J. E. (1982). An analysis of the incidence of special class placement: The masses are burgeoning. *Journal of Special Education, 17*, 141-147.

Algozzine, B., & Ysseldyke, J. E. (1981). Special education services for normal children: Better safe than sorry. *Exceptional Children, 48*, 238-243.

Anderson, T. K., & Kratochwill, T. R. (1988). Dissemination of behavioral procedures in the schools: Issues in training. In J. C. Witt, S. N. Elliott, & F. M. Gresham, (Eds.) *Handbook of behavior therapy in education* (pp. 217-244). New York: Plenum.

Apter, S. J. (1982). *Troubled children/troubled systems.* Elmsford, NY: Pergamon Press.

Apter, S. J., & Conoley, J. C. (1984). *Childhood behavior disorders and emotional disturbance.* Englewood Cliffs, NJ: Prentice Hall, Inc.

Becher, R. M. (1986). Parent involvement: A review of research and principles of successful practice. In L. G. Katz (Ed.). *Current topics in early childhood education* (Vol. VI, pp. 85-122). Norwood, N.J.: Ablex.

Bergan, J. R. (1977). *Behavioral consultation.* Columbus, OH: Charles E. Merrill.

Bergan, J. R., & Kratochwill, T. R. (1990). *Behavioral consultation and therapy.* New York: Plenum.

Bergan, J. R., & Tombari, M. L. (1976). Consultant skill and efficiency and the implementation and outcomes of consultation. *Journal of School Psychology, 14*, 3-13.

Brown, D., Pryzwansky, W. B., & Schulte, A. C. (1987). *Psychological consultation: Introduction to theory and practice.* Boston: Allyn and Bacon.

Caplan, G. (1970). *The theory and practice of mental health consultation.* New York: Basic Books.

Cataldo, M. F. (1984). Clinical considerations in training parents of children with special problems. In R. F. Dangel & R. A. Polster (Eds.), *Parent training* (pp. 329-357). New York: Guilford Press.

Chamberlain, P., Patterson, G., Reid, J., Kavanaugh, K., & Forgatch, M. (1984). Observation of client resistance. *Behavior Therapy, 15*, 144-155.

Christenson, S., Ysseldyke, J. E., & Algozzine, B. (1982). Institutional constraints and external pressures influencing referral decisions. *Psychology in the Schools, 19*, 341-345.

Coates, R. D. (1989). The regular education initiative and opinions of regular education teachers. *Journal of Learning Disabilities, 22*, 532-536.

Conoley, J. C. (1987). Strategic family intervention: Three cases of school-aged children. *School Psychology Review, 16*, 469-486.

Curtis, M. J., & Anderson, T. (1976). *The Consultant Observation Assessment Form* (COAF). Unpublished measure. University of Cincinnatti, Cincinnatti, OH.

Curtis, M. J., & Meyers, J. (1988). Consultation: A foundation for alternative services in the schools. In J. L. Graden, J. E. Zins, & M. J. Curtis (Eds.), *Alternative educational delivery systems: Enhancing options for all students* (pp. 35-48). Washington DC: National Association of School Psychologists.

Drabman, R. S., Hammer, D., & Rosenbaum, M. S. (1979). Assessing generalization in behavior modification with children: The generalization map. *Behavioral Assessment, 1*, 203-219.

Elliott, S. N. (1986). Children's ratings of the acceptability of classroom interventions for misbehavior: Findings and methodological considerations. *Journal of School Psychology, 24*, 23-35.

Epps, S., Ysseldyke, J. E., & Algozzine, B. (1983). Impact of different definitions of learning disabilities on the number of students identified. *Journal of Psychoeducational Assessment, 1*, 341-352.

Fuchs, D., & Fuchs, L. S. (1989). Exploring effective and efficient prereferral interventions: A component analysis of behavioral consultation. *School Psychology Review, 18*, 260-283.

Gettinger, M. (1988). Methods of proactive classroom management. *School Psychology Review, 17*, 227-242.

Graden, J. L., Casey, A., & Christenson, S. L. (1985). Implementing a prereferral intervention system. Part I: The model. *Exceptional Children, 51*, 377-384.

Gresham, F. M. (1989). Assessment of treatment integrity in school consultation and prereferral intervention. *School Psychology Review, 18*, 37-50.

Hoover-Dempsey, K. V., Bassler, O. C., & Brissie, J. S. (1987). Parent involvement: Contributions of teacher efficacy, school socioeconomic status, and other school characteristics. *American Educational Research Journal, 24*, 417-435.

Idol, L., Paolucci-Newcomb, P., & Nevin, A. (1986). *Collaborative consultation*. Rockville, MD: Aspen.

Johnson, S. M., Bolstad, O. D., & Lobitz, G. K. (1976). Generalization and contrast phenomena in behavior modification with children. In E. J. Mash, L. A. Hamerlynck, & L. C. Handy (Eds.), *Behavior modification and families*. New York: Brunner/Mazel.

Kauffman, J. M. (1989). The regular education initiative as Reagan-Bush education policy: A trickle-down theory of education of the hard-to-teach. *Journal of Special Education, 23*, 256-278.

Kazdin, A. E. (1982). Symptom substitution, generalization, and response covariation: Implications for psychotherapy outcome. *Psychological Bulletin, 91*, 349-365.

Kratochwill, T. R. (1985). Selection of target behaviors in behavioral consultation. *Behavioral Assessment, 7*, 49-61.

Kratochwill, T. R., & Bergan, J. R. (1990). *Behavioral consultation in applied settings: An individual guide*. New York: Plenum.

Kratochwill, T. R., & Sheridan, S. M. (1990). Advances in behavioral assessment. In C. R. Reynolds & T. B. Gutkin (Eds.). *Handbook of school psychology* (2nd ed., pp. 328-364). New York: Wiley.

Kratochwill, T. R., Sheridan, S. M., & Van Someren, K. R. (1988). Research in behavioral consultation: Current status and future directions. In F. West (Ed.), *School consultation: Interdisciplinary perspectives on theory, research, training, and practice* (pp. 77-102). Austin, TX: University of Texas Press.

Kratochwill, T. R., & Van Someren, K. R. (1985). Barriers to treatment success in behavioral consultation: Current limitations and future directions. *Journal of School Psychology, 23*, 225-239.

Lentz, F. E., & Shapiro, E. S. (1986). Functional assessment of the academic environment. *School Psychology Review, 15*, 346-357.

Mannino, F. V., & Shore, M. F. (1975). The effects of consultation: A review of empirical studies. *American Journal of Community Psychology, 17*, 275-282.

Martens, B. K., & Witt, J. C. (1988). Expanding the scope of behavioral consultation: A systems approach to classroom behavior change. *Professional School Psychology, 3*, 271-281.

Medway, F. J. (1979). How effective is school consultation: A review of recent research. *Journal of School Psychology, 17*, 275-282.

Medway, F. J., & Updyke, J. F. (1985). Meta-analysis of consultation outcome studies. *American Journal of Community Psychology, 13*, 489-505.

Meyers, J., Parsons, R. D., & Martin, R. (1979). *Mental health consultation in the schools*. San Francisco: Jossey-Bass.

National Association of School Psychologists/National Coalition of Advocates for Students (1985). *Advocacy for appropriate educational services for all children*. Washington DC: Author.

Pray, B., Kramer, J. J., & Lindskog, R. (1986). Assessment and treatment of tic behavior: A review and case study. *School Psychology Review, 15*, 418-429.

Rogers-Warren, A., & Warren, S. F. (Eds.). (1977). *Ecological perspectives in behavior analysis*. Baltimore: University Park Press.

Rosenfield, S. (1990). Taking a position on "appropriate educational services." *School Psychology Quarterly, 5*, 46.

Sarason, S. B., & Doris, J. (1979). *Educational handicap, public policy, and social history: A broadened perspective on mental retardation*. New York: Macmillan.

Schein, E. H. (1969). *Process consultation: Its role in organizational development*. Reading, MA: Addison-Wessley.

Schmuck, R. A., & Runkel, P. J. (1972). Organizational training. In R. A. Schmuck (Ed.), *Handbook of organizational development in schools*. Palo Alto: Mayfield.

Sheridan, S. M. (1990, August). *Behavioral consultation with parents and teachers: Conceptual and research considerations.* Paper presented at the 98th annual convention of the American Psychological Association, Boston.

Sheridan, S. M., Kratochwill, T. R., & Elliott, S. N. (1990). Behavioral consultation with parents and teachers: Delivering treatment for socially withdrawn children at home and school. *School Psychology Review, 19,* 33-52.

Voeltz, L. M., & Evans, I. M. (1982). The assessment of behavioral interrelationships in child behavior therapy. *Behavioral Assessment, 4,* 131-165.

Von Brock, M. B., & Elliott, S. N. (1987). Influence of treatment effectiveness information on the acceptability of classroom interventions. *Journal of School Psychology, 25,* 131-144.

Wahler, R. G. (1975). Some structural aspects of deviant child behavior. *Journal of Applied Behavior Analysis, 8,* 27-42.

Wahler, R. G., & Dumas, J. E. (1984). Changing the observational coding styles of insular and noninsular mothers: A step toward maintenance of parent training effects. In R. F. Dangel & R. A. Polster (Eds.), *Parent training* (pp. 379-416). New York: Guilford.

Wahler, R. G., & Fox, J. J. (1981). Setting events in applied behavior analysis: Toward a conceptual and methodological expansion. *Journal of Applied Behavior Analysis, 14,* 327-338.

West, J. F., & Idol, L. (1987). School consultation (Part I): An interdisciplinary perspective on theory, models, and research. *Journal of Learning Disabilities, 20,* 388-408.

Witt, J. & Elliott, S. N. (1982). The response-cost lottery: A time efficient and effective classroom intervention. *Journal of School Psychology, 20,* 155-161.

Witt, J. C., & Elliott, S. N. (1985). Acceptability of classroom management strategies. In T. R. Kratochwill (Ed.), *Advances in school psychology* (Vol. 4, pp. 251-288). Hillsdale, NJ.: Lawrence Erlbaum.

Witt, J. C., Elliott, S. N., & Martens, B. K. (1984). Acceptability of behavioral interventions used in classrooms: The influence of amount of teacher time, severity of behavior problem, and type of intervention. *Behavioral Disorders, 9,* 95-104.

Ysseldyke, J. E., Algozzine, B., & Epps, S. (1983). A logical and empirical analysis of current practices in classifying students as handicapped. *Exceptional Children, 50,* 160-166.

Ysseldyke, J. E., Algozzine, B., Richey, L., & Graden, J. L. (1982). Declaring students eligible for learning disability services: Why bother with the data? *Learning Disability Quarterly, 5,* 37-44.

Zins, J. E., & Curtis, M. J. (1984). Building consultation into the educational service delivery system. In C. A. Maher, R. J. Illback, & J. E. Zins (Eds.), *Organizational psychology in the schools: A handbook for professionals.* Springfield, IL: Charles C. Thomas.

Zins, J. E., Curtis, M. J., Graden, J. L., & Ponti, C. R. (1988). *Helping students succeed in the regular classroom.* San Francisco: Jossey-Bass.

15

MODELS FOR INTEGRATION

Joni Alberg
Research Triangle Institute

The mandates of Public Law 94-142 enacted in 1978 (Education of All Handicapped Children Act of 1975) guarantee that "to the maximum extent possible" students with disabilities should be educated with students who do not have disabilities. One of the primary challenges for educators initially and currently regarding implementation of PL 94-142 is to determine when integrated educational opportunities can occur and to maximize those opportunities for students with disabilities. This challenge is enhanced by the need to develop specific general education programs that address the growing cultural and racial diversity of the total student population. General education students' abilities, cultures, interests, and needs in classrooms and schools across the country are becoming increasingly heterogeneous and the inclusion of students with disabilities in these classrooms and schools compounds this heterogeneity. It is clear that although many approaches for educating students with diverse needs and abilities in the same educational setting already exist, there is a need to assist educators who are in the process of addressing this challenge by providing information and guidance.

It is important to understand that no one approach can be used by all schools to establish integrated educational opportunities for students with diverse abilities. It follows then, that flexibility will be needed when choosing from among the variety of approaches that can be followed to enhance learning for all students in the same educational setting.

Education as a whole incorporates many ways of imparting knowledge. Educational researchers and practitioners have developed numerous models applicable to an array of instructional situations. These models, developed for both general and special education, provide many options from which schools may choose. With this information available, the most crucial task for schools is to choose the approaches and models which will work best to help individual students achieve their personal best within the school system.

Because there is great diversity among the educational models from which schools may choose, a strategy or framework for examining and selecting from among them can be very helpful. Such a framework for grouping, or classifying, models helps to clarify the nature and focus of model implementation, making it easier for schools to select the type of model that will fit with or replace existing programs and help to provide successful student response to integration. For example, in the previous chapters in this section, three models, each providing distinctly different strategies for accommodating student needs within the general education classroom, are presented. Sheridan and Kratochwill explain how behavioral consultation can be used to improve indirect service-delivery to students with special needs in general education settings by providing consultative support and assistance to teachers. Implementation of this model requires that a behavioral consultant work with teachers to help them develop strategies and skills to manage student behavior, focusing on the professional development of teachers through consultation. Carnine discusses the benefits of using a highly structured approach to instruction and a nontraditional sequence of topic presentation to teach mathematics to students with diverse abilities and needs. Direct Instruction follows an instructional approach that requires a highly specified presentation of instruction and a sequential change in the curriculum, providing an alternative to traditional curriculum. Slavin and Stevens describe the use of specific cooperative learning techniques to facilitate instruction for heterogeneous groups of students within the same class. Implementation of this cooperative learning model requires that classroom instruction shift from the traditional teacher to instruction that is guided by the students themselves.

These three educational models are distinctively different in the approaches they take to teaching students with diverse abilities in general education settings. Some of these methods have greater value for some specific school settings and they are all quite different. Clearly, there is a need to develop a map to guide educators in choosing the best route for their schools.

This chapter includes such a map. Although some models such as those described in the previous chapters have more empirical support than others, examples of divers educational models will be used to illustrate a framework for organizing models and, thus, facilitating their examination and selection. The need to organize the large number of

available models into manageable groupings has resulted in the development of a framework by the Center for Educating Students with Handicaps In Regular Education Settings (CESHIRES)[1] for classifying various educational models. This framework organizes models according to primary approaches to educational change, i.e., the total teaching and learning compendium as well as school organization on every level of the educational process that would be affected if a model were implemented. For example, implementation of Slavin and Stevens' cooperative learning model will affect the instructional methods currently being used by shifting the teaching role to the student. Thus, this framework also provides an indication of the nature of the change(s) that will be required if a particular model is selected for implementation.

APPROACHES TO INTEGRATING STUDENTS WITH DIVERSE NEEDS

The American Heritage Dictionary (1982) defines "approach" as "the method used in dealing with or accomplishing something." With this definition in mind, CESHIRES (1989; 1990) developed a framework for classifying educational models according to the primary teaching approach followed by each model.

According to the CESHIRES framework there are two basic approaches, instructional and organizational, that most educational models follow. These classifications provide the general basis for distinguishing among the various models. Models following an instructional approach primarily focus on "what" is taught (the content) and "how" teaching occurs (the strategies

[1]The Center for Educating Students with Handicaps in Regular Education Settings was established at the Research Triangle Institute in North Carolina through a contract with the U.S. Department of Education's Office of Special Education Programs (Contract Number H588002301).

**Table 1: The Center for Educating Students with Handicaps in Regular Education
Settings (CESHIRES) Framework for Classifying Educational Models**

Approach:	Instructional				Organizational (class, building, district)	
Focus:	Content		Method		Structure	Procedure
	Academic/ Skill Subject Matter	Strategy/ Process Subject Matter	Teacher Directed	Student Guided	Grade/Class Configuration	Professional Development
					Student - Assignment	Shared Decision-Making

3/5/90 CESHIRES (Research Triangle Institute, NC Contract No. H588002301)

and methods of instruction). Instruction-al models can further be grouped according to the focus of the instruction. Is content the primary focus of the model, or does the model focus primarily on the use of a particular method to present content? Additionally, we can further define the classification of models by defining the type of content or the type of teaching method used. Instructional models are basically concerned with the classroom setting--what we want children to know and be able to do and how this knowledge is transmitted.

The organizational approach focuses on how schools are structured (including the organization of the classrooms, buildings, and the district as a whole) and on the procedures used to administer the educational programs of the school. Models that follow an organizational approach have a structural or procedural focus. Models having a structural focus emphasize the configuration of grade or class groupings. Models focused on procedures emphasize the way decisions are made, including the professional development of the school and district staff. The primary focus for models classified as following an organizational approach is on the entire support system that facilitates teaching and learning.

It should be noted that many models may contain components of more than one approach area. For example, a model may present a method for organizing the instructional staff of a school (organizational) while introducing new instruction-al strategies (instructional). The CESHIRES framework classifies models according to the primary approach they follow. This conceptual framework is intended as a general guide or map that can assist schools in identifying models for review and consideration. It also provides preliminary information about what will be required for model implementation.

In the following section, I briefly describe approaches presented in the CESHIRES framework. Model descriptions are provided as illustrations of each approach and should not be taken as recommendations or "how to's" for schools.

SELECTED MODELS

Although few educational models have been designed for the express purpose of integrating students with disabilities into general education settings, numerous models exist that have potential for facilitating integration. What can schools and districts do that will enable them to determine which model or models will work best for them? Schools must first determine what goals they wish to accomplish with regard to integrated educational programs. Is the goal to enhance existing integrated programs? Expand integrated opportunities? Improve the overall educational programs of the school or district so that all students have increased opportunities for academic and social achievement? Answers to these questions are needed before a school can even begin to choose a new instructional or organizational method. These goals may best be determined by a team comprised of administrators, teachers, support staff, parents, and where appropriate, students.

Once the goals have been established, the school needs to assess and define its role within the confines of the community and culture it serves. This contextual profile should contain such information as school or district philosophy, values of the community, stability of school staff and student populations, academic emphasis (including curriculum and textbook adoptions), and fiscal resources, as well as local, state, and district policies and procedures. The profile provides valuable information that can directly influence the selection and successful implementation of a model or models. In other words, understanding the nature and resources of the context for which an educational model is being sought will assist decision-makers in selecting an approach and model(s) that fit the context, thus ensuring a high probability of successful program implementation and individual goal attainment.[2]

Instructional Models

Instructional models focus on the design and delivery of instruction (i.e., methods and procedures) and the selection and use of instructional materials. According to the CESHIRES framework, instructional models can be broken down into those that focus on the content to be taught and those that focus on methods used to teach the content. As shown in Table 1, content models are classified as focusing on academic or skill content or on strategy or process content.

[2]For more detailed information about the steps in the process of choosing a model and about the models themselves, see CESHIRES (1990).

ACADEMIC/SKILL CONTENT MODELS. Educational models following an academic/skill content approach provide a focus on the presentation of academic content that differs from traditional curriculum content often breaking information into smaller units of learning, changing the learning sequence, etc. The following examples provide descriptions of two different types of academic/skill models.

- *Direct Instruction* (Becker, Engelmann, Carnine, & Rhine, 1981) is a comprehensive system of instruction designed to teach academic skills in one or more of a variety of subject areas (e.g., reading, language, spelling, writing, mathematics) at all grade levels (pre-K through postsecondary). In his chapter on Direct Instruction (DI) applied to mathematics, Carnine identified two major components of DI. The first, stresses effective teaching practices, including active instruction; systematic presentation of skills and concepts in small, easy-to-understand steps; guided practice; immediate feedback; and frequent student-teacher interactions. The second component, and according to Carnine the heart of the Direct Instruction system, is the use of curricular materials that were developed through careful analysis of each curriculum being taught. According to Carnine, the logical order of content presentation is as critical as the systematic delivery of instruction. The DI model has been demonstrated to be effective in producing significant academic gains for students with disabilities, bilingual students, and students identified as at risk (cf., Gersten, Woodward, & Darch, 1986; Becker, 1984; Gersten, Brockway, & Henares 1983). Frequent teacher-student interchanges; explicit presentation of material; guided practice; direct observation of student progress; and immediate feedback provide a structure for enabling each student to have an opportunity for the successful achievement of academic goals. DI requires a high degree of structure in the classroom and in the teaching process.

- The *High/Scope Curriculum* model (Hohmann, Banet, & Weikart, 1978) is designed to meet students' cognitive, social, affective, and physical development needs in kindergarten through third grade. According to Weikart (1988), the "fundamental premise of the curriculum is that children are active learners who construct their own knowledge from activities they plan and carry out themselves" (pp. 64). The High/Scope Curriculum revolves around 48 interrelated key experiences (e.g., active exploration with all senses, role playing, investigating and describing, making comparisons, planning and completing plans) with the primary emphasis placed on problem solving, independent thinking, social development, and relationships. The role of the teacher is one of facilitator and guide rather than the more traditional role of director. Teachers must organize the environment, provide materials for students, assist them in planning daily activities, and actively interact with them to extend planned activities to challenging levels. Developmental milestones are used to monitor child progress (Weikart, 1988), thus making it extremely conducive for use with students of varying developmental levels within the same classroom. Perhaps even more ideal would be the implementation of the High/Scope Curriculum in ungraded primary settings where stu-

dents of all abilities work and play side-by-side to achieve their own developmental milestones.

STRATEGY/PROCESS CONTENT MODELS. These are the second type of instructional content models. In addition to teaching academic content, strategy or process models teach students how to use higher-order thinking skills to access information rather then memorizing and repeating information provided by others. Instruction in learning strategies and processes for how to think and learn is especially appropriate for students with disabilities.

Models for teaching strategies or processes for thinking and learning provide a curriculum that must be first taught in isolation (i.e., in addition to the existing academic curriculum) and then applied in a variety of learning situations. These models require specific classroom time in order to teach these new techniques of learning and understanding. It is important to note that this time may encroach on time allocated for other subjects or activities.

- The *Strategies Intervention Model* (SIM) is a series of techniques, or strategies, that are taught to students to enable them to solve problems and complete tasks independently (Deshler, Warner, Schumaker, & Alley, 1983). Although originally designed for secondary students with learning disabilities, SIM has been used successfully with adults, students in upper elementary grades, and with students having a variety of disabilities as well as with students who have no disabilities. Specifically, students learn skills that allow them to meet immediate academic requirements and to generalize the skills to other situations and settings over time (Deshler & Schumaker, 1986). Use of SIM requires that time be set aside each day to teach the strategies and to practice transfer of skills to other situations. This means that a decision must be made to sacrifice other academic instructional time. In return, students acquire skills that will facilitate academic instruction at later times.

- *Tactics for Thinking* is a similar model developed for use in general education classes (Marzano & Arrendondo, 1986). Tactics provide a systematic approach to the introduction of thinking skills into school experience for students in grades K through 12. Tactics are grouped by type into three broad categories: learning to learn skills, content thinking skills, and reasoning skills. Tactics is based on three assumptions that distinguish it from other programs: (a) teaching of thinking should be overt, teacher-directed, and part of regular classroom instruction; (b) teaching of thinking must occur in conjunction with the teaching of content; and (c) direct teaching of thinking skills within formal education will necessitate a change in or restructuring of curriculum, instruction, and assessment techniques.

Instructional Method Models

Models that focus on instructional methods deal with the process of teaching. CESHIRES defines two types of teaching process models: those that are teacher directed and those that are student directed.

TEACHER DIRECTED MODELS. Models that can be classified as teacher directed use methods of instruction that can be applied to any curriculum and focus on how teachers present or deliver instruction.

- The *Contingencies for Learning Academic and Social Skills* (CLASS) program (Walker, Hops, & Greenwood, 1984) is another type of teacher directed model. CLASS, one program in the SUCCESS Program Series,[3] is a classroom behavior management program for acting-out students (i.e., those students who defy classroom rules, structures and procedures, and who exhibit excessive deviant behaviors such as disrupting class activities, noncompliance to teacher instructions and directions, inappropriate peer interactions, verbal or physical aggression, and destruction of property). The main purpose of CLASS is to produce rapid, significant, long-lasting changes in student behavior so that students are able to attend to academic instruction and learning. This model has been specifically designed to accommodate students with special needs in general education classrooms and requires the use of a teacher consultant to implement the program. The success of CLASS is dependent upon the following program components: a contracting procedure between the student, the teacher, and the class; parent involvement; group contingencies (the entire class receives a reward for the targeted student's improved behavior); teacher consultant assistance in implementing the program; and a systematic schedule for fading out the intervention components as the student is able to manage his/her own behavior without the program.

- *The Learning Styles Model* was developed as a method for improv-

3Success Using Contingencies to Create Effective Social Skills developed by Hill Walker, Charles Greenwood, and Hyman Hops.

ing instruction based on a belief in matching individual learning styles to instructional procedures and materials (Dunn & Dunn, 1978). Students' learning styles and preferences are diagnosed through self-report inventories, and teachers adjust their teaching styles and the organization of classrooms to accommodate the various learning styles of students. Thus, the individual needs of different students are said to be addressed within the same classroom.

STUDENT-GUIDED MODELS. These educational models focus on students as the facilitators of instructional delivery. Although teachers must organize and manage the process of student guided instruction, students assume primary responsibility for their own and other's learning. Cooperative learning, peer tutoring, peer modeling, and peer management all involve students assisting each other in the process of learning.

- *Cooperative learning*, as described by Slavin and Stevens in their chapter on cooperative learning and mainstreaming, is a method of instruction that involves small, heterogeneous groups of students working together to complete academic tasks. Peer tutoring, modeling, and management also involve students working together to complete academic tasks but rather than small groups, students work in pairs to complete academic tasks, model appropriate behaviors, or assist with daily routines. For example, peer tutors may assist with review and practice of words for a weekly spelling test; peer models may serve as models of appropriate behavior for students having difficulty on the playground or at lunch; and peer managers may help students who need special assistance in the bathroom, at lunch, or moving about

the school. The common focus for all of these peer methods is on students as deliverers of instruction.

Slavin and Stevens provide a description of what they refer to as "complex cooperative learning methods." According to these authors, the introduction of complex cooperative methods will result in comprehensive changes in curriculum. Slavin and Stevens describe two instructional models, Team Accelerated Instruction (TAI) and Cooperative Integrated Reading and Composition (CIRC), that are based on four central concepts: (a) *Students must be working toward a group goal* (students must have a reason to take one another's achievement seriously; the achievement of a group goal, with all members of the team contributing, provides the necessary motivation for cooperative learning); (b) *Individual accountability* (the team's success depends on the individual learning of all team members; this encourages teammates to tutor one another and make sure that everyone is adequately prepared for assessment activities; according to Slavin, this is one element that sets these models apart from many other cooperative learning methods); (c) *Equal opportunities for success* (students contribute to their teams by improving their own past performance; this ensures that each member is equally challenged to achieve their best); and (d) *Team rewards* (team members work together to master material at or above a designated criterion; when the team's criterion is reached, the team receives a certificate or other team rewards).

- *Classwide Student Tutoring Teams* (CSTT) is a student-guided model that was developed as an alternative instructional option to independent seat work and traditional drill and practice activities (Maheady, Harper, & Sacca, 1988). Classwide peer tutoring can be used at all grade levels with students having a wide range of abilities (e.g., Greenwood, Carta, & Hall, 1988). The CSTT model is based on the assumption that when students are given ample opportunities to respond to academic tasks and receive immediate feedback, they will increase their retention of information and improve their academic achievement. Students follow a structured tutoring procedure during team practice activities where students take turns acting as tutor and, tutees respond to questions or practice math facts or spelling words. Tutees are given immediate feedback in the form of points if a correct response is given or no points if an incorrect one has been given. The total number of points earned by each team from daily tutoring sessions plus scores on tests are publically posted in the class and the team(s) with the most points is rewarded.

Organizational Models

Organizational models focus on the development of systems and structures within schools and districts which provide the support for the delivery of instructional content. According to the CESHIRES framework organizational models can be broken down into two types: (a) those that focus on the structure of classrooms, buildings, and districts (e.g., how rooms are physically arranged; how staff/students are assigned; administrative organization within schools and within the district), and (b) those that focus on the procedures used to operate classrooms, buildings, and districts (e.g.,how decisions are made; responsibility for governance of classrooms and schools; administrative style of classrooms, schools, and districts).

STRUCTURAL MODELS. Structural models focus on the basic supports that

can enhance the teaching and learning process throughout a classroom, building, or district. At the classroom level, a structural model may provide a strategy for organizing students for instruction (e.g., assignments to groups); arranging furniture, materials, and instructional centers; and managing classroom procedures. At the school level structural models may offer strategies for assigning students to grades and classrooms (e.g., non-graded student groupings) or providing procedures for operating a variety of educational programs within the school.

• The *Comprehensive Local School* (CLS) is a model specifically designed to facilitate the integration of students with severe disabilities in the general education setting. In order to implement this model, schools must make a commitment to assigning all students to their neighborhood schools, providing special education services within the general education setting, and developing a comprehensive service delivery system that includes both school and community based instruction. The CLS is a multiphase service model that manifests itself differently for each of five age groupings (Sailor et al., 1989); these phases are described in Table 2.

PROCEDURAL MODELS. Educational models following a procedural approach to classroom, building, and district organization focus on the processes used to provide support to the teaching and learning process. These support processes include the procedures followed for decision making and the development of the professional skills of school and district staffs.

• *Behavioral Consultation*, as described by Sheridan and Kratochwill in their chapter, is a form of educational service delivery that provides an alterna-

Table 2: The Phases of the Comprehensive Local School Model

Phase I: Mainstreaming. Mainstreaming begins where infant intervention programs taper off and continues through kindergarten. Children with all types and ranges of disability are placed in the same classroom together with their nondisabled age mates. The primary academic emphasis is on the development of social and communication skills.

Phase II: Integration. Integration encompasses the early elementary school years (approximately first through fourth grades), where students with disabilities continue to be placed full-time with their nondisabled age mates and the development of a sustained social network is stressed.

Phase III: Community Intensive Instruction. Students in fifth through eighth grades are included in this phase. The instructional emphasis for students with severe disabilities begins to shift from full-time general education class instruction to instruction that is based in the larger community in which the school is located. Students with severe disabilities spend increasing amounts of time in non-school settings receiving training and instruction in independent living (e.g., mobility, domestic, recreational, and vocational settings).

Phase IV: Transition. This phase corresponds to the secondary program or grades nine through twelve. During this phase a heavy emphasis is placed on job training in integrated job sites. "Preparation for adult, post-school living and the world of work receive the most attention from the curriculum used during the phase of transition" (Sailor et al., 1989).

Phase V: Integrated Work and Community Living. This phase begins at around age 18, the age when most young people leave high school and move to post-secondary work and educational opportunities. The high school campus is no longer an appropriate setting at this phase. Rather, the community college campus becomes the setting of choice. Training for independent living and supported employment are highlighted.

tive service delivery option. This approach to delivering services may require schools to reconsider existing service delivery procedures, especially the delivery of psychological services. In this model, a behavioral consultant provides indirect service to students with problematic behaviors by (a) facilitating the consultation process (i.e., problem identification, problem analysis, treatment implementation, and treatment evaluation); (b) providing information and resources to teachers; and (c) ensuring that teachers provide services that benefit the students. Although the principle goal of the behavioral consultation model is to produce change in student behavior, the primary focus of the model is on increasing the skill, knowledge, confidence, and ability of teachers so that they are able to change problematic student behavior. To implement this model Sheridan and Kratochwill suggest that school personnel share a common understanding about and acceptance of the functions, objectives, advantages, and processes of behavioral consultation.

- *The Coalition of Essential Schools*, established in 1984 as a partnership between Brown University and a diverse group of secondary schools throughout the nation, is a school restructuring effort designed to modify priorities and simplify the structures of participating schools primarily through changes in the procedural aspects of schooling. According to O'Neil (1990) "each Coalition school proceeds independently, but they are united by their adherence to such principles as curricular design that promotes student mastery rather than content coverage, a personalized environment in which no teacher has more than 80 students, and student diplomas based on exhibition of mastery" (pp. 6). Although the efforts of the Coalition have been directed to secondary schools, the key principles upon which this model is based are applicable to schools at all levels. These principles ("Coalition of Essential Schools," 1988; Sizer, 1986; 1989) are described in Table 3.

SUMMARY

The CESHIRES framework for classifying models presented in this chapter provides educators with a map that can serve as a guide to the examination and selection of models that will facilitate the integration of students with disabilities in general education settings. Several models have been briefly described to provide examples of the various approaches included in the framework. Clearly, there are many additional models that can be implemented to help schools achieve their goals for integration of students with diverse needs and abilities in the same setting. Also, some models have more well-documented effectiveness than other models. On a final note, the approaches and models presented in this chapter provide methods to schools that will assist them in improving or expanding integrated educational opportunities for students with disabilities, but they will not eliminate the need for special education services.

NOTE

Preparation of this chapter was supported at least in part with Federal funds from the U.S. Department of Education under contract number H588002301. The content of this publication does not necessarily reflect the views or policies of the U.S. Department of Education nor does mention of trade names, commercial products, or organizations imply endorsement by the U.S. Government.

REFERENCES

American Heritage Dictionary (2nd ed.). (1982). Boston: Houghton Mifflin Company.

Becker, W. C., Englemann, S., Carnine, D. W., & Rhine, W. R. (1981). Direct Instruction Model. In R. Rhine (Ed.), Encouraging change in America's schools: A decade of experimentation (pp. 95-154). New York: Academic Press.

Becker, W. C. (1984, March). Direct Instruction--A Twenty Year Review. Paper presented at the XVI

Table 3: Principles of the Coalition of Essential Schools

1. An Essential School should focus on helping students to use their minds well.

2. The school's goals should be simple: that each student master a limited number of essential skills and areas of knowledge.

3. The school's goals should apply to all students.

4. Teaching and learning should be personalized to the maximum feasible extent.

5. The governing practical metaphor of the school should be student-as-worker.

6. The diploma should be awarded upon a successful demonstration of mastery for graduation.

7. The tone of the school should stress values of relaxed expectation ("I won't threaten you but I expect much of you"); trust, and decency (the values of fairness, generosity, and tolerance).

8. The principal and teachers should perceive themselves as generalists first and specialists second.

9. Ultimate administrative and budget targets should include total student loads per teacher of 80 or fewer pupils, substantial time for collective planning by teachers, competitive salaries for staff, and an ultimate per-pupil cost not to exceed that at traditional schools by more than 10 percent. Implementation of this model requires a significant commitment on the part of schools to the reorganization and restructuring of their total school program.

Annual Banff International Conference on Behavioral Science.

CESHIRES. (1989). *Plans for Year 2 documentation workshops.* Contract Number H588002301 Deliverable, October 31, 1989. Research Triangle Park, NC: Research Triangle Institute.

CESHIRES. (1990). *Model summary document.* Contract Number H588002301 Deliverable, May 31, 1990. Research Triangle Park, NC: Research Triangle Institute.

Coalition of Essential Schools. (1988). *Coalition of essential schools: Prospectus.* Providence, RI: Education Department, Brown University.

Deshler, D. D., Warner, M. M., Schumaker, J. B., & Alley, G. R. (1983). Learning strategies intervention model: Key components and current status. In J.D. McKinney & L. Feagans (Eds.), *Current topics in learning disabilities* (Vol. 1, pp. 245-283). Norwood, NJ: Ablex Publishing Corporation.

Deshler, D. D., Schumaker, J. B. (1986). Learning Strategies: An instructional alternative for low-achieving adolescents. *Exceptional Children, 52,* 583-590.

Dunn, R., & Dunn, K. (1978). *Teaching students through their individual learning styles: A practical approach.* Reston, VA: Reston Publishing Company.

Education of All Handicapped Children Act of 1975, 20 U. S. C. 1401 (1978).

Gersten, R. M., Brockway, M. A., & Henares, N. (1983). The Monterey DI program for students with limited English (ESL). *Direct Instruction News, 2*(4), 8-9.1.

Gersten R., Woodward, J., & Darch, C. (1986). Direct Instruction: A research-based approach to curriculum design and teaching. *Exceptional Children, 53,* 17-31.

Greenwood, C. R., Carta, J. J., & Hall, R. V. (1988). The use of classwide peer tutoring strategies in classroom management and instruction. *School Psychology Review, 17,* 258-275.

Hohmann, M., Banet, B., & Weikart, D. P. (1978). *Young children in action: A manual for preschool educators.* Ypsilanti, MI: High/Scope Educational Research Foundation.

Marzano, R. J., & Arrendondo, D. E. (1986). *Tactics for Thinking trainer's manual.* Aurora, CO: Mid-continent Regional Laboratory.

Maheady, L., Harper, G. F., & Sacca, M. K. (1988). Classwide peer tutoring programs in secondary self-contained programs for the mildly handicapped. *Journal of Research and Development in Education, 21*(3), 76-86.

O'Neil, J. E. (1990). Piecing together the restructuring puzzle. *Educational Leadership, 47*(7).

Sailor, W., Anderson, J., Halvorsen, A., Doerring, K., Filler, D. & Goetz, L. (1989). *The Comprehensive local school.* Baltimore, MD: Paul H. Brooks Publisher.

Sizer, T. R. (1986). Rebuilding: First steps by the Coalition of Essential Schools. *Phi Delta Kappan, 68,* 38-42.

Sizer, T. R. (1989). Diverse practice, shared ideas: The essential school. In H. J. Walberg & J. J. Lane (Eds.), *Organizing for learning: Toward the 21st century.* Reston, VA: National Association of Secondary School Principals.

Walker, H. M., Hops, H., & Greenwood, C. (1984). The CORBEH research and development model: Programmatic issues and strategies. In S. Paine, T. Bellamay, & B. Wilcox (Eds.), *Human services that work.* Baltimore, MD: Paul H. Brooks.

Weikert, D. (1988). Quality in early childhood education" In C. L. Warger (Ed.), *A resource guide to public school early childhood programs* (pp. 63-72). Alexandria, VA: ASCD.

PART IV

16

A RATIONALE FOR INTEGRATION AND RESTRUCTURING: A SYNOPSIS

William Stainback and Susan Stainback

University of Northern Iowa

The integration of all students into the mainstream of regular education and the restructuring of the education system to accommodate for integration is a controversial topic among both parents and educators today. As has been pointed out throughout the chapters in this book, although some professionals and parents agree with the integration movement, others have reservations. Despite these reservations, we believe that there are a growing number of reasons supporting the notion that integrated or inclusive schooling is a positive approach for all students.

The primary purpose of this chapter is to summarize why integration is a positive movement and why restructuring of education is necessary to achieve successful integration (Biklen, 1985; Forest, 1987; Gartner & Lipsky, 1987; Stainback, Stainback, & Forest, 1989; Stainback & Stainback, 1988, 1990; Villa & Thousand, 1988). A secondary purpose is to address some of the major concerns people have about integration and restructuring. Before doing so, however, we define integration and restructuring in education.

INTEGRATION AND RESTRUCTURING DEFINED

As defined here integration or inclusive schooling involves the inclusion of *all* students in the mainstream of regular education classes and school activities with their age peers from the same community. The basic underlying purpose of educating all students in the mainstream is to provide all students the opportunity to learn to live, work with, and gain an understanding of their age peers in natural, integrated educational and community settings. As noted by Vandercook, Fleetham, Sinclair, and Tettie (1988), "In integrated classrooms all children are enriched by having the opportunity to learn from one another, grow to care for one another, and gain the attitudes, skills, and values necessary for our communities to support the inclusion of all citizens" (p. 19).

However, to enable students and our society to profit from such integration, the educational structure of the schools will require some necessary changes. This is because successful integration rarely occurs unless all students, within the mainstream, are provided appropriate educational programs geared to their capabilities and needs as well as any support and assistance they and their teachers may need (Stainback & Stainback, 1989, 1990). Full inclusion does not mean that all students should be *dumped* into the mainstream without appropriate programs and support to meet their individual needs.

To achieve success, full inclusion of all available educational resources and support into the educational mainstream will be needed. This will require that special and regular educators come together to work toward and to achieve the goal of an effective and appropriate education for every student in the mainstream. Full inclusion does *not* mean that special educators are no longer necessary. Regular education with its current resources, knowledge base, and personnel cannot be expected to serve the needs of all students. It can only be done if current special educators and special education resources are joined up with and become a natural, integral part of the regular education mainstream. In other words, educational restructuring is necessary.

RATIONALE FOR INTEGRATION AND RESTRUCTURING

During the past several decades, the movement to place all students into regular neighborhood schools and classrooms has gained increased momentum world wide and is now occurring in the United States. There are a number of reasons. Before outlining several major ones, it should be stressed that at issue is *not* whether students should receive appropriate educational programs geared to their unique needs and the specialized tools and techniques they need from highly qualified school personnel and specialists to fulfill their potential. That this should occur is accepted by both those who advocate restructuring and those who do not. At issue is whether students should receive these services in integrated or segregated settings.

Benefits To Students

Although findings from some investigations have indicated that simply including students with disabilities into regular classrooms does not result in learning benefits (e.g. Marston, 1987), when they are provided appropriate educational programs and support in integrated settings, students tend to learn more than they do in segregated settings (e.g. Madden & Slavin, 1983). Thus, the key to success in integrated or inclusive classrooms is the provision of appropriate educational programs that challenge yet address the needs of all students, along with the provision of any necessary supports or related services students or teachers may need.

Although most of the research to date has been conducted with students labeled as having mild disabilities, Brinker and Thorpe (1983, 1984) found that students labeled severely retarded learn more of their IEP objectives in integrated settings and Strain (1983) found that students labeled autistic generalized newly acquired social behaviors considerably better in an integrated setting than in a segregated one. Strain found clear benefits for integration and concluded that "it is quite reasonable to question the predominant and pervasive segregation of autistic-like children into 'handicapped' only groups" (p. 3).

As with learning, attitude change toward students with disabilities can improve when appropriate guidance and direction is provided. That is, when given guidance from adults in integrated settings, students can learn to understand, respect, be sensitive to, and grow comfortable with individual differences and similarities among their peers (Voeltz, 1980, 1982). Students also can learn to interact, communicate, develop friendships, work together, and assist one another based on their individual strengths and needs (Forest, 1987; Strully, 1986, 1987; Stainback & Stainback, 1981; 1988; Vandercook, et al., 1988).

Another major benefit that occurs as a result of school integration is that it prepares students for integrated community living. The 1982 report of the *Dis-*

ability Rights, Education, and Defense Fund found "that regardless of race, class, gender, type of disability, or age at its onset, the more time spent in integrated public school classes as children, the more people achieved educationally and occupationally as adults" (Ferguson & Asch, 1989, p. 124). Some parents know this intuitively. One parent recently stated about her daughter's integrated education:

> When she's finished with school, she'll be able to be in some sort of integrated situation. She'll have social skills she wouldn't have had and an ability to function in more complex situations than she would've been able to do if she'd stayed segregated. (cited in Hanline & Halvorsen, 1989, p. 490)

To be accepted in the work place and the community at-large, people with disabilities need to learn how to function and perform in the "real, regular" world and interact with their peers. Equally important their peers need to learn how to interact and function with them. This cannot occur if educators place students with disabilities in segregated, special classes and, in effect separate students with and without disabilities in their school years. As noted by Flynn and Kowalczyk-McPhee (1989), " To be excluded, from an ordinary educational career and placed in a special education system probably means the person is destined for a special life style and special employment" (p. 30). And as a person with disabilities who was segregated in her school years stated: "I graduated...completely unprepared for the *real world* So I just stayed in the house all *day, a shut*-in, believing a job was out of the question.... Believe me, a segregated environment just will not do as preparation for an integrated life" (Massachusetts Advocacy Center, 1987, p. 4).

Avoids The Ill Effects of Segregation

A second reason for including all students into the mainstream is to avoid the ill effects of segregation inherent when students are placed in separate special schools or classes. Lack of self-confidence, lack of motivation, and lack of positive expectations for achievement are all products of segregated learning environments. As noted by Chief Justice Warren in the 1954 Brown v. Board of Education decision, separateness in education can

> generate a feeling of inferiority as to [children's] status in the community that may affect their hearts and minds in a way unlikely ever to be undone. This sense of inferiority...affects the motivation of a child to learn...[and] has a tendency to retard...educational and mental development. (Warren, 1954, p. 493)

Warren's concern was confirmed by a statement of a student who attended separate, special classes throughout his school years. He stated:

> The only contact we had with the "normal" children was visual. We stared at each other. On those occasions, I can report my own feelings: embarrassment.... I can also report their feelings: YECH! We, the children in the "handicapped" class, were internalizing the "yech" message--plus a couple of others. We were in school because children go to school, but we were outcasts with no future and no expectation of one. (Massachusetts Advocacy Center, 1987, p. 4-5)

Another student who moved from an integrated elementary class to a homogeneous, segregated class in junior high school also confirmed Chief Justice Warren's statement when she stated,

> I felt good when I was with my [elementary] class, but when they went and separated us that changed us. That changed our ideas, the way we thought about

each other, and turned us to enemies toward each other because they said I was dumb and they were smart. (Schafer & Olexa, 1971, p. 96)

Equality

The third and by far the most important reason for including all students into the mainstream is that it is the fair, ethical, and equitable thing to do. It deals with the value of EQUALITY. As was decided in the Brown v. Board of Education decision, SEPARATE IS NOT EQUAL. All children should be a part of the educational and community mainstream.

It is discriminatory that some students, such as those labeled disabled, must earn the right or be gotten ready to be in the regular education mainstream or have to wait for educational researchers to prove that they can profit from the mainstream, while other students are allowed unrestricted access, simply because they have no label. No one should have to pass anyone's test or prove anything in a research study to live and learn in the mainstream of school and community life. It is a basic right, not something one has to earn.

The basic premise of equality inherent in inclusive schooling was summarized on the floor of the United States Congress by Former Senator Lowell Weikert:

Authorities on disabilities have often said, and I have quoted them on this floor before, that the history of society's formal methods of dealing with people with disabilities can be summed up in two words: SEGREGATION and INEQUALITY. Psychologist Kenneth Clark, whose testimony about the damaging effects of segregation provided pivotal evidence in the landmark case of Brown versus the Board of Education, stated that "segregation is the way in which a society tells a group of human beings that they are inferior to other

groups of human beings in the society." As a society, we have treated people with disabilities as inferiors and made them unwelcome in many activities and opportunities generally available to other Americans. (Senator Lowell Weicker, 1988, p. 1)

It is discomforting to think that in the past we have actually decided that some children or adults should be excluded from our regular lives, classrooms, and communities. This exclusion has *not* been done maliciously, but rather with good intentions to help students; however, we cannot continue to overlook the effects of this segregation. If we truly want a fair, egalitarian society in which all people are considered to have equal worth and equal rights, we need to reevaluate how we operate our schools. If we want integration and equality for all people in our society, segregation in schools cannot be justified. If we want to do so, appropriate educational programs and related services can be provided in the mainstream. As noted by Forest (1988): "If we really want someone to be a part of our lives, we will do what it takes to welcome that person and accommodate his or her needs" (p. 3). When a single person, who has not broken any laws, is excluded from the mainstream of school and community life, we all become vulnerable.

CONCERNS

Throughout this book and in the professional literature, people have expressed concerns and reservations about integration and the restructuring of the schools. In this section we address several of the major concerns expressed by others in the literature and this text.

Regular Education Has Failed Pupils with Handicaps

CONCERN. The regular education system has failed students with disabilities before and that was the reason special education was developed (Lieberman, 1985; Messinger, 1985). By putting these students back into regular education again we cannot expect them to succeed, particularly given the problems regular education is currently experiencing.

RESPONSE. The regular education system failed in the past because the programs and accommodations needed by some students were simply not available in regular education. When they were developed, the accommodations and programs needed by students with disabilities were housed in a separate system of services--special education--and, according to the organizational rules and monetary restrictions, access to these programs and services was not possible for students in regular education. The only way students, whose needs were not met by the standard regular educational program, could become eligible for the educational services they needed was to be labeled, assigned to special education and in many cases segregated from their peers. The purpose of integration and restructuring is to allow every student the needed support and access to the services, materials and programs that fit his or her capabilities, interests and needs without having to be assigned a label, and removed from classmates and the mainstream of regular education.

Integration or mainstreaming without restructuring has lead to the common practice of focusing on the student's ability to fit into the existing regular education program. But as research and experience has indicated, students exhibit considerable variability in ability and learning characteristics (Stainback & Stainback, 1984), and if we want students to succeed to their maximum in the mainstream, educational restructuring is necessary to allow for programs to meet the needs of the students rather than maintaining a system that requires the student to fit the regular program. When

implemented appropriately, integration and inclusive schooling does *not* diminish the quality of services some students receive. Instead, it enhances quality services for all, including students with disabilities, by allowing all students access to any support and services deemed appropriate within the mainstream. That is, schools that have restructured have found that the integration of the best of special and regular education can help regular education become more flexible and adaptive to individual differences among all students, while at the same time allowing students with disabilities to receive the educational programs and specialized services and support they need in the mainstream (Williams, Villa, Thousand & Fox, 1989).

Because the educational system has failed some students in the past, there is no need to repeat our educational errors. As pointed out by Edmonds (1979) after extensive research on effective schools:

> We can, whenever and wherever we choose, successfully teach all children whose schooling is of interest to us. We already know more than we need in order to do this. Whether we do it will finally depend on how we feel about the fact that we haven't done it so far. (p. 29)

This will require that the knowledge base and resources in special and regular education be merged in order to identify appropriate but challenging goals and instructional programs within the mainstream for all students. It also will require that specialized support and assistance be provided, when and where necessary. But it can be done, if we have the will to do so.

Analogies to Race are Flawed

CONCERN. Some individuals maintain that many of the arguments for integration are flawed because they are based on the notion that people with disabilities are a minority group with the same civil rights as other minorities. For example, Kauffman (1989) states that "equating ethnic origin with disability is demeaning to racial groups" (p. 261). He goes on to state:

> The civil rights issue for racial and ethnic minorities is one of access to the same services provided to others, regardless of their characteristics; the civil rights issue for handicapped students, however, is one of access to a differentiated education designed specifically to accommodate their special characteristics even if accommodation requires separation. (p. 262)

Thus, according to this position, people with disabilities do not have the same civil rights as other minorities.

RESPONSE. Hahn (1989), a political scientist at the University of Southern California and a well known disability rights advocate explains the minority-group civil-rights perspective,

> Although relatively little attention has been devoted to the controversy in the special education literature, the study of disability is currently experiencing a massive conflict between opposing paradigms that may have a critical impact on the fate of this discipline and related areas. The conventional approach to research on this subject has been shaped by a "functional limitations" model...however, this orientation has been challenged by a "minority group" paradigm.... While the functional limitations model views disability primarily as a personal misfortune, the minority group perspective considers it a source of collective discrimination. Similarly, whereas the functional limitations orientation tends to prescribe compensatory adaptations as a principle remedy for

their difficulties, the minority group approach contends that solutions to the major problems of disabled Americans can be found through the strict enforcement of legal guarantees of freedom and equality. (pp. 225-229)

Hahn (1989) explains how these paradigms influence educational services:

> The logical implications of the functional limitations and the minority group paradigms, therefore, appear to indicate alternative educational strategies. From the former perspective, which locates the principal problem within disabled individuals, a primary task is the remediation of their functional deficits to the maximum extent possible. Hence, attempts are made to provide disabled young people with the skills that they must acquire in order to be productive in an environment that is usually not adapted to their interests or needs. The success of these efforts is measured by the comparability of proficiency displayed by such students and by their nondisabled peers. However, the characterization of disabled individuals by functional deficiencies has meant that remedies that focus solely on this dimension of their problems can never be fully successful. By contrast, the minority group model ascribes the source of the basic problem of disability to external instead of internal phenomena, and strives to adapt the environment to the aspirations of disabled people rather than to adapt the individual to the demands of the environment. (p. 229)

Hahn goes on to note that:

> From a minority group perspective, the principle change to be

sought in education policy is the "mainstreaming" or integration of disabled students into regular classrooms. The foundations for this effort were laid in the historic 1954 United States Supreme Court decision in Brown vs. Board of Education. (p. 233)

According to Hahn and other people with disabilities who are disability rights advocates (e.g. Ferguson & Asch, 1989; Snow, 1989; Worth, 1988) as well as a growing number of parents and professional educators (e.g. Biklen, 1985; Bushwell & Schaffner, 1990; Forest, 1987; Gartner & Lipsky, 1987; Strully, 1986, 1987) people with disabilities are a minority group and should be afforded the same rights as other minority groups. The U.S. Congress apparently agrees. Although not focused directly on education issues, the Senate recently approved the *Americans with Disabilities Act* that "is to provide a clear and comprehensive national mandate to end discrimination against individuals with disabilities giving them the same protection in our society available to other individuals protected by civil rights laws"("Senate Overwhelmingly Approve," 1989, p. 1). In the Senate debate on the act, proponents:

> likened it to the Civil Rights Act of 1964, which prohibited racial or religious discrimination. Some turned the clock back further: to the freeing of the slaves. Senator Tom Harkin, D-Iowa, one of the measure's chief sponsors, calls it a "20th century Emancipation Proclamation for people with disabilities". ("Congress on Verge," 1989, p. B1)

The *Americans with Disabilities Act* was approved by Congress and signed into law by the President on July 13, 1990. Thus, the notion that people with disabilities do not have the same civil rights as others is fast becoming outdated.

It should be stressed here that Hahn (1989) and other disabilities rights advocates are not advocating that students with disabilities simply be dumped into regular education classes, but rather that integration be *coupled* with a restructuring of regular education classes to meet the unique needs of all students, including those with disabilities. Contrary to popular opinion, research has indicated that the majority of regular educators are willing to join special educators in making regular classes more flexible and conducive to the needs of students with disabilities, *if* they are involved in the planning process and have choices about the design and types of support and assistance they will receive (Myles & Simpson, 1989).

Labels Are Needed to Protect Services

CONCERN. A major point that troubles those reluctant to accept full integration is the often associated emphasis on the delabeling of students. To quote a Council for Children with Behavioral Disorders (1989) statement:

> It remains unclear how students can be assured of receiving designated services if their eligibility is not determined. If eligibility decisions are not made, it might then be assumed that all students would be eligible for all services. That students should receive all services is a proposal which can hardly be taken seriously. If all students are eligible for all services but only some students receive them, then both eligibility decisions and special services become covert. (p. 204)

Other professionals have gone so far as to say that "without labels, we must simply ignore students' differences" (Kauffman, 1989, p. 264).

RESPONSE. First, it should be noted that integration can occur without doing away with labels and eligibility for special services. In fact, this is what most often happens at the present time. Students from special education are integrated into regular classes, but continue to receive special services within the mainstream.

However, although this is a step toward greater integration and inclusion of students in the educational mainstream, it does not promote total or complete inclusion. For full integration, the abolition of eligibility criteria for education and related services based on disability labels is necessary. This should not be misinterpreted to mean that full inclusion denies the reality that some students are deaf, blind, autistic, or have Down Syndrome, cerebral palsy and the like. Rather, it recognizes that students with any one or more of these characteristics are unique individuals and they do not necessarily require the exact same educational programs, services and accommodations needed by other students with the same or similar characteristic. Students with these and other characteristics definitely should receive an education geared to their unique needs and capabilities as should all students. But the education and related services any student receives in the public schools should be based on his or her specific interests, needs, and capabilities, not on a label such as black/white, male/female, sighted/nonsighted, disabled/nondisabled, or retarded/gifted. Any such label is not specific enough to be able to identify the specifics of an educational program a student may need. In education when we group people together or provide a program for students based on any such label, we run the risk of stereotyping a student's educational needs according to the label assigned rather than identifying and providing the best programs, supports and resources the individual student requires to achieve his/her maximum potential. When students or any others are approached according to a categorical affiliation, they are denied the individual

consideration they deserve. As noted by Reynolds and Balow (1972): "In all society there is a rising revulsion against simplistic categorization of human beings" (p. 357).

Doing away with the categorizing or labeling of students in education can lead to focusing on more educationally relevant individual differences among students rather than ignoring differences. As noted by Lilly (1979), for instructional purposes it is more effective to view students as individuals. Once we begin looking at students as individuals, the data available concerning their instructional needs is far more specific and precise than a special or regular label or any other categorical label, making such labels virtually useless for educational purposes.

Doing away with student labels also would *not* lead to all students being eligible for all services. As proposed in the inclusive schooling literature (e.g. Stainback & Stainback, 1990), students would be eligible for services based on their interests, needs, and capabilities. Those students who needed a service based on their individual interests, needs, and capabilities would receive it and those who did not would not. Finally, there would be no need to be covert about it. Eligibility criteria (i.e. individual interests, needs, and capabilities) should be openly and clearly stated to everyone.

It should be emphasized here that the issue is *not* whether disability categories are of benefit from a medical research standpoint or for other reasons such as disability insurance or reserved parking spaces in a parking lot. The issue also is not whether we can draw lines and divide students into special and regular needs students or disabled and nondisabled students. Everyone knows we can and it may be of benefit for some purposes. The issue is whether educators should approach and educate children according to a categorical affiliation (e.g. normal, blind, retarded, behaviorally disordered) or whether they should approach and educate all students as individuals.

Finally, because it has been proposed that public school classrooms be integrated and reliance on disability labels as a way of determining the instructional needs of students be reduced does not mean that students could never be grouped for instructional purposes as Kauffman (1989) asserts. As noted many times before, students may occasionally need to be grouped for teaching and learning based on the student's prior learning, the concepts being taught, and the teacher's preparation (Biklen, 1985; Gartner & Lipsky, 1987; Forest, 1987; Stainback, Stainback, & Forest, 1989). But occasionally grouping students for instruction based on their specific learning needs is not the same as grouping students by categorical labels into special and regular classes or into vocational and college bound tracks for most of the day over a long period of time. The reader is referred to Stainback, Stainback, and Forest (1989) and Stainback and Stainback (1990) for further information.

Excellence and Equity Are Incompatible

CONCERN. Some educators believe that excellence and equity are mutually exclusive. According to this position, excellence as a goal profits and can be expected to be achieved only by the "best" students. Treating students equitably, an underlying tenet of integration and inclusive schooling, is counterproductive to the achievement of excellence. As recently stated by one special educator: "Excellence and equity are always competing issues; what is gained in one is lost in the other. Excellence requires focusing support on the most capable learners; equity requires the opposite" (Kauffman, 1989, p. 267).

RESPONSE. The position that only "the most capable learners" can achieve excellence and that excellence and equity are incompatible is based on different assumptions about educational excellence than are held by many inclusive schooling advocates. The belief that excellence and equity are incompatible infers a definition of educational excellence that assumes that only some students can achieve excellence. As perceived by these authors, this notion that *only* some students can achieve excellence is counterproductive to meeting the educational needs of all students. It also promotes psychologically unhealthy elitist attitudes for the predefined group of students it supports.

Integration or inclusive schooling is based on the premise that excellence and equity are not incompatible; that is, all students can excel in integrated schools and classrooms when they are supported to learn and achieve according to their highest potential. This position assumes that every student is capable of contributing to society and can excel when given appropriate educational supports and learning opportunities to meet his or her unique learning needs. This view of excellence, however, recognizes criteria for outstanding performance as variable rather than standardized across students and based on the individual needs, interests and capabilities of each student. This approach to promoting excellence is a more humane and realistic educational practice because it fosters educational excellence for every student, not just an elite group, and also recognizes and capitalizes on the unique talents, gifts and abilities inherent in every child.

Further, excellence in education is reflected in how successful the system of educational services being offered achieves the goals inherent in the public provision of education to all children. The goal often stated for providing a free and appropriate education is to promote the development of positive contributing members of a *democratic and integrated, egalitarian society*. This cannot be achieved when excellence in education is held as an option for only some students within the student population. In addition, an integrated, democratic and egalitarian society can not be achieved by operating segregated schools. As a well known researcher on desegregation noted over a decade ago; "If we want a segregated society, we should have segregated schools. If we want a desegregated society, we should have desegregated schools" (Jencks, 1972, p. 106).

If we do want an integrated society in which everyone is expected to live together and contribute, and we do not want an elitist or segregated society, the best option is to establish a research agenda for the future to maximize the effectiveness of instruction for all students, including those with disadvantages and disabilities, in integrated schools and classrooms. As noted by Sarason (1982) it is not a good teaching strategy to attempt to teach a value, but then implement practices directly opposed to that value. For instance, it is not logical to focus on excellence for only some or divide and separate students yet try to teach them the values of integration, respect for individual differences, and how to live and work together in an integrated society.

In our opinion, it would be unconscionable for parents, educators, and the general public to adopt a position that children must be separated in order to achieve excellence for some and equity for others. All children can excel and the schools should focus on achieving *both* excellence and equity for all.

Special Education Programs Ensure Appropriate Services

CONCERN. Without maintaining special education, one cannot ensure that all students will receive appropriate educational programs and services in regular education.

RESPONSE. As personnel from special education are integrated into regular

education, they can join many concerned and caring regular educators to help ensure that all students, including those traditionally ill-served and underserved in the past, are served appropriately in regular education. Because of the integration of personnel as well as students, there will be an increased number of concerned and caring adults in regular education. This will help increase, rather than reduce, the probabilities that all students will receive a free and appropriate education.

In addition, it is possible, if we so choose, to protect the rights of all students legally, including those labeled as having disabilities, to receive appropriate educational programs and ancillary services in regular classes and regular education. One way to accomplish this would be to advocate for and achieve a modification of PL 94-142 to require that every child be provided a free and appropriate educational program and related services in regular education. For instance, the title of the law might be changed from "The Education of All Handicapped Children's Act" to "The Education for All Students Act." This modified law could require that all students receive a free and appropriate education within the mainstream of regular education. As a consequence, when a team from a state department or a federal agency monitored a school district, if *any* student was not receiving an appropriate program or services within regular education, then the school district would be in violation of the law. In this way, the law would ensure that all students, including those with disabilities, received a free and appropriate education in regular education.

Although it is imperative to support and protect the rights of students with disabilities to receive the programs and services they need to progress in school, it is also essential not to overlook the need to protect the rights of *all* students to receive the programs and services they need to progress in school. Too often many students not labeled as having a disability have fallen through the proverbial educational cracks, receiving a less than adequate education for them to succeed in school and later in society. It is not possible to conceive of a single child whose right to a free and appropriate education should not be protected. Protecting the rights of *all* children to a free and appropriate education is more fair and equitable than protecting any one or several categories of students' rights. As noted by Sapon-Shevin (1987), to achieve true equality in our schools, all students--not just selected categories of students--need educational programs that meet their unique needs.

Such protection can take place in a restructured and integrated system by strong and consistent advocacy to guarantee that programs and services are offered in the public schools to meet *all* students needs and to ensure that some students are not underserved or ill-served. As soon as we protect the rights of all students to receive an appropriate education, the needs of students traditionally classified as disabled, disadvantaged, or any other classification will be protected, because no student can be denied the services and programs she or he needs.

Finally, it should be noted that if, as a society, we decide not to offer a free and appropriate education to all students, then it will remain necessary to divide students into those eligible for a free and appropriate education and those who are not, based on labels such as nonhandicapped and disabled. But even if, as a society, we should decide not to offer a free and appropriate education for all students, integration can and should occur and students with disabilities will be protected in integrated classrooms by PL 94-142. The guarantees to a free and appropriate education and related services provided by PL 94-142 to students with disabilities do not stop when integration occurs.

The issue is not about which is most important--protecting quality instruction for students with disabilities or integration. They are *both* important. Thus, the task facing special educators is how to integrate ourselves into regular education and work side-by-side with regular educators to be sure that quality instruction is available to all students, including those ill-served and underserved in the past, in the mainstream of school life.

DISCUSSION

When racial integration in the schools began in the late 1950's and early 1960's there were numerous rationales given as to why it was not a good idea or would not work: "black students will be rejected by white teachers and students;" "it's not in their best interest;" "the schools are not ready;" "we need more analysis and study;" and "it's a Communist plot." The justifications that have been offered in this book and elsewhere (e.g. Vergason & Anderegg, 1989) for continuing to place students with disabilities into segregated, special classes and schools are also numerous. A few examples include: "regular education is not prepared;" "integration is a Reagan-Bush plot to reduce funds to students with disabilities;" "there is a need for further analysis and study;" "we need to maintain a continuum of services;" "students with disabilities need special treatments and interventions;" and "educational achievement is more important than placement."

But none of these arguments can really justify segregating students with disabilities or any other students from the mainstream of school and community life. An analogy may make this point clearer.

> At the time of the American Civil War, should Abraham Lincoln have asked to see the scientific evidence on the benefits of ending slavery? Should he have consulted with "the experts," perhaps a sociologist, an economist, a political scientist? Of course not. Slavery

is not now, and was not then, an issue for science. It is a moral issue. But, just for a moment, suppose that an economist had been able to demonstrate that Blacks would suffer economically, as would the entire South, from emancipation. Would that justify keeping slavery? And suppose a political scientist had argued that Blacks had no experience with democracy, they were not ready for it. Would that have justified extending slavery? Or imagine that a sociologist could have advised Lincoln against abolishing slavery on the grounds that it would destroy the basic social structure of Southern plantations, towns, and cities. All of the arguments might have seemed "true." But could they really justify slavery? Of course not. Slavery has no justification. (Biklen, 1985, pp. 16-17)

Although arguments can be made about Lincoln's motivation and the abolition of slavery did not actually occur until Amendment 13 became law, the above analogy nevertheless points out that some things are simply morally and ethically wrong. Those parents, professionals, politicians, and community members who have entered the struggle for the integration of all students into the mainstream have made a value judgement that integrated education is the best and most humane way to proceed. From their perspective, the point just made about slavery applies also to current segregationist practices in schools throughout America. If we want an integrated society in which all persons are considered of equal worth and as having equal rights, segregation in the schools can not be justified. That is, no defensible excuses or rationales can be offered, and no amount of scientific research can be conducted that will in the final analysis justify segregation. Segregation has no justification. As Gilhool (1976) has noted, "Separation is

repugnant to our constitutional tradition. Integration is a central constitutional value--not integration that denies difference but, rather, integration that accommodates difference; appreciates it and celebrates it" (p. 8).

A few years ago, some parents and educators were saying that they thought it may be possible to educate all students in the mainstream of America's schools. Now, growing numbers of people are convinced that it can be done, *given that the mainstream is sensitive to individual differences and teachers and students are provided adequate support and assistance.* The reason is that it is beginning to be done successfully in some schools in the U.S., Canada, Italy, and a number of other countries (Berrigan, 1988, 1989; Biklen, 1988; Blackman & Peterson, 1989; Forest, 1988; Porter, 1988; Schattman, 1988; Stainback & Stainback, 1988; Vandercook, York, & Forest, 1989; Villa & Thousand, 1988; York & Vandercook, 1989). Basically, these schools have identified appropriate but challenging goals within the mainstream for students with diverse needs rather then requiring them all to learn the exact same thing or always function at the same level of proficiency as their peers. They also have worked to provide teachers and students the support and assistance they need to make successful integrated education a reality. See Stainback, Stainback, and Forest (1989) and Stainback and Stainback (in press) for a review of specific and practical procedures some schools have used to make integrated education a reality for all students.

But it will be difficult to achieve success on a widespread basis if, as a society, we are unwilling to: (a) provide each student the support necessary for him or her to be in the mainstream, and (b) adapt and adjust, when necessary, the mainstream to accommodate all students. The key is our *willingness* to visualize, work for, and achieve a mainstream that is adaptive and supportive of everyone. Few people, including those classified as disabled, want to be in a mainstream that does not meet their needs and make them feel welcome and secure. Thus, it is essential that we make the mainstream flexible and sensitive to the unique needs of all students and that we foster friendships for students who lack friends in the mainstream. This is why restructuring is so critical. With restructuring, the literally billions of dollars now spent on segregated, special education programs and the hundreds of thousands of educators currently working in segregated, special settings could be integrated into regular education to help make the mainstream supportive, flexible, and adaptive to the individual needs of all students.

Finally, it should be emphasized that saying it can be done is not the same as saying it will be easy. Segregation has been practiced for centuries and there are entrenched attitudes, laws, policies, and educational structures that work against achieving full inclusion of all students on a wide spread basis. In addition, because a second system of education (i.e. "special" education) has operated for so long, many schools unfortunately do not know at the present time how to adapt and modify the curriculum and instructional programs to meet diverse student needs, deal with behavioral difficulties, and provide the tools, techniques, and supports some students need to be successful in the mainstream. Thus, achieving full inclusion of all students is likely to be a very challenging undertaking. But the goal of having inclusive schools where everyone belongs, has friends, and is provided appropriate educational programs and supports is far too important not to accept the challenge.

If integration is valued, as noted by Bogdan (1983): "Does mainstreaming work? is a silly question...Where it is not working, we should be asking what is preventing it from working and what can be done about it" (p.427).

REFERENCES

Berrigan, C. (1988, February). Integration in Italy: A dynamic movement. *TASH Newsletter*, 6-7.

Berrigan, C. (1989). All students belong in the classroom: Johnson City Central Schools, Johnson City, New York. *TASH Newsletter, 15*(1), 6.

Biklen, D. (1985). *Achieving the complete school.* New York: Columbia University Press.

Biklen, D. (Producer). (1988). *Regular lives* [video]. Washington, DC: State of the Art.

Blackman, H. & Peterson, D. (1989). *Totally integrated neighborhood schools.* LaGrange, Ill: LaGrange Department of Special Education.

Bogdan, R. (1983). 'Does Mainstreaming Work?' is a silly question. *Phi Delta Kappan, 64*, 427-428.

Brinker, R., & Thorpe, M. (1983). *Evaluation of integration of severely handicapped students in regular classrooms and community settings.* Princeton, NJ: Educational Testing Service.

Brinker, R., & Thorpe, M. (1984). Integration of severely handicapped students and the proportion of IEP objectives achieved. *Exceptional Children, 51*, 168-175.

Bushwell, B., & Schaffner, B. (in press). Families supporting inclusive schooling. In W. Stainback & S. Stainback (Eds.) *Support networks for inclusive schooling: Making interdependent, integrated education a reality.* Baltimore: Paul H. Brookes.

Congress on verge of passing landmark disabilities act. (1989, December). *Waterloo Courier*, p. Bl.

Council for Children with Behavioral Disorders. (1989). Position statement on the regular education initiative. *Behavioral Disorders, 14*, 201-208.

Edmonds, R. (1979). Some schools work and more can. *Social Policy, 9*(2), 28-32.

Ferguson, P., & Asch, A. (1989). Lessons from life: Personal and parental perspectives on school, childhood, and disability. In D. Biklen, A. Ford, & D. Ferguson (Eds.), *Disability and society* (pp. 200-236). Chicago: National Society for the Study of Education.

Flynn, G., & Kowalczyk-McPhee, B. (1989). A school system in transition. In S. Stainback, W. Stainback, & M. Forest (Eds.). *Educating all students in the mainstream of regular education (pp. 29-43).* Baltimore: Paul H. Brookes.

Forest, M. (1987). *More education integration*. Downsview, Ont: G. Allan Roeher Institute.

Forest, M. (1988). Full inclusion is possible. *IMPACT*, 1, 3-4.

Gartner, A., & Lipsky, D. (1987). Beyond special education. *Harvard Educational Review, 57*, 367-395.

Gartner, A., & Lipsky, D. K. (1987). Beyond special education: Toward a quality system for all students. *Harvard Educational Review, 57*, 367-395.

Gilhool. (1976). Changing public policies. In M. Reynolds (Ed.), *Mainstreaming (pp. 8-13)*. Reston, VA: Council for Exceptional Children.

Hahn, H. (1989). The politics of special education. In D. Lipsky & A. Gartner (Eds.) *Beyond special education (pp. 118-135)*. Baltimore, MD: Paul H. Brookes.

Hanline, M., & Halvorsen, A. (1989). Parent perceptions of the integration transition process: Overcoming artificial barriers. *Exceptional Children 55*, 487-493.

Jencks, C. (1972). *Inequality*. New York: Basic Books.

Kauffman, J. M. (1989). The regular education initiative as Reagan-Bush education policy: A trickle down theory of the hard-to teach. *Journal of Special Education, 23*, 256-279.

Lieberman, L. (1985). Special and regular education: A merger made in heaven? *Exceptional Children, 51*, 513-517.

Lilly, S. (1979). *Children with exceptional needs*. New York: Holt, Rinehart & Winston.

Madden, N., & Slavin, R. (1983). Mainstreaming students with mild academic handicaps: Academic and social outcomes. *Review of Educational Research, 53*, 519-569.

Marston, D. (1987). The effectiveness of special education. *Journal of Special Education, 21*, 13-27.

Massachusetts Advocacy Center, (1987). *Out of the mainstream*. Boston: Author.

Messinger, J. (1985). A commentary on "A rationale for the merger of special and regular education". *Exceptional Children 51*, 510-513.

Myles, B. S., & Simpson, R. L. (1989). Regular educators' modifications preferences for mainstreaming mildly handicapped children. *Journal of Special Education, 22*, 479-491.

Porter, G. (Producer). (1988). *A Chance To belong* [video]. Ontario, Canada: Downsview (Canadian Association for Community Living).

Reynolds, M., & Balow, B. (1972). Categories and variables in special education. *Exceptional Children, 39*, 357-366.

Sarason, S. (1982). *The culture of the school and the problem of change*. Boston: Allyn & Bacon.

Sapon-Shevin, M. (1987). Giftedness as a social construct. *Teachers College Record, 89*, 39-53.

Schafer, W., & Olexa, C. (1971). *Tracking and opportunity*. Scranton, PA: Chandler.

Schattman, R. (1988). Integrated education and organization change. *IMPACT, 1*, 8-9.

Senator Lowell Weicker on the Americans with Disability Act (1988, July). *D. C. Update TASH Newsletter, 3*, 1.

Senate Overwhelmingly Approves Americans with Disabilities Act. (1989). *D. C. Update TASH Newsletter, 4*, 1-2.

Snow, J. (1989). Systems of support: A new vision. In S. Stainback, W., Stainback, & M. Forest (Eds.), *Educating all students in the mainstream of regular education* (pp. 221-234). Baltimore: Paul H. Brookes.

Stainback, S., & Stainback, W. (in press). *Facilitating learning for all students: Curriculum considerations in the inclusive classroom*. Baltimore: Paul Brookes.

Stainback, S., & Stainback, W. (1988). Educating students with severe disabilities in regular classes. *Teaching Exceptional Children, 21*, 16-19.

Stainback, S., Stainback, W., & Forest, M. (Eds.). (1989). *Educating all students in the mainstream of regular education*. Baltimore: Paul H. Brookes.

Stainback, W., & Stainback, S. (1981). A review of research on interaction between severely handicapped and nonhandicapped students. *Journal of the Association for Persons with Severe Handicaps, 6*, 23-29.

Stainback, W., & Stainback, S. (1984). A rationale for the merger of special and regular education. *Exceptional Children, 51*, 102-11.

Stainback, W., & Stainback, S. (1990). *Support networking for inclusive schooling: Interdependent, integrated education*. Baltimore: Paul H. Brookes.

Stainback, W., & Stainback, S. (1989). Using qualitative data collection procedures to investigate supported education issues. *Journal of the Association for Persons with Severe Handicaps, 14,* 271-278.

Strain, P. (1983). Generalization of autistic children's social behavior change: Effects of developmentally integrated and segregated settings. *Analysis and Intervention in Developmental Disabilities,3,*23-24.

Strully, J. (1986, October). *Our children and the regular education classroom: Or why settle for anything less than the best?* Paper presented to the 1986 annual conference of the Association for Persons with Severe Handicaps, San Francisco, CA.

Strully, J. (1987, October). *What's really important in life anyway? Parents sharing the vision.* Paper presented at the 14th Annual TASH Conference. Chicago, IL.

Vandercook, T., Fleetham, D., Sinclair, S., & Tettie, R. (1988). Cath, Jess, Jules, and Ames ... A story of friendship. *IMPACT, 2,* 18-19.

Vandercook, T., York, J., & Forest, M. (1989). *MAPS: A strategy for building a vision.* Minneapolis: Institute on Community Integration.

Vergason, G., & Anderegg, M. (1989). Bah, Humbug, an answer to Stainback & Stainback. *TASH Newsletter,15*(11), 8-10.

Villa, R. & Thousand, J. (1988). Enhancing success in heterogeneous classrooms and schools: The power of partnership. *TeacherEducation and Special Education, 11,*144-153.

Voeltz, L. (1980). Children's attitudes toward handicapped peers. *American Journal of Mental Deficiency, 84* 455-464.

Voeltz, L. (1982). Effects of structured interactions with severelyhandicaps peers on children's attitudes. *American Journal of Mental Deficiency, 86,* 380-390.

Warren, E. (1954). *Brown v. Board of Education of Topeka.* 347 U.S. 483, 493.

Williams, W., Villa, R., Thousand, J. & Fox, W. (1989). Is regular class placement reallythe issue? *The Journal of the Association for Persons with Severe Handicaps, 14,*33-335.

Worth, P. (1988, December). *Empowerment: Choices and change.* Paper presented at the 15th Annual TASH Conference, Washington, D.C.

York, J., & Vandercook, T. (1989). *Strategies for achieving an integrated education for middle school aged learners with severe disabilities.* Minneapolis: Institution on Community Integration.

FRAMING THE REI DEBATE: ABOLITIONISTS VERSUS CONSERVATIONISTS

Douglas Fuchs and Lynn S. Fuchs

George Peabody College of Vanderbilt University

As we write, fires have charred 23,576 acres of Yosemite National Park in California (Aftermath of Forest Fires, 1990). If we may think of the REI as a forest fire, then we suggest that special educators' concerns about teacher referrals, testing, categorical labels, fragmented services, overlapping administrative systems, and accountability are the yellowing bracken, fallen branches, deep-piled pine needles, the dry tinder that feeds the conflagration. The catalytic spark as well as the oxygen keeping the fires alive, we believe, is the full-inclusion, or integration, movement closely associated with the Association for Persons with Severe Handicaps (TASH). We believe that the integration movement's elemental driving force is reflected in the REI's most basic question: Do we abolish or conserve special education's cascade of services?

DEFINING THE ISSUE AND IDENTIFYING THE PLAYERS

To be sure, the REI is associated with many additional and important questions such as "How can we reduce the frequency of regular educators' referrals?" "By what means might we enhance the psychometric adequacy and instructional relevance of our tests?" and "Why

don't we have more persuasive evidence of special education effectiveness?" But none throws off heat like the question of whether to eliminate or preserve the continuum of services and, implicitly, the notion of the least restrictive environment (LRE). It is this pivotal question that creates a meaningful divide among many of the major players in the REI debate: *Abolitionists*, who argue for the elimination, or dramatic diminution, of the cascade of services, and *Conservationists*, who wish to preserve special education's current structure as well as the LRE principle.

We developed Figure 1 to distinguish Abolitionists from Conservationists, and to underscore the important gradations of each. We will explore the nature of these gradations, but first we must share caveats and admonitions about our Figure 1. Most important, we are unsure of the accuracy of our placement of each writer. Although we would be surprised if our positioning was off by more than one placement to the right or left, we view the figure only as heuristic. Second, and in the same vein, the demarcations on the continuum were drawn purposely to convey ordinal, rather than equal interval, relationships. Third, to add comprehensiveness to the illustration, we have included writers in addition to those whose chapters constitute this volume. Because we were presumptuous enough to pigeon-

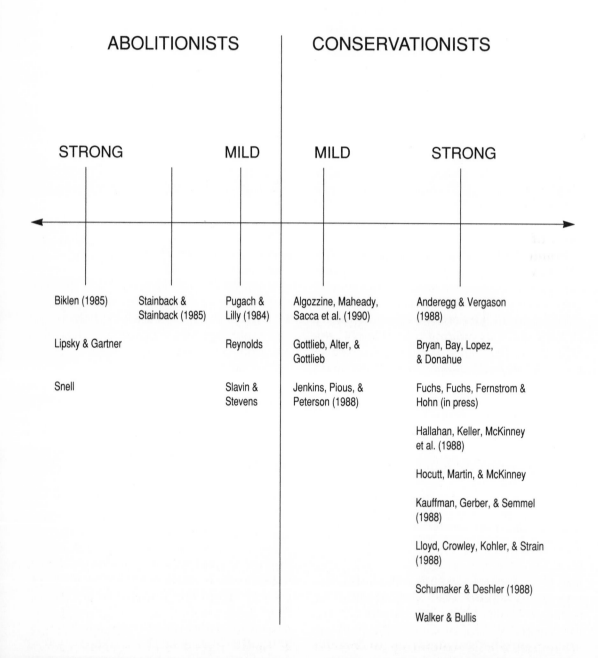

Figure 1: The range of views on the REI.

hole so many, we have decided to treat ourselves similarly. Hence, we, too, are included in the figure.

Abolitionists

We believe there are three variants of Abolitionist. The strongest view is exemplified by Lipsky and Gartner, who denounce special education as a categorical failure. Moreover, they would have us believe it harbors evil intent. An absence of data on students decertified by special educators nationwide, for example, is attributed to the purported fact that "students labeled as handicapped and served in special education programs are not expected to achieve and, as a result, to return to general education" (p. 44). Lipsky and Gartner's recommendation is a complete and immediate elimination of the cascade of services to wit: "The concepts of Least Restrictive Environment, a continuum of placements, and a cascade of services, were progressive when developed but do not today promote the full inclusion of all persons with disabilities in all aspects of societal life nor do they serve as guiding principles for the education that is the necessary means toward that goal's achievement" (p. 52).

Reynolds presents a mild Abolitionist view, one that differs in several ways from a strong position. First, in contrast to Lipsky and Gartner's blanket condemnation of the field, Reynolds focuses his criticism on services provided mildly handicapped pupils. Whereas he writes that categorical approaches to the education of mildly handicapped students cannot be justified, he implies elsewhere (e.g., Reynolds, 1988) that they *are* justifiable for children with more severe disabilities. Second, we believe he implicitly has recognized the importance of separate services for some children. And third, whereas Lipsky and Gartner call for an immediate restructuring of special education, Reynolds and associates (e.g., Wang, Rubenstein, & Reynolds, 1985)

have argued for a more deliberate time line, one that permits experimentation because, as Wang et al. confessed, "We doubt that anyone really knows how to design [needed reforms] with precision and credibility" (p. 66).

Between Lipsky and Gartner and Reynolds are Stainback and Stainback (1985) and other Abolitionists who argue explicitly for a partial roll back of the cascade of services. They call for the elimination of separate schools and facilities; for all children to be educated in their home schools through use of extant self-contained classrooms, resource rooms, and regular classes.

Conservationists

Most Conservationists defend special education against the type of categorical condemnations made by Lipsky and Gartner. For example, arguing that Biklen and Zollers (1986), Gartner and Lipsky (1989), and others have unfairly characterized special education as ineffective, Kauffman contests the idea that *all* pull-out programs have *always* failed. He cites a recent Harris poll, which indicates (a) that 94% of teachers believe education for students with disabilities is better now than 12 years ago, and (b) that 77% of parents of children with disabilities are satisfied with special education services. Similarly, with respect to students with behavior disorders, Walker and Bullis state special education effectiveness has been demonstrated many times and in many ways.

By definition, Conservationists support the preservation of the cascade of services. To provide an appropriate education to all children with disabilities, which is the promise made to their parents in PL 94-142, Conservationists (e.g., Bryan, Bay, Lopez-Reyna, & Donahue; Hocutt, Martin, & McKinney; Kauffman, Walker, & Bullis) recognize that separate instruction is sometimes necessary. The continuum of services ensures the delivery of this separate instruction. Does such a position imply that all Conservationists think that every special educator is effective, that all special education placements are necessary and none is overly restrictive, that all true special educators wear baseball caps proclaiming, "If it ain't broke, don't fix it?" No. Many, if not all, understand the current need for reform. But they also agree with the statement that necessary modifications "can occur within a framework of realities and protections for handicapped children" (Kauffman, p. 64).

What, then, distinguishes the milder from stronger Conservationists? At least two things. First, a greater willingness to describe special-education problems (see, for example, Gottlieb, Alter, and Gottlieb's critique of current testing and mainstreaming practices); and second, a more strident call for reform (see Gottlieb et al.'s recommendation that special educators consider large-scale, full-time mainstreaming programs). Gottlieb et al., together with Jenkins, Pious, and Peterson (1988), Algozzine, Maheady, Sacca, O'Shea, & O'Shea, (1990), and other mild Conservationists are distinguished from mild Abolitionists by the latter group's more explicit recommendation for a restructuring of special education, or a co-mingling of special and regular education monies. (Although Jenkins et al. [1988] have discussed a need for a unified system, they were describing the coordination of special education and remedial services; there was no explicit call for the elimination of special services to students with mild disabilities, nor advocacy of the full-time placement of such pupils in a regular classroom.)

Two Observations

COMMON GROUND. In several important ways, Abolitionists and Conservationists are adversaries. At the same time, however, they do not represent mutually exclusive camps. Common ground exists, especially regarding an identification of certain problems associated with special education. Conservationists like Gottlieb et al. express the same dissatisfaction as Lipsky and Gartner over the infrequency with which mainstreaming occurs; Sheridan and Kratochwill and Reynolds concur that there is too much testing with too little payoff for instruction; Gottlieb et al. and Reynolds both decry testing and labeling practices that, in Reynolds's words, attempt to offer "remote dispositional analyses" of students, rather than describing educational environments and focusing on instruction that works; Bryan et al. and Kauffman join Slavin and Stevens and Lipsky and Gartner in acknowledging the need for a major restructuring of regular education; and finally, we and other Conservationists share Lipsky and Gartner's concern that special education must be held more accountable for student outcomes. Thus, whereas the two groups' respective recommendations or solutions are clearly distinguishable, they often point to many of the same problems besetting the field.

DIFFERENT CONSTITUENCIES. A second, unrelated observation, and one to which we will return, is that Abolitionists tend to have different constituents than Conservationists. That is, the children and adults in whom the two groups have professional interest are dissimilar. By and large, Abolitionists work with persons with severe mental retardation. This is especially true of the stronger Abolitionists such as Snell and the Stainbacks. Conservationists typically do not work with mentally-challenged individuals. (A notable exception is Gottlieb and his associates who have worked with children described as educable mentally retarded.) This difference should not be taken to mean that Abolitionists and Conservationists are professionally invested in severe and mild disabilities, respectively. The efforts of Kauffman and Walker and their respective colleagues on behalf of seriously emotionally disturbed children and Bryan's and Hallahan's work in severe learning disabilities substantiates the wrong-headedness of such a dichotomy. Thus, Abolitionists tend to be associated closely with a relatively narrow constituency, whereas Conservationists collectively are associated with individuals representing a greater range (in type and degree) of disabilities.

IDEALISTIC VERSUS PRAGMATIC VIEWS ON REGULAR EDUCATION

The considerable difference between Abolitionist and Conservationist recommendations for special education is rivaled by the major disjunction between their respective understandings of regular education--a situation which, as suggested toward the end of this chapter, is more than coincidental. In comparison to Conservationists, in our opinion, Abolitionists are more idealistic than pragmatic, more prone toward advocacy than analysis.

Abolitionist Idealism

FUTURE-ORIENTED. Snell's, and Lipsky and Gartner's chapters focus on the future, not the past, except when pointing out special education's purported failures. Snell, for example, exhorts us to develop a vision of a more inclusive regular education (pp. 145). Lipsky and Gartner express similar faith in regular education's inherent goodwill and capability when they report that it currently is in the throes of a second, and more promising, wave of reform. Why more promising? Because, according to the authors, the second reform effort has shifted its focus from state capitols to school district and building levels. That is, the new wave addresses "the roles of the adults-- teacher empowerment, school-based management, and parental choice" (p. 49), in contrast to the previous wave that, presumably, did not.

This upbeat future-orientation seems based on a belief that if regular education historically mistreated many children with disabilities, it is a matter of little relevance now. The purported changes reshaping regular education renders its track record moot. Lipsky and Gartner point to cooperative learning and peer tutoring as representative of the type of paradigmatic shift of which they say regular education is capable (p. 50); that is, new processes of teaching and learning that involve "students in the active work of preparing material, sharing information with other students, acting as tutors, monitoring their own performance..." (p. 50).

NONEMPIRICAL. Lipsky and Gartner's (perfunctory) discussion of cooperative learning and peer tutoring reveals another feature of the typical Abolitionist perspective on regular education; namely, a tendency to be uncritical and nonempirical. With respect to cooperative learning, Lipsky and Gartner suggest that it, like peer tutoring, is a relatively new practice that should be encouraged because it "has been found in *extensive research* [our emphasis] to offer both affective and cognitive benefits" (p. 50). Yet, Slavin and Stevens, two people quite closely associated with cooperative learning, have been up front about the number of experiments they and their associates have conducted on the Cooperative Integrated Reading and Composition (CIRC) model: "Two studies have evaluated the impact of the full CIRC program" (Slavin & Stevens, p. 186).

Relatedly, Tateyama-Sniezek (1990) conducted an extensive review of the cooperative learning literature to answer two questions. First, how many cooperative learning studies sought to improve the academic achievement of handicapped students? Her answer: 12. Second, how many reported statistically significant gains? Her answer: only 6. Slavin, Stevens, and their colleagues' work on CIRC is pertinent here. In the first of two evaluations of a fully-imple-mented version, they found that across all study participants "effects...were quite positive" (Slavin & Stevens, p. 186). But no significant differences were obtained for "academically" handicapped and remedial students (p. 186). In the second more ambitious evaluation, "effects of the CIRC program on the reading achieve-ment of special and remedial reading stu-dents were much more positive than in Study 1." (p. 187). Table 6 of Stevens, Madden, Slavin, and Farnish (1987, p. 450) shows that, among four contrasts of handicapped experimentals and controls, two (involving measures of language ex-pression and mechanics) were *not* sig-nificant at the conventional probability level (p <.05); the remaining two (involv-ing measures of reading comprehension and vocabulary) were marginally so. In a footnote to their Table 6, the authors write that only 6 handicapped experimen-tal students and 14 handicapped controls participated in this second evaluation.

Does the foregoing indicate that cooperative learning has not worked for disabled students and that we should reject Lipsky and Gartner's suggestion of encouraging its implementation in schools? No. We, and many other Con-servationists, believe cooperative learn-ing, peer tutoring, and other programs hold promise for mainstream students, for those with and without disabilities. We disagree, however, with Abolitionists such as Lipsky and Gartner that such programs are tried-and-true means of large-scale, full-time mainstreaming. More to the point, we believe the forego-ing underscores two related Abolitionist tendencies. First, research is not regarded critically; there is scant effort to distinguish between experimental inter-ventions that have been field tested suffi-ciently for large-scale use with certain disabled students (e.g., Team-Assisted Individualization) and those that have not (e.g., CIRC). Second, some stronger Abolitionists use research in a self-serv-

ing manner. We agree with Kauffman (1990) that such practice seems to reflect an attitude that "Research isn't really very important because we already know what to do. We know what to do because we know what is right, irrespective of the data" (pp. 2-3).

CREDULOUS. Snell's, and Lipsky and Gartner's optimistic view of regular education is more than ahistorical and nonempirical; it reflects a naive belief about change: Once regular education is made more accommodating of student diversity, it will remain that way. Take, for example, Snell's disappointment over New Hampshire's decision to appeal the *Timothy W. v. Rochester School District* case before the Supreme Court. Noting that the Court eventually rejected New Hampshire's effort, Snell writes, "Despite the outcome of *Timothy W.*, many parents and professionals were dismayed that the educability battle was reopened in 1989" (p. 134). It was a battle, says Snell, that "many thought had been won in the 1970s" (p. 134). Moreover, like Snell, Lipsky and Gartner do not discuss how they would *maintain* the current and purported widespread interest in regular education restructuring, or if regular education were to change as dramatically as they an-ticipate, what they would do to ensure that the gains took hold rather than be uprooted by the vicissitudes of time.

Snell's and Lipsky and Gartner's ap-parent view of change and reform is like a white wall painted blue; once done, it is an accomplished immutable fact. As Conservationists, we suspect that strong Abolitionists may not recognize that the battle for children with disabilities, like efforts to preserve the Bill of Rights, is ongoing. The watchword must be vigilance and the strategies developed in support of special needs children must reflect cautiousness, allowing for the likelihood that, as has happened before, public enthusiasm over public education will wane. If restructuring occurs, the cascade of services is eliminated, and all children with disabilities and remedial students, are placed in regular classrooms, how do Abolitionists propose safeguarding their education over the long haul? What happens when the nation slips into economic depression or goes to war? How will students with disabilities fare when the public, and its elected officials, lose its supposedly strong interest in education in favor of clean air, farm programs, housing, AIDS, or campaign financing?

Advocacy

With a handful of notable exceptions, we believe Abolitionists distinguish themselves more as advocates than as analysts. They have helped develop large, energetic, grassroots organizations, and have lobbied skillfully in state capitols and Washington, DC. At least several factors have contributed to their success: They tend to focus on a single issue; they identify with a precisely-defined constituency; and they use effective rhetoric.

THE ISSUE. As mentioned previously, full-inclusion is the Abolitionists' touchstone, if not their exclusive concern. Snell illustrates this when she writes, "Most leaders in special education of persons with severe disabilities support ... inclusive education as being central to further improvements in school integration" (p. 143). Conservationists, on the other hand, believe there exists a *multiplicity* of important issues, and that successful integration strategies must be comprehensive. Compare Snell's focused concern with the Conservationist view of Hocutt et al.: "Consideration of ...placement to the exclusion of all other factors should not be the primary consideration in the education of handicapped students" (p. 25). Similarly, Bryan et al. write:

> We recognize that embedded in the notion of reconceptualization [of regular education] are issues

such as: Who will educate these children; and, to what extent will they be educated with nonhandicapped youngsters? These issues, however, are peripheral to the task. What is central is a careful consideration of program content, structure, and methods of instruction." (p. 127-128)

THE CONSTITUENCY. Most strong Abolitionists identify professionally with children and adults with severe mental retardation. Moreover, there is an indication that at least some doubt whether many other children with disabilities are really disabled. Kauffman, for example, reminds us that former Assitant Secretary of Education, Madeline Will, wrote, "Recent studies suggest that a significant percentage of the children served in the special learning disability category are not handicapped" (see Kauffman, p. 62); and that Wang, Reynolds, and Walberg have opined that "two-thirds of the children enrolled in special education have relatively minor problems, most or all of which could be addressed by general education" (see Kauffman, p. 62). How many Abolitionists believe that mildly handicapped students are not really handicapped? How many think that such an assignation wrongs not just the children affected directly by the labeling, but those with severe disabilities affected indirectly by the wasted expenditure of much needed monies on a population not in need?

A perspective shaped by a single issue and informed by a narrow constituency can lead to similarly narrow solutions. One example seems to be the "specialized instructional unit," described by Snell. The specialized instructional unit was developed to facilitate the integration of children with severe disabilities into LREs, including the regular classroom. Snell indicates it is more than related services; rather, it denotes the delivery of functional skills instruction by a trained teacher or assistant; implementation of a transition plan during a student's high school years; and ongoing program monitoring and modification, including intensive consultation from speech, occupational, and physical therapists (see p. 160). What strikes us as noteworthy about this approach, more so than its cost, is the time and energy it demands of many school personnel, especially the classroom teacher. At what point does an advocate's understandable, but focused caring about one student become disregard for his or her classmates?

THE RHETORIC. Like many strong Abolitionists, Lipsky and Gartner make heavy use of the subjunctive mood (in contrast to Conservationists' typical use of the indicative); their chapter is chock-full of wishes, conditions, and contrary-to-fact statements. Their prescriptions, moreover, are described most generally; there is little serious effort to make them concrete, qualify them, or make them operational. (In contradistinction, see Carnine's specific discussion of the problems associated with the application of instructional technology in regular classrooms.) The following is illustrative of Lipsky and Gartner's use of the subjunctive and the vagueness of their recommendations for change:

> The next and third [sic] wave of school reform needs to increase the productivity of students as workers in their own learning. Giving students respect, building upon their knowledge, providing them control over the learning process and appropriate materials, helping them to see the connection between subjects, encouraging cooperation among students are the necessary predicates to the increases in student learning, the bases for school improvement that will produce enhanced school outcomes of substantial magnitude

for all students, including those now labelled as handicapped (p. 49).

Furthermore, some Abolitionists sometimes write misleadingly. Snell claims, "Current averaged placement statistics show that 26% of students with disabilities are placed in regular classes; 41% are served in resource rooms; 24.9% are served in separate classes within a regular education building..." (p. 136). As defined on page 27 of *The Tenth Annual Report* (Annual Report to Congress, 1988), "regular class" means a child receives special education and related services for less than 21% of the school day; "resource room" denotes services provided for 60% or less and 21% or more; "separate class" indicates services for more than 60% of the day. Thus, although it is possible for a student with a regular class placement to participate in special education pull-out, it also is possible that one with a resource room assignment participates in regular classroom activity. Our experience in schools suggests that many children in resource rooms spend a portion of their time in the mainstream, which, if true nationally, means that many more handicapped children than suggested by Snell are in the mainstream full- or part-time.

One last point, here. As indicated by Hocutt et al., among all children with disabilities in public school, those in regular, resource, and special classes total 91%; only 9% currently are served elsewhere. Although this does *not* suggest to us, or to most Conservationists, that we should rest on our laurels and discontinue efforts to place more children on regular school campuses, it makes plain that an overwhelming majority already are there.

Conservationist Pragmatism

IS REGULAR EDUCATION WILLING? Many idealistic Abolitionists regard special education as *expendable* largely because they believe regular education is expandable. That is, mainstream education is (or can become) willing and able to accommodate greater student diversity, including the integration of all, or most, children with disabilities. Conservationists, especially those of a stronger strain, are skeptical of this proposition, a stance based on knowledge of regular education's checkered past and of the problems besetting it now. Davis (1989) noted that many special educators feel "a genuine concern that regular education still is not ready--in either attitude or instructional capabilities--to adequately meet the needs of students with special needs" (p. 443). Regarding attitude, Walker and Bullis remind us that "The public schools' record of effectively accommodating students with behavior disorders ...is close to abysmal" (p. 178). In part this is because classroom teachers have expressed a negative view of mainstreaming generally and of students with "externalizing behavioral characteristics" in particular.

IS REGULAR EDUCATION ABLE? Many conservationists are equally dubious about regular education's collective capacity for accommodation. Kauffman, Gerber, and Semmel (1988), like Davis, claim most classroom teachers lack the time and training, besides the right attitude, to work effectively with extremely low-achieving students. Full inclusion, they say, will demand too much from an already overburdened profession, and that there is nothing currently, as there has been little in the past, in the way of resources or incentives to facilitate or motivate teachers to higher levels of pedagogic performance.

Closely related to this question of regular education's capacity to mainstream all, or most, students is the issue of diversity. Figure 2 displays the reading performance of 118 second- through fifth-grade students constituting 31 different mainstream classrooms in 6 schools, that were located in either a suburban-rural or urban school district. The group included students with learning disabilities, low-achieving students without disabilities, and average-achieving pupils. All were participants in a 14-week class-wide peer tutoring project, directed by Deborah Simmons and us. Immediately preceding and following the students' project involvement, they were asked to read aloud from two 400-word passages (see Fuchs, Fuchs, & Hamlett, 1989, for details).

The figure, which depicts students' scores at pretesting and posttesting, is remarkable, we believe, for the diversity of performance it documents, a diversity that is obvious at pretesting and posttesting as well as in the changes from pretesting to posttesting. Regarding this last performance dimension, the figure shows that some pupils increased their initial score by nearly 200 words, whereas others *reduced* their initial performance by 50 words. Although this variation in pre-to-post change no doubt reflects many factors, we believe it may be interpreted in part as a response to the class-wide peer tutoring. As such, it underscores the differences in academic capacity, background knowledge, motivation, attentiveness, etc. that characterize the typical mainstream classroom. It is this dramatic, if not daunting, heterogeneity with which regular teachers must contend, as well as the documented failure of many to do so previously, that contributes to the Conservationists' penchant for analysis instead of advocacy; to their insistence on seeing carefully tested blueprints for change before supporting a policy of placing all children in regular classrooms.

Analysis

On page 25, Hocutt et al. call for more analysis, rather than advocacy, of the potential benefits of increased mainstreaming and for more consideration of the barriers in regular education that prevent the implementation of

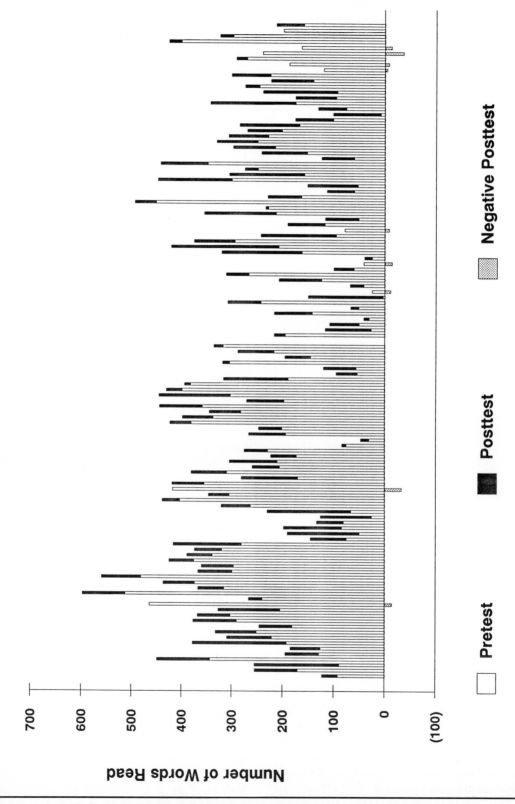

**Figure 2: Diversity in mainstream students' performance: Number of words read correctly
in three minutes.**

mainstreaming. Kauffman (1990) strikes a similar chord:

> A lot of the rhetoric about special and general education these days has taken on the characteristics of the political context of the 1980s: It is based on image and surface appeal; it is simplistic, reducing complex issues to a couple of key phrases; it carefully avoids logical analysis and questions about the meanings of its slogans. As painful and anxiety-provoking as it may be, we must start asking ourselves and others some questions that call for deeper analysis of issues. If we don't, who will? (p. 13)

Conservationists are more likely to engage in analysis than Abolitionists. Such analysis takes many forms, including a problem orientation, a tendency to look critically (as opposed to negatively) at research, and to engage in making policy with both a sense of history and a sense of the possible.

A PROBLEM ORIENTATION. Carnine addresses head-on the issue of student diversity discussed above. His analysis illustrates how such heterogeneity complicates the central task of providing instructionally effective programs in mainstream environments. One salient problem described by Carnine is whether to make important mathematical relationships explicit for average and below-average students, thereby possibly holding back the above-average students. On page 173, he presents a figure, which shows hypothesized relations between (a) the importance of Direct Instruction, and (b) a task's degree of cognitive complexity for special education, below-average, and above-average students. On highly complex tasks, he posits that Direct Instruction is "moderately" to "greatly" important for all; on low complexity tasks, it remains "greatly" important for special needs stu-

dents, is still "moderately" important for below-average pupils, and is "slightly" to "moderately" important for average and above-average students.

An even larger problem, according to Carnine, is how to bridge the gap between typical educational practice and those implied by Direct Instruction. An important part of Direct Instruction is interactive teaching. Although facilitating scripts are provided, such teaching remains very demanding. "The [teacher] interactions," writes Carnine, "are governed, in nature and amount, by the performance of the students. Thus, the teacher is continually deciding (a) how to relate what students have learned to any current confusions, and (b) how much demonstration and guided practice to provide, given the typical spread of student abilities" (p. 173).

A CRITICAL PERSPECTIVE ON LARGE-SCALE MAINSTREAMING PROGRAMS. Whereas some Abolitionists encourage use of relatively narrow integrationist strategies (e.g., Snell's espousal of the specialized instructional unit), others like Gartner and Lipsky (1989) advocate more comprehensive programs such as the Adaptive Learning Environments Model and various versions of cooperative learning. Many Abolitionists, especially strong adherents, have given their unconditional approval to these strategies as a means of accomplishing full inclusion (e.g., Biklen & Zollers, 1986; Gartner & Lipsky, 1989). In contrast, both mild and strong Conservationists are far more critical of the data supposedly validating such programs, far less enthusiastic about the likelihood of their success as large-scale mainstreaming strategies (e.g., Anderegg & Vergason, 1988; Bryan & Bryan, 1988; Fuchs & Fuchs, 1988; Hallahan et al., 1988; Lloyd, Crowley, Kohler, & Strain, 1988).

CAN SCHOOL REFORM BALANCE EQUITY WITH EXCELLENCE? Many Abolitionists and Conservationists differ as dramatically over the portents of reform for the education of disabled children as they do about the merits of extant large-scale mainstreaming programs. Whereas Lipsky and Gartner believe reform will make full inclusion considerably more likely, Hocutt et al. and other Conservationists claim just the opposite is true. According to Hocutt et al., equity and excellence are the two major values giving intellectual vigor to the reform. But discussions of equity nearly always are limited to poor, minority, and inner-city nonhandicapped children (see p. 24). And concerns about excellence are rooted in the view that public schools have failed the so-called disadvantaged and middle-class children. Hocutt et al. write:

> The silence about the needs of, or outcomes for, handicapped children in the current reform movement is deafening. Until and unless this movement toward excellence is accompanied by fundamental changes in the organization of schools...and by effective staff development, it will be extremely difficult for even the ablest exceptional students to 'measure up' to expectations fostered by the school reform movement. (p. 24)

EXPLAINING IDEALISTIC VERSUS PRAGMATIC ORIENTATIONS

Clean and Unclean Slates

We believe there are at least two ways to account for the contrasting Abolitionist and Conservationist perspectives on mainstream education. Abolitionist idealism is due in part to the fact that children with severe mental retardation have had little or no history in regular education. Prior to the past decade, these children were barred by many school districts from a public education, let alone entry into mainstream classrooms. To the children and their parents and advocates, mainstream education must represent a new frontier. And like all new frontiers (in this country, anyway), its very existence engenders a *can-do* optimism and compels us to challenge it and eventually tame it.

In contrast, mildly handicapped students, and some students more severely disabled, but not mentally challenged, have experienced regular education. They typically started there, had trouble, and were booted out. Many Conservationists' skepticism toward regular education is born of close-up observation of many educators' unwillingness or inability to work with these children; of the blatant intolerance, and sometimes visceral dislike expressed by many teachers toward them; of arbitrary and adamant refusals to permit the return of these pupils, even if only for part of the school day, to their classrooms. Thus, Abolitionist and Conservationist viewpoints clash because, in an important sense, they and the students for whom they tend to speak, have very different histories with regular education: For many Abolitionists, their orientation reflects a literal lack of history; for Conservationists, their pragmatism reveals a cautiousness based on past frustrations and disappointments.

Different Means and Ends

A second explanation concerns Abolitionist and Conservationist goals. In a general sense, parents, teachers, and others involved in the education of students with disabilities appear to wish the same things for these children, irrespective of type and degree of disability. They want them to feel good about themselves as kids and as students; to have friends who regard them with respect; to develop appropriate relations with adults; and to obtain knowledge and skills that will make future successes more likely. If we think about these goals more carefully, however, we realize that they tend to stand for very different things. Take the last goal mentioned: "to obtain knowledge and skills that will make future successes more likely." *Which* body of knowledge and *which* set of skills we define as important depends largely on *which* children we have in mind, just as our notion of the successes for which we are preparing them changes as a function of whether we are discussing a severely mentally challenged student or one, say, with a comparatively mild behavior disorder.

More specifically, mainstream goals for children with severe mental retardation tend to be social and attitudinal in nature. Snell writes:

> Probably the three most important and reciprocal benefits from integration ... are (a) the development of social skills ... across all school age groups, (b) the improvements in the attitudes that non-disabled peers have for their peers with disabilities, and (c) the development of positive relationships and friendships between peers as a result of integration. (pp. 137-138)

In contrast, Conservationists' goals for children with whom they work almost always highlight an academic component. Conservationists argue that, for these children, success in the mainstream means achieving at least passing grades. This is implicit in the following discussion by Bryan et al.

> We hope to maximize the likelihood that students with learning disabilities can emerge from their school experience with the knowledge and skills necessary to live independently, with positive feelings about themselves, and with optimistic views about their abilities to do well in adult endeavors. (p. 128)

Thus, although Abolitionist and Conservationist goals, or ends, may sound similar, they in fact tend to be different. As such, they require different means, which, in turn, have contrasting implications for what is required of regular education. Because the needs of students with relatively ambitious scholastic goals are primarily academic, these students, we believe, weigh heavily on the consciousness and conscience of the well-meaning regular classroom teacher. Their instruction is the teacher's responsibility; their different learning characteristics are the teacher's problems. In this way, disabled students with relatively ambitious goals, in comparison to those with severe mental retardation and their social-oriented objectives, constitute more of a challenge to the mainstream teacher and to the principle of integration. This point is illustrated with clarity, if not with irony, in the Ed Smith School in Syracuse, N.Y., a school aptly described by Lipsky and Gartner (p. 53) as a showcase for integration practices. Whereas many children with severe disabilities are integrated in mainstream classes there, most children with mild and moderate disabilities--those with relatively ambitious academic goals--receive their education from special educators in pull-out programs.

EPILOGUE

Abolitionists (e.g., Lipsky and Gartner, p. 53), like some conservative Baptist ministers here in our adopted home town, seem fond of battle metaphors. We'll piggyback on their favored imagery by suggesting that, for many Conservationists, regular education remains a foreign and hostile territory, neglecting many children with disabilities. PL 94-142, with its declaration of a free and appropriate education and its cascade of services and LRE principle, represented in 1975 the capturing of a beachhead for children with disabilities. It is time to gather our energies and courage; validate comprehensive integration strategies; pressure mainstream administrators and teachers for greater accommodations; move inland! But as we mount this new offensive, we, like any general worthy of his rank, must make certain that the beachhead remains secure. It's the beachhead, after all, that provides supplies and, in a worse case scenario, guarantees a safe retreat. The cascade of services is a source of strength and a safety net for the children we serve. Let's not lose it.

REFERENCES

Aftermath of forest fires. (1990, August 18). *The New York Times*, p. 8.

Algozzine, B., Maheady, L., Sacca, K C., O'Shea, L., & O'Shea, D. (1990). Sometimes patent medicine works: A reply to Braaten, Kauffman, Braaten, polsgrove, and Nelson. *Exceptional Children, 56.* 552-557.

Anderegg, M. L., & Vergason, G. A. (1988) An analysis of one of the cornerstones of the Regular Education Initiative. *Focus on Exceptional Children, 20,* 1-7.

Annual Report to Congress. (1988). *Tenth annual report to Congress on the implementation of the Education of the Handicapped Act.* Washington, D.C.: U.S. Department of Education.

Biklen, D. (1985). Getting started. In D. Biklen (Ed.), *Achieving the complete school* (pp. 1-29). New York: Teachers College.

Biklen, D., & Zollers, N. (1986). The focus of advocacy in the LD field. *Journal of Learning Disabilities, 19,* 579-586.

Bryan, J. H , & Bryan, T. H. (1988). Where's the beef? A review of published research on the Adaptive Learning Environments Model. *Learning Disabilities Focus, 4*(1), 9-14.

Davis, W. E. (1989). The Regular Education Initiative debate: Its promises and problems. *Exceptional Children, 55,* 440-447.

Fuchs, D., & Fuchs, L. S. (1988). Evaluation of the Adaptive Learning Environments Model. *Exceptional Children, 55,* 115-127.

Fuchs. D., Fuchs, L. S., Fernstrom, P., & Hohn, M. (in press). Toward a responsible reintegration of behaviorally disordered students. *Behavioral Disorders.*

Fuchs, L. S., Fuchs, D., & Hamlett, C. L. (1989). Monitoring reading growth using student recalls: Effects of two teacher feedback systems. *Journal of Educational Research, 83,* 103-111.

Gartner, A., & Lipsky, D. K. (1989). *The yoke of special education: How to break it.* Rochester, N.Y.: National Center on Education and the Economy.

Hallahan, D. P., Keller, C. E., McKinney, J. D., Lloyd, J. W., & Bryan, T. (1988). Examining the research base of the regular education initiative: Efficacy studies and the Adaptive Learning Environments Model. *Journal of Learning Disabilities, 21,* 29-35, 55.

Jenkins, J. R., Pious, C. G., & Peterson, D. L. (1988). Categorical programs for remedial and handicapped students: Issues of validity. *Exceptional Children, 55,* 147-158.

Kauffman, J. M. (1990, April). What happens when special education works? The sociopolitical context of special education research in the 1990s. Invited address, Special Interest Group: Special Education Research, annual meeting of the American Educational Research Association, Boston.

Kauffman, J. M., Gerber, M. M., & Semmel, M. I. (1988). Arguable assumptions underlying the Regular Education Initiative. *Journal of Learning Disabilities, 21,* 6-12.

Lloyd, J. W., Crowley, E. P., Kohler, F. W., & Strain, P. S. (1988). Redefining the applied research agenda: Cooperative learning, prereferral, teacher consultation, and peer-mediated models. *Journal of Learning Disabilities, 21,* 43-52.

National Commission on Excellence in Education. (1983). *A nation at risk.* Washington, D.C.: U.S. Government printing Office.

Pugach, M., & Lilly, S. M. (1984). Reconceptualizing support services for classroom teachers: Implications for teacher education. *Journal of Teacher Education, 35,* 48-55.

Reynolds, M. C. (1988). A reaction to the JLD special issue on the Regular Education Initiative. *Journal of Learning Disabilities, 21,* 352-356.

Schumaker, J., & Deshler, D. (1988). Implementing the regular education initiative in secondary schools: A different ball game. *Journal of Learning Disabilities, 21,* 36-42.

Stainback, S., & Stainback, W. (1985). *Integration of students with severe handicaps into regular schools.* Reston, VA: The Council for Exceptional Children.

Stevens, R. J., Madden, N. A., Slavin, R. E., & Farnish, A. M. (1987). Cooperative Integrated Reading and Comprehension: Two field experiments. . *Reading Research Quarterly, 22,* 433-454.

Tateyama-Sniezek, K. M. (1990). Cooperative learning: Does it improve the academic achievement of students with handicaps? *Exceptional Children, 56,* 426-437.

Wang, M. C., Rubenstein, J. L., & Reynolds, M. C. (1985). Clearing the road to success for students with special needs. *Educational Leadership, 43,* 62-67.

Author Index

Subject Index